Building Portals with the Java Portlet API

JEFF LINWOOD, DAVE MINTER

Apress®

ISBN (pbk): 1-59059-284-0

Printed and bound in the United States of America 9 8 7 6 5 4 3 2

Lead Editor: Steve Anglin

Technical Reviewer: Carsten Ziegeler

Project Manager: Kylie Johnston

Copy Edit Manager: Nicole LeClerc

Copy Editor: Liz Welch

Production Manager: Kari Brooks

Production Editor: Ellie Fountain

Compositor: Kinetic Publishing Services, LLC

Proofreader: Nancy Sixsmith

Indexer: James Minkin

Artist: Kinetic Publishing Services, LLC

Cover Designer: Kurt Krames

Manufacturing Manager: Tom Debolski

Distributed to the book trade in the United States by Springer-Verlag New York, Inc., 233 Spring Street, 6th Floor, New York, NY 10013 and outside the United States by Springer-Verlag GmbH & Co. KG, Tiergartenstr. 17, 69112 Heidelberg, Germany.

In the United States: phone 1-800-SPRINGER, e-mail `orders@springer-ny.com`, or visit `http://www.springer-ny.com`. Outside the United States: fax +49 6221 345229, e-mail `orders@springer.de`, or visit `http://www.springer.de`.

For information on translations, please contact Apress directly at 2560 Ninth Street, Suite 219, Berkeley, CA 94710. Phone 510-549-5930, fax 510-549-5939, e-mail `info@apress.com`, or visit `http://www.apress.com`.

The source code for this book is available to readers at `http://www.apress.com` in the Downloads section.

Contents at a Glance

Contents

Foreword

The phenomenal amount of information that networked computers can present to us is both the marvel and the bane of our time. Knowledge is commonly supposed to be power, but the reality is that we are often drowning in data, overwhelmed rather than enabled. The inexorable rise in the volume of facts and figures at our disposal should be A Good Thing, but unless we have the right tools to manage this information, we will struggle to keep our heads above water, let alone take full advantage of the data.

Arguably the single most important challenge in the computing world today is to provide users with the means to stay on top of the information they require. Connectivity is no longer enough—merely providing someone with a web browser and an Internet connection is roughly akin to supplying them with a small dinghy in order to circumnavigate the globe.

Two elements are crucial to solving this problem successfully: aggregation and selectivity. Aggregation technologies make multiple sources of information available in one place. Selectivity is the ability to exercise control over what is presented, and is necessary to exploit aggregation without being overwhelmed.

Search engines are the archetypical aggregation success story—the Internet would be orders of magnitude less useful without the ability to search the entire Web from one place. However, search engines are weak when it comes to selectivity. They necessarily cast their net very wide, which inevitably means that searches tend to return a lot of irrelevant data. This places the burden on users to sift through the results for data of value.

Search engines continue to improve their selection capabilities, with increasingly sophisticated algorithms for determining which pages are likely to be most relevant. However, search engines inevitably run up against the problem that different individuals are likely to be looking for different things when feeding in the same query. For example, someone I know was recently looking for information on dressage horses, and while the majority of results Google returned when she searched for "stallion german" were equine, a few of the results were catering to an entirely different market.

Recently, user-driven aggregation has been gaining ground, most notably in the form of RSS aggregators. These lack the all-encompassing reach of a search engine, but score much higher on selectivity—they retrieve information only from sources in which users have expressed an interest. This highly selective form of aggregation enables us to keep abreast of updates across hundreds of web sites without having to spend all day, every day visiting those sites in the browser.

The Java portlet architecture provides a framework for building systems that present users with the information they need. It offers the two key ingredients for success: aggregation (portals can aggregate information from multiple portlets) and selectivity (the architecture allows administrators and users to be selective about their sources of information by choosing which portlets will appear).

Moreover, portlets allow information from all kinds of sources to be aggregated, so a portal's reach is potentially much greater than that of either a web search engine or an RSS feed. Of course, portlets are available to handle both web content and RSS feeds, but portlets can also allow information from web services to be added to a portal, or from legacy systems. If you can retrieve information from a system with Java code, you can write a portlet for it.

Dave and Jeff have provided a comprehensive guide to the portlet architecture in this book. But of course, this technology will never be used in isolation—its basic purpose is to integrate diverse sources of information. Accordingly, they also describe the main technologies you are likely to come across when building portals. This book offers a guide to the various incompatible versions of RSS, shows you how to integrate the Lucene search engine into your site, and discusses various content management technologies.

Since the portlet specification is a fairly recent addition to the suite of Java specifications, very little portal-aware software exists right now. This means that for the time being, a lot of portlet development will involve integrating existing code into new portal environments. This book therefore provides a fully worked example, showing the effort required to take the open source YAZD forum software and wrap it as a portlet.

In short, the portlet specification provides the tools for building web sites that will enable users to exploit the potential of the information available to them, and this book tells you all you need to know to build great portals.

Ian Griffiths
Developer, consultant, and teacher
`www.interact-sw.co.uk/iangblog/`

About the Authors

Jeff Linwood is a software developer and consultant with the Gossamer Group (`www.gossamer-group.com`) in sunny Austin, Texas. Jeff has been in software programming since he had a 286 in high school. He was caught up with the Internet when he got access to a Unix shell account, and it has been downhill ever since. Jeff coauthored *Pro Struts Applications* (Apress, 2003), and was a technical reviewer for *Enterprise Java Development on a Budget* (Apress, 2004) and *Extreme Programming with Ant* (SAMS, 2003). He has a chemical engineering degree from Carnegie Mellon University.

Dave Minter is a freelance integration consultant and developer from rainy London, England. The first computer that he encountered was a Wang 2200 minicomputer, which at the time was roughly the same size as he was. Since then, he has worked for the largest of blue chip companies and the smallest of startups—encountering Jeff during the dotcom frenzy along the way. These days, he makes his living explaining to companies how they can build systems that "just work." He has a computer studies degree from the University of Glamorgan.

About the Technical Reviewer

Carsten Ziegeler is a member of the Apache Software Foundation and as such is involved in various open source communities, like Cocoon, Avalon, and Excalibur. He is a member of the Apache Portals project management committee and committer of the Pluto and the WSRP4J project.

In paid life, Carsten is the chief architect of the Open Source Group at S&N AG, Paderborn, Germany. The focus is on Java-based middleware functionality such as web frameworks, component architectures, and portal solutions and technologies.

The liaison to Apache started in 2000 when Carsten became committer of the Cocoon project and started to play an important role in designing and developing the current architecture. A major contribution to Cocoon is the standard-compliant Cocoon Portal.

Acknowledgments

THIS BOOK would not have been possible without the energy and enthusiasm of the Apress staff, especially John Zukowski for his decision to let us write it; Kylie Johnston, our project manager; and Steve Anglin, our editor. Special thanks to Liz Welch for a superb job of copyediting our chapters.

We owe particular thanks to Ian Griffiths (the gurus' guru) for his foreword to this book, and we owe a debt of gratitude to Carsten Ziegeler, our technical reviewer, whose comments have without exception been both pertinent and pithy.

Jeff would like to thank Karl Weinmeister, for his ideas on what should be in a portal development book, and Skip Walker, for reviewing the Single Sign-On material. Jeff would also like to thank his family for being supportive.

Dave would like to thank his parents for their patience with his little hobby, and his girlfriend Kalani Seymour for her tolerance and good humor as deadlines came and went. Thanks also to Bruce Robinson for the mug shot.

Any errors in the ensuing content are, of course, entirely our own doing.

Introduction

IT SHOULD BE possible to build a portal by plugging components from different vendors into a portal from any vendor. These components are portlets, and we explain how to build them in this book.

The noble aim of the portlet specification—which arose from Sun's Java Community Process with the collaboration of Sun, IBM, BEA, and others—was to simplify the process of tying applications into a portal by allowing them to cooperate. That so many vendors have come together to standardize their existing proprietary solutions bodes well for the future of this technology.

We believe that portlets and the portlet API will become at least as important to Java application developers as the servlet API has been because portlets make building a truly integrated system that much easier. Any new portal development projects should select a portal that supports the portlet API because independent software vendors now need to write portlets for only one API, not a dozen.

Both of us enjoy working with new technology, and there are a lot of new standards for portals, content management systems, business rules, and web services. We hope that you will enjoy learning about portal development as much as we enjoyed writing this book!

Who This Book Is For

This book is for developers who already have a command of the basics of web application development in Java. Ideally, you will have had some exposure to servlets and JSP pages. No prior knowledge of portlets or portal development is required. Some very basic knowledge of XML is useful.

All of our examples use standards or use open source software, so it will not be necessary for you to purchase any software to get started with portlet development. Because the portlet API is a standard, you can begin development on a free, open source portal, and then migrate your applications to a commercial portal.

This book is not an academic text—our focus is on providing extensive examples and taking a pragmatic approach to the technology that it covers.

How This Book Is Organized

We realize that many of our readers will be familiar with servlets and some of the core concepts of portlets when they come to this book. We recommend to such readers that they familiarize themselves with the following chapter guide so that they can quickly refer to the subjects they are interested in.

We have also tried to ensure that a portlet novice will find that these chapters are logically ordered, with the more advanced subjects covered only when the basics have been described in detail.

You will find the source code for the book's examples on the Apress web site (`www.apress.com`), on the Downloads page.

Chapter 1: Introduction to Portals and Portlets

This chapter outlines the basic concepts and terms that you will encounter in the book. We talk in broad terms about the strengths and weaknesses of portlets, and we give you an overview of some of the technologies that we cover more fully in later chapters.

Chapter 2: Portlet Basics

This chapter provides an example of a simple portlet, discusses how it works, and demonstrates how to build the application. We then introduce the open source Pluto portal and show how you can deploy the example portlet on Pluto.

Chapter 3: The Portlet Life Cycle

In this chapter, we discuss how a portlet interacts with a portal, from initialization to removal. We provide a simple example that walks you through the stages of the portlet life cycle, as well as a more complex example that illustrates the issues of multithreaded portlet applications.

Chapter 4: Portlet Concepts

This chapter introduces many of the basic portlet concepts for the first time, or in more detail, and much of the API is examined in depth. An example ties many of these concepts together to demonstrate file upload to a portlet.

Among many other topics, the chapter discusses

- Request and response objects
- Attributes and properties
- The portlet context

- Locales and internationalization
- Logging
- The API versioning scheme
- Sessions
- Default and custom modes
- Default and custom window states

Chapter 5: Using Servlets and JavaServer Pages with Portlets

Chapter 5 demonstrates how to invoke and include content from servlets and JSP pages. Session management, the creation and processing of HTML forms, and the portlet tag library are all addressed. We provide an example of a to-do list portlet to illustrate these techniques.

Chapter 6: Packaging and Deployment Descriptors

In this chapter, we show you how to use the portlet deployment descriptor. We also demonstrate XDoclet's portlet integration, which lets us build and deploy portlets easily.

Chapter 7: Portal and Portlet Configuration

This chapter describes the standard configuration information available to a portal and the portlets it contains. It discusses

- The `PortalContext` class
- Portal properties
- Window states and portlet modes configuration
- The `PortletConfig` class
- Portlet preferences

Chapter 8: Security and Single Sign-On

This chapter demonstrates how to integrate a portlet with a Single Sign-On solution using Kerberos as an example. We also discuss many of the other authentication and authorization technologies that are available to a portlet developer.

Chapter 9: RSS and Syndication

You'll learn how a portlet can incorporate syndicated links from other sites and how an application can present its own links to similarly capable external sites.

Chapter 10: Integrating the Lucene Search Engine

Lucene is a powerful, open source search engine. We show you how to create an index with Lucene, and then how to build a portlet that searches content in that index.

Chapter 11: Personalization and User Attributes

This chapter examines the information available to personalize portlets for the current user, and we describe the limited but useful facility for persisting user data. We discuss the use of a rules engine to govern portlet content decisions.

Chapter 12: Web Services for Remote Portlets (WSRP) and Application Syndication

We discuss the Web Services for Remote Portlets (WSRP) specification, and then tie WSRP into the broader problem of application syndication.

Chapter 13: Exposing an Existing Application As a Portlet

This chapter demonstrates how an existing real-world application, the YAZD forum software, can swiftly be converted into a portlet application using the techniques described in earlier chapters.

Chapter 14: Charting with JFreeChart

We apply the open source JFreeChart project to provide professional data-charting capabilities within a portlet.

Chapter 15: Content Management Systems

In our final chapter, we discuss integrating content management systems (CMSs) into portlets. We provide an overview of the new JSR 170 Java Content Repository API specification for CMS integration. WebDAV is a standard protocol for working with content management systems, and we build a portlet client for a WebDAV server.

CHAPTER 1

Introduction to Portals and Portlets

THIS BOOK IS FOR SOFTWARE developers and designers who develop Java applications for portals. We cover version 1.0 of the Java portlet API, also known as Java Specification Request (JSR) 168. Portlets are the individual components that provide content for a portal. Portals aggregate one or more portlets into web pages, which are usually personalized or customized for individual users or groups of users. Some portals also support mobile devices and voice support.

Before the release of this portlet API, each portal had a different API for developing portlets. Most Java portal vendors will support the JSR 168 standard in addition to their existing proprietary API. If you develop your portlets to the new portlet API standard, you can deploy them on any JSR 168-compatible server, just as any compatible servlet container can deploy servlets.

You may use the open source portal server Apache Pluto to run the portlets we write in this book. You are able to deploy your portlets on any other portals that support the standard, because none of the portlets will use any proprietary features. We use several open source software components to provide additional functionality beyond the portlet API.

Some of the problems we provide solutions for in later chapters are personalization, portal deployment, Single Sign-On (SSO), content syndication, and the porting of an existing application into a portal infrastructure. In this chapter, we discuss portals, information architecture, and background on the portlet API.

Providing a Solution with Portals

Usually, the decision to build a portal environment is made at a high level within an organization after users become frustrated with using applications that are not integrated and are not immediately visible. Other times, a project involving an extranet for suppliers and customers gets started, and the easiest way to aggregate security for all of these new users is through a portal's SSO feature. In this book, we do not discuss the business case for a portal within an organization. We wrote this book for developers and architects who have chosen to use a portal server that implements the Java portlet API and need to solve technical problems.

From a technical perspective, a portal provides a solution for aggregating content and applications from various systems for presentation to the end user. The users do not need to know how the content or functionality is provided; they just want to enjoy the benefits of a single web site and all of its services. Typically, a portal has an integrated user interface and an SSO approach for security. The software developer's job is to take all of the systems that provide these services and add interfaces to them to work with the portal. Portlets are the individual components displayed in the portal. Prior to the introduction of the standardized portlet API, portlets had to be custom-developed for each portal server because the API was different for each server. The leading portal vendors joined to create a standard to promote portal technology. Inside the Java Community Process (JCP), the name of the standard for the first version of the Java portlet API is JSR 168. Future versions of the portlet API will have different JSR numbers.

One of the problems for the designer or architect in charge of the portal project is that the existing systems do not always separate cleanly into presentation and business logic layers. Also, consider portal security and personalization when examining existing applications. In this book, we port an existing web application into a portlet application, so you can learn from some of our portlet integration problems. New software projects that integrate with the portal can use a services-oriented architecture with exposed web services, a stand-alone web application, or a portlet.

Portal projects have two major technical components designed in parallel: application architecture and information architecture. Both of these will flow from business requirements, and they require an integrated approach. If the portal applications do not support the common information architecture, the users will have a substandard experience. We discuss creating an information architecture for a portal environment in the next section.

Designing the Portal's Information Architecture

Moving all of your applications into a portal does not accomplish anything if your users are not able to solve their problems. One of the first steps for deploying a portal solution effectively is to gather requirements from the users and design the information architecture for your portal project. The information architecture includes the content displayed through the portal, the user interface, the available portlets, metadata, a search engine, and a classification system or taxonomy. The portal's information architecture defines the user-centered approach to the portal, while the technical architecture is what the developers use to build the portal. Aligning these two forces is a difficult task, but it is necessary for a successful project.

If you have not identified all of the users of the portal system yet, try to account for at least the three main types of users for a portal project: customers, suppliers, and employees. Most portal projects utilize phases or stages, with the initial phases usually being deployed only to a smaller group of users, usually side by side with existing systems. This will lower the risk profile for the project and cut initial support costs.

Identifying Content for the Portal

The business requirements for the portal determine the different collections of content. The content could be in content management or document management systems, in a database, on another web server, on the file system, or in any number of other places. Not all of your content is going to be web-ready, and you may need to write adapters to translate legacy content to XML or HTML. Some portal content may be syndicated using Rich Site Summary (RSS) feeds.

Another set of requirements determines who has access to what content. This can be set up with access rights, with pieces of content mapped into content collections, and users assigned into groups that can access these collections. Your content management system may already have all of this access control built in, and part of the portal project could be to integrate the portal authentication with the content management system security. Other implementations may have to build content security functionality on top of the portal's security model.

Identifying the Metadata for the Content

Most organizations do not have an enterprise-wide standard for their content metadata yet. Creating one makes the portal project much easier. Metadata is any descriptive information about content that can provide context, such as the title, creator, timestamp, or description. Traditionally, content cataloging has been a field where librarians excel, but it is certainly possible for content creators to learn how to provide correct metadata.

One standard for metadata is the Dublin Core Metadata Element Set (`www.dublincore.org/documents/dces/`). This set of 15 metadata elements contains fields for

- Title
- Creator
- Subject
- Description

- Publisher
- Contributor
- Date
- Type
- Format
- Identifier
- Source
- Language
- Relation
- Coverage
- Rights

The metadata can be stored inside the HTML document within `<META>` tags, as elements in an XML document, in a database, or in a Resource Description Framework (RDF) file that is separate from the content file.

If your content repositories do not have this information, you will need to create the metadata from the existing content. This can be a time-consuming manual process, but commercial tools for metadata extraction are available.

Designing the User Interface

Most portals (including the open source Apache Jetspeed 2 portal) are customizable using a set of skins, or themes, that provide look and feel. The HTML and style sheets for the portal are contained in the skin. The layout of the initial portal page the users will get when they log in is usually customizable through the administration tool. Many users will not customize the layout of this page, even if allowed, so an effective design is important. Determine which applications or content sources are going to be used most often (e-mail, human resources, engineering documents, etc.). Build prototypes of the proposed screens, and let users interact with the portal functionality.

From a technical perspective, changing the portal layout or look and feel after deployment is very simple, but the end users may require additional training and notification that the site layout is going to change. Some end users will always be resistant to change, even if it would improve their productivity, and this affects possible redesigns.

Creating an Effective Search Engine

We look at integrating the open source Jakarta Apache search engine Lucene with a portlet in Chapter 10. Your search engine should index as many of your content sources as possible, but it will probably need to be broken down into different collections for different classes of users. The metadata for the content will become fields in Lucene's search index for advanced searching. Commercial search engine vendors should provide portlets that plug into any portal server that implements the standard.

Portal Application Architecture

The information architecture leads to the technical architecture of a portal project. Part of the portal architect's job is to link the two together into a coherent design. For instance, if the business users require a natural language search engine or a structured view of all content in the system, the technical components used to build the portal must reflect this.

All portals that are compatible with the portlet API will have a similar structure. The portal will need to run inside a servlet container such as IBM WebSphere or Apache Tomcat. Because each portlet application deployed on the portal is also a web application, the servlet environment serves any web resources such as servlets or JavaServer Pages (JSP) files. The portal is responsible for providing administrative functionality, a layout for the portlets on the portal page, and the execution of the portlets within a portlet container. The portlet container may be a separate piece of software, but most portal implementations will integrate the container into the portal. Just as a servlet container is responsible for executing servlets, the portlet container will execute any portlets. The portlets have an execution life cycle that we will discuss in Chapter 3.

In this book, we use the terms *portal* and *portal server* interchangeably to reference the server-side application that runs the portlets, manages users, and displays portal pages.

Each visitor to the portal will receive a portal page, which will contain one or more portlets in a customizable layout. These portlets could be commercial portlets that integrate with your existing systems, open source portlets customized for your installation, or custom portlets you have created. Portlets are as easy to create as servlets, and your servlet programming background will help in creating effective portlets.

Building Portlets with the Portlet API

Portlets are components written in Java against the portlet API. The Java classes in the portlet API are in the `javax.portlet` package. Each portlet takes a request from the portal container and returns a response. The response contains content that the portal container will display as part of the portal page sent to the end user. Portlets may include JSP pages, Velocity templates, or another presentation layer technology. Just as with servlets, few developers will put any content directly into the Java code for any nontrivial portlets. In this book, we will use HTML inside of the portlet's Java code until we explain how to use JSP pages inside a portlet in Chapter 5.

The portlet container is responsible for sending requests from the portal to the portlet, and then passing the portlet response back to the portal. It also manages the initialization of the portlet, along with other life cycle events. The portal is responsible for taking the content from the portal container for each portlet and building a web page for the end user. The portal handles the layout, aggregation, and any personalization or SSO security features.

The portlet application is a standard Java 2 Enterprise Edition (J2EE) web application, with the addition of portlet classes and a portlet deployment descriptor named portlet.xml. The directory structure of the portlet application is the same as a web application's layout. A web application archive (WAR) file is also the format used for packaging the portlet application. The portal vendor is responsible for providing deployment and administration tools.

The standard build and packaging tools provided with your choice of Java programming environment or integrated development environment (IDE) for web applications are usable for building portlet applications. We are using the open source Java build tool Ant in this book. If you are not familiar with Ant, we recommend you check out *Java Development with Ant* by Erik Hatcher and Steve Loughran (Manning, 2002) or *Extreme Programming with Ant* by Glenn Niemeyer and Jeremy Poteet (Sams, 2003). Another source to check is the Apache Ant Manual on the Ant web site (`http://ant.apache.org/`).

Our example portlets deploy into the open source portal Apache Pluto (`http://jakarta.apache.org/pluto`), although they will work on any compatible implementation of the portal. Apache Jetspeed (`http://portals.apache.org/jetspeed-2/`) is a full-featured open source portal from Apache. There are currently two versions of Jetspeed: Jetspeed 1 does not support the Java portlet API, and Jetspeed 2 does support JSR-168. EXO (`www.exoplatform.org`) is another open source portal that supports the new Java portlet API, and it also supports Struts and JavaServer Faces (JSF). Most of the commercial Java portal vendors will have implementations of the Java portlet API out already or shortly. Some bundle JSR-168 support into a new version, and others are releasing support as an add-on module.

Providing Technical Solutions with Portals

Portal implementations usually involve a wide variety of interesting technical problems. Because they are generally systems for integrating a range of business systems, content stores, and web applications, the goals for the portal project are usually specific to the installation. Some of the goals that typically come up are integrating a search engine with the portal and providing an SSO interface for security. Other common development tasks for portal projects include extending personalization across all of the portal's applications, integrating content management systems, and creating portlets for systems that were not designed for portals.

In this book, we discuss all of these problems, plus several others, and provide solutions that work within a portal environment. Our hope is that you will be able to take our solutions and make them work for your problems.

Security and Single Sign-On

The portlet API has a basic security model based on the servlet security model. Security is an area that is going to depend heavily either on the proprietary features of your chosen portal, or on leveraging a third-party product that can handle a unified security model.

Single Sign-On is a key requirement for most portal projects, and we cover the different strategies that can be used for SSO projects. We cover SSO in Chapter 8.

Content Syndication and RSS

One common requirement for a portal deployment is to implement content syndication on the portal for multiple sources of content. This content could be from a content management system; from an internal groupware application; or from external sources like Reuters, Yahoo!, or CNN. In this book, we discuss using the RSS format for syndicating content on channels. The RSS portlet can consume RSS feeds that other sites publish.

We also discuss the mechanics of publishing an RSS feed for an existing content store. Our search engine integrates with RSS, so a content feed constantly updates a list of the top hits for a given search. This is useful for creating ad hoc knowledge management systems within your organization.

We will discuss RSS and content syndication in more detail in Chapter 9.

Searching Content from the Portal

In this book, we use the open source search engine Lucene from the Jakarta Apache project to create a portlet for searching content in a Lucene index. Our Lucene search portlet is compatible with any content indexed with Lucene. We demonstrate how to create a simple index from content on the file system. We also deliver the content for the search results inside the portlet.

We create the Lucene search portlet in Chapter 10.

Portals and Web Services

Portals are a natural fit for a services-oriented architecture. Portlets contain the user interface and controller logic, and call out to a service to retrieve information or execute a transaction. These services run on any platform that supports a Simple Object Access Protocol (SOAP) web services API, and the portlet calls out to them using a Java SOAP toolkit like Axis from the Web Services Apache project, or Glue from webMethods. These services can interface with existing mainframe or client server applications, and new enterprise applications should expose a SOAP web services API.

Figure 1-1 shows an example of a portal and web services architecture for a school or university. The enterprise systems for student information and course scheduling have a web services layer that exposes core functionality to the portlets. The web-based courseware service acts as a stand-alone service that can supply content to users of the portal. A desktop application uses SOAP to access the course scheduling system.

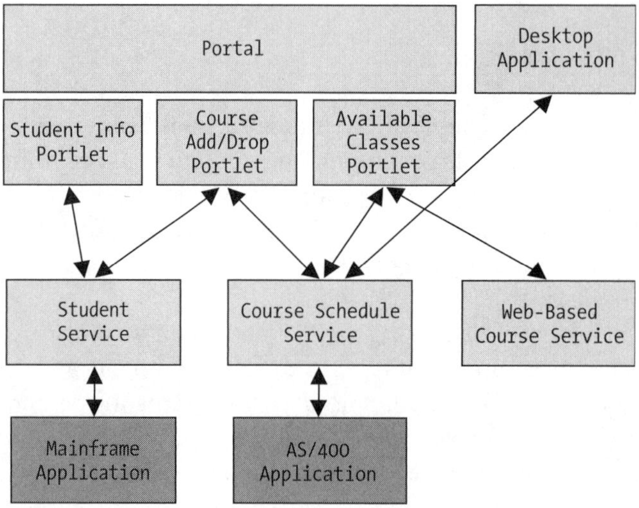

Figure 1-1. Example web services and portal architecture

Web Services for Remote Portlets (WSRP)

Another approach is to create a distributed portal infrastructure. A portal that supports the Web Services for Remote Portlets (WSRP) standard can display portlets from other WSRP-enabled portals. The producer portal publishes its available portlets to a registry, and a consumer portal can display a remote portlet from the registry. The protocols for displaying a portlet from a remote location were standardized with the WSRP specification from the Organization for the Advancement of Structured Information Standards (OASIS). We will cover WSRP in Chapter 12.

Integrating Existing Applications into the Portal

There are several approaches to bringing existing applications into a portal environment. The application can have a WSRP layer written on top, and host itself as a portlet producer. Another approach that uses SOAP is to completely write a thin web services layer on top of the core functionality, and then develop a portlet for that application.

For Java applications that do not have a services layer to expose, or where the value of the application is in the user interface, it makes sense to consider rewriting the application as a portlet or set of portlets. The business logic and persistence can be factored out of the existing application as it is rewritten. This creates a common base layer for both the new portlet user interface and the existing user interface.

Non-Java applications will have to be exposed using SOAP or another cross-platform API. For mainframe and AS/400 character mode applications, several commercial screen scraper products can translate a terminal interface into calls to and from a Java application. The portal may use a proxy portlet to serve existing web-based applications through the portal. The proxy portlet receives a request from the portal's end user and translates it into a web request for the existing application. The existing application responds to the proxy portlet's request with a response, which the proxy portlet then translates into a response for the portal. The portal aggregates that response with the rest of its content to produce a page for the end user. Some of the issues to consider when designing a proxied system like this one are SSO and security, personalization, a consistent look and feel, and the ability to keep track of sessions at the proxy portlet level.

We convert a web-based open source message board to use portlets in Chapter 13. We used the open source forums package YAZD as the beginning of our project. YAZD is built on a servlet and JSP architecture. We built a controller portlet that dispatches requests to the appropriate JSP page.

Using Charts in the Portal

Business intelligence and other analytical applications often use charts to communicate information. Some portal projects create “digital dashboards” that represent the current state of the organization for managers—for instance, a sales manager could see outstanding sales calls for each salesperson, sales margins for products, and profit projections for the quarter. We use the open source charting product JFreeChart to develop charts for portlets in Chapter 14.

Content Management and Portlets

In Chapter 15, we discuss two standards for communicating with content management systems: the Java Content Repository API and the WebDAV protocol. We create a portlet that uses the WebDAV protocol to integrate with a content management system. In this chapter, we use the open source WebDAV client library from the Apache Slide project to build our portlet.

Summary

Portal projects that use standards are going to be easily portable to new portal containers, and developers can use portlets from third-party vendors to create their portals. Before starting work on the production version of your portal, develop an information architecture from the user’s perspective. It should show how the portal is going to look, what it is going to do, and what problems it solves. Start small, with a prototype or deployment to a limited number of users, and build out from there, to ensure that your portal deployment scales.

> **NOTE** *The authors created a web site for this book at* `www.portalbook.com`*. We will have interesting articles, sample portlets, and more information about upcoming portal standards and APIs.*

CHAPTER 2

Portlet Basics

We are ready to start developing our first portlet applications. This chapter contains a quick primer on portlet development, packaging, and deployment descriptors. The open source Apache Pluto portal supports the portlet API, and you will learn how to deploy and run portlets on Pluto. We also cover the programming concepts we use in these first simple portlets, to get you up to speed on developing solutions with portals.

If you are familiar with servlet development, the details of portlet development will be pretty easy. The authors of the portlet specification purposely made portlets similar to servlets so that developers would not have to stretch too far to learn the new API. The hard part of portlet development is design and architecture for the portal and its portlets—instead of working on one Java 2 Enterprise Edition (J2EE) application, multiple applications need to be integrated into a portal.

For developers who are not familiar with JavaServer Pages (JSP), we recommend *Beginning JSP 2: From Novice to Professional* (Apress, May 2004). We use JSP and JSP tags for our portlet applications, so some experience with those is useful. If you have not used the servlet API, you do not need to know it to do portlet development, or to understand our examples.

The portlets in this chapter will be portable to any JSR 168–compliant portal server. Portlet deployment is going to vary based on your portal vendor's provided tools—some may pick up portlet applications from a directory, others may need a command-line tool, and some may use a web-based GUI to allow remote deployment and administration. In any case, the concepts used for development are the same.

We are going to use the terms *portlet, portlet application, portlet container,* and *portal* in this chapter. Portlets are individual classes that process requests from a user and return content for display inside a portal. Portlet applications are standard J2EE web applications that include portlet classes and the portlet.xml portlet deployment descriptor. The portlet container is part of a portal, and it instantiates and executes the portlet classes. Portals aggregate the output of one or more portals into a portal page, which is served to a user. When the user selects a link or submits a form on the portal page, the portal processes the request and then sends requests to all of the portlets on the page. We explain more about portlet request handling in this chapter, so don't worry if this seems a little confusing now.

First Portlet

Let's now jump into our first portlet. You can compile this portlet class, package it with the deployment descriptors, and deploy it on your portal to see it run. Often the hardest part of developing with a new technology is just getting something compiled and running on a server. In this book, we are going to limit our example portlets to the concepts being described, so our ideas do not get lost in implementation details. This portlet is about as basic as a portlet can be.

The following listing (FirstPortlet.java) is a very simple portlet that displays the same message every time it is rendered in a portal page. Every portlet must implement the `Portlet` interface. Your portlets should extend the `GenericPortlet` abstract class, which implements `Portlet` itself. That way, you can take advantage of the methods on the `GenericPortlet` class, which we will discuss further on. The `Portlet` and `GenericPortlet` classes are in the `javax.portlet` package, just like the rest of the classes in the portlet API. Figure 2-1 shows the portlet running on Pluto.

```
package com.portalbook.portlets;

import java.io.IOException;
import java.io.Writer;

import javax.portlet.GenericPortlet;
import javax.portlet.PortletException;
import javax.portlet.RenderRequest;
import javax.portlet.RenderResponse;

public class FirstPortlet extends GenericPortlet
{
    protected void doView(RenderRequest request, RenderResponse response)
        throws PortletException, IOException
    {
        response.setContentType("text/html");
        Writer writer = response.getWriter();
        writer.write("Help, I'm a portlet, and I'm trapped in a portal!");
    }
}
```

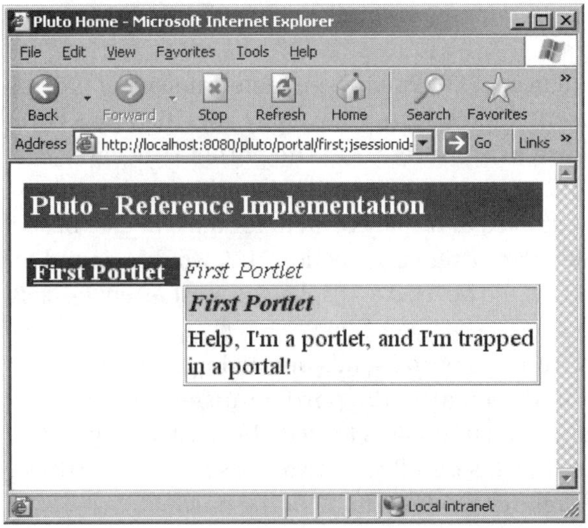

Figure 2-1. Our `FirstPortlet` *portlet running on Apache Pluto*

As you can see, there is a lot of similarity between this simple portlet and an equally simple servlet. Both use request and response objects. The `getWriter()` methods on a portlet response and a servlet response are analogous. The portlet throws a `PortletException` instead of a `ServletException`. The content types on each response are similar. There are several notable differences, however, even with this simple example.

Request Handling

Portlets handle requests differently than servlets. With a servlet, there is one request per response—a browser asks for a URL, and the servlet container processes the HTTP request and passes `HTTPServletRequest` and `HTTPServletResponse` objects to the servlet. Then the servlet normally calls its `doGet()` or `doPost()` methods to generate a response, and the response is sent back to the client's web browser.

With portals, there can be one or more portlets supplying content for each portal page served to the user's web browser. Even though the end user can click a link or submit a form for only one portlet at a time, the other portlets may still need to refresh their content to reflect any changes that have been made in the meantime to the underlying data model that would be reflected in the content. Because of this, portlets must handle two different types of requests: an action request and a render request. You can think of the *action request* as asking the portlet to do something, and the *render request* tells the portlet to display its contents based on its current state.

The portal processes the end user's HTTP request to determine what type of request was specified by the user. The requests are usually specified by a URL generated by a portlet, also known as a portlet URL. The portlet URL can either be an action URL or a render URL. You use the action URL to change the state of the portlet, while the render URL is used to display content for the end user based on the current state of the portlet. For instance, an action URL would be used to delete an e-mail, but a render URL would be used to display the most recent e-mails a user had received.

Each action URL requested from the portal sends one action request to the portlet that supplied the URL, and then after the portlet finishes processing the action request, the portal sends render requests to all of the portlets displayed on the portal page. An action request is handled in two phases. Render URLs requested from the portal send render requests to all of the portlets.

Portlets have two request-handling methods. The first is the `processAction()` method on the `Portlet` interface in the `javax.portlet` package, which is used for handling action requests:

```
public void processAction (ActionRequest request, ActionResponse response)
    throws PortletException, IOException
```

The second is the `render()` method on the `Portlet` interface, which is used for handling render requests:

```
public void render (RenderRequest request, RenderResponse response)
    throws PortletException, IOException
```

Portlet request handling is covered in more detail in the next chapter, along with the rest of the portlet life cycle.

For our first portlet, we only handled render requests. We overrode the `doView()` method on the `GenericPortlet` class. The `GenericPortlet` class is an abstract implementation of the `Portlet` interface. As you saw, we can easily extend `GenericPortlet` to create our own portlets. We discuss `GenericPortlet` in more detail in the `GenericPortlet` section of this chapter.

The doView() Method

The `doView()` method in the `FirstPortlet` class is the only method we overrode from the abstract base class `GenericPortlet`. It's similar to a `doGet()` or `doPost()` method on a servlet, but not exactly the same. Three modes for portlets are defined in the standard: VIEW, EDIT, and HELP. Only the VIEW portlet mode is required; the EDIT and HELP modes are optional.

- **VIEW:** Used to display the current contents of the portlet and allow interaction. You will use this mode for most of your portlet development.
- **EDIT:** Used to allow the user to edit preferences for the portlet to customize its behavior, provide connection data, or conduct similar tasks.
- **HELP:** Used to provide help to the user on using or customizing the portlet.

Other custom modes provided by the portal server are possible. For more on portlet modes, see Chapter 4.

Each mode has a corresponding method, `doView()`, `doEdit()`, or `doHelp()`, inherited from the `GenericPortlet` class. The method signature of the `doView()` method on the `GenericPortlet` abstract class is

```
protected void doView(RenderRequest request, RenderResponse response)
    throws PortletException, IOException
```

When a portlet receives a render request, the `render()` method from the `Portlet` interface class is called. For portlets that subclass the `GenericPortlet` abstract class, the `render()` method sets the title for the portlet, and then calls the `doDispatch()` method on the `GenericPortlet` class:

```
protected void doDispatch (RenderRequest request, RenderResponse response)
    throws PortletException, IOException
```

The `doDispatch()` method checks the portlet's window state to see if it should display any content. The window state for a portlet could be normal, maximized, or minimized. The user can choose to display a portlet in an expanded, full-page view (maximized), its normal layout, or shrunk to a small or nonexistent state (minimized). The portlet determines what content will be displayed, but the actual behavior of the portlet on the page is up to the portal server to decide. For more on window states, see Chapter 4.

If the window state isn't minimized, the `doDispatch()` method delegates the request object and the response object to the appropriate method based on the portlet mode (`doView()`, `doEdit()`, or `doHelp()`).

Building the Portlet Application

The portlet class will need to be packaged as part of a portlet application to be deployed into a portal, like a servlet class would need to be packaged up as part of a web application archive (WAR) file. A portlet application is also a web application, which you should already be familiar with. The difference is that a portlet application contains portlet classes and the portlet deployment descriptor (portlet.xml) in addition to any servlets, JSPs, HTML pages, images, style sheets, and the web application deployment descriptor.

The portal's servlet engine or application server processes and serves anything that is not a portlet in the portlet application. For instance, Pluto would run the portlets in the web application, but any servlets or images would be served by Tomcat. The portlet could include images in the portlet's content, but the portlet container would not directly serve them.

The portal application has the same directory structure as a web application. The WEB-INF directory under the portal application root directory holds the classes and libraries needed to run the portlet. The portal container will look in the WEB-INF/classes directory for portlet classes, or in the WEB-INF/lib directory for Java libraries.

The WEB-INF directory will also contain two deployment descriptors. The web application deployment descriptor, web.xml, contains a description of the web resources used in the portlet application. The portlet application deployment descriptor, portlet.xml, is used to describe the portlets and resources available to the portal container. For portlet applications, web.xml serves the same purpose as it does for web applications.

The web.xml web application deployment descriptor is used to describe several settings for the portlet application. These include the name, description, and any security role mappings that are used for controlling access to the portlet. This is the web.xml we are going to use when we package up the portlet application. The web.xml file your portal deploys into the servlet container may not match this web.xml, because the portlet container may inject its own properties and settings into the file. Each portal vendor may take a slightly different approach to application deployment and modification, so rather than edit files directly on the file system, we deploy portlet application archives into the portal.

```
<?xml version="1.0" encoding="UTF-8"?>
<!DOCTYPE web-app PUBLIC "-//Sun Microsystems, Inc.//DTD Web Application 2.3//EN"
                          "http://java.sun.com/dtd/web-app_2_3.dtd">
<web-app>
  <display-name>First Portlet</display-name>
  <description>This is the first portlet.</description>
</web-app>
```

The web.xml deployment descriptor is also used for describing any servlets included in the portlet application. To describe portlets, we use the portlet.xml deployment descriptor.

Here is the portlet.xml web application deployment descriptor for the `FirstPortlet` portlet application:

```
<?xml version="1.0" encoding="UTF-8"?>
<portlet-app xmlns="http://java.sun.com/xml/ns/portlet/portlet-app_1_0.xsd"
```

```
    version="1.0" xmlns:xsi="http://www.w3.org/2001/XMLSchema-instance"
    xsi:schemaLocation="http://java.sun.com/xml/ns/portlet/portlet-app_1_0.xsd➥
 http://java.sun.com/xml/ns/portlet/portlet-app_1_0.xsd">
    <portlet>
        <description>First Portlet for the Apress Portlet book by Jeff Linwood➥
 and David Minter.</description>
        <portlet-name>FirstPortlet</portlet-name>
        <display-name>First Portlet</display-name>
        <portlet-class>com.portalbook.portlets.FirstPortlet</portlet-class>
        <expiration-cache>-1</expiration-cache>
        <supports>
            <mime-type>text/html</mime-type>
            <portlet-mode>VIEW</portlet-mode>
        </supports>
        <portlet-info>
            <title>First Portlet</title>
            <short-title>1st Portlet</short-title>
            <keywords>First, Portlet</keywords>
        </portlet-info>
    </portlet>
 </portlet-app>
```

The portlet deployment descriptor has to comply with the portlet API XML schema definition file. One basic best practice is to use a validating XML editor any time you edit a deployment descriptor—it is too easy to edit one with a regular text editor like Notepad or vi and accidentally forget to escape an entity or something similar.

The `<portlet-app>` element of the deployment descriptor is the root of the XML document. The root is the container for information about the portlets in the portlet application. It also contains any custom portlet modes, custom window states, user attributes, or security constraints that the portlet application supports. For our first portlet, we are only going to describe a portlet.

The next element in the portlet.xml deployment descriptor is `<portlet>`, which represents one of the available portlets in the portlet application. There can be more than one `<portlet>` element under a `<portlet-app>` element. We define each portlet that could be included in a portal here as a `<portlet>` element.

We go on to give the portlet an optional description, which could be used by the portal to display information about the portlet to a portal administrator or users who are customizing their portal page to include relevant portlets. We will use our `<description>` element to include some information about the portlet. The `<description>` element is optional.

The next element underneath `<portlet>` is `<portlet-name>`, which is required. This name has to be unique across all portlets in the portlet application. The portal will use it for internal purposes to differentiate portlets in a portlet application. The portal can also use the portlet name to display a name to the end user, if the <display-name> element is not defined.

> **TIP** *Although the portlet name has to be unique within a portlet application, it is possible that one portal could have portlets in different portlet applications with the same name. It is also possible that you could install the same portlet application on a portal twice, in different contexts. The portal will use a combination of the portlet application context and the portlet name to refer to the portlet. As an aside, you can also have the same portlet in more than one place in the portal page.*

The <display-name> element contains a name that is suitable for presenting to the user or administrator. Unlike the <portlet-name> element, it does not have to be unique, and it is not a required element in a portlet.xml deployment descriptor.

We need to specify the Java class we are going to use for this portlet in the <portlet-class> element. The class name specified here should be a fully qualified class name. The class itself either should be in a directory under WEB-INF/classes, or packaged up in a JAR file in the WEB-INF/lib directory of the portlet application. These are the same requirements for packaging a class as the J2EE web application packaging standard. The <portlet-class> element is required in the portlet.xml deployment descriptor.

The <expiration-cache> element in the deployment descriptor controls caching for the portlet's content. We discuss caching in Chapter 4.

Each portlet is expected to contribute part of the portal page. For most application development, portlets will produce HTML or XHTML content. Other content types are possible for portlets, such as WML for wireless applications. Portlets will need to set the content type on the render response object. In our first portlet, we set the content type to "text/html", for returning HTML content.

For HTML or XHTML content, portlets need to support a limited set of HTML elements. The content a portlet returns is integrated into the portal page, which already has <HEAD>, <BODY>, <HTML>, and <TITLE> elements. The portlet should not use any of those elements, or the <BASE>, <FRAME>, or <FRAMESET> HTML tags.

All portlets should return valid content, with matched HTML tags, where appropriate. The portlet also shouldn't rely on any particular HTML (like tables) rendered in the portal page.

The <supports> element defines the supported portlet modes for each Multipurpose Internet Mail Extensions (MIME) type. Each portlet definition requires at least one <supports> element, but can have more if needed to support markup types such as HTML, text, or WML. The <supports> element contains a supported MIME type, and one or more supported portlet modes. The

`<mime-type>` element is required. The MIME type is usually text/html, but any MIME type supported by the portal is possible. The `<portlet-mode>` elements are the list of supported portlet modes (VIEW, EDIT, HELP, or custom) for the portlet. For our first portlet, we are only going to be supporting HTML output with the VIEW portlet mode.

Portal vendors may provide easy-to-use tools to create and edit portlet.xml deployment descriptors with their products. These tools may make application assembly easier, but it is still essential to learn about the format. For more on the portlet.xml deployment descriptor, see Chapter 6.

Packaging

We compiled and packaged the portlet application into a WAR file. You can use any tools you like to compile your portlet application. We used Apache Ant (`http://ant.apache.org`) to build our WAR file. The `FirstPortlet` class is in the WEB-INF/classes/com/portalbook/portlets directory. Our portlet.xml and web.xml deployment descriptors are in WEB-INF, and the manifest.mf manifest file is in the META-INF directory.

Deploying

We installed Apache Pluto (`http://portals.apache.org/pluto`) to run our portlet application. Apache Pluto is the open source reference implementation of the JSR 168 portlet API. The Pluto portal is very basic and not suitable for enterprise portal projects, but it is a good test platform for your portlets. Pluto requires a recent version of Apache Tomcat (`http://jakarta.apache.org/tomcat`); check the Pluto release notes and installation instructions on the Pluto web site for more details.

> **NOTE** *At the time of this book's writing, Pluto did not have a downloadable, compiled release. We had to install Apache Maven (*`http://maven.apache.org`*) and download Pluto's source code from CVS to create a compiled version. Check the Pluto web site for news about a version 1.0 release. If a compiled release is not available when this book is published, the authors will post on our web site,* `www.portalbook.com`*, a detailed HOWTO for getting Pluto running.*

Pluto's deployment process is not terribly easy, and there are three distinct steps after you get Pluto running on your machine. The first is to set up Apache Maven (`http://maven.apache.org`). Check the Pluto installation instructions to determine which version of Maven to install.

The next step is to run the Pluto deployment tool with your portlet application. This is straightforward. From your Pluto directory, run the following command, with the directory containing your WAR file where we have DIRECTORY:

```
maven deploy -Ddeploy=DIRECTORY\first.war
```

After you deploy your portlet application, the next step is to modify two Pluto configuration files so Pluto will display your portlet. These configuration files are located in your TOMCAT_HOME/webapps/pluto/WEB-INF/data directory.

The first configuration file is the portletentityregistry.xml file, which contains portlet and portlet application definitions. Inside this file, you will map portlet applications to an ID with the `<application id="first">` element. There can be more than one `<application>` elements. The `<definition-id>` element identifies the name of the web application on Tomcat that contains the portlet, in this case `first`.

Each application contains one or more `<portlet>` elements, which identify individual portlets. Put the name of the web application, a period, and then the name of the portlet as one string in the `<definition-id>`:

```
<?xml version="1.0" encoding="UTF-8"?>
<portlet-entity-registry>
    <application id="first">
        <definition-id>first</definition-id>
        <portlet id="firstportlet">
            <definition-id>first.FirstPortlet</definition-id>
        </portlet>
    </application>
</portlet-entity-registry>
```

The other configuration file, pageregistry.xml, describes how the portal page looks. The important part of this file is the fragment `p1` that identifies the portlet. The value of the portlet property must be a valid application ID, a period, and a valid portlet ID from that application, all concatenated together.

```
<?xml version="1.0"?>
<portal>
    <fragment name="navigation"
 class="org.apache.pluto.portalImpl.aggregation.navigation.TabNavigation">
    </fragment>
    <fragment name="first" type="page">
        <navigation>
            <title>First Portlet</title>
            <description>...</description>
        </navigation>
        <fragment name="row" type="row">
```

```
            <fragment name="col1" type="column">
                <fragment name="p1" type="portlet">
                    <property name="portlet" value="first.firstportlet"/>
                </fragment>
            </fragment>
        </fragment>
    </fragment>
</portal>
```

Running

Running Pluto after you deploy the portlets is simple. Just start up Tomcat, and go to the /pluto/portal path for your Tomcat installation (usually `http://localhost:8080/pluto/portal`). Select the link that says "first", and your first portlet should be up and running!

Portlet Programming 101

Before we move on to our next example, there are several classes in the portlet API we should cover. The `GenericPortlet` class is a useful abstract base class we can use for all of our portlets to provide default portlet functionality. The portlet uses the `PortletRequest` interface and its two subclasses, `ActionRequest` and `RenderRequest`, to retrieve information about the end user's request to the portlet, portlet configuration, and the portal's settings. The portlet uses `PortletResponse`, and its corresponding subclasses, `ActionResponse` and `RenderResponse`, to send output to the portal container, set portlet render parameters, and to pass information to the portal or portlet container.

We are not going to cover the request and response objects in full in this chapter—for more on internationalization, portal settings, and other topics, see Chapter 4. This rest of this chapter concentrates on the most commonly used aspects of the request and response objects, including the interplay between portlet actions and portlet rendering. We follow up with a more involved example of a portlet that posts information to itself, changes its own title used by the portal page, and includes images in its HTML content.

GenericPortlet

We are going to use the `GenericPortlet` class in the `javax.portlet` package as the base class for all of our portlets. `GenericPortlet` implements both the `Portlet` and the `PortletConfig` interfaces from the portlet API. We have already touched on the `Portlet` interface, but we will explain the `PortletConfig` interface in later chapters.

You will not have to know anything about PortletConfig for this example. We can either extend GenericPortlet directly or extend a class that already extends GenericPortlet. If you have portlets with related functionality, you should probably develop your own base portlet classes that extend GenericPortlet. For instance, if you are integrating a customer relationship management (CRM) system with your portal, you might have a portlet that displays active sales cycles, and another portlet that has sales contact information. If both of these use a similar connection to a back-end CRM system, you could put the connector functionality into a common base portlet class. Of course, abstracting that functionality into a class that does not use the portlet API at all would be even better, to leverage the common code with Swing or web applications.

One unlikely reason to use a different base class would be if you were using a portal container that provides functionality beyond the standard portlet API. If you were going to use these proprietary features, you might need to extend a portlet class that the portal vendor provides. As far as we know, no currently existing portals support this scenario, but it would be one reason to use a different base portlet class.

Portlets that subclass the GenericPortlet class get implementations of the default functionality for a portlet, which makes developing easier. The portlet will have to override at least one of the methods on the GenericPortlet abstract class to provide the desired functionality.

With any upgrade to the portlet API, you should check the GenericPortlet class to see what has changed between versions. If your classes extend the GenericPortlet abstract class, they will likely pick up default implementations of any new methods added to the Portlet interface, but that does not necessarily mean you should accept these defaults.

You may need to override the doDispatch() method for one of two reasons. The first would be to support any custom modes the portal vendor provided for the server. The doDispatch() method can only delegate to the doView(), doEdit(), and doHelp() methods. The second reason would be to support content display for the minimized window state.

Portlet Requests

The portlet container passes the portlet request and response objects to the portlet whenever the portlet handles a request. Both the render() and processAction() methods on a portlet take portlet request and response objects as arguments. The portlet can get details about the client's request, access information about the state of the portlet, and query the portlet for details of its configuration from the portlet request object.

Two different request objects are used in the portlet API. One is an object that implements the ActionRequest interface, which is an argument to the portlet's processAction() method. The other is a RenderRequest object, which the portlet container passes to the `render()` method. Both subclass the `PortletRequest` interface, which contains the common methods and fields for the `ActionRequest` and `RenderRequest` interface classes. Either type of request is possible when a user performs an action with a portlet. We discuss where to use action requests and render requests in more depth in Chapter 4.

Portlets can set parameters on portlet URLs to pass information in a request when the user clicks on a link that contains a portlet URL. These parameters are name/value pairs, with `String` objects representing both the name and the value. The parameters are accessible through a set of methods on the request object. You would use portlet request parameters just as you would use HTTP parameters in a normal web application.

One important point to make clear is the distinction between action requests and render requests. If parameters are passed to a portlet in an action request, they are not passed to a subsequent render request. This is to allow actions that carry out a discrete operation on the underlying data model or state of the portlet. An example of a task for an action would be sending an e-mail. You probably would not want an e-mail to be sent every time the user refreshes the portal's web page.

If an action wishes to set parameters for a render request, it can set render parameters itself on the action response. The portlet container takes the render parameters from the action response and puts them on the portlet's render request. Render parameters remain valid for a portlet, even if a request is passed to another portlet on the same page. When the user triggers an action request, the portlet is responsible for setting the render parameters used by future requests. If a portlet receives a render request, it will use the new render parameters for any subsequent render requests, until the portlet receives a new user-initiated request.

NOTE *Sun has reserved the javax.portlet. prefix for any of its own uses that require setting parameters. Don't use any parameters that start with javax.portlet in your portlets, and you should be fine.*

For more on portlet requests, see Chapter 4.

Portlet Response

A portlet uses a portlet response object to return content to the portal container, change the state of the portlet or the portal, and to pass any other information needed by the portal to build a portal page. Similar to the portlet request object, the `PortletResponse` interface class is the base class for both the `ActionResponse` interface and the `RenderResponse` interface.

You encode URLs to other resources in the portlet application, such as HTML files, images, JSP pages, servlets, or style sheets, so the portlet container can process the URL to aid in processing. Your portlet should use the encoded URL for any instance of a URL in the portlet's rendered content.

Portlets will need to set the content type of the response to one of the allowed content types from the request. Portlets can use the `setContentType()` method on the `RenderResponse` object to set the content MIME type:

```
public void setContentType(String type)
```

A portlet can ask the request for the default content type supported by the portal, or it can get a list of all of the content types supported by the portal. The deployment descriptor defines the content types a portlet can support, and portals must only ask for those supported content types from a portlet. The `getResponseContentType()` method on a `PortletRequest` object returns the content type that the portal would like to use:

```
public String getResponseContentType()
```

To get a list of all content types supported for displaying content from the portlet, use the `getResponseContentTypes()` method, which is also on the `PortletRequest` object:

```
public java.util.Enumeration getResponseContentTypes()
```

After a portlet has defined the content type it is going to use to render the markup fragment, the portlet will need to write its content to an output. Like a servlet, portlets can use either output streams or writers, both from the Java I/O library. The output stream is useful for writing byte output for the portal page, but its use is going to be very rare for a portlet. Do not use portlets for serving generated images or other binary content directly. Instead, write the generated content to disk and serve it as a static URL, or use a servlet to write binary data. For instance, use a charting servlet to generate dynamic images. The image HTML tags in the portlet's content would point to the servlet.

Most portlets should use the `getWriter()` method on the `RenderResponse` object to write out textual content to the portal page as a markup fragment:

```
public java.io.PrintWriter getWriter() throws java.io.IOException
```

The portlet can write to its output stream, or its writer, but not both during one render request.

For more on portlet response objects, see Chapter 4.

Enhancing the Portlet

We are going to make some improvements to our first portlet to demonstrate some more capabilities of the portlet API. Almost every portlet will refer to external resources such as images, JavaScript source files, or style sheets. We include an image in our portlet's content to demonstrate how to use other web resources that are bundled in the portlet application archive.

We will add a form that lets the end user edit the content and title displayed by the portlet. The portlet's EDIT portlet mode will let the user change the portlet's settings. We will also provide a brief message in the portlet's HELP portlet mode. All portals support these portlet modes, and users will expect to use them to change settings and get helpful information. The form is going to have to post back to the portlet, so we will use portlet URLs to create an action request for the portlet. We are also going to change the title that the portal will display for the portlet. We will need to override the default title handling that `GenericPortlet` provides.

Setting the Portlet Title

The portlet can specify the title to display in the portal page programmatically. By default, a portlet that subclasses the `GenericPortlet` class will set the title on the portlet itself from the portlet's resource bundle. Each portlet can have a resource bundle to hold descriptive data for internationalization purposes. The initial specification defines three different data elements for the resource bundle: title, short title, and keywords.

We could override the `getTitle()` method on the `GenericPortlet` class to provide our own title-handling code. For our advanced portlet in this chapter, we do just that. If we did not want to create our own method, we could set the title ourselves in the resource bundle.

The resource bundle is part of the portlet.xml deployment descriptor. The `<portlet-info>` element holds the resource bundle data. If you are using a resource bundle on the classpath, the `<resource-bundle>` element in the deployment descriptor should be used to provide a name.

Here is an excerpt from a portlet.xml deployment descriptor that shows a resource bundle with a title, short title, and keywords:

```
<portlet-info>
    <title>First Portlet</title>
    <short-title>1st Portlet</short-title>
    <keywords>First, Portlet</keywords>
</portlet-info>
```

Another way to change the title is the `setTitle()` method on the `RenderResponse` class. You can call this method from the portlet's `render()` method:

```
public void setTitle(String title)
```

Call the `setTitle()` method before the portlet's output is completely written out.

Portlet URLs

A portlet can create a URL that targets itself in the portlet container. These URLs are called portlet URLs. A portlet URL will reference the instance of the portlet in the portal page—if there are two portlets on the page with the same class, they will have different portlet URLs.

The portal container is responsible for the creation of the part of the portlet URL that references the portlet in the portal page, and for parsing the portlet URL into parameters for the portlet request.

The portlet creates `PortletURL` objects that represent portlet URLs. The portlet can use one of two methods on the `RenderResponse` class to create these `PortletURL` objects:

```
public PortletURL createRenderURL();
public PortletURL createActionURL();
```

We can use the `createActionURL()` method to make action URLs for HTML forms or links. These action URLs are useful for processing actions on the portlet.

Each portlet can add portlet URLs to content with no parameters, or they can set a parameter on a `PortletURL` object using the `setParameter(String name, String value)` method:

```
public void setParameter (String name, String value)
```

To set more than one value on a parameter, use the `setParameter(String name, String[] values)` method on the `PortletURL` class:

```
public void setParameter (String name, String[] values)
```

Portlets can also prepare all parameters at once in a `java.util.Map` object. The keys for the parameter map need to be `String` objects, and the values for the parameter map need to be `String` arrays. Use the `setParameters()` method on the `PortletURL` class to set the parameter map:

```
public void setParameters(java.util.Map parameters)
```

In addition, portlet URLs can specify that the portlet would like security enabled for the communication between the portal and the end user's browser. The `setSecure()` method takes an argument of `true` to enable security, or `false` if encryption is not needed by the portlet:

```
public void setSecure (boolean secure) throws PortletSecurityException
```

You can also use portlet URLs to set portlet modes or window states for the link. We cover these in more detail in Chapter 4.

Processing Action Requests

How does the portlet action request handling work? A portlet displays content with a link to an action URL, with or without parameters, or with a form that submits to an action URL. The portal processes the action URL, and passes an action request with any parameters to the portlet's `processAction()` method. The `processAction()` method takes any steps needed for the action. If the state of the portlet needs to change, the `processAction()` method can set render parameters on the action response that will be valid for the portlet for every subsequent render request from another portlet action on the page.

For our advanced portlet, we are going to set up an HTML form in the EDIT mode of the portlet. This form will submit to an action URL, which the portlet's `processAction()` method will handle as an action request.

The doEdit() method

The `doEdit()` method on the `AdvancedPortlet` class we've written contains the code used to display a form to users when they select the EDIT mode for the portlet. They can select the EDIT mode through the user interface that the portal provides—each portal will do this somewhat differently, but the details are not up to the portlet. The portlet can create links in its content that change the portlet's mode to EDIT, and we cover this in more detail in Chapter 4.

```
protected void doEdit(
    RenderRequest renderRequest,
    RenderResponse renderResponse)
    throws PortletException, IOException
{
    renderResponse.setContentType("text/html");

    Writer writer = renderResponse.getWriter();

    //get the existing parameters to use as defaults.
    String title = renderRequest.getParameter("title");
    String contents = renderRequest.getParameter("contents");

    if (title == null)
    {
```

```
            title = "";
        }

        if (contents == null)
        {
            contents = "";
        }

        writer.write("<H1>Portlet Settings</H1>");
        writer.write("<FORM ACTION=");
        writer.write(renderResponse.createActionURL().toString());
        writer.write(">");

        writer.write(
            "Title: <INPUT TYPE=text NAME=title VALUE='"
                + title
                + "' SIZE=25>");
        writer.write(
            "Contents: <INPUT TYPE=text NAME=contents VALUE= '"
                + contents
                + "' SIZE=25>");
        writer.write("<P>");
        writer.write("<INPUT TYPE=submit>");
        writer.write("</FORM>");
    }
```

The `doEdit()` method first sets the content type and gets the writer. Then the portlet checks for any render parameters on the request. It uses these render parameters, `title` and `contents`, to set the defaults for the HTML form. The HTML form is displayed by writing strings to the `PrintWriter` object of the portlet. We set the value of the HTML `<FORM>` element's `ACTION` attribute to an action URL we create and then immediately render as a `String`.

Next, we add two HTML `<INPUT>` elements with the default values, if any, and a submit button for the form. We end the HTML `<FORM>` element to provide valid content. The tags in the portlet's markup fragment should be balanced.

The interesting part of this method is the form itself, and how it points back to the portlet.

Pointing the Form to the Portlet

The HTML form's action needs to point to the portlet. The details of how a URL points to a specific instance of a portlet are up to the portal container, so rather than creating a URL ourselves, we use the portlet's render response object to create a portlet URL for an action request. A portlet URL that creates an action request is also called an action URL.

If a link that passes parameters in the portlet request needs to be created, use the `setParameter()` or `setParameters()` methods on the `PortletURL` object. Do not try to use string manipulation or additions to the URL in HTML to add parameters to the portlet URL. Because the portal may process the URL after the content is received from the portal's render method, portlet URLs should not necessarily be considered valid or complete URLs.

Processing the Action

The `processAction()` method of our portlet accepts the input from the form we displayed in the EDIT mode. Our VIEW and HELP modes do not have forms, so we have to worry only about handling the input from the EDIT mode's form.

```
public void processAction(
    ActionRequest actionRequest,
    ActionResponse actionResponse)
    throws PortletException, IOException
{
    //check for parameters
    String title = actionRequest.getParameter("title");
    if (title != null)
    {
        actionResponse.setRenderParameter("title", title);
    }

    String contents = actionRequest.getParameter("contents");
    if (contents != null)
    {
        actionResponse.setRenderParameter("contents", contents);
    }
}
```

This method should be called only from the Submit button on the edit page, but we need to check to see that the parameters we expect are in the `ActionRequest` object.

If a parameter does not exist, when we ask the `ActionRequest` object for that missing parameter, we will get a return value of null. If we get a non-null value for a parameter, we are going to set a render parameter with the same name as the action parameter on the `ActionResponse` object. This allows us to maintain state. In more complicated portlets, we would do additional work based on the input parameters, and would not necessarily set the same parameters we received from the action request as render parameters on the action response.

When the processAction() method is complete, the portal will proceed to send render requests to all of the portlets that are currently being displayed in the portal page.

Our portlet's render() method (inherited from GenericPortlet) will be called, which will in turn set the title for the portlet and then delegate content processing to the doDispatch() (also inherited from the GenericPortlet) method. The doDispatch() method will then look at the portlet mode and call the appropriate doView(), doEdit(), or doHelp() method on our portlet.

Setting the Title

The GenericPortlet base class has a getTitle() method that looks in the portlet's resource bundle to determine the portlet's title. We are going to override the getTitle() method on the GenericPortlet class to do our own processing. Our getTitle() method will check the render request object for a parameter called title. This method returns a string to the render() method, which then sets the title on the render response object:

```
protected String getTitle(RenderRequest renderRequest)
{
    String title = renderRequest.getParameter("title");
    if (title != null)
    {
        return title;
    }
    //else return a default title, if we don't have one set yet.
    return "Advanced Portlet";
}
```

Our default title, if one has not been set in the EDIT mode yet, is "Advanced Portlet".

After we set the title for the portlet, the render() method will call the doDispatch() method, which then calls a content display method for the current portlet mode.

Displaying the Content

Our doView() method displays the content for the portlet that will appear when the portlet starts. For design purposes, use the VIEW mode for most user interaction with the portlet. Our doView() method looks at the parameters on the render request object for the contents parameter. If it finds that parameter, it replaces the default portlet contents with the new contents that a user set in the EDIT mode of the portlet.

Here is the doView() method on our AdvancedPortlet class:

```
protected void doView(
    RenderRequest renderRequest,
    RenderResponse renderResponse)
    throws PortletException, IOException
{
    renderResponse.setContentType("text/html");
    Writer writer = renderResponse.getWriter();
    String contents = renderRequest.getParameter("contents");
    if (contents != null)
    {
        writer.write(contents);
    }
    else
    {
        //return the default contents
        writer.write("This is the default portlet contents.  To change ");
        writer.write("this message, edit the portlet's settings.");
    }

    writer.write("<p>");
    writer.write(
        "<IMG SRC="
            + renderResponse.encodeURL(
                renderRequest.getContextPath() + "/images/picture.jpg")
            + ">");

    writer.write("<p>");
    writer.write(
        "<IMG SRC=http://www.greenninja.com/images/teton1-small.jpg>");
}
```

Our doView() method also writes HTML to display two images in the content. The first image is loaded from the portlet application. Another web site (www.greenninja.com) serves the second image. Both of the pictures are static images.

Including an Image in the Portlet Content

Our portlet needs to display an image when it is in VIEW mode. It is easy to include an image in the portlet display if another machine serves the file—it is just a normal <IMG> HTML tag:

```
<IMG SRC="http://www.myserver.com/images/Sailboat.jpg">
```

If the image is packaged into a portlet application along with the portlet classes and any servlets, JSP files, or style sheets needed, including it in the portlet gets a little more complicated. We cannot just use relative links to static files that could be served up from the portlet application because the portal could be using the URL of the portal page for any purpose it needs—the URL on the end user's web browser may not necessarily correspond to the context path of the deployed portlet application.

Here is the relevant portion of our doView() method:

```
writer.write(
    "<IMG SRC="
        + renderResponse.encodeURL(
            renderRequest.getContextPath() + "/images/picture.jpg")
        + ">");
```

We will need to ask the portlet request for the context path of the running portlet, which we can use to construct links to the files included in the portlet application. The deployment of the portlet application on the portal determines the portlet application's context path. For example, if the portlet application archive file is called myapp.war, the portal administrator might have assigned the context path to be /myapp when deploying the portlet application on the portal. The portal would refer to the path /myapp to find the portlet application.

The getContextPath() method on the PortletRequest interface class is used to obtain the context path to build links:

```
public String getContextPath()
```

Because the portal could be using the URL to embed any information it needs for itself, we will need to ask the portal to encode the URL that the portlet renders for its display in HTML. We can use the encodeURL() method on the PortletResponse object that was passed as an argument to our doView() method:

```
public String encodeURL (String path)
```

Any external resources in the portlet application that are referenced as URLs in the portlet's displayed HTML content need to be referred to like the directions for the image in the AdvancedPortlet. This includes JavaScript source files, Cascading Style Sheet (CSS) files, images, Flash objects, and other multimedia elements.

The doView() method will be used much more often than the doHelp() method, which services the HELP portlet mode.

The doHelp() Method

The doHelp() method is very straightforward. It simply displays a basic help message in its content. We have already covered the portlet concepts used here in the opening section of this chapter, on our first portlet.

Here is the doHelp() method on our AdvancedPortlet class:

```
protected void doHelp(
    RenderRequest renderRequest,
    RenderResponse renderResponse)
    throws PortletException, IOException
{
    //return a helpful message
    renderResponse.setContentType("text/html");

    Writer writer = renderResponse.getWriter();
    writer.write(
        "This portlet allows you to change its content and title.");
}
```

The AdvancedPortlet class is the only Java class we have created for this portlet application. Now let's create a portlet application deployment descriptor to describe our portlet.

The portlet.xml Deployment Descriptor

The deployment descriptor for this portlet application includes all of the elements that were in the portlet.xml from the first portlet in this chapter, and we added support for several new portlet deployment descriptor elements:

```
<?xml version="1.0" encoding="UTF-8"?>
<portlet-app xmlns="http://java.sun.com/xml/ns/portlet/portlet-app_1_0.xsd"
 version="1.0"
 xmlns:xsi="http://www.w3.org/2001/XMLSchema-instance"
 xsi:schemaLocation="http://java.sun.com/xml/ns/portlet/portlet-app_1_0.xsd ➥
http://java.sun.com/xml/ns/portlet/portlet-app_1_0.xsd">
```

```
    <portlet>
        <description>Advanced Portlet Description</description>
        <portlet-name>AdvancedPortlet</portlet-name>
        <display-name>Advanced Portlet</display-name>
        <portlet-class>com.portalbook.portlets.AdvancedPortlet</portlet-class>
        <expiration-cache>-1</expiration-cache>
        <supports>
            <mime-type>text/html</mime-type>
            <portlet-mode>VIEW</portlet-mode>
            <portlet-mode>EDIT</portlet-mode>
            <portlet-mode>HELP</portlet-mode>
        </supports>
        <supported-locale>en</supported-locale>
        <portlet-info>
            <title>Advanced Portlet</title>
            <short-title>Adv. Portlet</short-title>
            <keywords>Advanced</keywords>
        </portlet-info>
    </portlet>
</portlet-app>
```

The advanced portlet needs to support the EDIT and HELP portlet modes, along with the VIEW mode we used in the first portlet. The portal will provide access to the different supported portal modes. Portals should allow access only to the modes the portlet supports, and remove any user interface elements that allow access to the unsupported modes for a portlet.

We also included the <supported-locale> element in the deployment descriptor. The <supported-locale> element is used to support multilingual portals that allow the user to choose a favorite language and see their portlets in that language if supported. Portals could also use the <supported-locale> element for the user's customization of portal pages. Portlets could be organized in a catalog by language. Our portlet supports only English.

The <portlet-info> element is used to specify metadata about the portlet. The <title> element is used to specify a title that the portal can use when it displays the portlet. The <short-title> element is a briefer version of the title. Our portlet also supplies a keyword with the <keywords> element. Portals could allow end users to search through the portlet catalog for a term that matches one of the keywords for a portlet. The keywords could also be displayed in the catalog as helpful information.

Here is the complete code listing for our AdvancedPortlet class:

```
package com.portalbook.portlets;

import java.io.IOException;
import java.io.Writer;
```

```
import javax.portlet.ActionRequest;
import javax.portlet.ActionResponse;
import javax.portlet.GenericPortlet;
import javax.portlet.PortletException;
import javax.portlet.RenderRequest;
import javax.portlet.RenderResponse;

public class AdvancedPortlet extends GenericPortlet
{

    protected void doEdit(
        RenderRequest renderRequest,
        RenderResponse renderResponse)
        throws PortletException, IOException
    {
        renderResponse.setContentType("text/html");

        Writer writer = renderResponse.getWriter();

        //get the existing parameters to use as defaults.
        String title = renderRequest.getParameter("title");
        String contents = renderRequest.getParameter("contents");

        if (title == null)
        {
            title = "";
        }

        if (contents == null)
        {
            contents = "";
        }

        writer.write("<H1>Portlet Settings</H1>");
        writer.write("<FORM ACTION=");
        writer.write(renderResponse.createActionURL().toString());
        writer.write(">");

        writer.write(
            "Title: <INPUT TYPE=text NAME=title VALUE='" + title + "' SIZE=25>");
        writer.write(
            "Contents: <INPUT TYPE=text NAME=contents VALUE= '"
                + contents
                + "' SIZE=25>");
```

```
        writer.write("<P>");
        writer.write("<INPUT TYPE=submit>");
        writer.write("</FORM>");

    }

    protected void doHelp(
        RenderRequest renderRequest,
        RenderResponse renderResponse)
        throws PortletException, IOException
    {
        //return a helpful message
        renderResponse.setContentType("text/html");

        Writer writer = renderResponse.getWriter();
        writer.write(
            "This portlet allows you to change its content and title.");
    }

    protected void doView(
        RenderRequest renderRequest,
        RenderResponse renderResponse)
        throws PortletException, IOException
    {
        renderResponse.setContentType("text/html");
        Writer writer = renderResponse.getWriter();
        String contents = renderRequest.getParameter("contents");
        if (contents != null)
        {
            writer.write(contents);
        }
        else
        {
            //return the default contents
            writer.write("This is the default portlet contents.  To change ");
            writer.write("this message, edit the portlet's settings.");
        }

        writer.write("<p>");
        writer.write(
            "<IMG SRC="
                + renderResponse.encodeURL(
                    renderRequest.getContextPath() + "/images/picture.jpg")
                + ">");
```

```
        writer.write("<p>");
        writer.write(
            "<IMG SRC=http://www.greenninja.com/images/teton1-small.jpg>");
    }

    protected String getTitle(RenderRequest renderRequest)
    {
        String title = renderRequest.getParameter("title");
        if (title != null)
        {
            return title;
        }
        //else return a default title, if we don't have one set yet.
        return "Advanced Portlet";
    }

    public void processAction(
        ActionRequest actionRequest,
        ActionResponse actionResponse)
        throws PortletException, IOException
    {
        //check for parameters
        String title = actionRequest.getParameter("title");
        if (title != null)
        {
            actionResponse.setRenderParameter("title", title);
        }

        String contents = actionRequest.getParameter("contents");
        if (contents != null)
        {
            actionResponse.setRenderParameter("contents", contents);
        }
    }

}
```

Web.xml Deployment Descriptor

Our web.xml deployment descriptor's format did not change from the first portlet, although we updated the display name and description:

```
<?xml version="1.0" encoding="UTF-8"?>
<!DOCTYPE web-app PUBLIC "-//Sun Microsystems, Inc.//DTD Web Application 2.3//EN"
```

```
                                   "http://java.sun.com/dtd/web-app_2_3.dtd">
<web-app>
  <display-name>Advanced Portlet</display-name>
  <description>An advanced portlet.</description>
</web-app>
```

Packaging and Deploying

We packaged the advanced portlet the same way we packaged the first portlet. We also deployed the advanced portlet with the same deployment tool and command line, substituting our new WAR file's path.

You will need to add the new portlet application to the portletentityregistry.xml file that we edited for the first portlet. With both portlet applications, it should look like this:

```
<?xml version="1.0" encoding="UTF-8"?>

<portlet-entity-registry>
    <application id="first">
        <definition-id>first</definition-id>
        <portlet id="firstportlet">
            <definition-id>first.FirstPortlet</definition-id>
        </portlet>
    </application>
    <application id="advanced">
        <definition-id>advanced</definition-id>
        <portlet id="advancedportlet">
            <definition-id>advanced.AdvancedPortlet</definition-id>
        </portlet>
    </application>
</portlet-entity-registry>
```

We also added the advanced portlet to the pageregistry.xml file. The portal will display the first portlet side by side with the advanced portlet:

```
<?xml version="1.0"?>
<portal>
    <fragment name="navigation"
 class="org.apache.pluto.portalImpl.aggregation.navigation.TabNavigation">
    </fragment>
    <fragment name="first" type="page">
        <navigation>
            <title>First Portlet</title>
            <description>...</description>
```

```
        </navigation>
        <fragment name="row" type="row">
            <fragment name="col1" type="column">
                <fragment name="p1" type="portlet">
                    <property name="portlet" value="first.firstportlet"/>
                </fragment>
                <fragment name="p2" type="portlet">
                    <property name="portlet" value="advanced.advancedportlet"/>
                </fragment>
            </fragment>
        </fragment>
    </fragment>
</portal>
```

After editing these files, we restarted Tomcat.

Running

When you reload the portal page, you will see the portlets running next to each other in the portal page. Figure 2-2 shows both portlets running in one portal page.

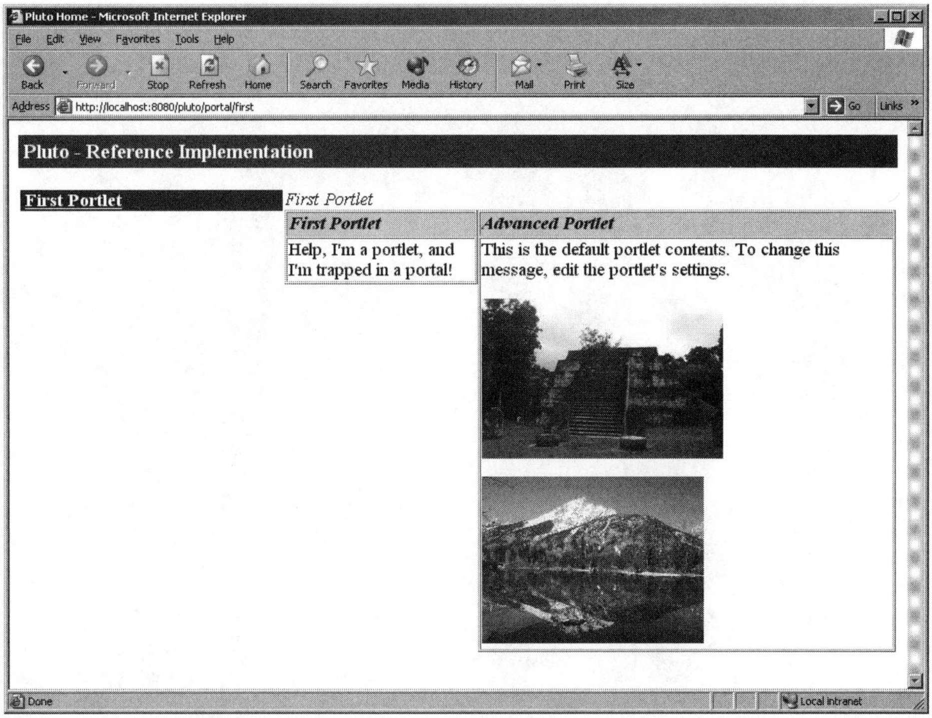

Figure 2-2. The first portlet and the advanced portlet on the same portal page

Summary

We have built two simple portlets and packaged them into portlet application archives for distribution. You can deploy either portlet application on any portal container that complies with the Portlet API 1.0 standard. We discussed the `PortletRequest`, `PortletResponse`, and `GenericPortlet` classes from the portlet API. We also covered several basic concepts for portlet development in this chapter. In the next chapter, we will discuss the life cycle of a portlet, including initialization, request handling, and destruction.

CHAPTER 3

The Portlet Life Cycle

As we've seen in earlier chapters, portlets are conceptually very similar to servlets. Like servlets, they can only operate within a container. Both have obligations that their design must satisfy to allow them to interact with their container, and both demand clearly specified behavior from their containers.

The portlet's obligations are, broadly speaking, to provide implementations of specific methods, to respond appropriately when these are invoked by the container, and to handle error conditions gracefully.

This chapter describes the container's interactions with a portlet, starting with its creation and concluding with its destruction. It also considers the constraints that are incumbent upon both the portlet and the container at each step in this life cycle.

The Portlet Interface

To demonstrate the basic steps in the life cycle, let's first look at a simple portlet that implements the `Portlet` interface directly. Portlets need to implement this interface, either directly, or indirectly by extending a class that has already implemented the interface.

Here is a devastatingly simple portlet example:

```
package com.portalbook.crawler;

import java.io.*;
import javax.portlet.*;

public class SimplePortlet
   implements Portlet {

   public SimplePortlet() {
   }

   public void destroy() {
      portletCounter--;
   }
```

```
public void init(PortletConfig config)
   throws PortletException
{
   portletCounter++;
}

public void processAction(
      ActionRequest request,
      ActionResponse response)
   throws PortletException, IOException
{
   actionCounter++;
}

public void render(
      RenderRequest request,
      RenderResponse response)
   throws PortletException, IOException
{
   renderCounter++;

   response.setTitle("Simple Portlet");
   response.setContentType("text/html");
   PrintWriter out = response.getWriter();
   out.write("The server has instantiated " +
         portletCounter +
         " copies of the portlet<br>");

   out.write("This portlet has been rendered " +
         renderCounter +
         " times (including this one)<br>");

   out.write("This portlet has received " +
         actionCounter +
         " action requests<br>");

   PortletURL action = response.createActionURL();
   out.write("Click <a href=\"");
   out.write(action.toString());
   out.write("\">here</a> to trigger an action.<br>");
}
```

```
    private static int portletCounter = 0;
    private int renderCounter = 0;
    private int actionCounter = 0;
}
```

The portlet.xml file for the simple portlet follows:

```
<?xml version="1.0" encoding="UTF-8"?>
<portlet-app
   xmlns="http://java.sun.com/xml/ns/portlet/portlet-app_1_0.xsd"
   version="1.0"
   xmlns:xsi="http://www.w3.org/2001/XMLSchema-instance"
   xsi:schemaLocation="http://java.sun.com/xml/ns/portlet/portlet-app_1_0.xsd
   http://java.sun.com/xml/ns/portlet/portlet-app_1_0.xsd">
   <portlet>
      <description>PortletBook Simple Portlet</description>
      <portlet-name>simple</portlet-name>
      <display-name>Simple Portlet</display-name>
      <portlet-class>com.portalbook.crawler.SimplePortlet</portlet-class>
      <expiration-cache>-1</expiration-cache>

      <supports>
         <mime-type>text/html</mime-type>
         <portlet-mode>VIEW</portlet-mode>
      </supports>

      <supported-locale>en</supported-locale>
      <portlet-info>
         <title>Simple Portlet</title>
         <short-title>Simple</short-title>
         <keywords>Simple, Example</keywords>
      </portlet-info>
   </portlet>
</portlet-app>
```

This portlet tracks the number of instances of the class that are being maintained by the portlet container at any given time, it counts the number of times that the specific instance has been rendered, and it counts the number of action requests that have been handled by the specific instance.

In the last section of this chapter, we will build a more realistic portlet application that demonstrates some of the issues involved in a threading application, and that builds upon the GenericPortlet class to make more complex portlet reactions possible.

Overview

It shouldn't come as much of a surprise to find that the life cycle of a portlet is broadly the same as that of a servlet. Servlets are generally responsible for rendering complete pages, and portlets are generally responsible for rendering fragments of pages, so there's an obvious correlation.

The life cycle of a portlet therefore breaks down into the following stages:

1. Creation of the portlet
2. Processing of a number of user requests (or possibly none)
3. Removal and garbage collection of the portlet

Creation of the Portlet

The creation of the portlet is probably the most complex "phase" in the life cycle since it involves three quite distinct steps. However, two of them—loading and instantiation—are very familiar Java concepts.

Loading the Classes

The container is able to load the classes required by the portlet at any point prior to invocation of the constructor.

A portlet application often consists of many classes and libraries, for which the actual portlet class is a relatively minor part of the whole. However, the portlet represents the user's way of interacting with the application. As such, it must have access to the rest of the application. The specification therefore demands that the portlet be loaded by the same classloader as the rest of the portlet application.

This guarantees that the servlets and other resources of the application may be accessed by the portlet that integrates it into the portal.

As with any class, at load time the class attributes will be initialized to their default values, so our variable `portletCounter` will be set to zero.

Invoking the Constructor

A portlet is required to provide a public default constructor—that is to say, a constructor taking no parameters.

Loading and instantiation (invoking the constructor) can take place either when the container starts the portlet application or when the container determines that the portlet is needed to service a request.

The option for delayed loading presents a benefit when a portlet will be used infrequently and consumes substantial resources, since they will not be acquired until they are actually needed. The trade-off is against performance, since the time taken by the portlet to service a request will be increased by the time taken to initialize its resources—but this will affect only the first user of the portlet. Where a portlet is initialized with the portlet application, the hit is taken "up front" when the application starts.

Our (minimal) constructor looks like this:

```
public SimplePortlet() {
}
```

It's hard to say anything interesting about our sample constructor. The normal instance initialization will take place, so that before the invocation of the constructor the attributes `renderCounter` and `actionCounter` will be set to zero, but then it does nothing, and, in fact, this is completely normal for a portlet implementation.

Initializing the Portlet

The container is required to initialize the portlet once it has been loaded and instantiated.

Although there's nothing to prevent you from doing useful initialization in the constructor, the configuration information isn't available to you until the `init()` method is called. As well as simplifying the implementation of the container, this allows the complete API of the portlet to be defined by the `Portlet` interface (interfaces don't allow the signature of the constructor to be specified):

```
public void init(PortletConfig config) throws PortletException
```

The `init()` method is passed an object implementing the `PortletConfig` interface. This object will be unique to the portlet definition and provides access to the initialization parameters and the `ResourceBundle` configured for the portlet in the portlet definition.

The `init()` method on a portlet instance is called only once by a portlet container.

Until the `init()` method has been invoked successfully, the portlet will not be considered active, so static initialization of the class should not trigger any methods that make this assumption. For example, the static (class rather than object scope) initializers of your class should not invoke connections to a database.

In our example, the `init()` method increases the number of portlet instances noted in the `portletCounter` attribute:

```
public void init(PortletConfig config)
            throws PortletException
{
            portletCounter++;
}
```

In a larger application, this method would be populated with code to extract configuration information in order to establish resources such as database connections and background threads. Our crawler example in the final section will demonstrate the initialization of a background thread in its `init()` method.

Exceptions During Initialization

The initialization process is error-prone. You are likely to be making connections to resources that may be unavailable and over which you have no control. For example, your database server might be unavailable. Without a mechanism for handling such errors, your portlet could end up in an invalid state. As you would expect, the usual exception-handling mechanism comes into play here.

The `init()` method is permitted to throw a `PortletException`. If it does so, the container is allowed to reattempt to load the portlet at any later time.

When constructing an `UnavailableException`, the portlet can provide a message describing the problem. In this case, the portlet must not be restarted. Use this exception if a configuration setting of the portlet will have to be changed to get the portlet work to properly. For instance, the portlet may require version 9 of a database to connect to, but the database it tried connecting to was version 7.

```
public UnavailableException(String text)
```

For example:

```
throw new UnavailableException("The database has been decommissioned");
```

Alternatively, you can specify a minimum period of time (in seconds) during which no attempt must be made to restart the portlet:

```
public UnavailableException(String text, int seconds)
```

For example:

```
throw new UnavailableException("The database is not currently available",5);
```

If the duration of the resource unavailability cannot be determined but is still considered to be a temporary problem, the portlet should return a zero or negative time.

For example:

```
throw new UnavailableException("A website resource could not be reached",0);
```

If any other PortletException is thrown, the container is allowed to attempt to restart the portlet at any time after the error. The container may either reuse the original instance, or discard the original and re-create it.

If a portlet needs to throw an exception from its initialization method, it must free any resources that it successfully acquired up to that point before doing so—this is because the destroy() method will not subsequently be called, as the portlet is considered to be uninitialized.

Request Handling

Once the portlet has been initialized, it is waiting for interactions with the users of the portal.

The container translates requests from the users of the portal into invocations of the render() and processAction() methods, thus elegantly breaking down the user requests into actions that command the portlet to change the state of its underlying application and render requests that display the application in its current state at any given point.

Users trigger actions by clicking on action URLs or submitting HTML forms that post data to an action URL. Upon receiving the action request from the user, the portal must invoke (via the container) the appropriate portlet's processAction() method. Once this method has completed, it must call the render() method for all of the portlets on the page. It is not required to invoke the render() methods in any particular order.

Users trigger render requests by either triggering action URLs as described previously, or by triggering a render URL. Again, upon receiving a request for a render URL from a user, the portal must invoke the render() method on all of the portlets in the page but is not obliged to follow any particular order.

The only exception to the invocations of the render() method as described is (optionally) for portlets that are cached by the portal and for which the state has not changed.

Since a single portlet is generally handling requests from multiple users, it must be able to handle simultaneous requests on different threads in each of these methods. In addition, it must not rely on any particular ordering of the calls to these methods.

Because the portlet cannot maintain all of the state information for a session, it is the container's responsibility to manage this and provide it when these methods are called.

Both action requests and render requests are similar, but each takes different classes for arguments. The action request cannot write any content to the portlet's response, because its ActionResponse does not have access to the output. The signatures of the two methods are very similar. First, here is the `processAction()` method signature:

```
public void processAction(
   ActionRequest request,
   ActionResponse response)
throws PortletException, IOException
```

And here is the `render()` method signature:

```
public void render(
   RenderRequest request,
   RenderResponse response)
throws PortletException, IOException
```

Each method receives a request object and a response object tailored to its function. In each case, the request represents the state of the session for the user, and the response object allows the method to interact with the portlet's response.

The `RenderRequest` object will not generally need to change the state of the underlying portlet application, so it provides the portlet with the information necessary to produce a view of it in its current state.

Specifically, these include

- The state of the portlet window (minimized, maximized, etc.)
- The mode of the portlet (e.g., VIEW mode)
- The context of the portlet
- The session associated with the portlet (including authorization information)
- The preferences information associated with the portlet
- Any render parameters that have been set on a render URL from a posted Form, or that have been set during the `processAction()` method

The `ActionRequest` object represents an opportunity to change the state of the portlet based on its current state, so this provides everything offered by the `PortletRequest` along with direct access to the content of the HTTP request made by the user of the portal.

Note that `ActionRequest` and `RenderRequest` are both interfaces, so it is the responsibility of the container to provide concrete implementation classes giving access to the appropriate information

To respond to `processAction()` the portlet should update its `ActionResponse` object. This provides methods to

- Redirect the client to a new page
- Change the mode of the portlet
- Add or modify rendering parameters for the user's session

You change the state of the portlet's container window in the portal. To respond to `render()`, the portlet should update its `RenderResponse` object. This provides methods to

- Render content into the container window displayed in the user's view of the portal
- Render URLs into that content, which will invoke actions on the portlet

Again, `ActionResponse` and `RenderResponse` are interfaces, and the container must provide a suitable implementation to be used by the portlet.

Here is our sample `processAction()` method:

```
public void processAction(
        ActionRequest request,
        ActionResponse response)
    throws PortletException, IOException
  {
    actionCounter++;
  }
```

The example `processAction()` makes only a trivial change to the state of the portlet; it increments the counter of actions handled, so it does not have to inform the container of any changes via the response.

Our sample `render()` method looks like this:

```
public void render(
        RenderRequest request,
        RenderResponse response)
    throws PortletException, IOException
  {
    renderCounter++;

    response.setTitle("Simple Portlet");
    response.setContentType("text/html");
    PrintWriter out = response.getWriter();
    out.write("The server has instantiated " +
          portletCounter +
          " copies of the portlet<br>");
```

```
        out.write("This portlet has been rendered " +
              renderCounter +
              " times (including this one)<br>");

        out.write("This portlet has received " +
              actionCounter +
              " action requests<br>");

        PortletURL action = response.createActionURL ();
        out.write("Click <a href=\"");
        out.write(action.toString());
        out.write("\">here</a> to trigger an action.<br>");
    }
```

Because our sample portlet does not need to tailor its view to the different users of the system, it is able to ignore the request parameter, which contains the user-specific (session) state information. It does, however, need to render its current state to the browser, and must specify the type of content that it will produce.

Our sample portlet demonstrates an important relationship between the portlet and the portal: one portlet can be rendered multiple times on a single page. If an instance of the portlet is placed in a portal page in two distinct places, the portlet will be loaded once, rendered multiple times (twice each time the portal page as a whole is rendered), and destroyed once.

The last few lines of this example method are of particular interest, since they demonstrate how to provide a mechanism by which actions (and thus calls by the container to `processAction()`) can be rendered:

```
PortletURL action = response.createActionURL ();
```

This retrieves an object from the response object provided in the parameters of the `render()` method, which can render a URL representing a specific action. Our example has only one type of action, but methods such as `addParameter()` can be called on the `PortletURL` object to differentiate between calls to the various actions that you want to implement.

Again, `PortletURL` is an interface, and it is the responsibility of the container to provide a suitable implementation.

It is not appropriate to hardcode a URL into your portlet since the precise details of the mappings between URLs and portlets are configurable by the administrator of the portal. In addition, portlet URLs distinguish between different instances of a portlet running inside of a portlet. The portlet URLs are usually prefixed with a namespace or another unique ID. These details will be specific to the portal in which your portlet is running, so if you want to make your portlet compatible between portals (and even between versions of the same portal) you should always rely on the `createActionURL()` method.

Destroying the Portlet

The `destroy()` method will not be invoked until all other initialization or processing threads on the instance have completed. It will be invoked when the container determines that the portlet is no longer required—the container is not required to keep the portlet in service for any specific period of time.

The container invokes the `destroy()` method to release any resources that have been retained by the portlet. The portlet will then be de-referenced by the container and the garbage collector will be free to remove the portlet object from memory.

The `destroy()` method is guaranteed to be called (unless initialization failed with an exception), so this is also an appropriate place in which to notify other parts of the application that the portlet is becoming unavailable.

Finalizers should not be used since their invocation is not guaranteed.

Destroying our example portlet looks like this:

```
public void destroy() {
   portletCounter--;
}
```

Our example portlet uses the `destroy()` method to reduce the count of its running instances in the class attribute `portletCounter`.

Threading Issues

In this final section, we demonstrate the life cycle of a portlet that uses background threads of execution in a web crawler application.

Handling Concurrent Requests

Because the portlet container will handle concurrent requests from clients by invoking the methods on the portlet on separate threads of execution, your portlet must be able to handle any combination and number of simultaneous calls to `render()` and/or `processAction()`.

You must therefore implement your portlet to handle these concurrent requests safely. In practice this is not usually too tricky—all the information you need to process a request is provided in a thread-safe manner in the parameter list, so if your portlets don't use instance variables and they don't access other resources external to the portlet, your application will automatically be thread-safe.

It is guaranteed that your `init()` method will be called only once at the beginning of the life cycle and that no other methods will be invoked by the container until `init()` completes successfully, so your `init()` method does *not* have to be thread safe.

Your `render()` and `processAction()` methods will be invoked with request and response objects. These are guaranteed to be unique to that invocation of the method *during the lifetime of the method*. Containers are likely to recycle these objects once the method in question has completed, so retaining a reference to them outside the scope of the method to which they were passed may result in unexpected behavior.

Our Thread-Safe Crawler

Our crawler class is implemented to be thread safe. It implements `Runnable` so it can be created and started within a background thread.

Once the crawler is running, it can be queried at any time. The `get` methods return unmodifiable sets so it is not possible for the client to externally alter their state.

The crawler can be stopped by an external thread by calling the `stopCrawler()` method. This is essential so that our portlet can be unloaded safely.

Our crawler implementation follows, with a running commentary. Although this illustrates the functionality that's needed in a web crawler, you should note that it is a demonstration application only. We make a lot of assumptions and take shortcuts that would not be acceptable in a commercial product.

```
package com.portalbook.crawler;

import java.io.*;
import java.net.*;
import java.util.*;

public class Crawler
   implements Runnable
{
```

Our simplest constructor creates an instance to crawl a given path. This will search only within the host of the path specified:

```
   public Crawler(String path)
      throws MalformedURLException
   {
      this(path,DEFAULT_LINK_DEPTH);
   }
```

This more complex constructor creates an instance to crawl a given path. It will search within the host of the path specified, and up to the specified number of sites (`depth`) away. If `depth` is 2, the crawler will look within the host of the path specified and within the hosts of sites referenced directly from this site, but no further:

```
public Crawler(String path, int depth)
   throws MalformedURLException
{
   this(new HashSet(
         Arrays.asList(
            new Object[]
               { new URL(path) })),
         new HashSet(),
         new HashSet(),
         new HashSet(),
         new HashSet(),
         depth);
}
```

This internal constructor is used directly or indirectly by the public ones to create the instance to crawl a given set of paths. It will search within the hosts specified, and up to the specified number of sites away from those sites. It will not search forbidden hosts, failed hosts, or already visited hosts:

```
protected Crawler( Set links,
                   Set visited,
                   Set visitedHosts,
                   Set forbidden,
                   Set failed,
                   int depth )
{
   this.links        = links;
   this.visited      = visited;
   this.visitedHosts = visitedHosts;
   this.forbidden    = forbidden;
   this.failed       = failed;
   this.currentHost  =
      (URL)links.iterator().next();
   this.depth        = depth;
}
```

Our crawler is designed to run as a thread, so it implements the `Runnable` interface. It can therefore be passed in as a parameter to a new `Thread` object.

When the start() method of the containing Thread object is called, the following run() method will be started on the background thread of execution:

```
public void run() {
```

This code flags that work is in progress:

```
    setStopped(false);
    try {
```

until we instruct the thread to stop, or it runs out of links to search, or it reaches the edge of the network of links that we're allowing it to search:

```
        while( !isStopped() &&
               (links.size() > 0) &&
               (depth > 0) ) {
```

This code gets the first link from the queue of links to search:

```
            URL link =
               (URL)links.iterator().next();
```

If the link is on a different host

```
            if( !isCurrentHost(link) ) {
```

this code goes to that host and searches the link (if we're allowed):

```
               crawlNewHost(link);
            } else {
```

This code crawls the link:

```
               crawl(link);
            }
        }
```

Normal or abnormal termination should flag that work has completed regardless:

```
    } finally {
        setStopped(true);
    }
}
```

> **TIP** *Most of the work of the crawler is carried out from within private methods. As with all good object-oriented designs, these hide the implementation details from the user of the class—this is particularly important with a multithreaded design, since you will need to carefully isolate any code that might cause problems if two different threads were to execute it simultaneously.*

This private method processes a buffer containing the contents of a robots.txt file and adds forbidden URLs to the appropriate list. The link for the robots.txt file is required to convert the relative disallowed paths into absolute URLs:

```
private void processRobotBuffer(
      StringBuffer buffer,
      URL link)
{
```

Now we prepare to gather up potential URL strings:

```
   List disallows = new ArrayList();
```

and look for `DISALLOW` tokens. Any token immediately following a `DISALLOW` is presumed to be (potentially) a path:

```
   StringTokenizer tokenizer =
      new StringTokenizer(buffer.toString());
   while(tokenizer.hasMoreElements()) {
      String element = tokenizer.nextToken();

      if( element.equalsIgnoreCase(DISALLOW) &&
          tokenizer.hasMoreElements() ) {

         String path = tokenizer.nextToken();
         disallows.add(path);
      }
   }
```

The following code iterates over the disallow tokens gathered and converts them into absolute paths and then URLs to forbid access:

```
   Iterator i = disallows.iterator();
   while(i.hasNext()) {
      String path = (String)i.next();
      try {
         URL disallowedURL = new URL(link,path);
         forbidden.add(disallowedURL);
```

```
            } catch( MalformedURLException e ) {
                // Couldn't form a URL from this.
                // No point disallowing access to a
                // link we can't access anyway.
            }
        }
    }
```

This private method determines the robots.txt file that governs access to the host on which the link resides, parses, and then disallows access to links as required by the robots specification; however, we're polite and assume that *any* link that's disallowed to *anybody* must be forbidden to us. This makes the logic slightly simpler but would not normally be done in a production system. The robots.txt information is cached with the host as the key, so we look it up only when we encounter the first link from a site:

```
    private void processRobots(URL link) {
```

If the host has been visited before, we're not obliged to reread the robots.txt file. If this is the first visit, however, we need to determine which paths to discard:

```
        HttpURLConnection connection = null;
        try {
            if( !visitedHosts.contains(link.getHost()) ) {
```

This code creates an HTTP connection to the link:

```
                URL robotLink = new URL(link,"/robots.txt");

                connection =
                    (HttpURLConnection)robotLink.openConnection();
```

This code gets the page:

```
                connection.setRequestMethod(GET);
                connection.setRequestProperty(
                        USER_AGENT,AGENT_IDENTIFIER);
```

And this reads the page into a buffer:

```
                InputStream input =
                    (InputStream)connection.getContent();
```

```
         BufferedReader reader =
            new BufferedReader(
               new InputStreamReader(input));

         int i = 0;
         StringBuffer buffer = new StringBuffer();
         String line = null;
         while((line = reader.readLine()) != null) {
            i++;
            buffer.append(line);
            buffer.append('\r');
         }
```

We now close the connection to the page and discard held resources:

```
         reader.close();
         connection.disconnect();
         connection = null;
```

Next we process the buffer to determine what links are permitted:

```
         processRobotBuffer(buffer,link);
      }
   } catch( IOException e ) {
```

Good. There is no robots.txt file, and we're allowed to view the site.
To ensure that the connection is always closed correctly, we use the following:

```
   } finally {
      if( connection != null ) {
         connection.disconnect();
      }
   }
}
```

This private method crawls a specified URL and adds all valid HREF entries to the queue of links to be crawled (unless they are denied by the appropriate robots.txt file or have already been crawled):

```
private void crawl(URL link) {
   HttpURLConnection connection = null;
   try {
```

Now let's check to see what is or isn't permitted on this host:

```
      processRobots(link);
```

This code creates an HTTP connection to the link:

```
connection =
   (HttpURLConnection)link.openConnection();
```

Now we get the page:

```
connection.setRequestMethod(GET);

String contentType = connection.getContentType();
if( (contentType != null) &&
     contentType.startsWith(TEXT_HTML) ) {

   InputStream input =
      (InputStream)connection.getContent();
```

And read the page into a buffer:

```
   BufferedReader reader =
   new BufferedReader(new InputStreamReader(input));

   int i = 0;
   StringBuffer buffer = new StringBuffer();
   String line = null;
   while((line = reader.readLine()) != null) {
      i++;
      buffer.append(line);
   }
```

To close the connection to the page and discard held resources, we use this code:

```
   reader.close();
   connection.disconnect();
   connection = null;
```

The next step is to process the page. This code assumes that the page is small enough to manage in memory:

```
   processBuffer(buffer,link);
} else {
   connection.disconnect();
   connection = null;
}
```

We've handled the item, so let's remove it from the queue of links:

```
        visited(link);
    } catch( IOException e ) {
```

The item caused a problem, so let's remove it from the queue:

```
        links.remove(link);
        failed.add(link);
    } finally {
```

To ensure that the connection is closed correctly, we use the following:

```
        if( connection != null ) {
            connection.disconnect();
        }
    }
}
```

This private method carries out actions once a link has been crawled. It removes the link from the queue of links to visit, adds it to the set of visited links, and adds its host to the set of visited hosts:

```
private void visited(URL link) {
    links.remove(link);
    visited.add(link);
    visitedHosts.add(link.getHost());
}
```

This private method processes a buffer containing an HTML page. The context is provided so that relative URLs can be resolved to their absolute URLs. HREFs within the HTML are extracted, converted to absolute URLs, and added to the queue of links to be crawled (if they have not already been visited and have not been forbidden by a robots.txt file):

```
private void processBuffer(StringBuffer buffer, URL url) {
```

Let's now prepare to gather up potential URL strings:

```
    List foundHREFs = new ArrayList();
```

And look for HREF tokens. Any token immediately following an HREF is presumed to be (potentially) a URL:

```
    StringTokenizer tokenizer =
        new StringTokenizer(buffer.toString(),DELIM);
```

```
while(tokenizer.hasMoreElements()) {
   String element = tokenizer.nextToken();

   if( element.equalsIgnoreCase(HREF) &&
       tokenizer.hasMoreElements() ) {

      String path = tokenizer.nextToken();
      foundHREFs.add(path);
   }
}
```

Now let's boil them down to absolute URLs:

```
Set absolute = new HashSet();
Iterator i = foundHREFs.iterator();
while(i.hasNext()) {
   String path = (String)i.next();

   try {
      URL toAdd = new URL(url,path);
      if( !toAdd.getProtocol().equalsIgnoreCase("http") ) {
```

If it's not a link beginning with "http" then it's not a protocol we're interested in:

```
      } else {
         absolute.add(toAdd);
      }
   } catch( MalformedURLException e ) {
```

If we encounter a `MalformedURLException`, then the crawler must have tried to load an invalid path. We should ignore the URL as it's probably a typo:

```
   }
}
```

Let's now remove all the URLs that we're not allowed to visit for one reason or another:

```
absolute.removeAll(forbidden);
```

And remove all the URLs that we've already visited anyway:

```
absolute.removeAll(visited);
```

We'll add the remainder to the visit queue:

```
    links.addAll(absolute);
}
```

The following private method crawls a link that is on a host other than the one currently being processed. The simplest way to effect this is to instantiate a new crawler specifying the appropriate URL, but to pass it the information on visited and forbidden hosts so that already crawled links can be ignored. Note that we reduce the permitted depth by 1 for this next crawler so that it can't creep too far away from the original link. Eventually we'll reach 0, and there's no point in instantiating the crawler because it would simply complete immediately.

```
private void crawlNewHost(URL url) {
    Set links = new HashSet();
    links.add(url);
    if( depth > 1 ) {
```

Now let's create a new crawler to crawl the external link:

```
        Crawler crawler =
            new Crawler(links,
                        visited,
                        visitedHosts,
                        forbidden,
                        failed,
                        (depth - 1));
```

The new crawler should be stopped whenever this crawler is stopped:

```
        addListener(crawler);
```

This code flags that the URL has been visited:

```
        crawler.run();
    }

    this.links.remove(url);
}
```

This private method adds a crawler to a set of crawlers that are children of this crawler so that they can all by stopped when this one is stopped:

```
private void addListener(Crawler crawler) {
    stopListeners.add(crawler);
}
```

This private method stops all the crawlers that are children of this crawler:

```
private void notifyStopCrawlers() {
   Iterator i = stopListeners.iterator();
   while(i.hasNext() && depth > 0) {
      Crawler crawler = (Crawler)i.next();
      crawler.setStopped(true);
   }
}
```

This method allows the owner of the crawler to test to see if the crawler is currently running:

```
public boolean isStopped() {
   return stopped;
}
```

This method allows the owner to stop the crawler:

```
public void stopCrawler() {
   setStopped(true);
}
```

The following private method sets the flag that causes the crawler to stop, and if it's set to true, it instructs any child crawler threads to stop as well:

```
private void setStopped(boolean stopped) {
   if(stopped) notifyStopCrawlers();
   this.stopped = stopped;
}
```

The next method allows the owner of the crawler to retrieve the set of links (as URL objects) that the crawler has encountered so far and that were valid. Access to the set of visited URLs is synchronized, and a copy is returned, so that it is not possible for two threads to try to access the set simultaneously. By pursuing this policy for all of the publicly accessible stores of data provided by the crawler, we make it thread safe with very little use of synchronization. Judicious use of the synchronized keyword is important because it carries a significant performance penalty. While this isn't a big deal for our crawler (which is not limited by processing speed so much as by bandwidth), getting good responsiveness is often the primary goal when using threads:

```
public Set getVisitedURLs() {
   synchronized(this.visited) {
      return new HashSet(this.visited);
   }
}
```

Similarly, this code allows the owner to retrieves the set of hosts (as Strings) that the crawler has encountered so far:

```
public Set getVisitedHosts() {
   synchronized(this.visitedHosts) {
      return new HashSet(this.visitedHosts);
   }
}
```

The following code retrieves the set of links as URLs that the crawler was forbidden to search by their associated robots.txt files:

```
public Set getForbiddenURLs() {
   synchronized(this.forbidden) {
      return new HashSet(this.forbidden);
   }
}
```

Next we retrieve the set of invalid links as URLs that the crawler could not search (usually because of a network problem of some sort, such as "404 Host Not Found"):

```
public Set getFailedURLs() {
   synchronized(this.failed) {
      return Collections.unmodifiableSet(this.failed);
   }
}
```

This private method determines if a given link falls within the set of links being crawled by this crawler's instance:

```
private boolean isCurrentHost(URL url) {
   return currentHost.getHost().equalsIgnoreCase(url.getHost());
}
```

This field identifies the host that this crawler is searching:

```
private URL currentHost;
```

These fields are used to stop this thread and its child threads:

```
private Set stopListeners = new HashSet();
private boolean stopped = true;
```

These fields maintain information on where we've been so far:

```
    private Set links;
    private Set visited;
    private Set visitedHosts;
    private Set forbidden;
    private Set failed;
    private int depth;
```

The following are String constants required by the application mostly during tokenization or protocol negotiation:

```
    private static final String DELIM      =  "\t\r\n\" <>=";
    private static final String TEXT_HTML  = "text/html";
    private static final String GET        =  "GET";
    private static final String HREF       =  "HREF";
    private static final String HTTP       =  "HTTP:";
    private static final String DISALLOW   = "DISALLOW:";
    private static final String USER_AGENT = "User-Agent";
```

This is the "official" name of this agent for identification in the logs of the servers we're searching:

```
    private static final String AGENT_IDENTIFIER="WoolGatherer";
```

Finally, we specify the default search depth to be used if the single-argument constructor is used:

```
    private static final int DEFAULT_LINK_DEPTH = 1;
}
```

Here is the portlet.xml file for the crawler portlet:

```
<?xml version="1.0" encoding="UTF-8"?>
<portlet-app
 xmlns="http://java.sun.com/xml/ns/portlet/portlet-app_1_0.xsd"
 version="1.0"
 xmlns:xsi="http://www.w3.org/2001/XMLSchema-instance"
 xsi:schemaLocation="http://java.sun.com/xml/ns/portlet/portlet-app_1_0.xsd
 http://java.sun.com/xml/ns/portlet/portlet-app_1_0.xsd">
    <portlet>
       <description>Link Crawler</description>

       <portlet-name>crawler</portlet-name>
       <display-name>Link Crawler</display-name>
```

```
        <portlet-class>
            com.portalbook.crawler.CrawlerPortlet
        </portlet-class>

        <init-param>
            <name>crawlPath</name>
            <value>http://localhost:8080/</value>
        </init-param>

        <expiration-cache>-1</expiration-cache>

        <supports>
            <mime-type>text/html</mime-type>
            <portlet-mode>VIEW</portlet-mode>
        </supports>

        <supported-locale>en</supported-locale>

        <portlet-info>
            <title>Link Crawler Portlet</title>
            <short-title>Crawler</short-title>
            <keywords>Crawler, Link, Checker</keywords>
        </portlet-info>

    </portlet>
</portlet-app>
```

The GenericPortlet Abstract Class

Portlets are allowed to be displayed in the three standard modes—VIEW, EDIT, and HELP. They do not have to support any of them except VIEW. Many do not require any action handling. This results in a lot of boilerplate code to handle the requests for each of these modes and render the response.

The `GenericPortlet` abstract class therefore provides an initial framework around which you can build your custom portlet. At its simplest, a portlet derived from `GenericPortlet` must implement a constructor, a `getTitle()` method, and a `doView()` method. `GenericPortlet` then provides your application with a variety of helper methods that you will make frequent use of. It is generally recommended that you override `GenericPortlet` rather than directly creating your own implementation of the `Portlet` interface.

`GenericPortlet`'s `render()` method calls the `doDispatch()` method. This method determines the current mode of the portlet render request, and calls `doView()`, `doEdit()`, and `doHelp()` as appropriate (the modes that are permissible for a portlet are configured in its deployment descriptor). The `processAction()` method throws an exception if invoked, so your class must override this if you wish to handle any actions.

Since our crawler portlet provides only a view method and does not accept any actions, `GenericPortlet` provides the perfect starting point.

Our Threaded Crawler Portlet

Our crawler overrides `GenericPortlet`; this will simplify the implementation of our very conventional design.

The constructor is empty:

```
public CrawlerPortlet() {
   super();
}
```

The `init()` method retrieves the path from which the crawler will start from the portlet configuration:

```
String path = (String)config.getInitParameter("crawlPath");
```

It then creates a new crawler object, and invokes it on a background thread:

```
crawler = new Crawler(path);
Thread background = new Thread(crawler);
background.start();
```

Our code does not need to retain a reference to the thread object, since this will not be manipulated directly, but it does retain a reference to the crawler object, since it will need to access its methods in order to retrieve information and ultimately stop the crawler.

When the portlet is eventually unloaded by the container, the `destroy()` method will be invoked:

```
public void destroy() {
   crawler.stopCrawler();
   crawler = null;
}
```

This method cleans up the portlet's resources by stopping the crawler. The crawler's thread will exit, and no further action will be necessary (the container will manage the removal of the portlet from memory).

When running, the portlet may be required to render itself into its container and then onto the portal itself. This process would typically be triggered by the user browsing to a page on which the portlet is configured to be displayed.

The render() method of the Portlet interface will be invoked. This is caught by the GenericPortlet implementation, and it instead sets the title (which it determines by invoking getTitle()) and then invokes doDispatch(). The default implementation gets the title from the ResourceBundle of the PortletConfig of the portlet, but we will override this to return a specific string without requiring configuration:

```
protected String getTitle(RenderRequest request) {
   return "Link Crawler";
}
```

doDispatch() is provided as a default implementation by GenericPortlet. It determines the mode of the portlet (VIEW, EDIT, or HELP) and then calls the doView(), doEdit(), or doHelp() method as appropriate in order to render the portlet in its appropriate mode.

Our sample provides only a VIEW mode, so all render requests must result in a call to doView():

```
protected void doView( RenderRequest request, RenderResponse response)
      throws    PortletException,
                IOException
{
      response.setContentType("text/html");
      PrintWriter out = response.getWriter();

      out.write("<table><tr><td>");
      out.write("<h2>Crawler</h2>");

      out.write("<table cellspacing=\"0\"")
      out.write("border=\"1\">");
      out.write("<tr><td align=\"right\">")
      out.write("<i>Status</i></td><td><b>");
      out.write(
         crawler.isStopped() ? "stopped" : "running");
      out.write("</b></td></tr>");
      out.write("</table>");

      renderCollection(out, "Hosts Crawled",
         crawler.getVisitedHosts());

      renderCollection(out, "Links Visited",
         crawler.getVisitedURLs());

      renderCollection(out, "Failed Links",
         crawler.getFailedURLs());
```

```
        renderCollection(out, "Forbidden Links",
           crawler.getForbiddenURLs());

        out.write("</td></tr></table>");
}
```

Whenever doView() is invoked, we render a simple set of tables demonstrating the current state of the crawler running in the background. Appropriate headers for the response are rendered, and then the output print writer is retrieved from the response object and all output is generated using this.

Both of our examples have used inline HTML to render output to the portlet window. Although this is straightforward, you can see with this example that it rapidly makes the structure of the page difficult to follow. In Chapter 5, we discuss the option of delegating the rendering of the page to a servlet or JavaServer Pages (JSP) page instead.

The full implementation of our threaded portlet follows. Because our crawler implementation is thread safe, we have only to ensure that we start the crawler thread in the init() method, and stop it in the destroy() method, and that we don't start any additional threads during the lifetime of our portlet.

Here is the threaded crawler portlet in full:

```
package com.portalbook.crawler;

import java.io.*;
import java.net.*;
import java.util.*;
import javax.portlet.*;

public class CrawlerPortlet
   extends GenericPortlet
{
   public CrawlerPortlet() {
      super();
   }

   public void init(PortletConfig config)
   throws PortletException
   {
      String path =
         (String)config.getInitParameter("crawlPath");

      try {
         crawler = new Crawler(path);

         // Here we create and kick off the background
         // thread of execution.
```

```
        Thread background = new Thread(crawler);
        background.start();

    } catch( MalformedURLException e ) {
        throw new PortletException(
            "Portlet could not be initialised",e);
    }
}

public void destroy() {
    // Here we ensure that the background
    // thread is terminated safely.
    crawler.stopCrawler();
    crawler = null;
}

private void renderCollection(
        PrintWriter out,
        String title,
        Collection collection )
    throws IOException
{
    out.write("<table cellspacing=\"0\"");
    out.write("border=\"0\">");
    out.write("<tr><td><b>");
    out.write(title);
    out.write("</b></td></tr>");

    Iterator i = collection.iterator();
    while(i.hasNext()) {
        out.write("<tr><td>");
        out.write(i.next().toString());
        out.write("</td></tr>");
    }

    out.write("</table><br>");
}

protected void doView(
        RenderRequest request,
        RenderResponse response)
    throws  PortletException,
            IOException
{
```

```
        response.setContentType("text/html");
        PrintWriter out = response.getWriter();

        out.write("<table><tr><td>");
        out.write("<h2>Crawler</h2>");

        out.write("<table cellspacing=\"0\"");
        out.write("border=\"1\">");
        out.write("<tr><td align=\"right\">");
        out.write("<i>Status</i></td><td><b>");
        out.write(
           crawler.isStopped() ? "stopped" : "running");
        out.write("</b></td></tr>");
        out.write("</table>");

        // Note that while we can access an object running
        // in a background thread from the doView method,
        // we must not create a new thread of execution here.
        renderCollection(out, "Hosts Crawled",
           crawler.getVisitedHosts());

        renderCollection(out, "Links Visited",
           crawler.getVisitedURLs());

        renderCollection(out, "Failed Links",
           crawler.getFailedURLs());

        renderCollection(out, "Forbidden Links",
           crawler.getForbiddenURLs());

        out.write("</td></tr></table>");
    }

    protected String getTitle(RenderRequest request) {
        return "Link Crawler";
    }

    private Crawler crawler;
}
```

Summary

In this chapter, we have discussed the life cycle of a portlet. The portlet container calls the `init()` method on the portlet to initialize the portlet, the portlet handles any requests from the user, and the portlet is destroyed. The user can send either action or render requests, and we discussed the order in which these requests are handled. We also discussed error handling from the portlet's initialization phase.

Our web crawler example demonstrates how a portlet can create and manage a background thread. We discussed which methods on the portlet need to be made thread safe, and which objects are guaranteed to be unique during processing.

In the next chapter, we discuss the concepts that underlie the design of the portlet API and that account for the specifics of the portlet life cycle that we have just described.

CHAPTER 4

Portlet Concepts

THIS CHAPTER COVERS in detail several areas that you saw in Chapter 2. These core portlet concepts include portlet requests, portlet responses, portlet sessions, content markup types, window states, and portlet modes. In addition, we discuss caching, style sheets, and logging.

The examples in this chapter demonstrate interportlet communication using sessions, uploading a file through a portlet, and redirecting the user to another URL.

Portlet Requests

To expand on our discussion of portlet requests in Chapter 2, we will cover the portlet request. The `PortletRequest` interface in the portlet API represents the common functionality in an action request and a render request. The `ActionRequest` interface and the `RenderRequest` interface both extend `PortletRequest`.

The `PortletRequest` interface provides methods for accessing information about the user's request, such as the parameters on the request. Your portlet retrieves the user's session through the request, along with information about the portlet, the portlet application, and the portal. The portal provides information about the current state of the portlet, including the portlet mode and the current window state. The portlet can also retrieve and set attributes on the request.

Request Attributes

Request attributes are a way to pass Java objects between portlets, servlets, and JSP pages. These attributes are name/value pairs, with a `String` value representing the name and a `java.lang.Object` as the value. The request attributes are valid only for the action request and any subsequent render requests. As soon as the portlet receives another action request, the attributes are no longer available, and they will be replaced with the request attributes for the new action request. The portlet may set, remove, or retrieve attributes during action processing or during render processing.

The attributes may be passed to servlets or JSP pages that are included using the portlet's request dispatcher. The attributes on the `PortletRequest` are identical to the attributes accessed from the servlet or JSP page's `HttpServletRequest` object. The portlet will reflect any updates, additions, or removals inside a servlet or JSP when execution control returns to the portlet. We will discuss using servlets and JSP with portlets in more detail in Chapter 5.

The request attributes can be retrieved from the portlet request with the `getAttribute()` method on the `PortletRequest` interface. If there are no request attributes with the name passed in as an argument, the method will return null.

```
public Object getAttribute(String name)
```

To get the names of the attributes on the request, portlets may use the `getAttributeNames()` method. This method returns an `Enumeration` of the attribute names, or an empty `Enumeration` if there are no request attributes.

```
public Enumeration getAttributeNames()
```

Attributes may be set on the request with the `setAttribute()` method. This method takes the name of the attribute as a `String` and the value as an `Object`. The general naming convention for request attributes is the same as those used for naming Java packages. Portlets can overwrite attributes in the portlet request. If attributes need to be removed from the request, the `removeAttribute()` method is used.

```
public void setAttribute(String name, Object o)
public void removeAttribute(String name)
```

You can use request attributes or render parameters to pass information from an action request to a render request, or from a portlet to a servlet or JSP page. Both attributes and parameters are name/value pairs. The difference is that the value of an attribute can be any Java object, while the value of a parameter has to be a string or an array of strings. Request attributes are only available for the life cycle of the current request, so request attributes on an action request are not accessible from subsequent render requests. During action handling, any render parameters set on the action response will be accessible from subsequent render requests.

Request properties are another set of name/value pairs that are available through the request object, but request properties are read-only. The portlet uses request properties to obtain information about the request from the server. You can think of request properties as an extensible way for portals to provide information to portlets. Portlets would not use request properties to pass information back and forth, while they would use request attributes and request parameters for that purpose.

Request Properties

The portlet can access properties defined by the portal server or portlet container through the request object. These properties are up to the portal vendor to determine, and are not guaranteed to be portable between different portal servers. Request properties usually, but not necessarily, describe some aspect of the user's request that is not exposed anywhere else in the portlet API. Each property consists of a name and one or more values. The name and the values are all strings. The `getProperty()` method returns the value of the named property, or the first value of the property if there is more than one value.

```
public String getProperty(String name)
public Enumeration getProperties(String name)
public Enumeration getPropertyNames()
```

The `getProperties()` method returns an `Enumeration` of all available properties for a given name. Both the `getProperties()` and the `getProperty()` methods throw an `IllegalArgumentException` if the name passed is null. If there is no request property with that name, `getProperty()` returns null, and `getProperties()` returns an empty `Enumeration` object.

The portlet can ask the request for the names of all of the available request properties using the `getPropertyNames()` method. Requests that do not have any defined properties will return an empty `Enumeration`.

Request Parameters

Request parameters consist of a name as a `String` object, and one or more `String` objects as the value or values of the parameter. Sources of request parameters are parameters on portlet URLs, parameters on HTML forms, and render request parameters set during the action request processing. The parameters sent to the portlet for an action request are valid only while that action request is processed. Request parameters are valid for render request processing until the portlet gets another request for the portlet from the user. The portlet specification states that requests to change the portlet's window state or portlet mode from user interface elements on the portal page should not reset the render parameters for a portlet. We covered setting parameters on portlet URLs in Chapter 2.

Action requests and render requests both read parameters with the same methods from the `PortletRequest` interface. The `getParameter()` method returns the request parameter's value, given the name of a parameter. If a request parameter could have more than one value, the `getParameterValues()` method will return a String array with all of the values. For both of these methods, if there is no request parameter with that name, the returned value is null.

```
public String getParameter(String name)
public String[] getParameterValues(String name)
```

The getParameterNames() method returns an Enumeration of all the names of the request parameters. This method could be useful if your portlet accepts arbitrary input.

```
public Enumeration getParameterNames()
```

You may also work with the entire request parameters as a Map object, with the getParameterMap() method. This method will return a Map of the request parameter names and values. The values in the Map are String arrays. If there are no parameters on the request, the Map will be empty.

```
public Map getParameterMap()
```

We will discuss setting render parameters on the action response later in the chapter. These render parameters become the parameters for the render request of a portlet after the action request is called.

Context Path

The portlet request's context path is the part of the URL that corresponds to the portlet's context. For instance, if the URL is http://localhost/portal/MyPortletApp/MyPortlet, the context path would be /MyPortletApp. If there is a trailing slash on the end of the path, the trailing slash is not part of the context path. If you deploy the portlet application in such a way that it is accessible as the web root (http://localhost:8520/), the request will return an empty string for the context path.

```
public String getContextPath()
```

The context path is retrieved from the PortletRequest object using the getContextPath() method. This method is analogous to the getContextPath() method on the HttpServletRequest class.

Here is a very basic portlet that will display the context path for a portlet application:

```
package com.portalbook.portlets;
import javax.portlet.*;
import java.io.*;
```

```
public class ContextPathPortlet extends GenericPortlet
{
    public void doView(RenderRequest request, RenderResponse response)
        throws PortletException, IOException
    {
        response.setContentType("text/html");
        PrintWriter writer = response.getWriter();
        //write out the context path
        writer.write(request.getContextPath());
    }
}
```

After we deploy this portlet from a WAR file named concepts.war to a portlet application named concepts, its context path is /concepts.

Preferred Locales and Internationalization

The portal indicates which locale it would like to use for content. For instance, a user may have customized her view of the portal to provide Spanish-language content as her preferred locale. The `getLocale()` method on the `PortletRequest` interface returns the locale the portal would like for the content from the portlet. The `getLocales()` method returns all of the locales for which the portlet could provide content for the portal.

```
public Locale getLocale()
public java.util.Enumeration getLocales()
```

The portlet lists the locales it supports in its portlet.xml portlet deployment descriptor.

Retrieving the Scheme, Server Name, and Port

The `PortletRequest` class includes methods for retrieving the scheme of the URL used for the request, the server's host name, and the port number the server is listening on:

```
public String getScheme()
public String getServerName()
public int getServerPort()
```

Because portlets should invoke the `createRenderURL()` and `createActionURL()` methods to create portlet URLs for links, you will probably not use these three methods very often.

HTTPS Security

Portlets may ask the request if the connection between the end user and the portal is secure. Typically, this will mean the request was using HTTPS instead of plain HTTP. The `isSecure()` method on the `PortletRequest` object returns true if the request is secure and false if it is not:

```
public boolean isSecure()
```

A portlet URL may indicate that it needs a connection in a secure mode with the `setSecure()` method on the `PortletURL` object. The method takes an argument of `true` for requiring security or `false` for not requiring security. If the portal does not support the requested security mode, this method will throw a `PortletSecurityException`:

```
public void PortletURL.setSecure(boolean secure) throws PortletSecurityException
```

Typically, in a servlet environment, a servlet might catch an insecure request for secure content, and then redirect the browser to a URL that uses HTTPS. Because a portal page embeds the portlet, the portlet has to rely on the portal to create portlet URLs with the HTTPS scheme embedded in the link.

Request Security

We describe how to use the `PortletRequest` object's `getAuthType()`, `getRemoteUser()`, `isUserInRole()`, and `getUserPrincipal()` methods in Chapter 8. The portlet security model is similar to the servlet security model, although security roles are in the portlet deployment descriptor.

Render Request

The `render()` method on the `Portlet` interface takes a `RenderRequest` object as one of the arguments. `RenderRequest` extends `PortletRequest`, but adds no additional methods in version 1.0 of the portlet API.

Action Request and File Uploading

The request object passed to the `processAction()` method on the `Portlet` interface is an action request, represented by the `ActionRequest` interface. `ActionRequest` extends the `PortletRequest` interface and adds several methods.

Two methods exist for reading the body of an HTTP request, `getReader()` and `getPortletInputStream()`. Both of these methods will throw an

IllegalStateException if the HTTP POST was from a form with the "application/x-www-form-urlencoded" Multipurpose Internet Mail Extensions (MIME) type, because the portlet container translated the body of the request into the portlet request parameters. Once the body is read by the portlet container, the getReader() method, or the getPortletInputStream() method, it is unavailable to be read by another method.

```
public InputStream getPortletInputStream() throws IOException
public BufferedReader getReader() throws UnsupportedEncodingException➥
IOException
```

Application/x-www-form-urlencoded is the default MIME type for an HTTP form that posts to a server. To avoid the IllegalStateException, and to determine whether to get a Reader or an InputStream, the portlet accesses the request body's MIME type with the getContentType() method:

```
public String getContentType()
```

Portlets may ask the action request which character encoding was used with the getCharacterEncoding() method. If the portlet needs to change the encoding type from what was specified in the HTTP request, the setCharacterEncoding() method allows the portlet to do so, if the body has not already been accessed using a Reader or translated into request parameters. The getContentLength() method returns the size of the HTTP request's body content. If the portal is unable to determine how big the HTTP request body is, the getContentLength() method will return a value of -1.

```
public String getCharacterEncoding()
public void setCharacterEncoding(String enc) throws UnsupportedEncodingException
public int getContentLength()
```

The methods on the ActionRequest interface all relate to the body of the end user's HTTP request. This is going to be most useful for reading files uploaded to the portlet using the browser-based file upload mechanism. For portlets, this behavior is similar to that of servlets—file uploads are expected to conform to RFC 1867, which is the "Form-Based File Upload in HTML" protocol.

The RFC specifies an extension to the <INPUT> HTML element to allow file uploading through an HTML form. The web browser submits the form with the HTTP POST method. The standard also requires an additional MIME type for uploaded content. The HTTP browsers that implement file upload should encode posted form information that could include uploaded files as the "multipart/form-data" MIME type. Standard HTML forms that POST to the server without uploaded files have a default encoding MIME type of "application/x-www-form-urlencoded".

For instance, an HTML form that has an input for uploading a file to a portlet could look like this example:

```
<form method="post" action="/portal/1/2/FileUploadPortlet" ➥
 enctype= "multipart/form-data">
   Upload File: <input type="file" name="fileupload">
   <br><input type="submit">
</form>
```

Content delivered by a portlet would use a portlet URL for the action, rather than a hardcoded action like the previous example.

Several open source or publicly available file upload libraries for servlets exist—you may already be familiar with some of them. We will use the Apache Jakarta Commons File Upload library, because Jeff Sackett has contributed several classes that allow portlets to use the file upload library. Instead of using an `HttpServletRequest` object to parse data, the portlet extensions use the `ActionRequest` object.

You can download the binary distribution or the source code of the 1.0 release from `http://jakarta.apache.org/commons`. The portlet file upload classes are distributed with the source code for this book, under the Apache Software License.

> **NOTE** *You can also download the portlet file upload classes from the authors' web site,* `www.portalbook.com`.

We are going to demonstrate using the Jakarta Commons File Upload library to process a file uploaded to a portlet running inside the portal. File uploading is the sort of utility code where open source advocate Eric S. Raymond's phrase "Given enough eyeballs, all bugs are shallow" (which he calls "Linus's Law") is very applicable.

Portlet File Upload Library Overview

There are three classes in the Commons File Upload library that we use in the file upload portlet. `PortletDiskFileUpload` manages the interaction with the portlet's action request and parses the request into a list of `FileItem` classes. The `FileItem` class is an object that represents either an uploaded file or a form input parameter. The class has a method for checking whether its object is a file or a form field. There are also methods for writing a file to disk, determining the size and content type of a file, and getting the name and value of the input parameters.

The `PortletDiskFileUpload` class also handles the temporary storage of any uploaded files. Files that are smaller than a specified size (default is 10KB) are stored in memory, and larger files are stored on the hard drive in a temporary repository. The `setSizeThreshold()` method sets the cutoff size for memory storage. The default location for the repository is the value of the Java system property `java.io.tmpdir`, which is the path to a temporary directory. The `setSizeMax()` method provides the size past which a file is to be rejected to conserve storage space or to defeat attacks on the server.

The `parseRequest()` method on the `PortletDiskFileUpload` class throws a `FileUploadException` if there are any problems uploading the file. Common problems are that an uploaded file exceeded the maximum file size allowed, there is a disk full error, or the request is not a multipart form submission.

File Upload Portlet

The file upload portlet uses the Jakarta Commons File Upload Library to process multipart form submissions. These submissions could include file uploads and regular HTML form parameters. Our example uses an HTML file upload input and an HTML text input for its form content. The form is the only content displayed to users when they first load the portlet. If the user submits the form back to the server, the portlet processes the inputs in the `processAction()` method.

The portlet first checks to see if the request's content type starts with "multipart/" There is a utility method called `isMultipartContent()` on the `PortletDiskFileUpload` object to do this check for us. We then set the maximum allowable file size and memory cutoff size for file uploads. Next, we parse the action request into a list of `FileItem` objects. If the `FileItem` object is a form field, we set a render parameter with the same name on the portlet's action response object.

If the `FileItem` object is an uploaded file, we get the size of the file, its content type, and the name of the field on the form used to submit the file. We set render parameters on the response with the size and content type of the file. Next, we write the file to a temporary directory under the name fileupload-portlet.tmp. The `FileItem` class has a method called `write()` that takes a `java.io.File` object as an argument. If you are using portlet file uploading to add content into a document management system, you can also get an input stream from the file item. We finish up by logging the location of the file, and setting the name of the file on the server as a render parameter. The portlet catches and logs exceptions that occur, and the portlet adds the error message to the action response as a render parameter.

When the portlet receives a render request after processing an action request, it will display any error messages. If there are no error messages, it will optionally display the value of the form input parameter sent to the action request, the size of the uploaded file, the file's content type, and the name of the file on the server.

If any of these items do not exist as render parameters on the request, they are not visible.

```
package com.portalbook.portlets;
import org.apache.commons.fileupload.PortletDiskFileUpload;
import org.apache.commons.fileupload.FileUploadException;
import org.apache.commons.fileupload.FileItem;
import javax.portlet.ActionRequest;
import javax.portlet.ActionResponse;
import javax.portlet.GenericPortlet;
import javax.portlet.PortletException;
import javax.portlet.PortletURL;
import javax.portlet.RenderRequest;
import javax.portlet.RenderResponse;
import java.io.IOException;
import java.io.Writer;
import java.io.File;
import java.util.*;
public class FileUploadPortlet extends GenericPortlet
{
    public static final String ERROR_NO_FILE = "ERROR_NO_FILE";

    public void doView(RenderRequest request, RenderResponse response)
        throws PortletException, IOException
    {
        response.setContentType("text/html");

        Writer writer = response.getWriter();

        String error = request.getParameter("error");
        String size = request.getParameter("size");
        String contentType = request.getParameter("contentType");
        String serverFileName = request.getParameter("serverFileName");
        String param1 = request.getParameter("param1");

        if (ERROR_NO_FILE.equals(error))
        {
            writer.write("Expected to process an uploaded file.<P>");
        }
        else if (error != null)
        {
            writer.write(error + "<P>");
        }
        if (serverFileName != null)
        {
```

```
            //portlet upload was a success if serverName is set
            writer.write("File Size: " + size + "<BR>");
            writer.write("Content Type: " + contentType + "<BR>");
            writer.write("File Name on Server: " + serverFileName + "<BR>");
        }
        if (param1 != null)
        {
            writer.write("Parameter 1: " + param1);
        }

        PortletURL actionURL = response.createActionURL();

        writer.write(
            "<form method='post' enctype='multipart/form-data'");
        writer.write(" action=' " + actionURL.toString() + "'>");
        writer.write("Upload File: <input type='file' name='fileupload'>");
        writer.write(
            "<br>Parameter 1: <input type='text' name='param1' size='30'>");
        writer.write("<br><input type='submit'>");
        writer.write("</form>");
    }
    public void processAction(ActionRequest request, ActionResponse response)
        throws PortletException, IOException
    {
        // Check the request content type to see if it starts with multipart/
        if (!PortletDiskFileUpload.isMultipartContent(request))
        {
            //set an error message
            response.setRenderParameter("error", ERROR_NO_FILE);
            return;
        }

        PortletDiskFileUpload dfu = new PortletDiskFileUpload();

        //maximum allowed file upload size (10 MB)
        dfu.setSizeMax(10 * 1000 * 1000);

        //maximum size in memory (vs disk) (100 KB)
        dfu.setSizeThreshold(100 * 1000);

        try
        {
            //get the FileItems
            List fileItems = dfu.parseRequest(request);
```

```
            Iterator iter = fileItems.iterator();
            while (iter.hasNext())
            {
                FileItem item = (FileItem) iter.next();
                if (item.isFormField())
                {
                    //pass along to render request
                    String fieldName = item.getFieldName();
                    String value = item.getString();
                    response.setRenderParameter(fieldName, value);
                }
                else
                {
                    //write the uploaded file to a new location
                    String fieldName = item.getFieldName();
                    String fileName = item.getName();
                    String contentType = item.getContentType();
                    long size = item.getSize();
                    response.setRenderParameter("size", Long.toString(size));
                    response.setRenderParameter("contentType", contentType);
                    String tempDir = System.getProperty("java.io.tmpdir");
                    String serverFileName = fieldName + "-portlet.tmp";
                    File serverFile = new File(tempDir, serverFileName);
                    item.write(serverFile);
                    response.setRenderParameter("serverFileName",
                        serverFileName);
                    getPortletContext().log(
                        "serverFileName : " + tempDir + "/" + serverFileName);
                }
            }
        }
        catch (FileUploadException fue)
        {
            String msg = "File Upload Exception: " + fue.getMessage();
            response.setRenderParameter("error", msg);
            getPortletContext().log(msg, fue);
        }
        catch (Exception e)
        {
            String msg = "Exception: " + e.getMessage();
            response.setRenderParameter("error", msg);
            getPortletContext().log(msg, e);
        }
    }
}
```

Portlet Response

The portlet sends a response object back to the portal after every request. The response contains the content fragment for the portlet, any requested portlet modes or window states, a new title if requested, and several other pieces of information we will discuss.

The `PortletResponse` interface contains the common functionality for the portlet's response to an action request and its response to a render request. There are only three methods on the `PortletResponse` interface: two for setting the response property values, and one for encoding the URL of portlet application resources. Most of the portlet response functionality is on the `RenderResponse` or `ActionResponse` interface.

Properties

The portlet API provides for an exchange of configuration properties between the portlet and the portal. The portal decides which properties it supports, so check your vendor's documentation. A property consists of a key with one or more values. The key and the values are `String` objects, with no restrictions on naming.

The `setProperty()` method on the `PortletResponse` object creates a new property, or replaces an existing property. If you need to add more than one value to a property, use the `addProperty()` method. Pass an existing key as one argument, and the added value as the other argument:

```
public void setProperty(String key, String value)
public void addProperty(String key, String value)
```

One example of using properties as part of the standard portlet API is caching. Portlets may set their cache timeout value as a property on the response, using the `portlet.expiration-cache` property. We discuss caching later in this chapter. The properties also support proprietary features in a portal.

URL Encoding

We discussed URL encoding in Chapter 2 briefly, but we wanted to emphasize the necessity of encoding URLs to resources within the portlet application. The portal may need additional information on the URL to identify which portlet on the page the resource is associated with, especially if there are two instances of the same portlet for a user. If the user's browser does not support cookies, the portal may need to rewrite the URL with the current session ID.

The `encodeURL()` method on `PortletResponse` takes the path to a resource inside the portlet application. The path may be either an absolute path to a resource on the server, or a full URL with the scheme, server, port (if necessary), and path.

```
public java.lang.String encodeURL(String path)
```

The path must start with a forward slash or be a complete URL, or the method will throw an `IllegalArgumentException`. Here is a code snippet from a portlet that is writing out a URL:

```
//encode a URL
writer.write(response.encodeURL("/images/mountain.jpg"));
```

The encoded URL will include any information the portal needs, if the path is to a resource on the server. If you pass a complete URL to the `encodeURL()` method, the portlet container will just return it as is, because the other server will have no record of the portlet user anyway.

Render Response

The `RenderResponse` object contains methods for working with the response during the render request handling phase. We discussed four of these methods in Chapter 2; see that chapter to learn about the `createActionURL()`, `createRenderURL()`, `setContentType()`, and `setTitle()` methods. We discuss content types later in this chapter.

The other methods on the render response allow the portlet to write content into the response, buffer the content, and retrieve the content type. Another method, `getNamespace()`, provides a unique ID for HTML and JavaScript elements on the page. The `getLocale()` method returns the locale the response is using for internationalization.

Writing Content

The render response provides two methods for writing content to the portal page: `getWriter()` and `getPortletOutputStream()`. Both require that the content type be set on the response before the portlet retrieves the response's writer or output stream. Once the portlet calls one of these methods on a response, the other one is unavailable and will throw an `IllegalStateException`.

The `getWriter()` method returns a `PrintWriter` object. The portlet can write text to the `PrintWriter`. This method is similar to its counterpart on the `HttpServletResponse` object.

```
public PrintWriter getWriter() throws IOException
```

You will probably never use the portlet output stream, because it supports binary output for image streams and other similar applications. Binary content does not integrate into an HTML portal page, so support is there for portals that might use other markup types. For instance, if a telephony portal used the portlet API, the portlet output stream could provide a WAV sound stream to the portlet output.

```
public OutputStream getPortletOutputStream() throws IOException
```

The portlet container may buffer the writer and the output stream, so output may not go to the user's web browser right away. The portlet manages the output buffering with several methods on the `RenderResponse` interface.

Buffering Output

The portlet container may buffer the output of the portlet for performance reasons. The portlet containers stores the portlet's output in a buffer. When the buffer is full, the portlet container will send the buffer's contents back to the end user's web browser. If the portlet is finished writing content, the portlet container will send the final incomplete buffer as well. For the most part, this buffering is going on behind the scenes of your portlet application. You may need greater control over output buffering if your portlet is taking a long time to accomplish a task, and the portlet is providing a status report.

The portlet may set its requested buffer size with the `setBufferSize()` method on `RenderResponse`. The portlet container will provide a buffer that is the same size or greater. After content has been written to the portlet's output, `setBufferSize()` will throw an `IllegalStateException`.

```
public void setBufferSize(int size)
```

The `getBufferSize()` method will return the buffer size used by the portlet container. Some portals will have buffering on by default, and the `getBufferSize()` method returns the size of the default buffer if the portlet has not called the `setBufferSize()` method. If there is no output buffering, this method returns a size of zero.

```
public int getBufferSize()
```

Portlets may flush the content stored in a partially full buffer to the user's web browser with the `flushBuffer()` method. Any errors while writing content will cause `flushBuffer()` to throw an `IOException`. This method commits the response, which means that the portal sent content to the user's web browser.

```
public void flushBuffer() throws IOException
```

To determine if the response is committed, the `RenderResponse` interface provides the `isCommitted()` method, which returns true if content has already been sent.

```
public boolean isCommitted()
```

If the response has not yet been committed, the portlet can reset the response, or just the content in the buffer. The `reset()` method throws away any response properties and the content in the response's buffer. If the portlet would like to keep the properties and just remove the content, it can use the `resetBuffer()` method.

Locale and Character Encoding

The render response supports portlet internationalization by providing two methods for determining the locale of the render response and the character encoding used by the render response's `PrintWriter` object.

```
public java.util.Locale getLocale()
```

See the "Preferred Locales and Internationalization" section, earlier in this chapter, for more about locales.

```
public String getCharacterEncoding()
```

The character encoding is the character set used for the text of the output.

Portlets and JavaScript

Portlets can use JavaScript in their content markup fragments, just like any other web page. One unique problem with content fragments in a portal page is that more than one instance of a portlet may be running. This means that any JavaScript variables or named HTML elements will appear more than once on the same page, which leads to unpredictable results. For instance, if you are using JavaScript mouse rollover code that sets the source URL for an HTML image, an image in another portlet might change instead. Two portlets developed independently may also inadvertently use the same names in their JavaScript code.

To solve this problem, the designers of the portlet API added the concept of namespaces to the render response. The portal assigns each portlet on the portal page a unique name, even if it is the same Java class as another portlet on the page. The actual name used by the portal does not matter for the portlet developer, because the `getNamespace()` method on the `RenderResponse` interface returns the name. The JavaScript methods, JavaScript variables, and any HTML elements referenced in JavaScript should begin with this namespace where they appear in the page.

```
public String getNamespace ()
```

One problem with this approach is that when JavaScript code is included as an external source file, the portal does not process the code. If the JavaScript source file references any elements in the portlet, it will not work because it does not know the namespace. One solution would be to include the JavaScript methods in the portlet's content fragment, so everything can begin with the portlet's namespace. The other alternative is to write your JavaScript methods so that they take a reference to a JavaScript element as an argument. The JavaScript method will use the prefixed name.

Action Response

The `ActionResponse` interface extends the `PortletResponse` interface and has methods for sending redirects, setting render parameters, and setting the window state and the portlet mode.

We discuss the window state and portlet mode functionality of the portlet later in this chapter. The functionality for both cuts across several classes in the portlet API. The methods on the `ActionResponse` interface for setting the window state and portlet mode are

```
public void setWindowState(WindowState state) throws WindowStateException
public void setPortletMode(PortletMode mode) throws PortletModeException
```

Both of these methods will throw an exception if the window state or portlet mode is invalid for the current portlet. In addition, if the action response sends a redirect to the client, both of these methods will throw an `IllegalStateException` if they are called after the `sendRedirect()` method in the action request handling step.

Send Redirect

Portlets that need to send the user's browser to an entirely different page may send a redirect as a response to the user's request. The redirect will completely leave the portal if the URL is to a page that is outside the portal or on another web server. The `sendRedirect()` method on the `ActionResponse` interface does not allow for any other methods on the `ActionResponse` interface to be called either before or after `sendRedirect()` is called. If the user's browser redirects to another web site or web application, the action response does not matter anymore anyway.

```
public void sendRedirect(String location) throws IOException
```

The argument on the `sendRedirect()` method is the path of the web page where the server redirects the user's browser. For instance, this path could be another web site (`www.apress.com`), or another path on the server (`/forums/home`). The path must be an absolute path, starting with a forward slash, or a complete URL with a scheme, server name, port, and path. If the location is a relative path, the `sendRedirect()` method will throw an `IllegalStateException`.

One reason your portlets may need to redirect the user to another page is to obtain access to pages protected by Single Sign-On (SSO) authentication. A common method of providing SSO is to redirect the user to a login page hosted on another server. The user authenticates to the SSO server, and receives an authentication token. Typically, the user goes to an SSO login page with a URL like `http://security.greenninja.com/login?url=http://portal.greenninja.com/portal`. Upon a successful login, the SSO page redirects the user to the URL from the parameter, with an authentication token passed as a parameter. The portal takes the authentication token and verifies its authenticity with the SSO server through another channel such as a web service or a Remote Method Invocation (RMI) connection. We discuss SSO in Chapter 8.

Our example of a portlet redirect simply redirects the user's browser to the Apress web site if the user selects the only link on the portlet. The link submits an action request, and the `processAction()` method sends a redirect back through the portal to the user's browser. The user will leave the portal entirely and will see only the Apress page. A friendlier approach would be to allow the user to open the Apress page in a new window from the portlet, using the standard HTML for setting a target on an `<A>` element:

```
package com.portalbook.portlets;

import java.io.IOException;
import java.io.PrintWriter;

import javax.portlet.ActionRequest;
import javax.portlet.ActionResponse;
import javax.portlet.GenericPortlet;
import javax.portlet.PortletException;
import javax.portlet.PortletURL;
import javax.portlet.RenderRequest;
import javax.portlet.RenderResponse;

public class RedirectPortlet extends GenericPortlet
{
    public void doView(RenderRequest request, RenderResponse response)
        throws PortletException, IOException
    {

        response.setContentType("text/html");
        PrintWriter writer = response.getWriter();

        PortletURL actionURL = response.createActionURL();
```

```
        writer.write("<a href='" + actionURL.toString() + "'>");
        writer.write("Redirect to APress</a>");
    }

    public void processAction(ActionRequest request, ActionResponse response)
        throws PortletException, IOException
    {
        response.sendRedirect("http://www.apress.com/");
    }
}
```

The redirect portlet example is very simple. As you can see, the only method we call in the portlet's `processAction()` method is the `sendRedirect()` method. The `doView()` method creates an action URL, and then provides an HTML link to trigger the action request.

Setting Render Parameters

Render parameters are useful to pass information about what occurred in the current action request handling phase to the render request. The portlet can then process the parameters on the render request to generate a content fragment to display to the user. Render parameters consist of a `String` object key and either a `String` object value or an array of `String` object values. These render parameters are valid during any render requests that follow the action request, until either a render request or an action request is made to the portlet. If the user refreshes the portal page or sends a request to another portlet, the render parameters are still valid. Because they are valid only until the portlet processes another request, they are very useful for providing information about how the current action request was processed. If there were any errors in the action request, they can be provided to the `render()` method through render parameters.

There are three methods on the `ActionResponse` that set render parameters:

```
public void setRenderParameter(String key, String value)
public void setRenderParameter(String key, String[] values)
public void setRenderParameters(Map parameters)
```

All of the methods will throw an `IllegalArgumentException` if any of the keys or values is null. The `setRenderParameter(String key, String value)` method sets a key/value pair, and the new value replaces any existing parameters with the same key. Another method, `setRenderParameter(String key, String[] values)`, takes an array of `String` objects as the value, in case your render parameter needs to be multivalued. If you need to assign all of the values at once, the `setRenderParameters (Map parameters)` method removes all existing render parameters and replaces them with the parameters in the `Map` object. The parameters in the `Map` should all be String/String array key/values pairs. This method will throw an IllegalArgumentException if any of the keys in the Map are not String objects or if any of the values in the Map are not String arrays. The setRenderParameters() method will also throw an IllegalArgumentException if the Map is null.

Portlet Context

Portlets will use the PortletContext object to get access to logging, resources, attributes, and initialization parameters, just like servlets in a web application would use a ServletContext object. The PortletContext object provides information and resources from the portlet application.

A portlet application context exists for each portlet application installed in a portal. If there is more than one portlet in a portlet application, they share an instance of the PortletContext object, and can use it to set and retrieve application-wide data. Servlets and JSP pages also share the contents of the PortletContext, through the ServletContext. Since the portlet application is also a web application, the servlets and JSPs deployed in the portlet application all use one context.

Retrieving the Portlet Context

You can retrieve the portlet context for a portlet's portlet application with the getPortletContext() method on the PortletConfig interface:

```
public PortletContext getPortletContext ()
```

The GenericPortlet class implements the PortletConfig interface, so any subclass of GenericPortlet may just call getPortletContext() on itself. If your portlet directly implements the Portlet interface, your init(PortletConfig config) method must retain a reference to the PortletConfig object.

Portlet Context Attributes

The attributes on the portlet context are shared data for the portlets and servlets in a portlet application. These attributes are name/value pairs, with a String object as the key and an Object as the value. The portlet can get access to the portlet context attributes from the PortletContext object.

If servlets are deployed as part of the portlet application, they will be able to access the same context attributes as part of their servlet context. Portlets will be able to access the data from servlets that use the attributes on the ServletContext object.

There are methods on the PortletContext object for retrieving the value of an attribute, retrieving the names of every portlet context attribute, removing an attribute, and setting an attribute's value:

```
public Object getAttribute(String name)
public Enumeration getAttributeNames()
public void removeAttribute(String name)
public void setAttribute(String name, Object object)
```

These attributes are different from the request attributes, even though the method names are similar. Each portlet application on the portal has one portlet context that is independent of individual users and sessions. All users can access the portlet context attributes, and they are valid until the portal server shuts down. The request attributes are valid on an action request only while the request is being processed and only valid on a render request until the user sends another request to the portlet.

In addition, portlet context attributes are only valid for the Java virtual machine they are running in. For portlet applications distributed across multiple servers, you will need to use another information store, such as a database.

Context Initialization Parameters

Portlets in the same portlet application share context initialization parameters. Rather than defining initialization parameters for each portlet with the same names and values, use context initialization parameters instead. These context initialization parameters are defined the portlet application's web.xml deployment descriptor, because they are also the context initialization parameters servlets would use. Any portlets or servlets in a portlet application may use these context initialization parameters.

The context initialization parameters are defined using <context-param> elements that are children of the <web-app> root element in the web.xml file. The following example demonstrates the use of two context parameters, named mailServer and fromAddress:

```
<web-app>
    ...
    <context-param>
```

```
        <param-name>mailServer</param-name>
        <param-value>mail.portalbook.com</param-value>
        <description>Address of the SMTP server.</description>
    </context-param>
    <context-param>
        <param-name>fromAddress</param-name>
        <param-value>info@portalbook.com</param-value>
        <description>Address used for the sender.</description>
    </context-param>
    ...
</web-app>
```

The getInitParameterNames() method on the PortletContext object returns the names of the context initialization parameters. The names are returned as an Enumeration of String objects. If there are no context initialization parameters for the portlet application, the method returns an Enumeration that is empty.

```
public Enumeration getInitParameterNames()
```

To retrieve an individual context initialization parameter, portlets may call the getInitParameter() method on the PortletContext object. The getInitParameter() method takes a non-null String as an argument with the name of the initialization parameter. It returns a String containing the value from the web.xml deployment descriptor. If the parameter is not defined, it returns null. If the argument passed to the method is null, the getInitParameter() method will throw an IllegalArgumentException.

```
public String getInitParameter(String name)
```

Portlets may also have their own initialization parameters that are specific to one portlet in a portlet application. These can be accessed from the PortletConfig object. See Chapter 7 for more details on using these portlet initialization parameters.

Accessing Resources and MIME Types

Because the portlet context corresponds to a servlet context, the methods for accessing files inside the portlet application and determining their MIME type work the same way in a portlet as they do in a servlet. We can use these methods to map the paths that a user would use to access a resource (image, JSP, movie, HTML) to a URL the portlet can use to load the resource. These URLs are valid only for reading from the file, but portlet containers may provide write access to the portlet for some URL schemes. The portlet API provides a way to access files that are part of the portlet application, whether they are in a WAR file or deployed on the file system. In either case, the portlet may use the `getResource()` method on the `PortletContext` to retrieve a URL to the file:

```
public URL getResource(String path) throws MalformedURLException
```

The path to the file must start with a forward slash. The resource is loaded relative to the portlet application. To load files in the WEB-INF directory, use a path like /WEB-INF/content/homePage.xml. If the resource does not exist, the URL will be null.

The portlet can directly access an `InputStream` for the resource with the `getResourceAsStream()` method on `PortletContext`. The semantics of the path are the same as the `getResource()` method, but this method returns an `InputStream` for convenience:

```
public InputStream getResourceAsStream (String path)
```

The portlet should not use either of these methods to load JSP pages from the web application. The portal would not process or execute the JSP pages when loaded as a resource. We discuss including JSP pages in the portlet's output in the next chapter.

If the MIME type for a resource in the portlet application is unknown, the portlet can ask the portlet context to determine the MIME type for a file. The `getMimeType()` method returns the resource's MIME type. Each portal will have a set of MIME type mappings. The web.xml deployment descriptor can contain any additional MIME types for the portlet application. The `path` argument is relative to the portlet application root, so "/WEB-INF/content/nav.html" would work.

```
  public String getMimeType(String path)
```

The `getResourcePaths()` method takes the partial name of a path as an argument. The method will create a `Set` of paths to resources that start with the path. You can use the `Set` to browse through the portlet application like a directory on a file system. If you pass in a "/" to signify the root of the portlet application, you will get a `Set` of the paths of any directories or files directly under the root. You can also pass in directory names.

One use for this method would be to load all configuration files in a directory, for instance, all properties files in the /WEB-INF/config/cms directory. It returns a null if there are no matching resources for the path.

```
public Set getResourcePaths(String path)
```

If your portlet runs on a portal that uses the file system for portlet application storage, you can get the path on the file system for a resource. The `getRealPath()` method takes the path to the resource inside the portlet application and returns the file system path. This method will return null if the resource does not exist, or if the portlet application is not on a file system.

```
public String getRealPath(String path)
```

These methods work the same way in the portlet environment as they do in the servlet environment, so if you come across an edge case not covered in the portlet documentation, check the servlet discussion groups or other servlet programming resources to see if anyone has had a similar problem.

Logging

The portlet may write log messages out to an event log. The portlet logging functionality is identical to the logging methods on the `ServletContext` class. Like servlet logging, the location of the log is dependent on the implementation of the container, and could be a text file, a database entry, or any other method the container provider chooses. There are two `log()` methods on the `PortletContext` class. The first logging method takes a `String` object as an argument, and writes the message it contains to the portlet's log:

```
public void log(String msg)
```

The other logging method also takes a `String` object that contains a message as an argument, as well as a `Throwable` object as an argument. This method is used for passing errors or exceptions to the portlet container's event log:

```
public void log(java.lang.String message, java.lang.Throwable throwable);
```

Instead of using the built-in logging functionality from the `PortletContext` object, we recommend that you use Apache's log4j (`http://logging.apache.org/log4j`) project for your logging. log4j's main features are the ability to format logging output, the ability to redirect logging output to multiple locations, and support for different levels of logging. The logging level for log4j can be raised or lowered dynamically on a per-class or per-package basis.

Accessing Portlet Container Information

A portlet can access some information about the portlet container through the PortletContext object. Other information about the portal server itself is available on the PortalContext object, which we discuss in Chapter 7. The getServerInfo() method on the PortletContext object returns a String object that contains the name and the version number of the portlet container:

```
public String getServerInfo()
```

The server information will be returned in this format: Portlet Container Name/Version Number, for instance, "Pluto/1.0".

Portlet API Versioning

The portlet may retrieve information about the version of the portlet API that the portlet container supports. This could be useful for supporting future changes. For instance, if a future version of the portlet API provides a new mechanism for accessing user information, the portlet could support this. If the portlet is running in a portlet container with an older version of the portlet API, it could fall back on some sort of legacy behavior or a compatibility layer.

The version data consists of a major version and a minor version. If the version supported is 2.1, the major version is 2, and the minor version is 1.

The two methods on PortletContext that return version information are:

```
public int getMajorVersion()
public int getMinorVersion()
```

When future versions of the portlet API are developed, you can decide whether to support the new features and behavior in your portlets. It is very likely that some functionality that is currently only available as a proprietary feature of one vendor's portal will be included in the standard, because portlet developers will benefit.

Including Servlets or JavaServer Pages

In the next chapter, we discuss including servlets or JavaServer Pages (JSP) in the servlet's response. The getRequestDispatcher() and getNamedDispatcher() methods on the PortletContext object are used to obtain PortletRequestDispatcher objects. These portlet request dispatchers are used to pass the portlet's render request and render response objects to servlets or JSP pages in the portlet application.

Sessions

A portlet application can track the user across multiple client requests for a portal page using sessions. Session tracking for portlets is similar to the session tracking used in the servlet API. For portlets, the portal is responsible for the mechanics of maintaining a session for the user across HTTP (which is a stateless protocol). The portal's session tracking could be done with HTTP cookies, URL rewriting, or another mechanism, but the portlet should not rely on or expect any particular method.

A portlet in a portlet application can get access to the session through a `PortletSession` object. The `PortletSession` object is available through the portlet's request object. There are two `getPortletSession()` methods on the `PortletRequest` object used for retrieving portlets. You use the first method to access the portlet session for the user, if one already exists. If the user's session has not been created yet, this method will create the new session and return it:

```
public PortletSession getPortletSession ()
```

The other method is useful if you need to determine whether there is a current `PortletSession` object:

```
public PortletSession getPortletSession (boolean create)
```

If the argument is `true`, this method has the same behavior as the first `getPortletSession()` method described earlier. If `false` is passed instead, the method will return null if a portlet session has not been created yet for this user. If a portlet session exists for this user, either of these methods will return the session.

Each `PortletSession` object is specific to a portlet application. Portals do not share portlet sessions between different portlet applications. Portlet sessions are also unique between different users of the portal.

Portlets can store objects in the session as attributes, referenced by the attribute name, a `String` object. There are two different scopes for placing and accessing objects: the application scope and the portlet scope. Session objects stored as portlet scope are for a given instance of the portlet on the portal page. If there is more than one instance of the portlet on a page, the portlet scope will be different for each. When an object is saved on the session in the portlet scope, it has a namespace prefix appended to the attribute name. The namespace is different for each instance of the portlet on the page. This does not hide the objects from other portlets in the session; if they get the names of all the attributes in the session, they will be able to see the portlet scope objects. Use this scope to avoid overwriting the session attributes of other portlets in the portlet application.

Any portlet in the portlet application can retrieve or modify any attributes in the user's session stored as application scope.

Portlets set session attributes with the two `setAttribute()` methods. Each method takes the name and value of the attribute. The only difference is which scope the attribute uses. The first method takes no scope argument, and the attribute belongs in the portlet scope. The next method takes an `int` value as the scope argument. There are two acceptable values for the scope: the static constants `PortletSession.PORTLET_SCOPE` and `PortletSession.APPLICATION_SCOPE`.

```
public void setAttribute(String name, Object value)
public void setAttribute(String name, Object value, int scope)
```

The portlet retrieves the attributes from the session using one of the two `getAttribute()` methods. Like `setAttribute()`, one takes an `int` value for the scope, and one assumes that it will look for the attribute in the portlet scope. Both return null if there is no session attribute with that name.

```
public Object getAttribute(String name)
public Object getAttribute(String name,int scope)
```

If you need the names of the attributes in the session, the two `getAttributeNames()` methods will provide an `Enumeration` of attribute names. One method takes the scope as an argument, and the method with no arguments uses the portlet scope.

```
public Enumeration getAttributeNames()
public Enumeration getAttributeNames(int scope)
```

To remove attributes from the session, you can use either one of the `removeAttribute()` methods. Each takes the name of the attribute to remove as an argument, and one requires a scope. If the attribute does not exist, nothing happens.

```
public void removeAttribute(String name)
public void removeAttribute(String name, int scope)
```

The portlet session shares all of its attributes with the web application session. If the portlet application uses servlets or JSP pages, the session available to those resources will have the same attributes, and the portlet reflects any changes to the attributes in the portlet session when control returns to the portlet.

Like the servlet API, objects may implement the `HttpSessionBindingListener` interface. These listener objects receive a notification when bound into a session or are unbound from a session. You will need to specify the session listeners in the web application deployment descriptor using the `<listener>` and `<listener-class>` XML elements.

Session Creation and Access Times

Portlet sessions provide the time when the user last accessed the session. You can use this to provide a session timeout countdown to users, to warn them that the portal will drop their session after an amount of time has passed.

The `getCreationTime()` method returns the time when the portal created the session. This time is in milliseconds since 1970.

```
public long getCreationTime()
```

The user's session has been inactive since the time in milliseconds since 1970 returned by the `getLastAccessedTime()` method. This is the time that the user's request was last received by the portal.

```
public long getLastAccessedTime()
```

Session Timeout and Invalidation

The portlet session uses the same mechanisms for session timeout as the servlet API. The portlet may programmatically set the length of inactivity in seconds that a session may have before being marked invalid. The `setMaxInactiveInterval()` method on the `PortletSession` interface takes the number of seconds as an argument that a given session has before it times out. The portlet may ensure that the session does not time out by setting this interval to a negative number.

```
public void setMaxInactiveInterval(int interval)
```

Sessions may also be invalidated by the portlet directly, using the `invalidate()` method. This is useful when a user is logging out of a system, and you want to explicitly destroy the session.

```
public void invalidate()
```

These session methods are similar to the methods on the `HttpSession`. The important difference is the existence of a portlet scope that allows more than one instance of a portlet to run at a time, and for portlets in the same portlet application to share information about the user's session.

Threading and Distributed Deployment Considerations

Because the portlet session is available to any portlets in the portlet application, it is possible for the portlets to access an object in the portlet session simultaneously. The portlet session does not synchronize access to its objects, so the portlet will need to manage any threading issues. The portlet session has the same thread model issues as the servlet session.

In addition to threading issues, portlet applications deployed in a distributed environment have the same considerations as distributed servlets. Because a user may switch from server to server between requests, a portlet that supports clustering must only put serializable objects in the portlet session. In addition, the portlet should not use any static variables to hold information. The actual movement of the session between different servers in the cluster is left up to the portal vendors to determine, and it will probably also depend on the application server deployed in the environment. Not all portals will support distributed deployment.

Portlet Session Utility

The portlet session utility class, `PortletSessionUtility`, is useful for working with the encoded session attributes in the portlet scope. (We discussed the different session scopes earlier.) The `PortletSessionUtility` provides two static methods for decoding session attributes. The first method, `decodeAttributeName()`, takes an encoded session attribute name and returns a decoded attribute name. If the session attribute is in the application scope, it does not need to be decoded, so the argument is just returned as the value.

```
public static String decodeAttributeName(String name)
```

The next method, `decodeScope()`, returns the scope of a portlet session attribute.

```
public static int decodeScope(String name)
```

The value returned is either `PortletSession.PORTLET_SCOPE` or `PortletSession.APPLICATION_SCOPE`. Both of these methods look at the name of the attribute to determine if it starts with the portlet scope namespace, which is "javax.portlet.p".

Sessions and Interportlet Communication

Portlets communicate with other portlets in the same portlet application through the user's portlet session. In the initial version of the portlet API, this is the only available interportlet communication functionality. Portal vendors may offer a proprietary way to pass messages or events between portlets. Future versions of the portlet API will probably provide a standard for communication.

If we have one portlet that has a list of employees, and another portlet that displays their insurance information, the portlets will share a reference to the current employee in the session. Both portlets must be in the same portlet application to share the session.

We will create a simple content browser tool that consists of two portlets. One will display a set of topics, and the other will display content. When the user clicks on a link in the topic browser, the portal page will refresh, the portal sends an action request to the topic portlet, and then the portal sends render requests to all of the portlets on the page. The topic portlet reads the `id` parameter from the action URL when the portlet processes the action request. The portlet then places the `id` parameter in the portlet session as the `contentId` parameter in the application scope. We named them differently here to make it clear that the parameter on the action request is distinct from the parameter on the portlet session. The render request and the other portlets in the portlet application do not have access to the action request parameters.

There are three key points to remember for interportlet communication using sessions:

- The portlet places the parameters in the session's application scope.
- Be sure not to enable caching for the portlets.
- Changes to the portlet session must occur during an action request to guarantee that the updates propagate to every portlet during the render request. There is no guarantee that the portlets render in any particular order. Synchronization is not required, because only one action request will be processed for each user at one time.

Our `TopicPortlet` class shows how to add a parameter to the session in the `processAction()` method to communicate with another portlet. We also use the `createActionURL()` method on the response to create action URLs for our content.

```
package com.portalbook.portlets.content;

import java.io.IOException;
import java.io.Writer;
import java.util.ArrayList;
```

```
import java.util.Iterator;
import java.util.List;

import javax.portlet.ActionRequest;
import javax.portlet.ActionResponse;
import javax.portlet.GenericPortlet;
import javax.portlet.PortletException;
import javax.portlet.PortletSession;
import javax.portlet.PortletURL;
import javax.portlet.RenderRequest;
import javax.portlet.RenderResponse;

public class TopicPortlet extends GenericPortlet
{
    List topics = new ArrayList();

    public void init()
    {
        topics.add("xerces");
        topics.add("lucene");
        topics.add("xalan");
        topics.add("jdom");
    }

    public void doView(RenderRequest request, RenderResponse response)
        throws PortletException, IOException
    {
        response.setContentType("text/html");
        Writer writer = response.getWriter();

        Iterator iter = topics.iterator();
        while (iter.hasNext())
        {
            String key = (String) iter.next();

            PortletURL actionURL = response.createActionURL();
            actionURL.setParameter("id", key);

            writer.write("<a href='" + actionURL.toString() + "'>");
            writer.write(key + "</a><br>");
        }
    }
```

```
    public void processAction(ActionRequest request, ActionResponse response)
        throws PortletException, IOException
    {
        PortletSession session = request.getPortletSession(true);
        String id = request.getParameter("id");
        session.setAttribute("contentId", id, PortletSession.APPLICATION_SCOPE);
    }
}
```

The `ContentPortlet` class checks the session for a parameter named `contentId` in the application scope. If the portlet finds the content ID, it displays the appropriate content. There is no `processAction()` method on this class—it expects that the new content piece will come from the session through the topic browser. If this portlet ran on its own, it would have no way of changing its content.

```
package com.portalbook.portlets.content;

import java.io.IOException;
import java.io.Writer;
import java.util.HashMap;

import javax.portlet.GenericPortlet;
import javax.portlet.PortletException;
import javax.portlet.PortletSession;
import javax.portlet.RenderRequest;
import javax.portlet.RenderResponse;

public class ContentPortlet extends GenericPortlet
{

    private HashMap contentMap = new HashMap();

    public void init()
    {
        contentMap.put("xerces", "Xerces is an open source XML Parser.");
        contentMap.put("lucene", "Lucene is a Java search engine.");
        contentMap.put("xalan", "Xalan is an open source XSLT engine.");
        contentMap.put("jdom", "JDOM is an open source Java XML parser.");
    }

    public void doView(RenderRequest request, RenderResponse response)
        throws PortletException, IOException
    {
```

```
        response.setContentType("text/html");
        Writer writer = response.getWriter();

        PortletSession session = request.getPortletSession(true);

        String contentId =
            (String) session.getAttribute(
                "contentId",
                PortletSession.APPLICATION_SCOPE);

        if (contentId == null)
        {
            writer.write("No content selected yet.");
        }
        else
        {
            if (contentMap.containsKey(contentId))
            {

                String content = (String) contentMap.get(contentId);
                writer.write(content);
            }
            else
            {
                writer.write("Content not found for: " + contentId);
            }
        }
    }
}
```

This example should demonstrate how portlets communicate with each other using the first version of the portlet API. This is an area to watch for innovations from a portal vendor. You may decide that you need to process an action in both portlets if something happens, which would require functionality that is not in the standard.

Content Markup Types

Each portlet supports one or more different markup standards for displaying content. Some of the possible markup types are HTML, WML, and XML. Each different markup is specified as a MIME type in the deployment descriptor. The HTML MIME type is text/html, the WML MIME type is text/vnd.wap.wml, and the MIME type for XML is text/xml.

Most portlets will support only one markup type, most likely HTML. Support for other markup types has been lukewarm, because of the ubiquity of HTML. Unless you absolutely need to support WML or another markup language for small footprint devices such as cell phones, PDAs, or other handheld devices, try to use HTML to accomplish the same goals. Keep your HTML simple and light, with minimal table markup and no reliance on CSS styles, colors, frames, or JavaScript. Writing HTML that degrades gracefully is a difficult task when the business units responsible for the portal demand the latest dynamic browser feature in the portlets, but save your users from their user interface nightmare, and rely on the HTML standards for portability.

Asking the Portal for the Supported Content Types

If a portlet allows access to multiple content markup types, the portlet may ask the portal which content type the portal prefers to use. The portlet may also ask the portal for a list of all of the supported markup types. In both cases, the portal will return only markup types that the portlet supports in its deployment descriptor.

The `getResponseContentType()` method on the `PortletRequest` object returns the default content type the portal will accept in the response. To get all supported content types, use the `getResponseContentTypes()` method on the `PortletRequest` interface. The supported content types are sorted in order of preference, with the default content type first.

```
public String getResponseContentType()
public Enumeration getResponseContentTypes()
```

Portlets may support all content types, and so may portals. Support of all content types is signified with either the "*" or "*/*" wildcards. For the special case where both the portlet and the portal support all content types, "*" or "*/*" is a valid response from the `getResponseContentType()` and `getResponseContentTypes()` methods.

Setting the Content Type on the Render Response

The portlet provides a content type for its markup fragment with the `setContentType()` method on the `RenderResponse` interface. If the portlet has already asked for a writer or an output stream, the content type is already set. The content type passed into the method as an argument has to be one of the content types returned by the `getResponseContentTypes()` method we discussed earlier.

```
public void setContentType(String type)
```

After the `setContentType()` method has been called on a render response, the `getContentType()` method will return the response's content type. If `setContentType()` has not been called yet, `getContentType()` will return a null value.

```
public String getContentType()
```

The content type on a response has to be set before the portlet retrieves the reader or output stream from the response.

Deployment Descriptor

The portlet can have a set of portlet modes for each content type it supports. The supported portlet modes map to the content types in the portlet's deployment descriptor. We discuss the deployment descriptor markup for content types and portlet modes in the next section.

Portlet Modes

These portlet modes are the different functions that a portlet container can ask a portlet to perform. The portlet container is responsible for telling the portlet which mode it is in. Each portlet can also change its mode based on the user input, if needed.

Portlet authors can decide which modes their portlets will support based on the markup type, but all portlets need to support the VIEW mode for all markup types. The VIEW mode is for normal operation, displaying content to the user and accepting requests. If any other modes are implemented by the portlet, they will need to be specified in the portlet.xml deployment descriptor for the portlet. The three standard modes defined in the Portlet specification are VIEW, EDIT, and HELP, and all portlet containers must support at least these three modes. The portlet container may define other modes, and the portlet can support them if needed. The portlet is not required to support any optional or custom portlet modes.

The portlet may support different portlet modes for each MIME type. For instance, if a portlet is running in a normal web-based portal, it could support the VIEW, EDIT, and HELP portlet modes. Portlets deployed on a wireless portal that output in WML might support only the VIEW mode.

Retrieving the Portlet Mode from the Request

The portlet can use the current portlet mode to determine which content to display. The portlet can also handle actions differently for each mode. In either case, the portlet can ask the portlet request for the current portlet mode. The `getPortletMode()` method on the `PortletRequest` object returns a `PortletMode` object.

```
public PortletMode getPortletMode()
```

The `PortletMode` object describes a portlet mode. Several static fields on the `PortletMode` object (VIEW, EDIT, and HELP) represent the three standard portlet modes. For portals that support custom modes (for instance, PRINT), the constructor on `PortletMode` can be called with the name of the custom mode (as a `String` object) as the sole argument to the constructor. The name of the portlet mode can be retrieved from the `PortletMode` object as a `String` by calling the `PortletMode`'s `toString()` method. The `PortletMode` class also overrides the `equals()` and `hashCode()` methods from the `java.lang.Object` class.

Methods for Portlet Modes on GenericPortlet

The `GenericPortlet` abstract portlet base class has several methods that may be used to support rendering content for portlet modes in a render request. The `doDispatch()` method asks the portlet request for the current portlet mode. The render request is then dispatched to the `doView()`, `doEdit()`, or `doHelp()` method as needed. If the window state was minimized, the portlet will not render anything. If custom portlet modes are required, the `doDispatch()` method will need to be overridden by any portlet class that extends `GenericPortlet`.

Required Portlet Modes

There are three required portlet modes: VIEW, EDIT, and HELP. All portals must support these modes, but portlets have to support only the VIEW mode. The VIEW mode is the default mode that the portlet will render content for. Portlets should use the VIEW mode for their typical behavior, such as displaying the weather. Because the default portlet mode for a portlet when it is first loaded is VIEW, any content will have to be in the VIEW mode. If your portlet needs to display content that would normally be in the EDIT portlet mode when it first loads, you should just display it as normal.

Our weather portlet would use the EDIT mode to allow the user to put in a different location, or to change the display to show a seven-day weather forecast. The EDIT mode should be used to provide a way to change the settings for the portlet's display or business logic.

The HELP portlet mode may be used to give the end user help content about the portlet. The HELP mode could display a single HTML file with some help, or it could be the entry into a more sophisticated help system with an index, a search engine, or other advanced features.

The portal container does not restrict the portlet from any behavior inside the portlet modes. You could add a form to allow the user to set preferences for the portlet inside the VIEW mode if you wanted. It would be bad form to do so, because the user expects that preferences are set through the available EDIT mode on the portlet. The decision to break up functionality into different mode should be based on usability and user expectations for behavior. Sending and receiving e-mail should belong in the VIEW mode, while the user's mail server settings should be changed in the EDIT mode.

Custom Modes

Portals can also provide custom modes that are proprietary to a vendor. The portlet API defines several extended modes that a portal vendor may implement—this standardized naming should make it easier to make the portlets that use these custom modes portable.

The suggested extended modes are:

- ABOUT
- CONFIG
- EDIT_DEFAULTS
- PREVIEW
- PRINT

The ABOUT portlet mode is useful for displaying information about the creator of the portlet, the version number, and the name of the portlet product. Portal administrators can use a portlet in CONFIG mode to change portlet preferences that are not able to be modified by portlet users. (For more on portlet preferences, see Chapter 7.) Portlets may provide a user interface to edit default settings for portlet preferences in the EDIT_DEFAULTS mode. Both the CONFIG and the EDIT_DEFAULTS portlet modes are meant for use by portal administrators.

The PREVIEW mode is used for displaying default content that shows how the portlet would look under real usage. Portlets should not try to make any database or other connections in PREVIEW mode, and should not rely on the portlet user. The PREVIEW portlet mode can be used for display in a portal's portlet catalog, or when the user customizes his home page. Portlets should use their most typical layout, with dummy text or plausible defaults.

Portals may support a printer-friendly mode for portlets called PRINT. In the PRINT mode, portlets should render content that is suitable for printing. This could mean that the portlet is stripped of any unnecessary navigation or input elements. For a content management portlet that displays content as HTML, the

VIEW mode might display links for editing or downloading a piece of content in addition to the content. The PRINT mode would just display the content itself.

The portal vendor will decide which portlet modes to support beyond the required modes. Portlets could implement these suggested modes, but portlets are not required to support them for operation. Usually, the portal page will show the appropriate GUI elements to switch between portlet modes for a portlet; only the allowed portlet modes will have elements.

Changing the Portlet Mode

The portlet can switch to another portlet mode during action request processing or when a user triggers a portlet URL that directs the portlet to enter a specific portlet mode. The end user can also switch the portlet mode by using a user interface element provided by the portal server. It is up to the portal to provide an indicator to the user that a portlet is in a given portlet mode, but it is not required. Of course, the portlet can also tell the user what portlet mode it is in as part of its display.

The `ActionResponse` object contains the `setPortletMode()` method, which takes a valid `PortletMode` object as an argument:

```
void setPortletMode(PortletMode portletMode)
```

If the portlet mode is custom, the portlet should ask the portlet request if the portlet mode is valid by using the `isPortletModeAllowed()` method on the `PortletRequest` object:

```
boolean isPortletModeAllowed(PortletMode mode)
```

The `setPortletMode()` method will throw a `PortletModeException` if the portlet mode is not valid or supported.

Links and forms can trigger a change to a new portlet mode. The portlet URL must have the portlet mode set on the URL using the `setPortletMode()` method on the `PortletURL` object. Like the `setPortletMode()` method on `ActionResponse`, it takes a `PortletMode` object as an argument, and if it is invalid or unsupported, the method will throw a `PortletModeException`.

Deployment Descriptor

The portlet.xml portlet deployment descriptor contains `<supports>` elements for each markup MIME type that a portlet could handle. The `<supports>` elements are children of the `<portlet>` XML element. Each `<supports>` element contains one `<mime-type>` element with the supported MIME type, and any supported portlet modes as `<portlet-mode>` elements. Because each portlet has to support the VIEW mode, you do not have to include the VIEW mode in the list of supported modes.

Here is a snippet of the portlet deployment descriptor for a portlet that supports the HTML and XML markup types with the VIEW, EDIT, and HELP portlet modes:

```
<portlet>
...
          <supports>
                  <mime-type>text/html</mime-type>
                  <portlet-mode>edit</portlet-mode>
                  <portlet-mode>help</portlet-mode>
          </supports>
          <supports>
                  <mime-type>text/xml</mime-type>
                  <portlet-mode>edit</portlet-mode>
                  <portlet-mode>help</portlet-mode>
          </supports>
...
</portlet>
```

The custom modes supported by the portlet are also specified with the `<portlet-mode>` element, in the same manner. A portlet application must specify all of the custom portlet modes that it uses in its portlet deployment descriptor.

```
<portlet>
...
          <supports>
               <mime-type>text/html</mime-type>
               <portlet-mode>edit</portlet-mode>
               <portlet-mode>print</portlet-mode>
          </supports>
...
</portlet>
```

In the previous example, the portlet uses the print custom portlet mode. If the portal does not support the PRINT mode, the portlet should provide the equivalent functionality in another manner, such as a link in the portlet's main navigation or menu. To support a custom portlet mode, the portlet has to define the custom mode under the `<portlet-app>` root XML element in the portlet deployment descriptor. The `<custom-portlet-mode>` element contains two child elements. The <description> element provides a readable description for the mode. The <name> child element is the name by which the portlet mode will be referenced. The <name> element needs to match the name of one of the portal's supported modes exactly.

The portlet deployment descriptor for a portlet that supports the PRINT, VIEW, and EDIT modes for the HTML markup type would look like this:

```
<portlet-app>
          <portlet>
...
                    <supports>
                           <mime-type>text/html</mime-type>
                           <portlet-mode>edit</portlet-mode>
                           <portlet-mode>print</portlet-mode>
                    </supports>
...
          </portlet>
          <custom-portlet-mode>
               <description>Printer-friendly content display for the portlet</description>
                 <portlet-mode>print</portlet-mode>
          </custom-portlet-mode>
...

</portlet-app>
```

This portlet will now be able to display content in the PRINT portlet mode. Before creating any portlet URLs that change the portlet mode to PRINT, the portlet should ask the portal which window modes are supported.

Getting the Supported Portlet Modes from the Portal

Because the portal can support custom portlet modes, the portlet API includes a method on the PortalContext object to get all of the supported portlet modes. The portlet can use this as another way to determine which portlet modes the portal allows. The getSupportedPortletModes() method will return an Enumeration of PortletMode objects that represent the available portlet modes on the portal. This method will always return the VIEW, EDIT, and HELP portlet modes, at the very least.

```
public Enumeration getSupportedPortletModes()
```

If the portlet supports custom portlet modes, it can use this method to find out if the portal supports the portlet modes, or it can ask the request if the portlet mode is supported with the `isPortletModeAllowed()` method on the `PortletRequest` object. In either case, the portlet specifies which custom modes it supports in its portlet application deployment descriptor.

Window States

The portal can display one or more portlets at a time on the portal page. These portlets can take up various amounts of screen space, and the portal container can tell the portlet what type of space it expects to fill. The portlet can use this information, called a window state, to determine how much information to display.

The portlet API specifies three different window states. Each portal may define custom window states for other uses. The portlet must explicitly support these custom window states and cannot use any window states that are not defined by the portal. Therefore, if you decide to support a proprietary window state, it may work on only one portal server.

NORMAL

The NORMAL window state is for portlets that appear on the portal page in their default setting—with other portlets. Most portlets will be displaying the most essential information to a user in this setting, and will not take up unnecessary screen real estate. For example, an e-mail portlet might inform the user that there are seven new e-mails, and provide a link to view them.

MAXIMIZED

The MAXIMIZED window state is for portlets that are the focus of the portal page—there probably are not any other portlets on the page, and the user has probably selected this portlet to work with from the main page. If we had an e-mail portlet, when the user clicked the new messages link the portlet was displaying in the NORMAL window state, the e-mail portlet would expand to MAXIMIZED, and display 20 e-mail subject headings from the user's inbox.

MINIMIZED

The MINIMIZED window state is for portlets that are not currently being displayed in the portal page, or may be displayed in a very small area of the page. For instance, a portal that is displaying a portlet in the MAXIMIZED window state might display the other active portlets in the MINIMIZED state along the bottom edge of the portal page, like the Microsoft Windows taskbar. This behavior is up to the portal vendor to determine, and your portal may have settings to customize the minimization behavior.

Our e-mail portlet might just display one line, saying "7 new messages" or a similar message. Setting the portlet title to something descriptive can also be useful for portlets that display only their title.

Custom Window States

You will need to add a `<custom-window-state>` element to the portlet.xml deployment descriptor for your portlet to support any portal-specific window states. For instance, your portlet may support a ONE_LINE window state that displays only one line of content, or it could support a dock window state, where each portlet renders a fixed-width, fixed-height window of content.

Processing the Appropriate Content for the Window State

The portlet can determine which window state the portlet is currently being displayed in with the `getWindowState()` method on the `PortletRequest` interface. The `getWindowState()` method returns a `WindowState` object that represents either one of the standard window states or a custom window state:

```
public WindowState getWindowState()
```

If your portlet extends `GenericPortlet`, you will need to override the `doDispatch()` method if you want to display any content when the portlet is minimized. Typically, you would either display nothing or display a one- or two-line version of the portlet's content. For our e-mail portlet, the minimized view might display only a message telling the user she has four new e-mails in her inbox. By default, the `doDispatch()` method does not call the `doView()`, `doEdit()`, or `doHelp()` methods when the portlet is minimized.

Inside any of the portlet mode rendering methods (`doView()`, `doEdit()`, `doHelp()`, or any custom portlet modes that are supported), you can check for the portlet's window state, and change the content displayed based on the current window state. You may use a different JSP page to display the content, or you could let the JSP page determine what to do with the window state.

Setting the Window State on the Response, Based on a User Action

The portlet can change the window state that it is in when it processes the action request. On the ActionResponse interface, the setWindowState() method takes a valid WindowState object as its only argument. The portlet will then render in that window state when the render request is processed. Any future render requests will use the new window state until the portlet changes it during the action handling phase, or the user initiates the change through the portal's interface.

A valid window state must be passed to the portlet. The portlet needs to support all standard window states. If the portal supports custom window states, and the portlet defines the custom window state as supported in the portlet.xml deployment descriptor, the change is valid. If the portlet wants to double-check that the window state is allowed, it can call the isWindowStateAllowed() method on the portlet's PortletRequest object.

```
public void setWindowState(WindowState windowState)  throws WindowStateException
```

If the window state is not supported, the WindowStateException is thrown by the setWindowState() method.

Getting Supported Window States

The portal also provides a list of supported window states to the portlet. The portlet may use these window states to determine how to handle any custom behavior. Any custom window states are not available to the portlet unless defined in the portlet deployment descriptor. The getSupportedWindowStates() method on the PortalContext object allows the portlet to retrieve all of the window states:

```
public Enumeration getSupportedWindowStates()
```

Similar to the getSupportedPortletModes() method, the getSupportedWindowStates() method will return an Enumeration of WindowState objects, including the standard window states and any custom window states the portlet supports. You are more likely to support custom portlet modes than custom window states, unless your portlet deploys in a non-web environment such as a mobile phone or a VoiceXML telephone portal.

Caching

A portlet may ask the portal container to cache its content for a given user. This cache is on a timeout expiration basis, which means that the content is fresh only for a specified length of time, and at the end of that time, the stale content will be refreshed with a call to the portlet to display content. Any request from the end user to the portlet will automatically invalidate the cache for that portlet, and the portlet's response to the user contains the cached content fragment.

The deployment descriptor for the portlet contains an XML element called `<expiration-cache>`, which is a child of the `<portlet>` element. The optional `<expiration-cache>` element contains the maximum number of seconds for the portlet's content timeout cache. The cache may be set to never expire with a value of `-1`. Refreshes to the portlet's content will occur only if the user sends a request to the portlet. If the portlet does not use the cache, the timeout cache value should be set to zero.

The portlet may also set its cache timeout value during a request if it has an expiration cache in its deployment descriptor. The portlet would change the `portlet.expiration-cache` property on the `RenderResponse` object to a new value. The name of the property is also a static constant `String` field on the `RenderResponse` object called EXPIRATION_CACHE.

A portal container does not cache information across multiple users, although the portlet may cache information for multiple users itself if performance is an issue. The two major issues with using caches for portlets are changes to back-end content invalidating the cached content, and memory usage. If your portlet relies on a database accessed by multiple users or by other applications, determine what the best trade-off is between reducing load on the server and possibly showing invalid content to the end user.

Some portals will not implement caching. If a portlet that supports caching runs on a portal that does not support caching, the portlet will run normally. The caching behavior is invisible to the portlet.

This is another good reason not to do anything that modifies the state of the portlet or the underlying data model in the render request handling methods on the portlet. You cannot necessarily control caching or guarantee that the portal will call the portlet's render method only once between action requests.

Style Sheets and the User Experience

Consider the user experience with the portal when designing individual portlet applications. The users should not have to be aware that the different portlets on the portal page they see represent discrete applications that were developed separately. One of the many advantages of moving enterprise applications into a portal environment is the ability to standardize on a common user experience, including Single Sign-On, a consistent look and feel, and a single start page.

Several different levels can be looked at for integrating the user interface of different portlets. Of course, not all portlets are going to be developed in-house, and for those portlets provided without source code, it will be difficult to customize the functionality without paying a third party. Most portlets will use the easily customizable JSP as the presentation layer technology.

The first and easiest layer of the portal user interface to integrate is the styles used to display the HTML in the portal page. We can create a consistent look and feel across all portlets by using the same Cascading Style Sheet (CSS) in all of the portlets. All portlets will share the same fonts, colors, text sizes, and other display elements of rendered HTML. The portal should provide a CSS style sheet that includes all of the standard portlet styles. For a complete list of these styles, see Chapter 12. Web Services for Remote Portlets (WSRP) and the portlet API share the same styles.

The next layer to integrate is a common terminology for the user interface items across portlets. Portlets can use the same or similar terms for user interface commands, navigation, and data display. If we have a portlet that allows browsing through a document management system that holds patent applications, and a portlet that lets us get training materials from the information technology department, both should share a common vocabulary.

There are several ways to go about creating a common terminology, and the approach you take probably will depend on how your development teams are structured more than anything else. The easiest way is for the developers of the first phase of the portal to hire usability engineers or human-computer interaction specialists to assist with the creation of the interface. These experts can recommend clear language for interface elements in the portlet. Other groups developing portlets can copy the language used in the first phase of portlet building, or bring in the usability experts for more consulting. You can abstract out the terms out into resource bundles that are maintained in a central repository, although this could end up creating a deadlock in some development organizations.

Another approach is to leverage the terminology created for existing web applications being ported to the portal environment. Development teams can then reconcile inconsistencies at the portal level with each other. A tester can be assigned to catalog the vocabulary currently in use, and terms that do not match a common vocabulary can either be added or changed to match existing terminology.

The final layer to integrate is process and navigation consistency. When users carry out tasks with a portlet, can they use that workflow to carry out the same task in another portlet? Developers who can create standards for process will cut down on end-user support costs and training for new portlets.

Summary

We have covered the core pieces of the portlet API in this chapter. Portlet requests provide information about the user's request to the portal. Portlet responses provide the methods needed for writing content fragments for the portal page. The user's portlet session contains attributes that are accessible by all portlets in a portlet application, or marked for use by only one instance of a portlet. Portlets should prefix JavaScript elements with a namespace, and the portlet should encode paths to images or other resources in the web application.

Portlets may support more than one portlet mode or content type. The portal provides several window states for portlets, and custom portlet modes or window states are possible. We have demonstrated uploading a file to a portlet, and using the session for interportlet communication.

CHAPTER 5

Using Servlets and JavaServer Pages with Portlets

The portlet application can use servlets and JavaServer Pages (JSP) in addition to portlets. These Java 2 Enterprise Edition (J2EE) resources can be created especially for the portlet application, or they can be part of a port of an existing J2EE application. Existing servlets and JSP will probably need to be edited to conform to the portlet markup rules for a content fragment. In this chapter, we discuss using servlets and JSP with a portlet. Most portlets will use JSP or another page display technology such as Apache Velocity to render content. Rendering content directly from a portlet is just as awkward as displaying HTML output from a servlet.

This chapter also examines using the portlet request dispatcher, which is used to include servlets or JSP inside the portlet. The portlet passes its render request and response objects to the servlet or JSP, and we cover the rules and exceptions for this pass-through. In addition, we explain how to handle any exceptions the servlet might throw inside the portlet. You'll also learn how to deploy servlets, JSP, and portlets together as an integrated web application.

We are not going to cover any web frameworks in this chapter. Apache Struts 2.0 and JavaServer Faces (JSF) will support portlet applications in the future. Most popular open source frameworks will probably release a portlet module or add-on. The biggest architectural difference is that portlets have to handle two requests (action and render) instead of just one (like a web application).

Portlets, Servlets, and JSP Design Goals

Most portlets should use JSP or another presentation technology (like Apache Velocity) to display their content The JSP page can share the portlet's session, request, and response objects easily, and there is a portlet JSP tag library to make some tasks easy.

In these cases, the portlet is going to act as a controller, and handle incoming action and render requests. The render requests will be processed and delegated to a JSP page, based on session attributes, request parameters, portlet modes, or window states. The action request handling phase of the portlet makes an excellent place to put a front controller that handles incoming command requests, while the `render()` method can determine which page to display.

The business logic for the portlet application should be encapsulated in classes that do not refer to classes from the `javax.portlet` package. This makes reuse easier in web applications, Swing applications, web services, or other portlet applications.

One factor to consider when assessing JSP reuse is that the portlet should be using styles defined in the portal's style sheet for all content. If your content all shares a similar look and feel across portlets, it makes the portal seem more integrated, and portal administrators can adjust the portal style sheet to reflect desired changes. These changes could include standard fonts, company colors, or larger default text sizes. If you reuse these JSP pages in a standard web application, you will need to have your own copy of a portlet-API compatible style sheet in the web application, to match the expected styles.

You also will have to be careful not to use portlet tags or classes inside the JSP if you want it to remain portable. For these reasons, it is probably not likely that you will be able to leverage much of the JSP pages directly for reuse. Some pages may lend themselves better than others. Try and encapsulate some common functionality into a JSP tag library that can be shared between different applications. Split the JSP pages into chunks of portable and nonportable code.

For exceptionally large applications (hundreds or even thousands of pages), you may want to look into a page-generation technology with templates. Using Apache Velocity (`http://jakarta.apache.org/velocity`) or another page template language, you could define certain chunks of the templates as portlet code and other parts as web application code. A simple generation tool that calls Velocity could generate JSP pages for both portlets and web applications, and store them in different folders. You could also use Velocity directly within a portlet, instead of JSP.

Portlet Request Dispatcher

Your portlet can use a portlet request dispatcher to include the content from a servlet or JSP page. The portlet request dispatcher translates the portlet's render request and render response into servlet requests and responses. Then the portlet request dispatcher passes those servlet objects to the appropriate servlet or JSP resource. The resource processes the render request as if the request was an `HttpServletRequest` and adds its content to the portlet's render response. Each portlet has access to a portlet request dispatcher through the portlet's `PortletContext` object. The portlet request dispatcher is an object the portlet container creates that implements the `PortletRequestDispatcher` interface. Here are the two methods for retrieving a `PortletRequestDispatcher` object from the `PortletContext` object:

```
public PortletRequestDispatcher getNamedDispatcher(String name)
public PortletRequestDispatcher getRequestDispatcher(String path)
```

Each of these methods retrieves a portlet request dispatcher for a servlet or JSP. The difference is how the resource is found in the web application. The `getNamedDispatcher()` method is used to get access to a servlet or JSP that is given a name in the web application deployment descriptor. It is also possible to name a servlet from your application server's administration tool; this is dependent on the application server used.

The `getRequestDispatcher()` method is used to access a resource relative to the portlet's context root. The `path` argument must start with a "/", and must be a valid path. For each of these methods, if the path or name is invalid, the methods will return null.

The `PortletRequestDispatcher` object is very similar to the `RequestDispatcher` object from the servlet API. The major difference is that servlets may either include another servlet or forward a request, while portlets may only include another servlet's response. A portlet may not forward a request to a servlet, because that means that control would not return to the portlet. The portlet remains in control when it includes a servlet or a JSP. When the servlet (or JSP) is finished writing output, control passes back to the portlet that included the servlet.

There is only one method on the `PortletRequestDispatcher` object:

```
public void include(RenderRequest request, RenderResponse response)
    throws PortletException, java.io.IOException
```

The `include()` method hides all of the details of loading and processing the servlet or JSP page, just like in the servlet API.

Request Dispatcher

A portlet may use a portlet request dispatcher to include the output of either a servlet or a JSP page. This example shows how to load a JSP page called homePage.jsp from the WEB-INF/jsp directory of your portlet application:

```
PortletContext portletContext = getPortletContext();
PortletRequestDispatcher prd =➥
    PortletContext.getRequestDispatcher("/jsp/homePage.jsp");
prd.include(request,response);
```

The `include()` method on the `PortletRequestDispatcher` object throws a `PortletException` or an `IOException`.

You may pass a query string on the path used for the `getRequestDispatcher()` method. For instance, our previous example could look like this:

```
PortletContext portletContext = getPortletContext();
PortletRequestDispatcher prd =➥
PortletContext.getRequestDispatcher("/jsp/homePage.jsp?personalize=NONE");
prd.include(request,response);
```

The rule to remember is that any parameters passed in the query string to the `PortletRequestDispatcher` override any existing parameters with the same name on the request object. This can be useful for providing temporary overrides of parameters for one JSP page, while keeping the portlet's parameters intact for use on other JSP pages and servlets.

If you would like to load a servlet through a request dispatcher, map the servlet to a path in your portlet application's web.xml deployment descriptor. Use the `<servlet-mapping>` element in the web.xml file, just as you would for a normal web application. Here is a snippet of code that includes a servlet with a request dispatcher:

```
PortletContext portletContext = getPortletContext();
PortletRequestDispatcher prd =➥
    portletContext.getRequestDispatcher("/patents");
prd.include(request,response);
```

Named Dispatcher

A named dispatcher is useful for loading servlets or JSP pages that have been given a name in the portlet application's web deployment descriptor. It also returns a `PortletRequestDispatcher` object. One important difference is that it is impossible to pass a query string to a servlet or JSP that is called through a named dispatcher.

If we have a servlet named SingleSignOnServlet, we could include it when we render the portlet, using code like the following:

```
PortletContext portletContext = getPortletContext();
PortletRequestDispatcher prd =➥
    PortletContext.getNamedDispatcher("SingleSignOnServlet");
prd.include(request,response);
```

One important point is that portlets may not be included in the output of another portlet using dispatchers. Rendering one portlet's content inside another portlet should be accomplished by calling methods directly to get content, providing access to the portlet's templates, or another form of direct access.

Including Content in the Portlet

The content returned by a servlet should be the same type of content that the portlet is writing out. In almost all cases, that will be character data, not binary data. If you need to serve binary data from a portlet, provide a link directly to the servlet from the portlet's content. This way, your portlet application can serve images, PDF files, and other binary data. For character data, use the `getWriter()` method on the servlet response.

Your servlet should not try to set the content type on its servlet response. The portlet is in control of the content type, and the servlet cannot affect it. Although your portlet sets the content type on its response, your servlet cannot get the content type from the servlet request. If your servlet works with different types of text content (XML, HTML, etc.), you will need to manage content types with request attributes or session parameters. You can always use two different servlet classes, of course.

Handling Exceptions Thrown by the Servlet or JSP

Portlets will need to be able to handle exceptions thrown by servlets or JSP pages that are included by the portlet. If the servlet or JSP throws an `IOException`, the `IOException` is passed unchanged to the portlet. Every other type of exception is encapsulated in a `PortletException` by the portlet container.

Either the portlet may catch these exceptions itself, or it may throw them to the portlet container, just like any other type of portlet exception.

Simple Portlet Example That Includes a Servlet

We are going to demonstrate how to include a servlet inside a portlet, using the named dispatcher and the request dispatcher. For simplicity, we are going to have only one servlet, and it is going to write only one line of content. We will include it once with a request dispatcher, and once with a named dispatcher.

When you run this simple `HelloPortlet` example in Pluto, it will look like Figure 5-1.

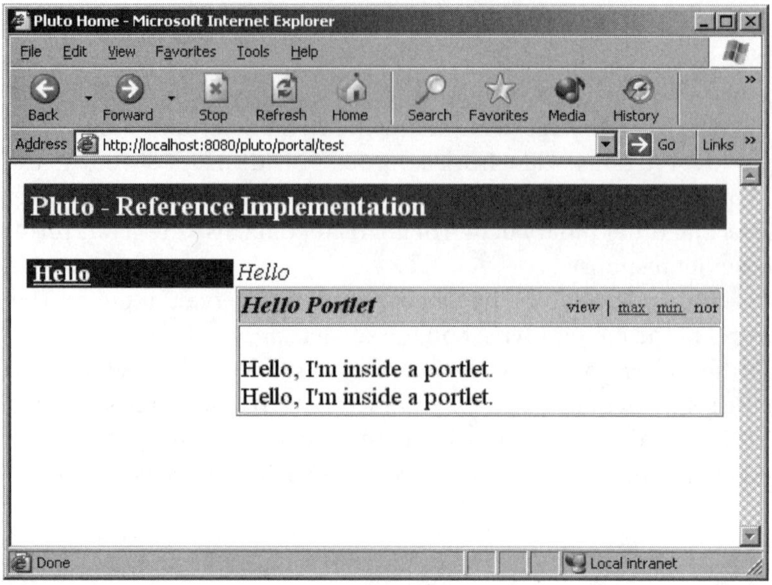

Figure 5-1. Our `HelloPortlet` *example showing two types of request dispatches to a servlet*

The servlet is named `HelloServlet` in the web application deployment descriptor, and it is mapped to the /hello URL. Here is the web.xml deployment descriptor for our portlet application, with the servlet description and mapping:

```
<?xml version="1.0" encoding="UTF-8"?>
<!DOCTYPE web-app PUBLIC "-//Sun Microsystems, Inc.//DTD Web Application 2.3//EN"
"http://java.sun.com/dtd/web-app_2_3.dtd">
<web-app>
    <display-name>First Portlet</display-name>
    <description>This is the first portlet.</description>
    <servlet>
      <servlet-name>HelloServlet</servlet-name>
      <servlet-class>com.portalbook.servlets.HelloServlet</servlet-class>
   </servlet>
   <servlet-mapping>
       <servlet-name>HelloServlet</servlet-name>
       <url-pattern>/hello</url-pattern>
   </servlet-mapping>
</web-app>
```

The `HelloPortlet` class is very simple. You can see how it sets up both of the portlet request dispatchers:

```
package com.portalbook.portlets;

import java.io.IOException;

import javax.portlet.GenericPortlet;
import javax.portlet.PortletContext;
import javax.portlet.PortletException;
import javax.portlet.PortletRequestDispatcher;
import javax.portlet.RenderRequest;
import javax.portlet.RenderResponse;

public class HelloPortlet extends GenericPortlet
{
    protected void doView(RenderRequest request, RenderResponse response)
        throws PortletException, IOException
    {
        response.setContentType("text/html");

        PortletContext portletContext = getPortletContext();
        PortletRequestDispatcher reqDispatcher =
            portletContext.getRequestDispatcher("/hello");
        reqDispatcher.include(request, response);

        PortletRequestDispatcher namedDispatcher =
            portletContext.getNamedDispatcher("HelloServlet");
        namedDispatcher.include(request, response);

    }
}
```

Next is our HelloServlet class, which writes only one line to its response. We do not include a content type in its output because the portlet already did.

```
package com.portalbook.servlets;

import java.io.*;

import javax.servlet.ServletException;
import javax.servlet.http.HttpServlet;
import javax.servlet.http.HttpServletRequest;
import javax.servlet.http.HttpServletResponse;

public class HelloServlet extends HttpServlet
{
```

```
    public void doGet(HttpServletRequest req, HttpServletResponse resp)
        throws ServletException, IOException
    {
        PrintWriter writer = resp.getWriter();
        writer.write("<BR>Hello, I'm inside a portlet.");
    }
}
```

Our portlet.xml deployment descriptor is very ordinary because it does not describe anything about the servlet:

```
<?xml version="1.0" encoding="UTF-8"?>
<portlet-app xmlns="http://java.sun.com/xml/ns/portlet/portlet-app_1_0.xsd"➥
    version="1.0" xmlns:xsi="http://www.w3.org/2001/XMLSchema-instance"➥
    xsi:schemaLocation="http://java.sun.com/xml/ns/portlet/portlet-app_1_0.xsd➥
    http://java.sun.com/xml/ns/portlet/portlet-app_1_0.xsd">
    <portlet>
        <description>Includes a Servlet</description>
        <portlet-name>HelloPortlet</portlet-name>
        <display-name>Hello Portlet</display-name>
        <portlet-class>com.portalbook.portlets.HelloPortlet</portlet-class>
        <expiration-cache>-1</expiration-cache>
        <supports>
            <mime-type>text/html</mime-type>
            <portlet-mode>VIEW</portlet-mode>
        </supports>
        <portlet-info>
            <title>Hello Portlet</title>
            <short-title>Hello</short-title>
            <keywords>Hello, Portlet</keywords>
        </portlet-info>
    </portlet>
 </portlet-app>
```

Request and Response Objects

The servlet or JSP that is included in the portlet's render response has partial, limited access to the portlet's `RenderRequest` and `RenderResponse` objects through the servlet or JSP's `HttpServletRequest` and `HttpServletResponse` objects. Many of the servlet methods either perform no operation or return null when used inside a portlet, because portlets have a higher level of abstraction than servlets. Other servlet methods call the equivalent method on the portlet objects. Table 5-1 lists the methods on the `HttpServletRequest`, and how they behave when included from a portlet.

Table 5-1. The Methods on an HttpServletRequest Object in a Portlet

Method Name	Method Description
`getAttribute()`	Returns the value of an attribute when given a name, or null. Calls `getAttribute()` on the portlet's `PortletRequest` object.
`getAttributeNames()`	Returns the names of the available attributes. Calls `getAttributeNames()` on the portlet's `PortletRequest` object.
`getAuthType()`	Returns the authentication scheme used. Calls `getAuthType()` on the portlet's `PortletRequest` object.
`getCharacterEncoding()`	Returns null; does nothing.
`getContentLength()`	Always returns 0.
`getContentType()`	Returns null; does nothing.
`getContextPath()`	Returns the context path associated with the portlet application on the portal. Calls `getContextPath()` on the portlet's `PortletRequest` object.
`getCookies()`	Returns cookies from properties on the portlet request.
`getDateHeader()`	Returns a date header from properties on the portlet request.
`getHeader()`	Returns header from properties on the portlet request.
`getHeaderNames()`	Returns header names from properties on the portlet request.
`getHeaders()`	Returns headers from properties on the portlet request.
`getInputStream()`	Returns null; does nothing.
`getIntHeader()`	Returns an integer header from properties on the portlet request.
`getLocale()`	Returns preferred locale for the portal. Calls `getLocale()` on the portlet's `PortletRequest` object.
`getLocales()`	Returns locales accepted by the portal. Calls `getLocales()` on the portlet's `PortletRequest` object.
`getMethod()`	Returns "GET".
`getParameter()`	Returns the value of the parameter from either the portlet request, or from the query string passed into the request dispatcher. The query string takes precedence.

Table 5-1. The Methods on an HttpServletRequest Object in a Portlet (continued)

Method Name	Method Description
`getParameterMap()`	Returns a map of name/value pairs of the parameters from the portlet request and the query string passed into the request dispatcher. The query string takes precedence.
`getParameterNames()`	Returns the names of the parameters from the portlet request and the query string passed into the request dispatcher.
`getParameterValues()`	Returns the values of the parameter from the portlet request and the query string passed into the request dispatcher. The query string takes precedence.
`getPathInfo()`	Returns the path and query used to get the portlet's request dispatcher.
`getPathTranslated()`	Returns the path and query used to get the portlet's request dispatcher.
`getProtocol()`	Returns null.
`getQueryString()`	Returns the path and query used to get the portlet's request dispatcher.
`getReader()`	Returns null; does nothing.
`getRealPath()`	Returns null.
`getRemoteAddr()`	Returns null.
`getRemoteHost()`	Returns null.
`getRemoteUser()`	Returns the login for the current user, or null if there is no login yet. Calls `getRemoteUser()` on the portlet's `PortletRequest` object.
`getRequestDispatcher()`	Same as Servlet 2.3 specification.
`getRequestedSessionId()`	Returns the request's session ID, or null if there is none. Calls `getRequestedSessionId()` on the portlet's `PortletRequest` object.
`getRequestURI()`	Returns the path and query used to get the portlet's request dispatcher.
`getRequestURL()`	Returns null.
`getScheme()`	Returns the name of the URL scheme used to call the portlet. Calls `getScheme()` on the portlet's `PortletRequest` object.
`getServerName()`	Returns the server's hostname. Calls `getServerName()` on the portlet's `PortletRequest` object.

Table 5-1. The Methods on an HttpServletRequest Object in a Portlet (continued)

Method Name	Method Description
`getServerPort()`	Returns an integer representing the server's port number. Calls `getServerPort()` on the portlet's `PortletRequest` object.
`getServletPath()`	Returns the path and query used to get the portlet's request dispatcher.
`getSession()`	Same as Servlet 2.3 specification
`getUserPrincipal()`	Returns a `Principal` for the current user, or null if the user isn't logged in yet. Calls `getUserPrincipal()` on the portlet's `PortletRequest` object.
`isRequestedSessionId FromCookie()`	Same as Servlet 2.3 specifications.
`isRequestedSessionId FromURL()`	Same as Servlet 2.3 specifications.
`isRequestedSessionId FromUrl()`	Same as Servlet 2.3 specifications; deprecated.
`isRequestedSessionId Valid()`	Returns the validity of the request's session ID. Calls `isRequestedSessionIdValid()` on the portlet's `PortletRequest` object.
`isSecure()`	Returns a Boolean indicating secure communication. Calls `isSecure()` on the portlet's `PortletRequest` object.
`isUserInRole()`	Same as Servlet 2.3 specification.
`removeAttribute()`	Removes an attribute on the request object. Calls `removeAttribute()` on the portlet's `PortletRequest` object.
`setAttribute()`	Sets an attribute on the request object. Calls `setAttribute()` on the portlet's `PortletRequest` object.
`setCharacterEncoding()`	Returns null; does nothing.

The servlet response object passed to the servlet or JSP by the portlet wraps the behavior of the portlet's `RenderResponse` object. Like the `RenderRequest` object, the `RenderResponse` object is similar to its servlet counterpart. Having a firm knowledge of Java servlet programming can go a long way in understanding portlet development and best practices. Table 5-2 describes the behavior of the methods on the `HttpServletResponse` object when a portlet includes content from a servlet or JSP.

Table 5-2. The Methods on the HttpServletResponse Object

Method Name	Method Description
addCookie()	Does nothing.
addHeader()	Does nothing.
addIntHeader()	Does nothing.
containsHeader()	Returns false.
encodeRedirectURL()	Returns null.
encodeRedirectUrl()	Returns null; deprecated.
encodeURL()	Returns an encoded URL for URL rewriting for session tracking.
encodeUrl()	Returns an encoded URL for URL rewriting for session tracking; deprecated.
flushBuffer()	Flushes the buffered output to the client for the response body, and commits the response.
getBufferSize()	Returns the size of the response buffer.
getCharacterEncoding()	Returns the character encoding used by the MIME body for the portlet's response.
getLocale()	Returns the portlet response's locale.
getOutputStream()	Returns the output stream for writing binary data.
getWriter()	Returns a writer for writing textual data.
isCommitted()	Returns true if the response has been committed.
reset()	Resets the buffer and the response properties, if the response has not been committed.
resetBuffer()	Resets the buffer if it hasn't been committed yet. Leaves properties alone. Useful for error message handling.
setDateHeader()	Does nothing.
setHeader()	Does nothing.
sendError()	Does nothing.
sendRedirect()	Does nothing.
setBufferSize()	Sets the buffer size used for the portlet's response body.
setContentLength()	Does nothing.
setContentType()	Does nothing.
setIntHeader()	Does nothing.

Table 5-2. The Methods on the HttpServletResponse Object (continued)

Method Name	Method Description
setLocale()	Does nothing.
setStatus()	Does nothing.

Request Parameters and Attributes

The request parameters from the portlet's render request object are available in the servlet or JSP as parameters on the servlet request object. The parameters are named the same, and can be accessed through the getParameter() method on the request object.

The same is true for attributes stored on the portlet's render request. The servlet or JSP will be able to access these attributes from the servlet request object.

Session Management Between a Portlet and a Servlet or JSP

All of the resources in a portlet application share a session for each user. Portlets will access the session through the PortletSession object, and servlets and JSPs will use their HttpSession objects. Any attributes stored on the session by a portlet are accessible through the HttpSession object, and any attributes stored by servlets or JSPs are accessible through the PortletSession object.

A portlet may share an object in the session for a servlet or a JSP by putting the object into the application scope. If the object is in portlet scope, the object will be in a namespace defined by the portlet container, and will not be easily accessible to the servlet or JSP. The object will still be an attribute on the session, but it would be tricky to decode the proper name. You should avoid trying to decode an out-of-scope attribute, because it will be container-specific—this would qualify as a hack.

Inside the portlet, you call the setAttribute() method on a PortletSession object like this:

```
PortletSession session = request.getPortletSession(true);
session.setAttribute("ContentManager", contentManager,➥
 PortletSession.APPLICATION_SCOPE);
```

From the JSP or servlet, you ask the `HTTPSession` object for an attribute called ContentManager, just as you normally would do for any other object on the session. In a servlet, it might look like this:

```
ContentManager contentMgr = (ContentManager) session.getAttribute("ContentManager");
```

Creating a Form in JSP

Your portlet's JavaServer Pages can use HTML forms just like stand-alone JSP pages. The two most important portlet practices are to use the POST method for all forms, and to set the action for the form to an action URL or a render URL for the portlet.

The POST method is necessary because the URL's query string may be used by the portlet container or portal to maintain information about the user's session. The POST method is safe for portlets (and any servlets or JSP pages they include) to use.

The HTML form will need to point back to the portlet that created the form so the portlet can process the request. The portlet can create `PortletURL` objects that can then create portlet URLs. There are two choices for creating a portlet URL: action URLs or render URLs. Inside the JSP page, you will need to use one of the portlet URL JSP tags to create a portlet URL. Either portlet URL JSP tag will output a URL, so you can just include a tag into your form's action. We discuss the portlet JSP tags in the next section. For more on portlet URLs, see Chapter 2.

Using the Portlet JSP Tag Library

JavaServer Pages can use the portlet tag library to access portlet functionality. Any JSP pages that are called from a portlet can use these tags to get access to portlet objects, create URLs for links to the current portlet, or provide a unique identifier for named HTML elements.

The recommended taglib declaration for any JSP pages that use the tag library is

```
<%@ taglib uri='http://java.sun.com/portlet' prefix='portlet'%>
```

In your web.xml application deployment descriptor, you will need to map the portlet taglib URI to the location of the tag library descriptor (TLD) file:

```
<taglib>
    <taglib-uri>http://java.sun.com/portlet</taglib-uri>
    <taglib-location>/WEB-INF/tags/portlet.tld</taglib-location>
</taglib>
```

You do not need to add anything to the portlet.xml deployment descriptor to enable the tag library, because the tags are for the JSP pages, which are processed by the JSP compiler and servlet engine.

The <defineObjects> JSP Tag

The `<defineObjects>` tag is used to define several objects from the calling portlet's request in the JSP page. You can use these objects from JSP scriptlets. The tag takes no attributes or content—it's always used in this form:

```
<portlet:defineObjects/>
```

The variables it defines are

```
PortletConfig portletConfig
RenderRequest renderRequest
RenderResponse renderResponse
```

These objects are the same ones that are included in the request object for a JSP or servlet in a portlet application. They can be accessed as request attributes from that request object. The `<defineObjects>` tag is a convenient shortcut for using these objects from a JSP.

Here is an example that uses the `renderRequest` variable from the `<defineObjects>` JSP tag:

```
<portlet:defineObjects/>
The host name of the server: <%=renderRequest.getServerName()%>
```

We can use any of the methods available on any of the objects that are defined, including retrieving other objects from the portlet API.

The <param> JSP Tag

The `<param>` portlet tag is used to provide parameters for the `<actionURL>` and `<renderURL>` tags. It represents a name/value pair. There are two required attributes on the `<param>` tag: `name` and `value`. You can set these to be whatever you need for your portlet development. Here is an example showing the `<param>` tag as part of an `<actionURL>` tag:

```
<portlet:actionURL>
    <portlet:param name="emailID" value="255"/>
    <portlet:param name="mvcAction" value="deleteEmailConfirm"/>
</portlet:actionURL>
```

The <actionURL> JSP Tag

The <actionURL> tag builds a URL that will send an action request to the portlet. The action request takes parameters that are supplied by including <param> tags inside the start and end pair of <actionURL> tags. The portlet container will process an action request for one portlet, and then send render requests to the other portlets on the page. For more on action requests, see Chapter 2.

Here is an example of how to use the <param> tag with the <actionURL> tag:

```
<portlet:actionURL>
    <portlet:param name="emailID" value="13"/>
    <portlet:param name="mvcAction" value="deleteEmail"/>
</portlet:actionURL>
```

In addition to the portlet parameters, the <actionURL> tag can take several optional attributes. All of these optional attributes also apply to the <renderURL> JSP tag, which we discuss in the next section of this chapter.

The windowState Attribute

The windowState attribute for the <actionURL> and <renderURL> tags can be set to one of the allowed window states for a portlet application running on this portal container. When the user follows the link, the portlet will appear in the specified window state, if it is a valid state for this portlet. Nonvalid states will result in a JSP exception. The standard window states are normal, maximized, and minimized. If the windowState attribute is not included, the portlet should keep its current window state. For more on window states, see Chapter 4.

If we were building this e-mail portlet, we might want the user to see the e-mail message in the largest space available in the portlet. We tell the portlet to use the maximized window state here:

```
<portlet:actionURL windowState="maximized">
    <portlet:param name="emailTo" value="jeff@portalbook.com"/>
    <portlet:param name="mvcAction" value="createEmail"/>
</portlet:actionURL>
```

The portletMode Attribute

The action request link tells the portlet to use a certain mode. This attribute is also optional, and if it is omitted, the portlet will retain its current mode. The portlet modes defined in the specification are VIEW, EDIT, and HELP. You may also use any custom portlet modes that your portal supports. Like window states, a nonvalid portlet mode will result in a JSP exception. We discuss portlet modes in detail in Chapter 4.

You can use the `portletMode` attribute to build links in JSP pages to help content in the portlet, to a properties configuration page, or to another portlet-defined mode. Here is an example of an `<actionURL>` JSP tag used to create a link to the EDIT mode of a portlet:

```
<portlet:actionURL portletMode="edit">
    <portlet:param name="mvcAction" value="deleteContactConfirm"/>
    <portlet:param name="contactID" value="155"/>
</portlet:actionURL>
```

The var Attribute

If you need to use the URL the `<actionURL>` tag creates in another place in your JSP, you can export the URL string to a page-scoped JSP variable. The `var` attribute is optional, and if you do not include it, the default behavior is to write out the URL string as output. If the `var` attribute is defined, nothing will be written as output when the tag is processed. This is useful if you need to output the same URL in several places.

We are going to use the `var` attribute to write out the JSP variable in a link further down the page:

```
<portlet:actionURL var="logoutLink">
    <portlet:param name="mvcAction" value="logout"/>
</portlet:actionURL>
...
<a href="<%=logoutLink%>">Logout</a>
```

For this example, the only place the logout URL will appear in the HTML is inside the link. The URL will not appear in the HTML where we created the action URL with the JSP tag. We could go on to create the logout link in several places in the HTML, using the `logoutLink` variable.

After we create the portlet URL as a variable, we are not allowed to modify the URL to add parameters or anything else. Everything should be done when the URL is created, or you may need to create more than one portlet URL in your JSP page.

The secure Attribute

If your portlet needs to run in an SSL connection, use the `secure` attribute to force the portlet to use the HTTPS protocol if available. The portlet can also be told to use a normal, insecure connection by setting the `secure` attribute to `false`. The `secure` attribute is optional, and takes either `true` or `false` as possible values. If there is no secure attribute on the <actionURL> or <renderURL> tag, the portlet must maintain its current connection (HTTP or HTTPS). If the portlet doesn't support HTTPS or another secure protocol, a JSP exception will be thrown. This could be a problem if the portlet is used with non-HTTP protocols, or with clients that support a very limited network stack (no SSL).

If we needed to secure confidential information from network snooping, we could use the secure attribute here in the <actionURL> tag:

```
<portlet:actionURL secure="true">
    <portlet:param name="mvcAction" value="viewBillingAccountInfo"/>
</portlet:actionURL>
```

All of these portlet attributes are also used for the <renderURL> tag.

The <renderURL> JSP Tag

You can create a URL for a portlet render request with the <renderURL> tag. This tag is very similar to the <actionURL> tag, except that it creates a render request for the current portlet instead of an action request. It uses the same portlet attributes as the <actionURL> tag, and is used in a similar manner. Here is an example that uses a render request to display an e-mail in the portlet:

```
<portlet:renderURL>
    <portlet:param name="emailID" value="689"/>
    <portlet:param name="mvcAction" value="viewEmail"/>
</portlet:renderURL>
```

The <namespace> JSP Tag

You use the <namespace> tag from the portlet tag library to create unique names for HTML objects. Because you could have multiple instances of a portlet rendered on one web page, JavaScript methods that locate HTML elements by their name might not find the correct object. For instance, an image displayed by the portlet could be rendered in HTML like this:

```
<img src="/images/display_on.jpg" name="display"/>
```

A mouseover or another event could trigger JavaScript code that changes this image's source file to /images/display_off.jpg:

```
<a href="/" onmouseover="document.display.src='/images/display_off.jpg';">Home</a>
```

This would work well if it were the only portlet on the page. If there are two copies of this portlet on the page, we'd have two images named display. Another portlet could also use that name for one of its images. To solve this mess, there is a JSP tag called `<namespace>` that provides a unique string for this instance of the portlet. The namespace comes from the `getNamespace()` method on the portlet's `RenderResponse` object. The `<namespace>` tag doesn't take any attributes or enclosed text, and is used like this:

```
<portlet:namespace/>
```

We would rewrite our image HTML to look like this:

```
<img src="/images/display_on.jpg" name="<portlet:namespace/>display"/>
```

And it might render like this:

```
<img src="/images/display_on.jpg" name="PORTLET0022340593display"/>
```

The `<namespace>` tag is completely dependent on the portal container used, and you should not rely on any specific formatting to parse out any data. Just use the `<namespace>` tag or the `getNamespace()` method on the portlet's `RenderResponse` object.

Our JavaScript event handler would be rewritten to look like this:

```
<a href="/"➥
onmouseover=➥
"document.<portlet:namespace/>display.src='/images/display_off.jpg';">Home</a>
```

Other web page elements that need to be prefixed with a namespace include JavaScript and VBScript functions, JavaScript and VBScript variables, and anything referenced by name using dynamic HTML.

To-Do List Portlet Example

We are going to create a more involved example portlet application that manages a to-do list. The user will be able to add tasks to the list, mark tasks as finished, edit tasks, or remove items from the to-do list.

We will use a portlet to control the application. The portlet will process any action requests to change the data model itself. When the portlet receives a render request, it will include JSP pages to render the content for the portal page.

We are going to use the portlet tag library, portlet modes, and request parameters. To keep the to-do list portlet simple, we won't have any persistent storage for the to-do list items. Persistence can be easily added in later using Hibernate, Torque, SQL statements, or anything else you choose.

Our portlet application has two Java classes: `ToDoListPortlet` and `ToDoItemBean`. It also contains four JSP pages, a web.xml deployment descriptor, and a portlet.xml portlet application deployment descriptor.

The ToDoItemBean Class

The to-do list portlet will use the `ToDoItemBean` class to represent individual to-do list items. This class will be the only business object we create. Nothing in this class will use the portlet API, so we can reuse the bean for another project outside a portlet API. Keeping business logic and objects separate from the portlet API or the servlet API usually makes code maintenance simpler in the long run. If you had a large enterprise application that had references to the servlet API in the business logic, it would probably be more difficult to port to a portlet application than one that was designed with separation of concerns.

The `ToDoItemBean` class has four fields: `description`, `priority`, `status`, and `submittedDate`. Each of these fields is private, but has public getter and setter methods.

```
package com.portalbook.portlets.todo;

import java.util.Date;

public class ToDoItemBean
{
    private String description;
    private int priority;
    private Date submittedDate;
    private boolean status;

    public String getDescription()
    {
        return description;
    }

    public int getPriority()
    {
        return priority;
    }

    public void setDescription(String string)
```

```
    {
        description = string;
    }

    public void setPriority(int i)
    {
        priority = i;
    }

    public boolean getStatus()
    {
        return status;
    }

    public void setStatus(boolean b)
    {
        status = b;
    }

    public Date getSubmittedDate()
    {
        return submittedDate;
    }

    public void setSubmittedDate(Date date)
    {
        submittedDate = date;
    }

}
```

We will use the `ToDoItemBean` class in the `ToDoListPortlet`, and in the JSP pages.

The ToDoListPortlet Class

The portlet application has only one portlet class: `ToDoListPortlet`. Let's discuss the action request handling first, and then move on to the render request handling.

The portlet stores a collection of `ToDoItemBean` objects in an `ArrayList` object for each user. This `ArrayList` object is placed in the user's session as an attribute called `ToDoList`. Because the portlet and the JSP pages share the same session attributes, if we store the list in the session as application scope, we can access it from either the portlet or the JSP pages. If we had used the portlet scope, the list object's name would be obscured by a namespace. You should store any session attributes you need in a servlet or JSP in application scope. Because we store the ArrayList in the session, if there is more than one instance of the to-do list portlet from the same portlet application on the portal page, they will share the same data.

Action Request Handling

The processAction() method of the ToDoListPortlet class processes requests created by links or forms in the JSP pages. For our portlet, these requests can have a command, which tells the portlet to carry out some operation on the user's data. In the to-do list portlet, these commands are NEW, DELETE, EDIT, MARK_FINISHED, and MARK_UNFINISHED. All of these commands would be passed in an action request in a parameter named COMMAND.

The portlet retrieves the current user's session, if it exists, and if one doesn't exist, it creates a new one to use. If the data list exists, the portlet pulls that out of the session; if it doesn't exist, the portlet creates a new data list.

The portlet then checks the request parameter named COMMAND for an action to take. If it finds an action, it executes that action. At the end of the method, the modified list is placed back in the user's session, where it can be found by the JSP pages.

Here is the processAction() method from the portlet class. At the end of the chapter, you'll find a full listing of all of the source code in this class.

```
public void processAction(ActionRequest request, ActionResponse response)
    throws PortletException, IOException
{
    //retrieve the to do list out of the user's session
    PortletSession session = request.getPortletSession(true);

    //the to do list is just stored as an ArrayList here, because
    //we are not going to persist it to a database or other storage.
    ArrayList list = (ArrayList) session.getAttribute("ToDoList",
            PortletSession.APPLICATION_SCOPE);

    //if the list doesn't exist, create an empty one.
    if (list == null)
    {
        list = new ArrayList();
    }

    //set up a very simple controller here, based on a
    //request parameter called COMMAND
    String command = request.getParameter("COMMAND");
    String itemParam = request.getParameter("ITEM_ID");
```

```
int itemId = -1;
if (itemParam != null)
{
    itemId = Integer.parseInt(itemParam);
}

if ("MARK_FINISHED".equals(command))
{
    ToDoItemBean item = (ToDoItemBean) list.get(itemId);
    item.setStatus(true);

}
else if ("DELETE".equals(command))
{
    list.remove(itemId);
}
else if ("MARK_UNFINISHED".equals(command))
{
    ToDoItemBean item = (ToDoItemBean) list.get(itemId);
    item.setStatus(false);

}
else if ("EDIT".equals(command))
{
    ToDoItemBean item = (ToDoItemBean) list.get(itemId);

    String desc = request.getParameter("DESCRIPTION");
    item.setDescription(desc);

    String priority = request.getParameter("PRIORITY");
    if (priority != null)
    {

        try
        {
            int p = Integer.parseInt(priority);
            item.setPriority(p);
        }
        catch (NumberFormatException nfe)
        {
            getPortletContext().log(
                "Error trying to format " + priority + " as a number.");
        }
    }
}
```

```
        else if ("NEW".equals(command))
        {
            ToDoItemBean item = new ToDoItemBean();

            String desc = request.getParameter("DESCRIPTION");

            if (desc == null)
            {
                return;
            }

            item.setDescription(desc);
            item.setStatus(false);
            item.setSubmittedDate(new java.util.Date());
            item.setPriority(0);

            list.add(item);
        }
        session.setAttribute("ToDoList", list,
PortletSession.APPLICATION_SCOPE);
    }
```

Displaying the To-Do List

The `doView()` method includes the homePage.jsp file in the portlet's response. We cover this JSP page in the next section of this chapter. The `doView()` method gets a request dispatcher from the portlet context for the /WEB-INF/jsp/homePage.jsp file. Then the portlet calls the `include()` method on the request dispatcher to add the content of the JSP page to the response. The `doView()`, `doEdit()`, and `doHelp()` methods are all very similar, because all of the content and presentation logic is contained in the JSP pages.

```
        protected void doView(RenderRequest request, RenderResponse response)
        throws PortletException, IOException
    {
        response.setContentType("text/html");

        PortletContext portletContext = getPortletContext();

        PortletRequestDispatcher prd =
            portletContext.getRequestDispatcher("/WEB-INF/jsp/homePage.jsp");
        prd.include(request, response);
    }
```

The doEdit() method also dispatches the request to a JSP page, but it checks the request parameter named DISPLAY to determine which page to include. By default, it displays the /WEB-INF/jsp/editPage.jsp file, which allows the user to choose a to-do list item to edit. When the portlet is first called, or it is switched into the VIEW portlet mode, this is the page it will display. We can construct links in the JSP pages to set the request parameter named DISPLAY to a value, and we check to see if we need to display the portlet page that allows editing of an individual to-do list item:

```
protected void doEdit(RenderRequest request, RenderResponse response)
    throws PortletException, IOException
{
    response.setContentType("text/html");

    String display = request.getParameter("DISPLAY");

    PortletContext portletContext = getPortletContext();
    if ("EDIT_PAGE".equals(display))
    {
        PortletRequestDispatcher prd =
            portletContext.getRequestDispatcher(
                "/WEB-INF/jsp/editItemPage.jsp");
        prd.include(request, response);
    }
    else
    {
        PortletRequestDispatcher prd =
            portletContext.getRequestDispatcher("/WEB-INF/jsp/editPage.jsp");
        prd.include(request, response);
    }
}
```

The doHelp() method works in the same way as the doView() method:

```
protected void doHelp(RenderRequest request, RenderResponse response)
    throws PortletException, IOException
{
    response.setContentType("text/html");

    Writer writer = response.getWriter();

    PortletContext portletContext = getPortletContext();

    PortletRequestDispatcher prd =➥
        portletContext.getRequestDispatcher("/WEB-INF/jsp/helpPage.jsp");
```

```
        prd.include(request, response);

    }
```

This portlet concerns itself with data operations and page display dispatching. In the next section, we discuss the JSP pages that display the content of the application. We also briefly introduce the Java Standard Tag Library (JSTL), which we use in the JSP pages but that does not have anything to do with portals or portlets.

Using the Java Standard Tag Library (JSTL)

We use the Java Standard Tag Library (JSTL) in our JSP pages for convenience. The JSTL tag library works the same way in a portlet application as it does in a web application. The to-do portlet will use the Standard Taglib 1.0.4 from the Jakarta Apache Taglibs project (`http://jakarta.apache.org/taglibs/doc/standard-1.0-doc/intro.html`).

> **TIP** *If you would like to learn more about the Java Standard Tag Library, check out* Beginning JSP 2 *(Apress, 2004) and* Pro JSP 2 *(Apress, 2003).*

Each of the four tag libraries that make up the standard tag library (core, formatting, XML, SQL) is represented by a Tag Library Descriptor (TLD) file. We are going to use the core and the formatting libraries in our to-do portlet. The c.tld and fmt.tld files from the Standard Taglib 1.0.4 binary distribution are in the portlet's WEB-INF/tld directory, along with the portlet.tld descriptor file. There are two required libraries from the Jakarta Standard Taglib distribution in the WEB-INF/lib directory: jstl.jar and standard.jar. These two libraries contain the classes that the tag libraries require.

We use several of the JSTL tags, and we also use the JSP expression language in our JSP pages.

The To-Do List Items Display

This JSP page, homePage.jsp, is included in the response for the portlet's VIEW mode. We import several tag libraries: the portlet tag library, the JSTL core tag library, and the JSTL formatting tag library. We also import several Java classes that we use inside the portlet.

We create a table to display the priority, description, creation date, and status of the to-do items. Then we use a tag from the JSTL core library called `<c:forEach>`

(we used `c` for the JSTL core namespace) to iterate through the `ToDoList` list object that was in our user's session. When we placed the `ToDoList` list object in our portlet session in the application scope, it became available to our JSP pages.

The `<c:forEach>` tag exposes a `LoopTagStatus` object that we named `status` in our JSP, which can be used to access the current count of the object. If we had built this portlet to use a database for storage, we would have used the primary key from the database here to ensure that the correct to-do list item would be used in the action request. Instead, with our nonpersistent to-do list, we use the position of the item in the `ArrayList` to identify it. To get this position, we use the `getCount()` method on the `LoopTagStatus` object. We place it into a variable called `itemId` that we can reference as a value for a JSP tag attribute.

For each of the to-do items in the list, we display the description using the `<c:out>` tag from the core JSTL tag library. The `<c:out>` tag can write the value of an expression to the output of the JSP page. Our `<c:forEach>` tag places the current item (represented by a `ToDoListBean`) into the expression variable called `item`. The `<c:out>` tag can use an expression from the JSTL expression language (EL) such as `${item.description}` to render the value of the `description` field on the `item` object.

We used the `<fmt:formatDate>` tag from the formatting tag library to display the creation date in a readable format. We specified the short date style, because we want to conserve room on the portal page.

Next, we checked the to-do list item's status to determine which message and portlet action link to display. We used the `<c:choose>`, `<c:when>`, and `<c:otherwise>` tags to simulate an `if...else` statement.

The interesting part of the status display is the link we use to change the status of the to-do item. The link is created with the `<portlet:actionURL>` JSP tag. We added two parameters to the action URL tag: one for the action command, and one for the item to modify.

At the bottom of the page, we included a simple form to add a to-do item to the list. It takes only the description as a parameter. The HTML form's action is a portlet action URL that is also created with the `<portlet:actionURL>` tag. We used the POST method for the form because it is required. Figure 5-2 shows the to-do list portlet running in VIEW mode.

```
<%@ page session="true" %>

<%@ taglib uri='/WEB-INF/tld/portlet.tld' prefix='portlet'%>
<%@ taglib uri="/WEB-INF/tld/c.tld" prefix="c" %>
<%@ taglib uri="/WEB-INF/tld/fmt.tld" prefix="fmt" %>

<%@ page import="java.util.*"%>
<%@ page import="javax.servlet.jsp.jstl.core.LoopTagStatus"%>

<table>
  <tr class="portlet-section-header">
    <td class="portlet-section-header">Description</td>
```

```
      <td>Priority</td>
      <td>Created Date</td>
      <td>Status</td>
    </tr>
  <c:forEach var="item"
              items="${ToDoList}"
              varStatus="status">
          <%
             LoopTagStatus status = (LoopTagStatus)➥
                 pageContext.getAttribute("status");
             String itemId = Integer.toString(status.getCount() - 1);
        %>
  <tr>
    <td><c:out value="${item.description}"/></td>
    <td><c:out value="${item.priority}"/></td>
    <td><fmt:formatDate value="${item.submittedDate}" dateStyle="short"/></td>
    <td>
      <c:choose>
        <c:when test="${item.status}">
          Complete <a href="<portlet:actionURL>
            <portlet:param name="COMMAND" value="MARK_UNFINISHED"/>
            <portlet:param name="ITEM_ID" value="<%=itemId%>"/>
          </portlet:actionURL>"
          >(change)</a>
        </c:when>
        <c:otherwise>
          Incomplete <a href="<portlet:actionURL>
            <portlet:param name="COMMAND" value="MARK_FINISHED"/>
            <portlet:param name="ITEM_ID" value="<%=itemId%>"/>
          </portlet:actionURL>"
          >(change)</a>
        </c:otherwise>
      </c:choose>
    </td>
  </tr>
  </c:forEach>

  </table>

  <form action="<portlet:actionURL>
    <portlet:param name="COMMAND" value="NEW"/>
  </portlet:actionURL>"
```

```
method="post">
  Description: <input type="text" size="30" name="DESCRIPTION">
  <br>
  <input type="submit" text="Create">
</form>
```

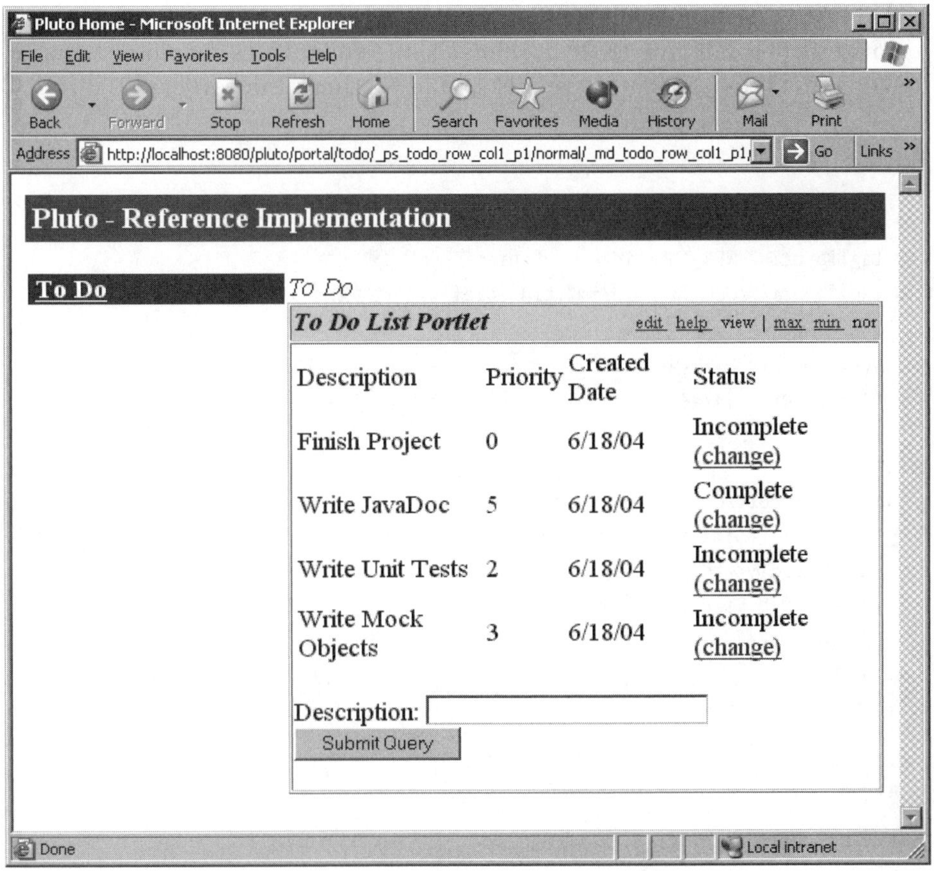

Figure 5-2. The VIEW mode for the to-do list portlet

The homePage.jsp page uses an item from the portlet session and the portlet action URL JSP tag in several places. We also used the JSTL to avoid JSP scriptlets as much as possible.

Editing the To-Do List Items

Much of the Edit All Items page (editPage.jsp) is similar to the Home page we just discussed. We are going to cover the differences in this section. This page is displayed if the user selects the EDIT mode from the portal page's user interface.

The Edit All Items page also iterates through all of the to-do items, and it displays edit and delete links for each one. The edit link is a portlet render URL generated from a `<portlet:renderURL>` tag. We used a render request because we are only going to display another page and not make any modifications to the object when the user clicks on the link. However, when the user selects the delete link, we want the to-do list object to be removed from the list for the user, so we use an action URL. If we had used a render URL, any time we refreshed the portal page it would try to delete that to-do list item again. Render URLs should not change the portlet's underlying data or model. Figure 5-3 shows the portlet's EDIT mode.

```
<%@ page session="true" %>

<%@ taglib uri='/WEB-INF/tld/portlet.tld' prefix='portlet'%>
<%@ taglib uri="/WEB-INF/tld/c.tld" prefix="c" %>
<%@ taglib uri="/WEB-INF/tld/fmt.tld" prefix="fmt" %>

<%@ page import="java.util.*"%>
<%@ page import="javax.servlet.jsp.jstl.core.LoopTagStatus"%>

<table>
  <tr class="portlet-section-header">
    <td class="portlet-section-header">Description</td>
    <td>Priority</td>
    <td>Created Date</td>
    <td>Status</td>
  </tr>
<c:forEach var="item"
              items="${ToDoList}"
              varStatus="status">
                <%
             LoopTagStatus status =➥
                 (LoopTagStatus) pageContext.getAttribute("status");
             String itemId = Integer.toString(status.getCount() - 1);
    %>
<tr>
  <td><c:out value="${item.description}"/></td>
  <td><c:out value="${item.priority}"/></td>
  <td><fmt:formatDate value="${item.submittedDate}" dateStyle="short"/></td>
  <td>
    <c:choose>
      <c:when test="${item.status}">

        Complete <a href="<portlet:actionURL>
          <portlet:param name="COMMAND" value="MARK_UNFINISHED"/>
```

```
            <portlet:param name="ITEM_ID" value="<%=itemId%>"/>
          </portlet:actionURL>"
          >(change)</a>
        </c:when>
        <c:otherwise>

          Incomplete <a href="<portlet:actionURL>
            <portlet:param name="COMMAND" value="MARK_FINISHED"/>
            <portlet:param name="ITEM_ID" value="<%=itemId%>"/>
          </portlet:actionURL>"
          >(change)</a>
        </c:otherwise>
      </c:choose>
    </td>
    <td>

          <a href="<portlet:renderURL>
            <portlet:param name="DISPLAY" value="EDIT_PAGE"/>
            <portlet:param name="ITEM_ID" value="<%=itemId%>"/>
          </portlet:renderURL>"
          >Edit</a>
    </td>
    <td>
          <a href="<portlet:actionURL>
            <portlet:param name="COMMAND" value="DELETE"/>
            <portlet:param name="ITEM_ID" value="<%=itemId%>"/>
          </portlet:actionURL>"
          >Delete</a>
    </td>
  </tr>
  </c:forEach>


  </table>

  <form action="<portlet:actionURL>
    <portlet:param name="COMMAND" value="NEW"/>
  </portlet:actionURL>"
  method="post">
    Description: <input type="text" size="30" name="DESCRIPTION">
    <br>
    <input type="submit" text="Create">
  </form>
```

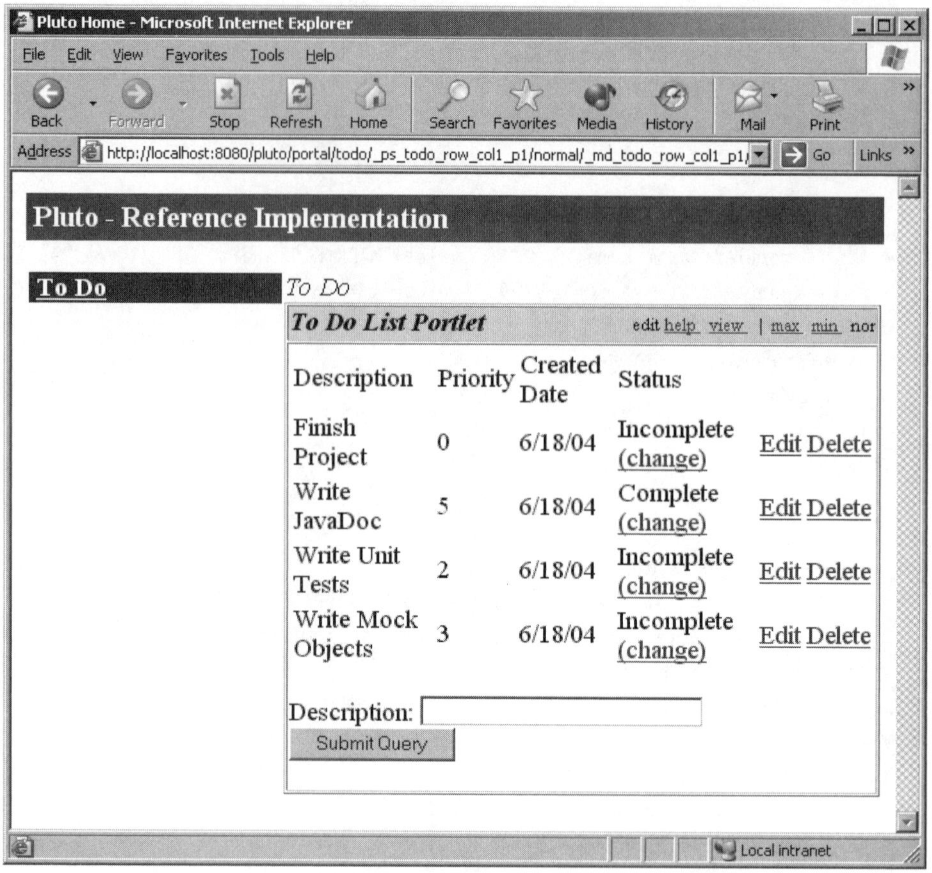

Figure 5-3. The to-do list portlet in EDIT mode

The Edit All Items page contains links to edit individual to-do list items. This uses a separate JSP page.

Editing a To-Do List Item

We can edit a to-do list item from the editItemPage.jsp page. Like the Edit All Items page, this JSP page is for the EDIT portlet mode. We create a form that sends an action request with the command EDIT to the portlet's action request handler, which updates the appropriate to-do list item. The form is populated with the contents of the to-do list item, using the `<c:out>` tag from the core JSTL tag library. We use the `<c:set>` tag to set the expression variable item to the `ToDoListBean` object from the `ToDoList` list.

This form also uses a `<portlet:actionURL>` JSP tag as the form's action, and we used the POST HTTP method for the form again (because it is required for portlets).

```
<%@ page session="true" %>

<%@ taglib uri='/WEB-INF/tld/portlet.tld' prefix='portlet'%>
<%@ taglib uri="/WEB-INF/tld/c.tld" prefix="c" %>
<%@ page import="java.util.*"%>

<c:set var="item" value="${ToDoList[param.ITEM_ID]}"/>
<a href="<portlet:renderURL portletMode="edit"/>">Back to Edit All Items</a>

<form action="<portlet:actionURL>
  <portlet:param name="COMMAND" value="EDIT"/>
  <portlet:param name="ITEM_ID" value="<%=request.getParameter("ITEM_ID")%>"/>
 </portlet:actionURL>"

method="post">
  Description: <input type="text" size="30"
  value="<c:out value="${item.description}"/>" name="DESCRIPTION">
  <br>
  Priority: <input type="text" size="2"
  value="<c:out value="${item.priority}"/>" name="PRIORITY">
  <br>
  <input type="submit" text="Create">
</form>
```

The Help Page

The simplest JSP page we created for the to-do list portlet application is helpPage.jsp, which contains only HTML. It will be displayed in the HELP portlet mode of the to-do portlet.

```
<H2>Help for To Do List Portlet</H2>

This portlet is a basic to do list.  The default
implementation does not store the to do items
in a database, so the items are lost when the user
logs off of the portal or the portal shuts down.
<p>
To add a new item, use the main screen to add a description of the task.
<p>
An item can be marked either finished or unfinished, and can be changed
at any time, by selecting the (change) link in the main view.
<p>
```

```
Each item has a priority, which should a positive integer, like 1 or 4.
This is useful for prioritizing one task over another.
<p>
The To Do List portlet also keeps track of the time when the to do item was
submitted.
<p>
To Do items may be edited or removed in the edit view, which can be accessed
from the portal page.
```

Because there is no functionality on this page, we do not have to use any scriptlets or portlet tags. If users want to navigate away from the help page, they can use the controls built into the portal page.

The portlet.xml Deployment Descriptor

Our application will have only one portlet, with one portlet class named `com.portalbook.portlets.todo.ToDoListPortlet`. The portlet.xml deployment descriptor will contain the required fields for our portlet, along with the supported portlet modes: VIEW, EDIT, and HELP.

```
<?xml version="1.0" encoding="UTF-8"?>
<portlet-app xmlns="http://java.sun.com/xml/ns/portlet/portlet-app_1_0.xsd"
 version="1.0"
 xmlns:xsi="http://www.w3.org/2001/XMLSchema-instance"
 xsi:schemaLocation="http://java.sun.com/xml/ns/portlet/portlet-app_1_0.xsd ➥
http://java.sun.com/xml/ns/portlet/portlet-app_1_0.xsd">
    <portlet>
        <description>To Do List Portlet</description>
        <portlet-name>ToDoPortlet</portlet-name>
        <display-name>To Do List Portlet</display-name>
        <portlet-class>com.portalbook.portlets.todo.ToDoListPortlet</portlet-class>
        <expiration-cache>-1</expiration-cache>
        <supports>
            <mime-type>text/html</mime-type>
            <portlet-mode>VIEW</portlet-mode>
            <portlet-mode>EDIT</portlet-mode>
            <portlet-mode>HELP</portlet-mode>
        </supports>
        <supported-locale>en</supported-locale>
```

```
        <portlet-info>
            <title>To Do List Portlet</title>
            <short-title>To Do</short-title>
            <keywords>To Do</keywords>
        </portlet-info>
    </portlet>
</portlet-app>
```

This portlet.xml deployment descriptor is very basic because we do not use any portlet preferences, more than one portlet, or more than one locale.

The web.xml Deployment Descriptor

The web.xml deployment descriptor is very simple because we do not have any servlets in this application:

```
<?xml version="1.0" encoding="UTF-8"?>
<!DOCTYPE web-app PUBLIC "-//Sun Microsystems, Inc.//DTD Web Application 2.3//EN"
                         "http://java.sun.com/dtd/web-app_2_3.dtd">
<web-app>
    <display-name>To Do List Application</display-name>
    <description>This portlet appplication manages a to do list.</description>
</web-app>
```

Directory Structure of the Application

Our directory structure for the to-do list portlet application is the normal web application structure. Our tag library JAR files are in WEB-INF/lib. The TLD files are in WEB-INF/tld. The JSP files are also under the WEB-INF directory, in WEB-INF/JSP. Our Java classes and deployment descriptors are in their usual place. Figure 5-4 shows our portlet application structure in the Eclipse IDE's Navigator window.

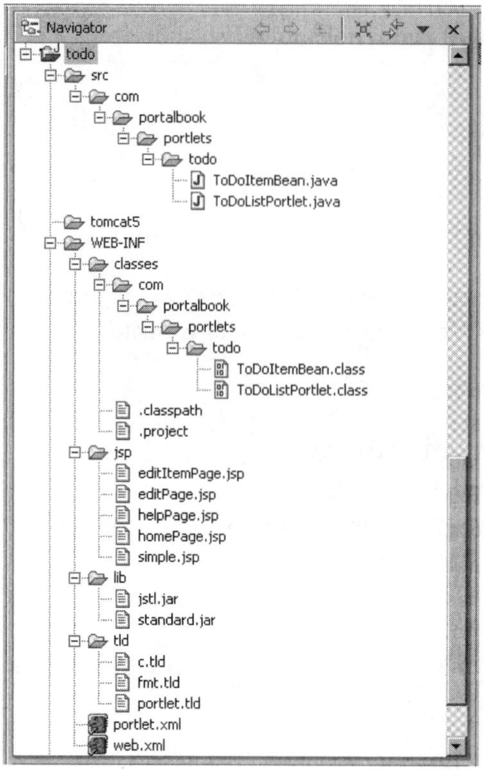

Figure 5-4. Directory structure of the to-do list portlet application

Complete Code Listing for the To-Do List Portlet

Here is the complete code listing for the to-do list portlet that we've discussed in this chapter:

```
package com.portalbook.portlets.todo;

import java.io.IOException;
import java.io.Writer;
import java.util.ArrayList;

import javax.portlet.ActionRequest;
import javax.portlet.ActionResponse;
import javax.portlet.GenericPortlet;
import javax.portlet.PortletContext;
import javax.portlet.PortletException;
import javax.portlet.PortletRequestDispatcher;
import javax.portlet.PortletSession;
```

```
import javax.portlet.RenderRequest;
import javax.portlet.RenderResponse;

public class ToDoListPortlet extends GenericPortlet
{

    public void processAction(ActionRequest request, ActionResponse response)
        throws PortletException, IOException
    {
        //retrieve the to do list out of the user's session
        PortletSession session = request.getPortletSession(true);

        //the to do list is just stored as an ArrayList here, because
        //we are not going to persist it to a database or other storage.
        ArrayList list = (ArrayList) session.getAttribute("ToDoList",
                PortletSession.APPLICATION_SCOPE);

        //if the list doesn't exist, create an empty one.
        if (list == null)
        {
            list = new ArrayList();
        }

        //set up a very simple controller here, based on a
        //request parameter called COMMAND
        String command = request.getParameter("COMMAND");
        String itemParam = request.getParameter("ITEM_ID");

        int itemId = -1;
        if (itemParam != null)
        {
            itemId = Integer.parseInt(itemParam);
        }

        if ("MARK_FINISHED".equals(command))
        {
            ToDoItemBean item = (ToDoItemBean) list.get(itemId);
            item.setStatus(true);

        }
        else if ("DELETE".equals(command))
        {
            list.remove(itemId);
        }
```

```
else if ("MARK_UNFINISHED".equals(command))
{
    ToDoItemBean item = (ToDoItemBean) list.get(itemId);
    item.setStatus(false);

}
else if ("EDIT".equals(command))
{
    ToDoItemBean item = (ToDoItemBean) list.get(itemId);

    String desc = request.getParameter("DESCRIPTION");
    item.setDescription(desc);

    String priority = request.getParameter("PRIORITY");
    if (priority != null)
    {

        try
        {
            int p = Integer.parseInt(priority);
            item.setPriority(p);
        }
        catch (NumberFormatException nfe)
        {
            getPortletContext().log(
                "Error trying to format " + priority + " as a number.");
        }
    }
}
else if ("NEW".equals(command))
{
    ToDoItemBean item = new ToDoItemBean();

    String desc = request.getParameter("DESCRIPTION");

    if (desc == null)
    {
        return;
    }

    item.setDescription(desc);
    item.setStatus(false);
    item.setSubmittedDate(new java.util.Date());
    item.setPriority(0);
```

```
                list.add(item);
            }
            session.setAttribute("ToDoList", list,
PortletSession.APPLICATION_SCOPE);
        }

    protected void doView(RenderRequest request, RenderResponse response)
        throws PortletException, IOException
    {
        response.setContentType("text/html");

        PortletContext portletContext = getPortletContext();

        PortletRequestDispatcher prd =
            portletContext.getRequestDispatcher("/WEB-INF/jsp/homePage.jsp");
        prd.include(request, response);
    }

    protected void doEdit(RenderRequest request, RenderResponse response)
        throws PortletException, IOException
    {
        response.setContentType("text/html");

        String display = request.getParameter("DISPLAY");

        PortletContext portletContext = getPortletContext();
        if ("EDIT_PAGE".equals(display))
        {
            PortletRequestDispatcher prd =
                portletContext.getRequestDispatcher(
                    "/WEB-INF/jsp/editItemPage.jsp");
            prd.include(request, response);
        }
        else
        {
            PortletRequestDispatcher prd =
                portletContext.getRequestDispatcher("/WEB-INF/jsp/editPage.jsp");
            prd.include(request, response);
        }
    }

    protected void doHelp(RenderRequest request, RenderResponse response)
        throws PortletException, IOException
    {
```

```
            response.setContentType("text/html");

            Writer writer = response.getWriter();

            PortletContext portletContext = getPortletContext();

            PortletRequestDispatcher prd =
                portletContext.getRequestDispatcher("/WEB-INF/jsp/helpPage.jsp");
            prd.include(request, response);

    }
}
```

Summary

Most of the portlets you develop will use servlets or JSP pages to display content for the portal page. The output of the servlets or JSP pages can be included in the portlet's render response. Servlets and JSP pages may only be included during the portlet's render request handling phase, not during action request handling. The portlet can share its session with any servlets or JSP pages, and objects may be passed between the two on either the request or the session.

CHAPTER 6

Packaging and Deployment Descriptors

PORTLET APPLICATION ASSEMBLERS need to package each portlet application into a web application archive (WAR) file for distribution and deployment. Each portlet application contains a web and a portlet deployment descriptor, and we discuss the formats used for each in this chapter. Several tools assist with the portlet assembly and packaging process. We briefly discuss the Ant build tool, and cover the XDoclet portlet extensions in more detail.

Portlet Application Packaging

The portlet application consists of the portlet classes, any libraries or resources, a web application deployment descriptor, and a portlet application deployment descriptor. Both deployment descriptors are contained in the portlet application's WEB-INF directory.

The application assembler packages the portlet application into a WAR file. The portlet application's WAR file structure is identical to that of a standard Java 2 Enterprise Edition (J2EE) web application, with the addition of a portlet.xml portlet application deployment descriptor and the portlet classes.

Versioning

Versioning each release of a portlet application can help you manage your portlet distributions. If you are releasing the WAR file to other groups or other organizations, the version can help you track down specific bugs for a release. You can also provide other information about the portlet application implementation, such as the title and vendor name.

The versioning standard for a portlet application WAR archive is the same one used for Java Archive (JAR) files. The versioning information belongs in the WEB-INF/MANIFEST.MF file in the WAR archive. There are six different pieces of metadata that describe the versioning for a portlet application: title, vendor, and version both for the implementation and for the specification. It is up to you to specify the titles, versions, and vendors. Some portals may have tools that track these versions for you, and they can be useful if there is no other version information in the WAR file.

Here is an example MANIFEST.MF file for a portlet application:

```
Manifest-Version: 1.0
Name: DocumentManagementPortlet
Specification-Title: WebDAV
Specification-Vendor: WebDAV
Specification-Version: 1.0
Implementation-Title: DocumentationManagementPortlet
Implementation-Vendor: PortalBook.com
Implementation-Version: 0.9.3
```

Portlet Application Deployment Descriptor Structure

An XML Schema named portlet-app_1_0.xsd specifies the structure of the portlet application deployment descriptor. Your portal should include a copy of this schema, either as documentation or for deployment descriptor documentation. The full schema is too large to reprint in this book (over 15 pages), but we used Altova's XML Spy XML editor to generate diagrams from the schema. We discuss each element in the schema, and give a pointer to the relevant chapter of this book. Future versions of the portlet API may extend or change elements of this schema, so when you upgrade to a portal that supports a newer version, check the release notes to see what changed.

portlet-app

The root element of the portlet application deployment descriptor is the `<portlet-app>` element. The `<portlet-app>` element contains any portlet definitions, custom portlet modes or window states, the supported user attributes for the portlet application, and the security constraints. This element represents a distinct portlet application that is self-contained and can be deployed on a portal with no dependencies. Figure 6-1 shows the XML Schema for this element.

There are two attributes on the `<portlet-app>` element. The first attribute is named `version`, and it is required. The value of the `version` attribute is the version of the portlet API that this portlet application supports. The deployment descriptor must be valid with that version of the portlet application deployment descriptor schema, but it may be invalid with future releases. Until a new version of the portlet API is released, this value will be 1.0. The other attribute, `id`, is optional.

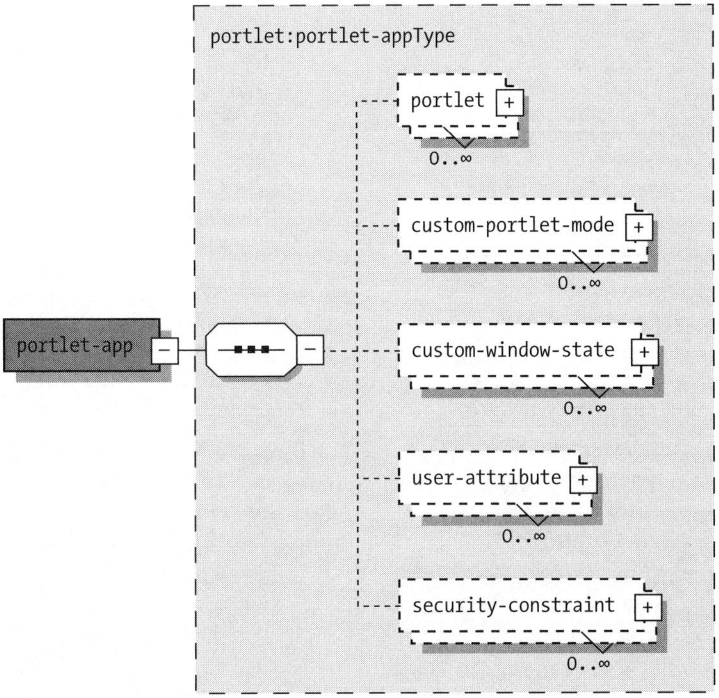

Figure 6-1. The <portlet-app> *XML Schema*

The <portlet-app> element may contain <portlet> elements, which represent portlet classes, <custom-portlet-mode> elements, <custom-window-state> elements, <user-attribute> elements, or <security-constraint> elements.

```
<portlet-app xmlns="http://java.sun.com/xml/ns/portlet/portlet-app_1_0.xsd" ➥
version="1.0" ➥
xmlns:xsi="http://www.w3.org/2001/XMLSchema-instance" ➥
xsi:schemaLocation="http://java.sun.com/xml/ns/portlet/portlet-app_1_0.xsd ➥
http://java.sun.com/xml/ns/portlet/portlet-app_1_0.xsd">
    <portlet>
        ...
    </portlet>
 </portlet-app>
```

portlet

The <portlet> element (see Figure 6-2) represents a portlet class and all of its metadata. The only attribute on the <portlet> element is id, and it is optional.

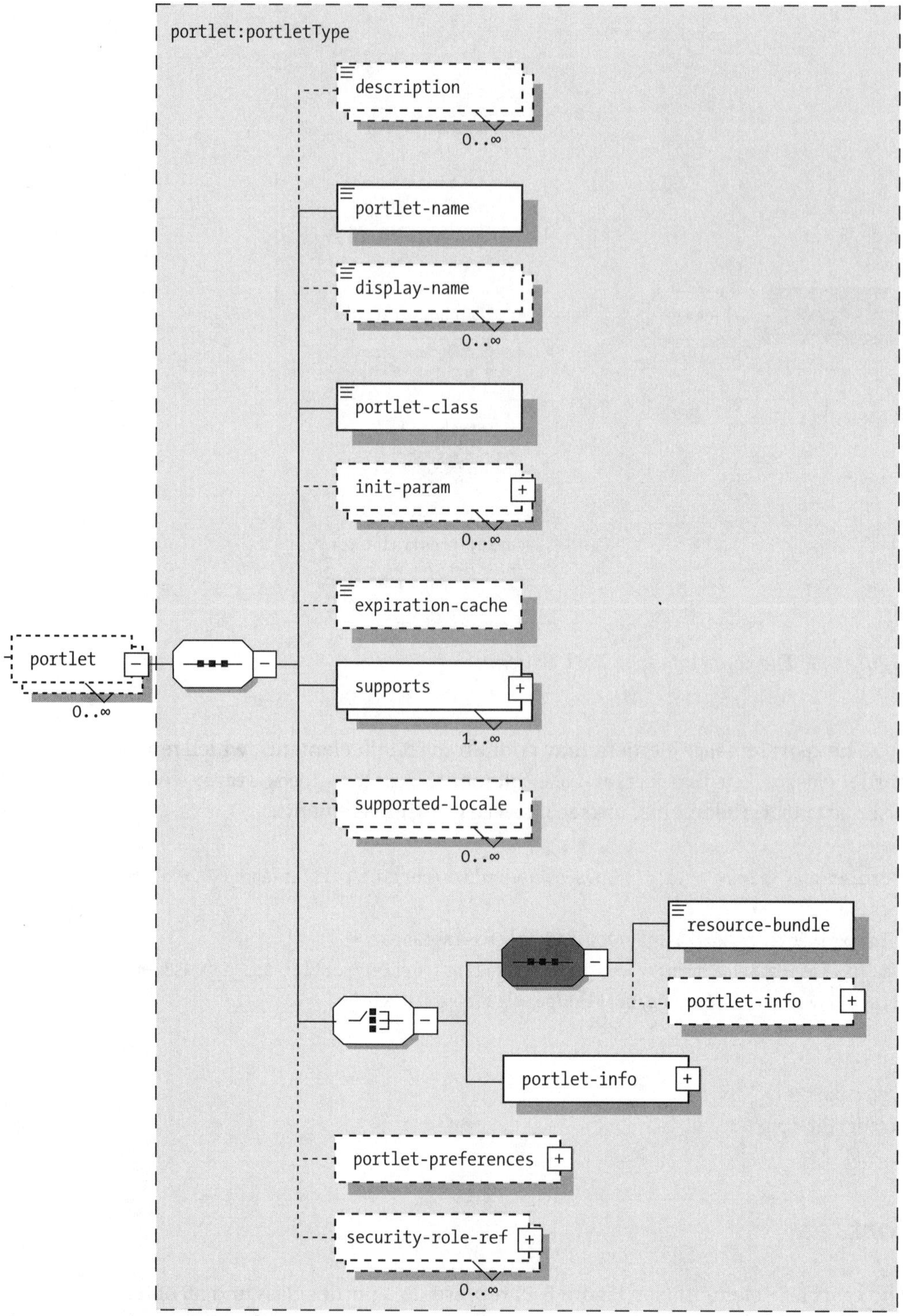

Figure 6-2. The `<portlet>` *XML Schema*

Each portlet may have an optional description, which is specified in the `<description>` element. Portal administration tools use the description to give some context about the portlet to a portlet application deployment.

> **TIP** *The* `<description>` *element is a child of many of the tags in the portlet deployment descriptor. Its use is optional, but it is very handy for documentation or portlet deployment tools.*

The `<portlet-name>` element is required for the portlet. Each portlet's name in the portlet application has to be unique. This name should not contain any spaces or non-web-friendly special characters.

The `<display-name>` element provides a human-readable name for portal administration tools. It is optional.

The class name of the portlet belongs in the `<portlet-class>` element, which takes a fully qualified Java class name, as shown here:

```
<portlet>
    <description>Preferences Validation Portlet</description>

    <portlet-name>PreferencesValidationPortlet</portlet-name>

    <display-name>Preferences Validation Portlet</display-name>

    <portlet-class>
com.portalbook.portlets.PreferencesValidationPortlet</portlet-class>
    ....
 </portlet>
```

Each portlet may have zero or more portlet initialization parameters, which are used to provide configuration information for all users. The `<init-param>` element (see Figure 6-3) has three child elements: `<description>`, `<name>`, and `<value>`. The `<name>` and `<value>` elements are required. For more on initialization parameters, see Chapter 7.

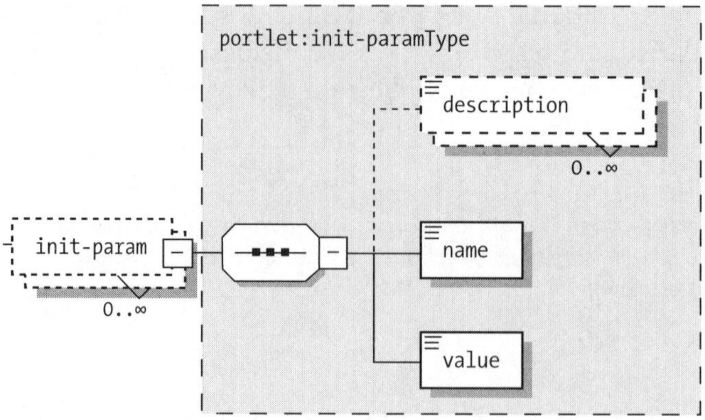

Figure 6-3. The `<init-param>` *XML Schema*

```
<init-param>
  <name>indexPath</name>
  <value>/java/index</value>
</init-param>
<init-param>
  <name>repository</name>
  <value>engineering</value>
</init-param>
```

The portlet container may cache the output of a portlet. The portlet defines the timeout it expects for the cache in the `<expiration-cache>` element. If the value is -1, the cached output is always valid:

```
<expiration-cache>0</expiration-cache>
```

The portlet may support more than one Multipurpose Internet Mail Extensions (MIME) type, and for each MIME type, the portlet needs to tell the portlet container which portlet modes are valid. These could be any of the standard portlet modes (VIEW, EDIT, HELP), or custom modes that are specified later in the deployment descriptor. Each MIME type should be specified only once, and there must be at least one MIME type for each portlet. The `<supports>` element (see Figure 6-4) groups MIME types, `<mime-type>`, and portlet modes, `<portlet-mode>`. The portlet modes should be a comma-delimited list of valid portlet modes. For more on portlet modes, see Chapter 4.

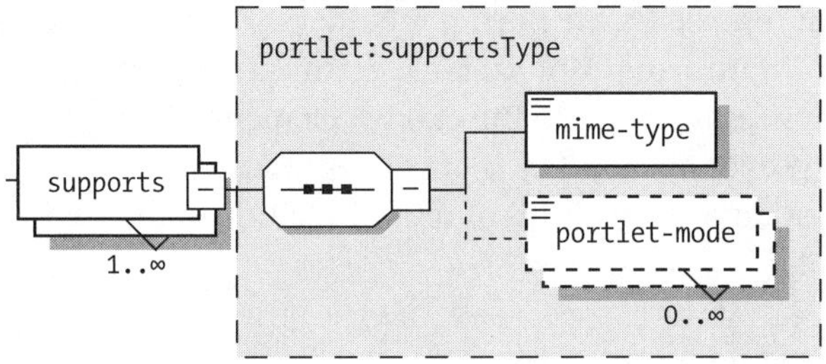

Figure 6-4. The `<supports>` *XML Schema*

```
<supports>
  <mime-type>text/html</mime-type>
  <portlet-mode>edit</portlet-mode>
  <portlet-mode>help</portlet-mode>
  <portlet-mode>view</portlet-mode>
</supports>
```

You may specify which locales the portlet supports with the `<supported-locale>` element. The element should contain the name of a valid Java locale. There can be more than one supported locale for a portlet. The portal may use these values to localize content for the end user:

```
<supported-locale>en</supported-locale>
```

The portlet metadata can also be localized with a resource bundle. The resource bundle should contain the information from the `<portlet-info>` tag (Figure 6-5), specified as javax.portlet.title, javax.portlet.short-title, and javax.portlet.keywords. The `<resource-bundle>` tag should contain the class name of the resource bundle. The bundle should be in the portlet application's classpath:

```
<resource-bundle>com.portalbook.Messages</resource-bundle>
```

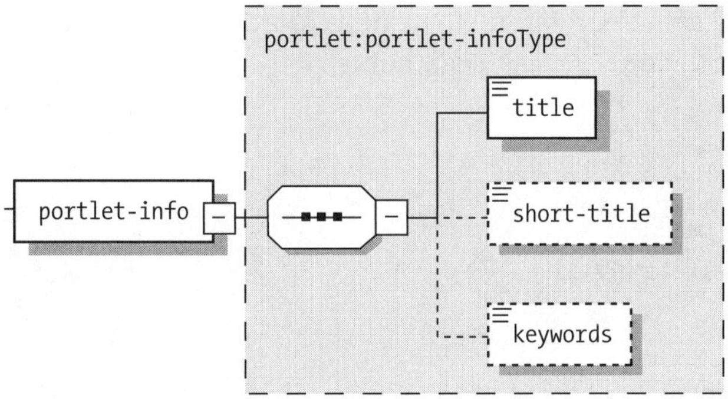

Figure 6-5. The `<portlet-info>` *XML Schema*

The <portlet-info> element represents the portlet metadata. There are three XML child elements that contain information: <title>, <short-title>, and <keywords>. The portlet's title bar uses the value in the <title> element, although some portlets will change the title dynamically. The short title is for mobile phones, PDAs, or other portal clients that do not have a lot of room for a title to display.

```
<portlet-info>
  <title>Taxonomy Portlet</title>
  <short-title>Taxonomy</short-title>
  <keywords>Taxonomy,Lucene</keywords>
</portlet-info>
```

The <portlet-preferences> element (Figure 6-6) contains zero or more <preference> elements and an optional <preferences-validator> element. The <preferences-validator> value should be the class name for a validator class. The <preference> element has a child <name> element, which is required, and zero or more optional initial values. There is also a read-only flag for preferences that cannot be modified. The preference value must be set in the deployment descriptor.

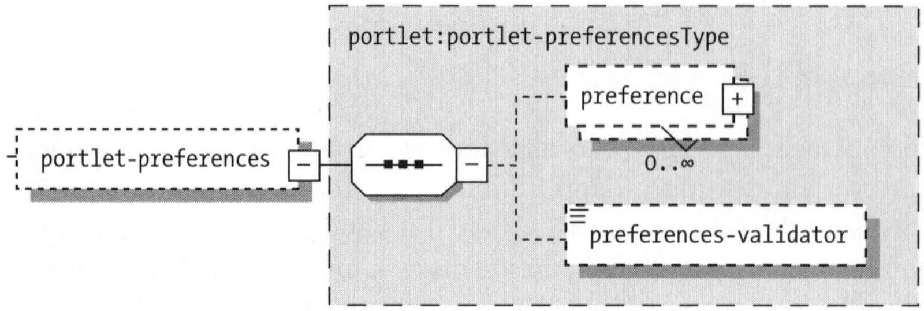

Figure 6-6. The <portlet-preferences> *XML Schema*

Each portlet preference name must be unique for the portlet. You may have portlet preferences with the same name for two or more portlets in a portlet application. For more on portlet preferences, see Chapter 7.

```
<portlet-preferences>
  <preference>
    <name>bookmark</name>
    <value>/content/marketing</value>
  </preference>

  <preferences-validator>
    com.portalbook.portlets.TaxonomyValidator
  </preferences-validator>
</portlet-preferences>
```

The <security-role-ref> element (Figure 6-7) maps portlet security roles to web application security roles. For more on portlet application security, see Chapter 8.

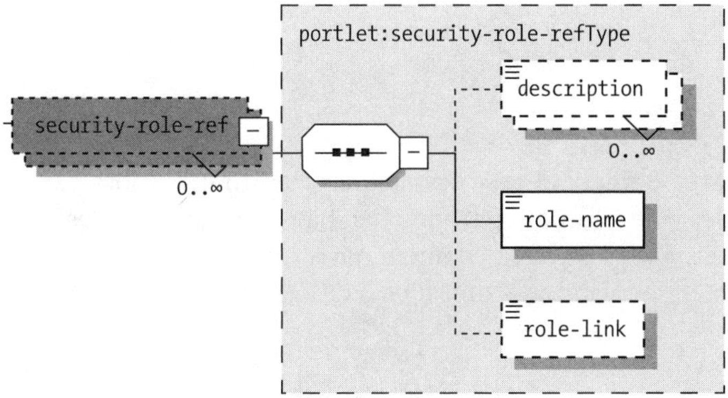

Figure 6-7. The <security-role-ref> *XML Schema*

```
<security-role-ref>
  <role-name>Administrator</role-name>
  <role-link>admin</role-link>
</security-role-ref>
```

custom-portlet-mode

The <custom-portlet-mode> element (Figure 6-8) defines a custom portlet mode that this portlet supports. Each portlet application can have as many custom portlet modes as it needs. The <custom-portlet-mode> element has a <portlet-mode> element that contains the name of the portlet mode, such as PRINT. The <description> element is optional.

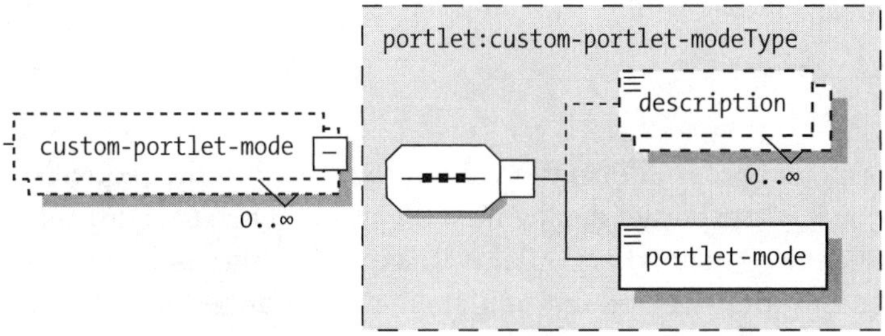

Figure 6-8. The <custom-portlet-mode> *XML Schema*

For more on custom portlet modes, see Chapter 4.

```
<custom-portlet-mode>
  <portlet-mode>PRINT</portlet-mode>
</custom-portlet-mode>
```

custom-window-state

The <custom-window-state> element (Figure 6-9) defines a custom window state supported by this portlet. The portlet application can have zero or more custom window states. The <custom-window-state> element has a <window-state> element that contains the name of the window state, such as ICON. The <description> element is optional.

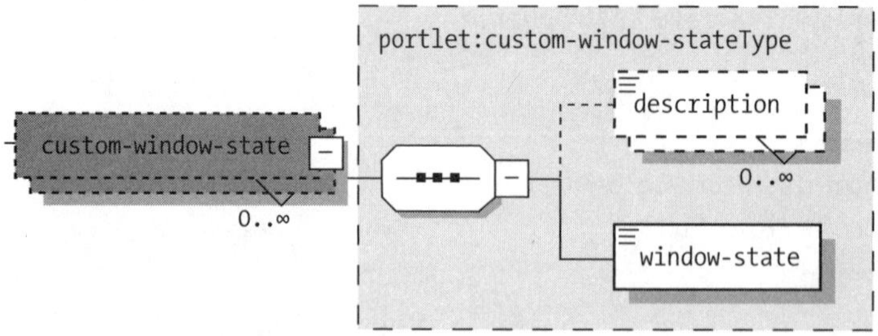

Figure 6-9. The <custom-window-state> *XML Schema*

For more on custom window states, see Chapter 4.

```
<custom-window-state>
  <window-state>docked</window-state>
</custom-window-state>
```

user-attribute

The portlet application can access information about the user, but the requested attributes must be explicit in the portlet deployment descriptor. Each user attribute the portlet requires needs to be defined in portlet.xml as a <user-attribute> element (Figure 6-10). The user attributes are optional, and there may be an unlimited number of them.

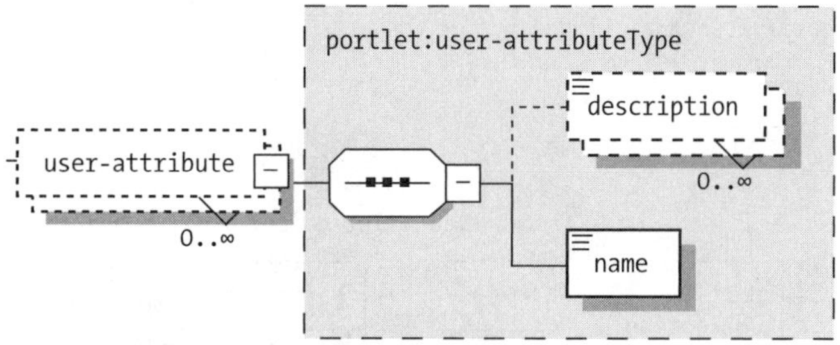

Figure 6-10. The `<user-attribute>` *XML Schema*

The `<user-attribute>` tag has a `<name>` child element, which must be unique for the portlet application. The `<description>` element is optional.

For more on user attributes, see Chapter 11.

```
<user-attribute>
  <name>user.name.given</name>
</user-attribute>
<user-attribute>
  <name>user.name.suffix</name>
</user-attribute>
<user-attribute>
  <name>user.home-info.postal.country</name>
</user-attribute>
```

security-constraint

The `<security-constraint>` element (Figure 6-11) has an optional display name, a portlet collection, and a user data constraint. The `<portlet-collection>` element has a set of `<portlet-name>` elements that reference portlets defined in the portlet application. The `<user-data-constraint>` element has a `<transport-guarantee>` element and an optional description.

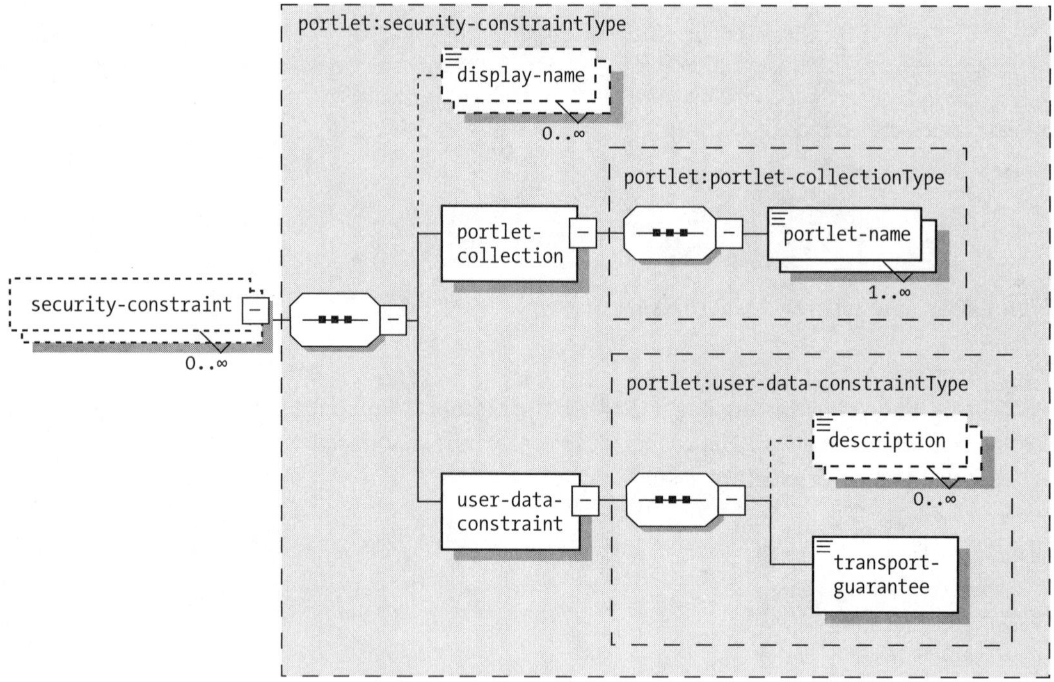

Figure 6-11. The `<security-constraint>` *XML Schema*

The `<transport-guarantee>` element may have a value of NONE, CONFIDENTIAL, or INTEGRAL. If the value is NONE, the portlets in the portlet collection do not require any transport-level security. The CONFIDENTIAL guarantee means that the data transmitted between the user and the portal cannot be seen by third parties. The INTEGRAL guarantee requires that another party cannot alter traffic between the user and the portal.

```
<security-constraint>
  <portlet-collection>
    <portlet-name>TaxonomyPortlet</portlet-name>
  </portlet-collection>
  <user-data-constraint>
    <transport-guarantee>INTEGRAL</transport-guarantee>
  </user-data-constraint>
</security-constraint>
```

Web Application Deployment Descriptor

Each portlet application needs a web application deployment descriptor named web.xml that resides in the WEB-INF directory. Three portlet application settings are common to the web application and belong in web.xml. The description should be specified in the <description> element. The <display-name> tag contains the name of the portlet application. Portlet security is controlled with the <security-role> tag, although the portlet application deployment descriptor also contains the <security-role-ref> tag for mapping roles.

In addition, any servlets or JSP pages descriptions belong in the web.xml file. We covered servlets and JSP in Chapter 5.

Some portlet containers will rewrite your portlet application's web.xml file as part of the deployment process, but this should not affect your portlet development. The following code snippet is from a web.xml deployment descriptor created during the Apache Pluto deployment process:

```
...
 <servlet>
   <servlet-name>ContentPortlet</servlet-name>
   <display-name>ContentPortlet Wrapper</display-name>
   <description>Automated generated Portlet Wrapper</description>
   <servlet-class>org.apache.pluto.core.PortletServlet</servlet-class>
   <init-param>
     <param-name>portlet-guid</param-name>
     <param-value>myapp.ContentPortlet</param-value>
   </init-param>
   <init-param>
     <param-name>portlet-class</param-name>
     <param-value>com.portalbook.portlets.content.ContentPortlet</param-value>
   </init-param>
 </servlet>
   ...
```

The web.xml deployment descriptor was generated from the values in the portlet.xml deployment descriptor.

XDoclet Portlet Support

XDoclet is an open source Java code-generation tool, with an Apache-style license. The XDoclet home page is located at `http://xdoclet.sourceforge.net/`. You need to download and install the XDoclet 1.2 package from SourceForge (`http://sourceforge.net/projects/xdoclet/`) to run the examples in this section. You also need Apache Ant 1.5 or greater (`http://ant.apache.org`) to run XDoclet. If you are not familiar with Ant, the online Apache Ant manual (`http://ant.apache.org/manual/index.html`) is a good place to start, as is *Enterprise Java Development on a Budget* by Christopher M. Judd and Brian Sam-Bodden (Apress, 2004).

We are going to use XDoclet to generate the portlet.xml deployment descriptor from our Java portlet class source code. Craig Walls wrote the portlet deployment descriptor integration for XDoclet, which speeds up the portlet application development process. To use XDoclet, you need to mark up your portlet classes with custom JavaDoc tags. XDoclet processes the JavaDoc tags and creates the deployment descriptor. The advantage is that the portlet description information belongs with the source code for the portlet class, so when you create or modify your portlet, it is easy to change the deployment descriptor information. For instance, if the class or package name changes, the generated deployment descriptor will contain the new name without any additional work on your part.

> **TIP** *Keep the XDoclet-generated files out of source control. Re-create any generated files during the build process, because they will be derived from source files that may have changed.*

After working through the XDoclet example in this section, you should have some idea of whether using XDoclet is worth integrating into your build process. The portlet application deployment descriptor is not so complicated that automating its generation with XDoclet saves a lot of time on a normal project. For complex development projects with many portlet applications and portlet classes, standardization on XDoclet makes more sense.

> **NOTE** *The main reason most developers use XDoclet is for generating Enterprise JavaBeans (EJB) classes. XDoclet cuts down on the number of Java classes that must be created and maintained for each EJB, so it can be a real time-saver. If you are interested in using XDoclet for EJB code generation, check out* Enterprise Java Development on a Budget *(Apress, 2004).*

We will show you how to set up a portlet class with XDoclet tags and then how to create an Ant build file that will generate a portlet.xml deployment descriptor. If you had more than one portlet class in your project with XDoclet tags, XDoclet will add all of them to the portlet.xml deployment descriptor.

XDoclet Tags for Portlets

We are going to reuse the `SessionPortlet` class from Chapter 4 for our XDoclet example. None of the Java code in the portlet needs to be modified for XDoclet support; we only have to add the XDoclet portlet tags to the class.

The first XDoclet tag we will use for `SessionPortlet` will be `@portlet.portlet`. This tag represents one portlet class in the portlet application. There are four parameters on the `@portlet.portlet` tag: `description`, `display-name`, `expiration-cache`, and `name`. These parameters correspond to several of the child elements of the

<portlet> tag in the deployment descriptor. The name parameter is required, and it corresponds to the <portlet-name> tag. The name of the portlet must be unique within the web application.

Here is the source code to the marked-up SessionPortlet class, with the @portlet.portlet tag. Notice that the XDoclet tag looks like the @author and @version JavaDoc tags in the source code. The @portlet.portlet tag takes up to four parameters, which can be specified on the same line as the tag name, or spread out over multiple lines. Each parameter has a name and a value—for this tag, all of the values are plain text.

```
package com.portalbook.xdoclet;

import java.io.IOException;
import java.io.PrintWriter;

import javax.portlet.GenericPortlet;
import javax.portlet.PortletException;
import javax.portlet.PortletSession;
import javax.portlet.RenderRequest;
import javax.portlet.RenderResponse;

/**
 * XDoclet example portlet
 *
 * @portlet.portlet
 *          description="This portlet demonstrates the use of the portlet session."
 *           display-name="Session Example"
 *           expiration-cache="0"
 *           name="SessionPortlet"
 *
 * @portlet.supports
 *           mime-type="text/html"
 *           modes="VIEW"
 *
 * @author Jeff Linwood and David Minter
 * @version 1.0
 */
public class SessionPortlet extends GenericPortlet
{
    public void doView(RenderRequest req, RenderResponse resp)
        throws PortletException, IOException
    {
        String newMessage = null;
```

```
        //set up for output
        resp.setContentType("text/html");
        PrintWriter writer = resp.getWriter();

        //get the session, or create it if needed
        PortletSession session = req.getPortletSession();

        //if there is already a value in the session, get it
        Object message = session.getAttribute("message");
        if (message == null)
        {
            //This is nothing in the session stored by the name 'message'
            newMessage = "Hi, This is the first visit to the portlet.";

        }
        else if (message instanceof String)
        {
            //change the message for repeat visitors
            newMessage = "Welcome back to this portlet!";
        }

        //Store it in the portlet session
        session.setAttribute("message", newMessage);

        //write it out
        writer.write(newMessage);
    }
}
```

As you can see, we now specify some of the metadata about the portlet in the Java class. We do not have to maintain this metadata in two different places; instead, we can just generate the portlet.xml deployment descriptor from the Java class.

Creating the Ant Build File with XDoclet Support

We've updated one of our standard portlet application Ant build files with XDoclet support. XDoclet can be run only from an Ant build file, because XDoclet is implemented as a set of Ant tasks. Here is a list of several of the available XDoclet Ant tasks:

- **EJBDoclet:** Used for generating local interfaces, home interfaces, application-server specific deployment files, and Struts/EJB integration code

- **WebDoclet:** Used for generating a web application deployment descriptor, JSP tag lib TLD files, struts-config.xml files for Struts, and servlet container-specific deployment files

- **HibernateDoclet:** Generates the bean to database mapping files for the open source persistence layer Hibernate

- **PortletDoclet:** Creates the portlet.xml deployment descriptor for a portlet application

To use any of these XDoclet tasks in an Ant build file, you will need to define the task in the build file with the `<taskdef>` element. We will use `<taskdef>` in our Ant build file to define the `<portletdoclet>` task. The `<portletdoclet>` task will use the `xdoclet.modules.portlet.PortletDocletTask` class from the XDoclet 1.2.x distribution. You will need to have downloaded and unzipped the XDoclet 1.2.x binary distribution somewhere on your file system so we can load the task. The portlet XDoclet task also requires the Java portlet API JAR file (portlet-api-1.0.jar) in the task's classpath. In our build file, we set up a classpath called xdoclet.portlet.classpath that references the JAR files in our XDoclet distribution and the portlet API JAR file. You will need to edit this classpath to point to these locations on your machine.

The `<portletdoclet>` task takes several attributes, the most important of which is `destdir`. The `destdir` attribute specifies the directory where XDoclet will generate the portlet.xml file. By default, XDoclet will not overwrite existing files, but if you set the `<portletdoclet>` element's `force` attribute to `true`, the new portlet.xml will overwrite an old portlet.xml. The `mergedir` attribute is the location of any additional XML files that will be merged into the generated portlet.xml. The portlet XDoclet supports custom window states, custom portlet modes, user attributes, and security constraints in the portlet deployment descriptor, if they are included in the XDoclet merge directory as XML files.

You will need to specify a set of Java source files for XDoclet to use to generate the portlet.xml. The `<portletdoclet>` task needs an Ant file set for the project's Java source code files. These can be anywhere, but in our Java build file, we used the regular source directory, with all Java classes. If your portlets are in one or two packages, or all of your portlet class names end in Portlet, you can use a more specific filter for the Ant file set include. Alternatively, you may also exclude certain classes from the file set if you have portlets with XDoclet markup that are not going to be deployed on the portal in this build. This could be useful in a scenario where you make different portlet application builds for production servers and development machines with the same Ant build file and source control repository.

The only subtask for the `<portletdoclet>` task is the `<portletxml>` subtask. The `<portletxml>` subtask will generate the portlet.xml from the XDoclet tags in the Java source code. Behind the scenes, it is filling in an XDoclet template with the correct information. The XDoclet template for portlet.xml is called portlet_xml.xdt, and it is available in the XDoclet source distribution or in the XDoclet portlet module JAR file. You do not ever need to edit this template, but if you are curious about how XDoclet works, the template is easy to understand.

The create-portlet-xml target is a dependency of our default Ant target, build-war, and it runs after compilation. That way, if our compilation fails, the build file does not generate a portlet.xml:

```
<?xml version="1.0" encoding="UTF-8"?>

<project default="build-war" name="xdoclet-build" basedir=".">
  <property file="build.properties"/>
  <property name="src.dir" value="src"/>
  <property name="build.dir" value="build"/>
  <property name="dist.dir" value="dist"/>
  <property name="classes.dir" value="${build.dir}/classes"/>
  <property name="lib.dir" value="lib"/>
  <property name="web-inf.dir" value="WEB-INF"/>
  <property name="web-inf.generated.dir" value="generated"/>
  <property name="war.name" value="xdocletexample"/>

  <property name="xdoclet.merge.dir" value="merge"/>

  <path id="xdoclet.portlet.classpath">
    <fileset dir="${xdoclet.install.dir}/lib">
        <include name="*.jar"/>
    </fileset>
        <fileset dir="${tomcat.shared.lib.dir}">
          <include name="*.jar"/>
        </fileset>
  </path>

  <target name="init">
    <mkdir dir="${build.dir}"/>
    <mkdir dir="${classes.dir}"/>
    <mkdir dir="${dist.dir}"/>
    <mkdir dir="${lib.dir}"/>
    <mkdir dir="${web-inf.generated.dir}"/>
  </target>

  <target name="compile" depends="init">
    <javac destdir="${classes.dir}" deprecation="true" debug="true" optimize="false">
      <src>
        <pathelement location="${src.dir}"/>
      </src>
      <classpath>
        <fileset dir="${lib.dir}">
          <include name="*.jar">
          </include>
        </fileset>
        <fileset dir="${tomcat.shared.lib.dir}">
          <include name="*.jar">
          </include>
        </fileset>
```

```
      </classpath>
    </javac>
  </target>

  <target name="create-portlet-xml">
    <taskdef name="portletdoclet"
             classname="xdoclet.modules.portlet.PortletDocletTask"
             classpathref="xdoclet.portlet.classpath"
     />

     <portletdoclet destdir="${web-inf.generated.dir}"
                    mergedir="${xdoclet.merge.dir}"
                    force="true"
     >
         <fileset dir="${src.dir}">
            <include name="**/*.java"/>
         </fileset>

         <portletxml/>
     </portletdoclet>
  </target>

  <target name="copy-portlet-xml">
    <copy file="${web-inf.generated.dir}/portlet.xml"
          todir="${web-inf.dir}"
     />
  </target>

  <target name="build-war" depends="compile,create-portlet-xml,copy-portlet-xml">
    <war destfile="${dist.dir}/${war.name}.war" webxml="WEB-INF/web.xml">
        <classes dir="${classes.dir}"/>
        <lib dir="${lib.dir}"/>
        <webinf dir="${web-inf.dir}"/>
    </war>
  </target>

  <target name="clean">
    <delete dir="${build.dir}"/>
    <delete dir="${dist.dir}"/>
    <delete dir="${web-inf.generated.dir}"/>
  </target>
</project>
```

You will need to edit the build.properties file referenced at the top of this Ant build file to correspond to your installation directories for the Tomcat shared library folder where you have the portlet API JAR (this could be any directory, not just Tomcat). You also need to update the XDoclet installation directory reference. Here is our example build.properties:

```
xdoclet.install.dir=/java/xdoclet
tomcat.shared.lib.dir=/java/tomcat/shared/lib
```

If the portlet API JAR is not in the task's classpath, the portlet XDoclet task will throw an error when the build is run. The API is necessary because XDoclet checks to see if the annotated class is an implementation of the `javax.portlet.Portlet` interface.

Running the Ant Build File

Once you have edited the build file to point to your portlet API JAR and XDoclet directory, you can run Ant to generate your portlet.xml and package your WAR file.

On a Windows XP machine with JDK 1.4 and Ant 1.5.1, the output looks like this:

```
C:\apress\packaging>ant -verbose -f xdoclet-build.xml create-portlet-xml

Apache Ant version 1.5.1 compiled on October 2 2002
Buildfile: xdoclet-build.xml
Detected Java version: 1.4 in: C:\java\j2sdk1.4.1_01\jre
Detected OS: Windows XP
parsing buildfile xdoclet-build.xml with URI = file:C:/apress/packaging/xdoclet-
build.xml
Project base dir set to: C:\apress\packaging
Build sequence for target 'create-portlet-xml' is [create-portlet-xml]
Complete build sequence is [create-portlet-xml, clean, init, compile, copy-portl
et-xml, build-war]

create-portlet-xml:
[portletdoclet] (XDocletMain.start                   47   ) Running <portletxml/>

[portletdoclet] Generating portlet.xml.

BUILD SUCCESSFUL
Total time: 3 seconds
```

Here, we ran Ant in verbose mode to show extra information. We also set the `verbose` attribute to have the value "true" on the `<portletdoclet>` task in the Ant build file, but that did not give us any extra information about the portlet.xml generation.

Generated Portlet.xml Deployment Descriptor

The generated portlet.xml deployment descriptor follows. As you can see, the generated XML has placeholders for the custom portlet modes, custom window states, user attributes, and security constraints:

```
<?xml version="1.0" encoding="UTF-8"?>

<portlet-app version="1.0" xmlns:xsi="http://www.w3.org/2001/XMLSchema-instance" ➥
  xsi:schemaLocation="http://java.sun.com/xml/ns/portlet/portlet-app_1_0.xsd ➥
  http://java.sun.com/xml/ns/portlet/portlet-app_1_0.xsd" ➥
  xmlns="http://java.sun.com/xml/ns/portlet">

    <portlet>
      <description>This portlet demonstrates the use of the portlet session.
      </description>
      <portlet-name>SessionPortlet</portlet-name>
      <display-name>Session Example</display-name>
      <portlet-class>com.portalbook.xdoclet.SessionPortlet</portlet-class>

      <expiration-cache>0</expiration-cache>
      <supports>
        <mime-type>text/html</mime-type>
        <portlet-mode>VIEW</portlet-mode>
      </supports>

      <portlet-info>
        <title></title>
      </portlet-info>

      <portlet-preferences>

      </portlet-preferences>
    </portlet>
     <!--
       To add custom portlet modes to the portlet.xml file, add a file to your
       XDoclet merge directory called custom-portlet-modes.xml that contains the
       <custom-portlet-mode></custom-portlet-mode> markup.
     -->
```

```
    <!--
        To add custom window states to the portlet.xml file, add a file to your
        XDoclet merge directory called portlet-custom-window-states.xml that contains the
        <custom-window-state></custom-window-state> markup.
    -->

    <!--
        To add user attributes to the portlet.xml file, add a file to your
        XDoclet merge directory called portlet-user-attributes.xml that contains the
        <user-attribute></user-attribute> markup.
    -->
    <!--
        To add security constraints to the portlet.xml file, add a file to your
        XDoclet merge directory called portlet-security.xml that contains the
        <security-constraint></security-constraint> markup.
    -->

</portlet-app>
```

> **NOTE** *There is a bug in XDoclet 1.2 with the portlet.xml generation module. The XML Schema location is not specified correctly, and the generated portlet.xml will not deploy properly on Pluto (and probably most other portlet containers). If this is not fixed in a release when this book goes to print, we will make a working XDoclet portlet module available from our web site (*`www.portalbook.com/`*).*
>
> *The generated portlet.xml file in this chapter uses the correct XML Schema location,* `xsi:schemaLocation="http://java.sun.com/xml/ns/portlet/portlet-app_1_0.xsd http://java.sun.com/xml/ns/portlet/portlet-app_1_0.xsd"`.

Other Portlet XDoclet Tags

In addition to `@portlet.portlet`, the other XDoclet tags for portlets are

- `@portlet.portlet-info`
- `@portlet.portlet-init-param`
- `@portlet.preference`
- `@portlet.preferences-validator`
- `@portlet.security-role-ref`
- `@portlet.supports`

All of these tags are for a portlet class, and are specified in the same place in the source code as the `@portlet.portlet` tag. None of them is required. All of the values for all of the parameters should be plain text.

The `@portlet.portlet-info` tag has three optional parameters: `title`, `keywords`, and `short-title`. There can be only one or none of each of these tags.

The `@portlet.portlet-init-param` tag takes two required parameters: `name` and `value`. The `description` parameter is optional. You may have zero or more portlet initialization parameters as XDoclet tags.

The `@portlet.preference` tag specifies portlet preferences. Any number of preferences is allowed, including none. There are two required parameters: `name` and `value`. The `read-only` parameter is optional.

There can be zero or one `@portlet.preferences-validator` XDoclet tags. This tag only requires one parameter, `class`, which is a Java class name.

The `@portlet.security-role-ref` tag has two required parameters: `role-link` and `role-name`. The `description` parameter is optional. A class may have zero or more of these tags.

The `@portlet.supports` tag specifies portlet mode to MIME type mappings. The tag has two required parameters: `mime-type` and `modes`. The `modes` parameter is a comma-delimited list of portlet modes. There may be zero or more of these tags in a class.

Extended XDoclet Example

We used the preceding XDoclet portlet tags to build a sample generated portlet.xml file for a taxonomy portlet. Here is the JavaDoc comment that belongs at the top of the class:

```
/**
 * @portlet.portlet
 *    name="TaxonomyPortlet"
 *    description="Browse Organized Content"
 *    display-name="Taxonomy Portlet"
 *    expiration-cache="0"
 *
 * @portlet.portlet-info
 *    title="Taxonomy Portlet"
 *    keywords="Taxonomy,Lucene"
 *    short-title="Taxonomy"
 *
 * @portlet.portlet-init-param
 *    name="indexPath"
 *    value="/java/index"
 *
 * @portlet.portlet-init-param
```

```
 *    name="repository"
 *    value="engineering"
 *
 * @portlet.preference
 *    name="bookmark"
 *    value="/content/marketing"
 *
 * @portlet.preferences-validator
 *    class="com.portalbook.portlets.TaxonomyValidator"
 *
 * @portlet.security-role-ref
 *    role-link="admin"
 *    role-name="Administrator"
 *
 * @portlet.supports
 *    mime-type="text/html"
 *    modes="edit,help,view"
 *
 */
```

Here is the generated portlet.xml deployment descriptor from those JavaDoc XDoclet tags:

```
<?xml version="1.0" encoding="UTF-8"?>

<portlet-app version="1.0" xmlns:xsi="http://www.w3.org/2001/XMLSchema-instance"➥
 xsi:schemaLocation="http://java.sun.com/xml/ns/portlet/portlet-app_1_0.xsd ➥
http://java.sun.com/xml/ns/portlet/portlet-app_1_0.xsd" ➥
xmlns="http://java.sun.com/xml/ns/portlet">

    <portlet>
      <description>Browse Organized Content</description>
      <portlet-name>TaxonomyPortlet</portlet-name>
      <display-name>Taxonomy Portlet</display-name>
      <portlet-class>com.portalbook.xdoclet.SessionPortlet</portlet-class>

      <init-param>
        <name>indexPath</name>
        <value>/java/index</value>
      </init-param>
      <init-param>
        <name>repository</name>
        <value>engineering</value>
      </init-param>
```

```
    <expiration-cache>0</expiration-cache>
    <supports>
      <mime-type>text/html</mime-type>
      <portlet-mode>edit</portlet-mode>
      <portlet-mode>help</portlet-mode>
      <portlet-mode>view</portlet-mode>
    </supports>

    <portlet-info>
      <title>Taxonomy Portlet</title>
      <short-title>Taxonomy</short-title>
      <keywords>Taxonomy,Lucene</keywords>
    </portlet-info>

    <portlet-preferences>
      <preference>
        <name>bookmark</name>
        <value>/content/marketing</value>
      </preference>

      <preferences-validator>
        com.portalbook.portlets.TaxonomyValidator
      </preferences-validator>
    </portlet-preferences>
    <security-role-ref>
      <role-name>Administrator</role-name>
      <role-link>admin</role-link>
    </security-role-ref>
  </portlet>
   <!--
     To add custom portlet modes to the portlet.xml file, add a file to your
     XDoclet merge directory called custom-portlet-modes.xml that contains the
     <custom-portlet-mode></custom-portlet-mode> markup.
   -->
  <!--
     To add custom window states to the portlet.xml file, add a file to your
     XDoclet merge directory called portlet-custom-window-states.xml
     that contains the <custom-window-state></custom-window-state>
     markup.
  -->
```

```
    <!--
      To add user attributes to the portlet.xml file, add a file to your
      XDoclet merge directory called portlet-user-attributes.xml that contains the
      <user-attribute></user-attribute> markup.
    -->
    <!--
      To add security constraints to the portlet.xml file, add a file to your
      XDoclet merge directory called portlet-security.xml that contains the
      <security-constraint></security-constraint> markup.
    -->

</portlet-app>
```

Summary

Portlet application packaging is similar to web application packaging—both use web application archive (WAR) files and web.xml web application deployment descriptors. Portlet applications add the portlet.xml portlet application deployment descriptor and portlet classes.

XDoclet is a code-generation tool that generates the portlet application deployment descriptor from JavaDoc tags in the portlet source code. The <portletdoclet> XDoclet Ant task is straightforward, and the XDoclet tags in the portlet correspond to the elements in the deployment descriptor. The XDoclet portlet module also supports portlet application-wide deployment descriptor information: custom portlet modes, custom window states, user attributes, and security role references.

CHAPTER 7

Portal and Portlet Configuration

The portlet API defines several interfaces for working with preferences and settings for the portal, the portlet application, and the current user of the portlet. Portlets access information about the portal that they are currently running in through the `PortalContext` object. The configuration settings for the application are available from the `PortletConfig` class. The portlet accesses and persists individual settings and preferences transparently with the `PortletPreferences` object.

In a typical portlet application, each user has preferences or configuration information that should be stored. You can use portlet preferences instead of creating a database table and code for each user. The portal may use a database or another form of storage to store the preferences, but the portlet does not need to know the details. Portlets that use proprietary portal features will have to determine whether the portal supports them with the portal context. You can use the `PortletConfig` class to determine any deployment-specific data for the application. Another information source is the `PortletContext` class, which we covered in Chapter 4. This class provides context-wide initialization parameters.

In this chapter, we are going to demonstrate how to use the portal context and portlet configuration and preferences to access configuration information from a portlet.

Using the PortalContext to Retrieve Information About the Portal

You retrieve information about the portal with the `PortalContext` object. In the current version of the portlet API, all of the portal information is read-only, so it is not possible to create nonproprietary administrative or management portlets just yet. Vendors could provide their own interfaces to set portal configuration data, or they could just bundle their own administrative portlets. Less-sophisticated portals will probably rely on administrators changing text or XML configuration files manually. The portal's internal configuration store is not directly accessible through the portlet API.

Portlets use the `PortalContext` object to determine which features beyond the portlet specification the portal supports. For instance, you may be able to develop a portlet that supports a custom mode for portlets if it is available, but otherwise defaults to making that content available through a link from the default VIEW mode.

All portlets have access to the PortalContext for the portal they are running in. The PortalContext object is made available to a portlet through the getPortalContext() method on the PortletRequest object:

```
public PortalContext getPortalContext()
```

Portlets access portal properties, supported modes, supported window states, and the name and version number of the portal software through the portal context.

Portal Properties

Each portal has a collection of portal properties, which contain information about the portal. Each portal vendor decides which portal properties to implement. Developers should not confuse portal properties with request properties. Each property is a name/value pair of String objects. The portal provides an Enumeration of all available property names:

```
public Enumeration getPropertyNames()
```

The portlet retrieves the value for a property using the getProperty() method:

```
public String getProperty(String name)
```

The getProperty() method returns null if there is no property with that name, and it throws an IllegalArgumentException if the name argument passed in is null.

Here is an example that will display all of the available portal properties in a portlet. The portlet API does not provide a way to let you modify these properties yet, so this portlet would only be useful for diagnostics:

```
package com.portalbook.portlets;

import java.io.IOException;
import java.io.Writer;
import java.util.Enumeration;

import javax.portlet.GenericPortlet;
import javax.portlet.PortalContext;
import javax.portlet.PortletException;
import javax.portlet.RenderRequest;
import javax.portlet.RenderResponse;

public class PortletConfigPortlet extends GenericPortlet
{
```

```
    protected void doView(RenderRequest request, RenderResponse response)
        throws PortletException, IOException
    {
        response.setContentType("text/html");

        Writer writer = response.getWriter();

        writer.write("<H2>Available Portal Properties</H2>");

        //get the Portal Context
        PortalContext portalContext = request.getPortalContext();

        //get the available portlet propertyNames
        Enumeration availablePropNames = portalContext.getPropertyNames();

        //check to see if there are more than zero property names
        if (!availablePropNames.hasMoreElements())
        {
            writer.write("There are no portal properties defined.<BR>");
        }

        //iterate through the property names, and output them
        while (availablePropNames.hasMoreElements())
        {
            String name = (String) availablePropNames.nextElement();
            if (name != null)
            {
                String value = portalContext.getProperty(name);
                if (value != null)
                {
                    writer.write(
                        "The value of property " + name +
                            " is " + value + "<BR>");
                }
                else
                {
                    writer.write(
                        "There is not a property value defined for " +
                            name + "<BR>");
                }
            }
        }
    }
}
```

Window States

Each portal vendor could support additional window states beyond the standard three (maximized, minimized, normal) defined by the portlet API.

Your portlets check the portal's defined window states through the `PortalContext` object by using the `getSupportedWindowStates()` method. This method will return an `Enumeration` of `WindowState` objects. If your portlet is going to support a proprietary window state, check to see if the portal supports the window state with this method. If possible, supply another way to access the functionality for portability.

```
public Enumeration getSupportedWindowStates()
```

For more on window states with portlets, see Chapter 4.

Portlet Modes

As with window states, portal vendors could have proprietary portlet modes that go beyond the three standard portlet modes from the portlet API (EDIT, HELP, VIEW).

A portlet also checks for supported portlet modes using the `getSupportedPortletModes()` method on the `PortalContext` object. This method returns an `Enumeration` of `PortletMode` objects, one for each supported portlet mode. As you would with window states, check this method for the supported portlet modes of the portal vendor if you are going to use a non-standard portlet mode:

```
public Enumeration getSupportedPortletModes()
```

If a portal supports a proprietary mode that corresponds to one of the functions of your portlet, add support for this portlet mode in the `render()` method of your base portlet. To support portals that do not have this mode, you can add a navigation link to the appropriate screens of your portlet that will provide your users with the same functionality but in the VIEW portlet mode. You could remove this link inside portals that support a graphical user interface (GUI) mechanism for switching to this portlet mode.

For more on portlet modes, see Chapter 4.

Portal Information

Portlets obtain the portal's vendor name and version number of the software from the `getPortalInfo()` method on the `PortalConfig` object:

```
public String getPortalInfo()
```

The portal information will be similar to this: Jetspeed/2.0. The name of the portal server software and the version number are required. The portal may include optional information after the server name and version number, and any optional portal information will be enclosed in parentheses.

The following example portlet will display the portal's information to the user in the VIEW portlet mode:

```
package com.portalbook.portlets;

import java.io.IOException;
import java.io.Writer;

import javax.portlet.GenericPortlet;
import javax.portlet.PortalContext;
import javax.portlet.PortletException;
import javax.portlet.RenderRequest;
import javax.portlet.RenderResponse;

public class PortalInfoPortlet extends GenericPortlet
{
    protected void doView(RenderRequest request, RenderResponse response)
        throws PortletException, IOException
    {
        response.setContentType("text/html");

        Writer writer = response.getWriter();

        writer.write("<H2>Portal Information</H2>");

        //get the Portal Context
        PortalContext portalContext = request.getPortalContext();

        //get the available portal information
        String portalInfo = portalContext.getPortalInfo();

        writer.write("The portal this portlet is running under is: ");
        writer.write(portalInfo);

    }
}
```

Using the PortletConfig Object

The portlet uses the `PortletConfig` object to access configuration information from the portlet.xml deployment descriptor. Your portlets should retrieve any information they need during the initialization stage in the portlet life cycle through the `init()` method on the `Portlet` interface. The `init()` method for a portlet takes a `PortletConfig` object as its argument:

```
public void init(PortletConfig portletConfig) throws PortletException
```

Portlets that extend `GenericPortlet` will implement the `PortletConfig` interface, which allows the portlet to access its configuration data directly. The `GenericPortlet` keeps the `PortletConfig` object it is passed by the portlet container; this `PortletConfig` object is accessible through the `getPortletConfig()` method on `GenericPortlet`:

```
public PortletConfig getPortletConfig()
```

It is unlikely that you will be using this method much, however, since the `GenericPortlet` implements the `PortletConfig` interface by calling out to the corresponding methods on its configuration object.

The portlet configuration consists of initialization parameters and portlet information, which could either be stored directly in the portlet.xml deployment descriptor or in a specified resource bundle.

The portlet's context is also accessed through the `getPortletContext()` method on the `PortletConfig` object. You use the portlet context to access resources, logging, and context attributes:

```
public PortletContext getPortletContext()
```

Because we covered the portlet context in Chapter 4, we are not going to cover the same material in this chapter. Some functionality on the portlet context, such as context attributes and the portlet API version, is relevant to portlet configuration. For instance, the `getServerInfo()` method on the `PortletContext` interface returns the portlet container's name and version number. You could use this in case some portlet containers are released with bugs that need workarounds.

Initialization Parameters

Initialization parameters specify configuration data for the portlet. You use them to provide default values for file paths, connection data, or other deployment-specific details. One point to note is that these are initialization parameters for all of the users of the portlet. User-specific configuration should be done with portlet preferences, which we discuss at the end of this chapter.

The initialization parameters are stored in the portlet.xml deployment descriptor. Each portlet could have zero or more initialization parameters. Each parameter consists of a name, a value, and an optional description. String objects represent both the name and the value.

Each `<init-param>` element in the portlet deployment descriptor represents one initialization parameter. The `<init-param>` elements are children of the `<portlet>` element. The initialization parameters section of a portlet deployment descriptor follows:

```
<portlet-app>
  <portlet>
    ...
    <init-param>
      <name>connectionPort</name>
      <value>9001</value>
    </init-param>
    <init-param>
      <name>connectionServer</name>
      <value>127.0.0.1</value>
    </init-param>
    ...
  </portlet>
</portlet-app>
```

A portlet accesses its initialization parameters through the `PortletConfig` object. The `getInitParameter(String name)` method takes the name of the initialization parameter as its argument, and returns the value of the initialization parameter as a `String` object. If the parameter does not exist in the deployment descriptor, the method will return a null value. If the name passed in as an argument is null, the method will throw an `IllegalArgumentException`.

```
public String getInitParameter(String name)
```

Your portlets should be aware of the names of the initialization parameters that they expect, but portlets can also retrieve the names of all of their initialization parameters. The `getInitParameterNames()` method on the `PortletConfig` object returns an `Enumeration` object that contains string values for each of the names of the initialization parameters. If no initialization parameters are defined, the `Enumeration` will be empty.

```
public Enumeration getInitParameterNames()
```

Getting the Resource Bundle of Portlet Metadata

Each portlet has a set of metadata associated with it to provide the title of the portlet, a shorter title for truncated displays, and keywords to describe the portlet in an administration tool. You will probably not need to get the resource bundle directly in your portlets—this information is most useful for the portal itself when it displays the portal in the aggregated page or when it presents a catalog of portlets for the user to choose from.

Either the metadata is specified directly in the deployment descriptor, or it could be specified in a resource bundle. There could be more than one resource bundle, and the portlet container will load the appropriate one based on the specified locale. If you need to support a multiple-language deployment, use resource bundles. The portlet container uses the standard rules for finding a resource bundle based on locale.

The `<portlet-info>` XML element is used to hold metadata defined in the portlet.xml deployment descriptor. Each `<portlet>` element may have one or none `<portlet-info>` elements as children. The `<portlet-info>` element has three children: `<title>`, `<short-title>`, and `<keywords>`. Each of these three elements should contain the text for the value of the metadata. Here is an example excerpt of a portlet.xml deployment descriptor with the `<portlet-info>` element:

```
<portlet-app>
  <portlet>
    ...
    <portlet-info>
      <title>Patent Classification Browser</title>
      <short-title>Classification</short-title>
      <keywords>Taxonomy,Legal,Patents</keywords>
    </portlet-info>
    ...
  </portlet>
</portlet-app>
```

Instead of specifying the metadata in the portlet.xml deployment descriptor, it is possible to create a resource bundle to store the information. This works well for internationalization. The `<resource-bundle>` element in the portlet.xml deployment descriptor should contain the name of the resource bundle, for example:

```
<resource-bundle>com.portalbook.portlets.PatentPortlet</resource-bundle>
```

The portlet accesses a resource bundle from the `getResourceBundle(Locale locale)` method on the `PortletConfig` interface. For the portlet's purposes, it does not matter whether the information was specified in the portlet deployment descriptor or the resource bundle. If the information is not found in the specified resource bundle, the portal container will use the values defined in the portlet deployment descriptor. If there is no resource bundle, the portlet container will create one from the inline portlet information values.

```
public java.util.ResourceBundle getResourceBundle(java.util.Locale locale)
```

There are three standard pieces of metadata in the first version of the portlet specification: title, short title, and keywords. Expect more to be added in the future as the specification evolves. The resource bundle keys and a description are listed here:

- **javax.portlet.title:** The title to be displayed in the portlet's title bar and other places in the portal GUI.
- **javax.portlet.short-title:** This is a shorter version of the title for use on truncated displays.
- **javax.portlet.keywords:** The keywords are a comma-separated list of words or phrases that describe the portlet. The keywords can be used in a portlet catalog so the user can find the appropriate portlet.

Here is an example showing the use of the resource bundle from a portlet:

```
package com.portalbook.portlets;

import java.io.IOException;
import java.io.Writer;
import java.util.Locale;
import java.util.ResourceBundle;

import javax.portlet.GenericPortlet;
import javax.portlet.PortletException;
import javax.portlet.RenderRequest;
import javax.portlet.RenderResponse;

public class ResourceBundlePortlet extends GenericPortlet
{
    protected void doView(RenderRequest request, RenderResponse response)
        throws PortletException, IOException
    {
        response.setContentType("text/html");

        Writer writer = response.getWriter();

        writer.write("<H2>Resource Bundle Values</H2>");
```

```
            //get the current Locale
            Locale locale = request.getLocale();

            //get the Resource Bundle
            ResourceBundle rb = getResourceBundle(locale);

            //get the title
            String title = rb.getString("javax.portlet.title");

            //get the short title
            String shortTitle = rb.getString("javax.portlet.short-title");

            //get the keywords
            String keywords = rb.getString("javax.portlet.keywords");

            //Output the title, short title, and keywords
            writer.write("Title: " + title + "<P>");
            writer.write("Short title: " + shortTitle + "<P>");
            writer.write("Keywords: " + keywords + "<P>");
        }
    }
```

The portlet.xml deployment descriptor for the resource bundle test portlet should be as follows:

```
<portlet-app xmlns="http://java.sun.com/xml/ns/portlet/portlet-app_1_0.xsd"➥
 version="1.0" xmlns:xsi="http://www.w3.org/2001/XMLSchema-instance"➥
xsi:schemaLocation="http://java.sun.com/xml/ns/portlet/portlet-app_1_0.xsd➥
http://java.sun.com/xml/ns/portlet/portlet-app_1_0.xsd">
  <portlet>
    <description>Resource Bundle Test</description>
    <portlet-name>ResourceBundlePortlet</portlet-name>
    <display-name>Resource Bundle Test</display-name>
    <portlet-class>com.portalbook.portlets.ResourceBundlePortlet</portlet-class>
    <expiration-cache>-1</expiration-cache>
    <supports>
      <mime-type>text/html</mime-type>
      <portlet-mode>VIEW</portlet-mode>
    </supports>
    <supported-locale>en</supported-locale>
    <portlet-info>
      <title>Resource Bundle Test Portlet</title>
      <short-title>Bundle</short-title>
      <keywords>Resource Bundle, Test, Portal Book</keywords>
```

```
    </portlet-info>
  </portlet>
</portlet-app>
```

Portlet Name

The portlet name is defined in the portlet deployment descriptor, in the <portlet-name> element. The <portlet> element contains only one <portlet-name> element, and the relevant part of the portlet deployment descriptor would look like this:

```
<portlet-app>
  <portlet>
    <portlet-name>Online Payments Portlet</portlet-name>
    ...
  </portlet>
</portlet-app>
```

The portlet accesses its name information with the `getPortletName()` method on the `PortletConfig` object. This method returns the name of the portlet as a `String`:

```
public String getPortletName()
```

Most portals provide a GUI for modifying the elements of a portlet deployment descriptor for the portlets deployed on the portal server. Some also provide a portlet application assembly tool to help create the deployment descriptor. For configuration settings that are stored on a per-user basis, the portlet can use preferences for storage, as you'll see in the next section.

Using Portlet Preferences

Portlets can save the user's preferences to a persistent store that is managed by the portal or portlet container. Instead of storing the user's settings in a database or in text files, you use portal preferences for portable storage.

Portals may implement a shared preferences database between clustered portal servers, so portlets could access preferences for a user from any server in the cluster. In some portals, we can do this by sharing the preferences database.

The preferences a portlet uses may be described in the portlet.xml deployment descriptor, but it is not necessary. Portlets can set any preferences they choose, even if they are not defined in the deployment descriptor. The deployment descriptor is used to provide defaults for the preference values, as well as to mark a portlet preference as read-only. The portlet cannot change the value of a read-only preference in the normal portlet modes, although it is possible that a portal server could provide a custom mode that allows read-only preferences to be changed.

Retrieving Preferences

Preferences are name/value pairs. The names of the preferences are `String` objects, and the values of the preferences are stored as arrays of `String` objects. All of the methods for accessing portlet preferences are on the `PortletPreferences` interface. You can use the `getPreferences()` method to retrieve the user's `PortletPreferences` object from the `PortletRequest` object:

```
public PortletPreferences getPreferences()
```

The portlet uses the `PortletPreferences` object for the current user to get a list of the user's preferences, to obtain a value of a preference, or to make changes to the preferences. The portlet can only store a user's preferences during the portlet's action request handling, in the `processAction()` method of the portlet.

To retrieve the names of the available preferences, use the `getNames()` method, which returns an `Enumeration` of `String` objects to represent the preference names, or an empty `Enumeration` if there are no preferences:

```
public Enumeration getNames()
```

If you prefer to use a `Map` object to work with portal preferences, you retrieve a `Map` containing the user's preferences. The names are `String` objects, and the values are `String` array objects. To make changes to the portlet preferences, you cannot use this `Map` object; instead, operate directly on the `PortletPreferences` object:

```
public Map getMap()
```

The values of any preference as a `String` array are available with the `getValues()` method, which takes the name of the preference and an array of `String` objects as the default value as arguments. If no value is specified for the preference, the default is returned. If a default value is already specified at the portal server, either through the deployment descriptor or through the portal administration, that default is returned instead of the default value passed as an argument here:

```
public String[] getValues(String key, String[] def)
```

Even though the preferences are stored in `String` arrays, the portlet API defines a shortcut method to retrieve the first value for the preference as a `String` object. The way default values are handled is similar to the `getValues()` method discussed earlier. The default value for this method should be a `String` object, rather than an array of strings:

```
public String getValue(String key, String def)
```

When retrieving preferences using the `getValue()` and `getValues()` methods, be sure to pass in a non-null value for the key, or each method will throw an `IllegalArgumentException`.

Setting and Removing Preferences

Portlets can create new preferences for users, or modify preferences that are not marked read-only. Portlets can also remove a preference for a user or, if the preference has a default, return it to that initial default value.

Before modifying a preference, a portlet should check to see whether the preference is marked read-only and is nonmodifiable by the end user. The `isReadOnly()` method on the `PortletPreferences` object takes the name of the preference as an argument and returns true if the preference is read-only. The preference can be marked read-only either in the deployment descriptor or through another administration tool provided by the portal container. If the preference is not in the deployment descriptor and the preference is not marked read-only by the portal container, the `isReadOnly()` method will return false. The portlet can modify or create the portlet preference.

```
public boolean isReadOnly(String key)
```

Portlets may set preferences during an action request. There are two methods for setting preferences, one for `String` object values and the other for `String` array values. Both will throw a `ReadOnlyException` if the preference is marked read-only in the deployment descriptor. These methods also must have a name for the preference that is not null, or they will throw an `IllegalArgumentException`. They may also throw that exception if the length of the name or the value is longer than the portal container allows.

```
public void setValue(String key, String value)  throws ReadOnlyException
public void setValues(String key, String[] values) throws ReadOnlyException
```

The portlet API provides the `reset()` method for removing portlet preferences. If a default value is specified for that preference, the preference cannot be removed but can only be reset to the default value. If the value is read-only, it cannot be removed or reset, and the `reset(String key)` method will throw a `ReadOnlyException`:

```
public void reset(String key) throws ReadOnlyException
```

The changes to the preferences must be committed to the database or other storage with the `store()` method on the `PortletPreferences` object. The `store()` method validates the preferences using a `PreferencesValidator` object if one is defined in the deployment descriptor. We discuss preferences validation in the next section of this chapter. If the validator finds the preferences to be invalid, the `store()` method will throw a `ValidatorException`, and none of the preferences will be stored. If any of the preferences fail to be stored for any reason, none of the new preference changes will be saved. The `store()` method will also throw an `IOException` if there is a problem with the persistence mechanism on the portal container level.

```
public void store() throws IOException, ValidatorException
```

The `store()` method works only when called during the action request handling step of the portlet. If any portlet preferences are created, changed, removed, or reset without calling the `store()` method successfully, the changes to the preferences are discarded when the action request handling phase is over.

Preferences Example

The following example reads the preferences for the portlet, and then displays them to the user. The portlet allows the user to set preferences for two different preference keys. The new values will overwrite any existing preferences for this portlet.

```
package com.portalbook.portlets;

import java.io.IOException;
import java.io.Writer;
import java.util.Enumeration;

import javax.portlet.ActionRequest;
import javax.portlet.ActionResponse;
import javax.portlet.GenericPortlet;
import javax.portlet.PortletException;
import javax.portlet.PortletPreferences;
import javax.portlet.PortletURL;
import javax.portlet.RenderRequest;
import javax.portlet.RenderResponse;

public class PreferencesPortlet extends GenericPortlet
{
    protected void doView(RenderRequest request, RenderResponse response)
        throws PortletException, IOException
    {
        response.setContentType("text/html");

        Writer writer = response.getWriter();
```

```
    writer.write("<H2>Portlet Preferences</H2>");

    //get the user's preferences
    PortletPreferences prefs = request.getPreferences();

    //Write the preferences out
    writer.write("<P>The user's current preferences:");
    Enumeration names = prefs.getNames();

    if (!names.hasMoreElements())
    {
        writer.write("<P>There are no preferences defined for this portlet.");
    }

    while (names.hasMoreElements())
    {
        String name = (String) names.nextElement();
        String value = prefs.getValue(name, "defaultValue");
        writer.write("<P>Name: " + name);
        writer.write("<BR>Value:" + value);
    }

    //create a form so preferences can be created
    writer.write("<P><H2>Set Preferences</H2><P>");
    PortletURL url = response.createActionURL();
    writer.write("<FORM METHOD='POST' ACTION='" + url + "'>");
    writer.write(
        "Preference 1: <INPUT NAME='pref1' TYPE='text' SIZE='30'><P>");
    writer.write(
        "Preference 2: <INPUT NAME='pref2' TYPE='text' SIZE='30'><P>");
    writer.write("<INPUT TYPE='submit'>");
    writer.write("</FORM>");

}

public void processAction(ActionRequest request, ActionResponse response)
    throws PortletException, IOException
{
    //get the preference values from the request
    String pref1 = request.getParameter("pref1");
    String pref2 = request.getParameter("pref2");

    PortletPreferences prefs = request.getPreferences();
```

```
            //set the preferences
            prefs.setValue("pref1", pref1);
            prefs.setValue("pref2", pref2);

            //store the preferences
            prefs.store();
        }
    }
```

Defining Preferences in the Deployment Descriptor

Initial values may be set for preferences in the portlet deployment descriptor, and these portlet preferences may also be marked read-only in the descriptor. You do not need to define preferences in the deployment descriptor; any preference can be created programmatically. Here is a section of a portlet deployment descriptor that populates two preferences with values for all users and declares one of them to be read-only:

```
<portlet-preferences>
  <preference>
    <name>WelcomeScreen</name>
    <value>Beginner</value>
    <modifiable>0</modifiable>
  </preference>
  <preference>
    <name>PreferredDatabases</name>
    <value>AccountActivity</value>
    <value>CustomerReturns</value>
    <value>HumanResources</value>
  </preference>
</portlet-preferences>
```

The `WelcomeScreen` preference is read-only, and the `PreferredDatabases` preference is populated with several values. You will need to determine which settings should be portlet-wide configuration settings and which should be user-configurable. In this case, it is conceivable that we could implement an advanced welcome screen in the future, and then provide a way for users to switch themselves. We also present users with a set of preferred databases as a set of defaults that can be updated by each user.

Preferences Validation

The user's preferences can be validated when stored by the portlet container, if you create a preferences validator. The portlet container will validate the preferences any time the portlet stores preferences. Also, the portlet container will validate the portlet's preferences if the portal allows users to edit their portlet preferences outside of the portlet with a vendor-supplied administrative portlet or other tools.

If the validation fails, none of the preferences is stored. The `store()` method on the `PortletPreferences` object either saves all of the preferences or none of them. In addition to a `ValidationException`, the `store()` method throws an `IOException` if the portal cannot access its preferences store or an `IllegalStateException` if called during render request handling.

Each portlet may define a validator that implements the `PreferencesValidator` interface in the portlet preferences section of the portlet.xml deployment descriptor:

```
<portlet-preferences>
  <preference-validator>com.portalbook.portlets.PreferencesValidator
  </preference-validator>
</portlet-preferences>
```

The `PreferencesValidator` interface only contains one method: `validate()`.

```
public void validate(PortletPreferences preferences) throws ValidatorException
```

The `validate()` method should be implemented with your validation logic for each of the preferences your portlet needs to verify. If there are any errors with the saved preferences, the `validate()` method should throw a `ValidatorException`, which is a subclass of `PortletException`. The `validate()` method will also need to be thread safe. The portlet container will create only one instance of the validator class for each portlet defined in the deployment descriptor.

The `ValidatorException` class has three public constructors:

```
public ValidatorException (String text, Collection failedKeys)
public ValidatorException (String text, Throwable cause, Collection failedKeys)
public ValidatorException (Throwable cause, Collection failedKeys)
```

All of the constructors take a `Collection` of failed keys as an argument. The `failedKeys` argument can contain all of the names of the preferences that failed validation or just the first key, or it can be null. It is your decision as the portlet author to decide what makes the most sense with your portlet application.

The portlet can check the `ValidatorException` that is thrown by the `store()` method on an instance of `PortletPreferences` for failed keys:

```
public void store() throws IOException, ValidatorException
```

The `getFailedKeys()` method on the `ValidatorException` class returns an `Enumeration` of the failed keys from the validation. As we said earlier, it is up to you to decide how to handle the failed keys behavior.

```
public Enumeration getFailedKeys()
```

PreferencesValidation Example

Now let's add validation to our preferences portlet. The `PreferencesValidatorPortlet` class demonstrates the use of preferences with a preferences validator. Our validation logic is very simple: the validator forces the stored values to have a length of at least four characters. Using regular expressions or a list of allowable values from a database would be easy to add, because all you would need to do is write a method for each preference name that validates the preference individually. Your method could then collect all of the keys that failed validation, and return them in the `ValidationException` as the `failedKeys` collection.

Let's also add a `try...catch` block around our call to the `store()` method on the `PortletPreferences` object in the portlet's `processAction()` method. If we catch a validation error, we add the validation error message and the failed keys to the session. If the `store()` method is successful, we remove the validation error and failed keys from the session. This way, our `render()` method will continue to show the validation errors until they are fixed.

In our `render()` method, we display the validator error message if we have one, and we also display a list of failed keys. We remind the user that none of the preferences was stored, as you can see when the code displays the previous preferences.

```
package com.portalbook.portlets;

import java.io.IOException;
import java.io.Writer;
import java.util.Enumeration;

import javax.portlet.ActionRequest;
import javax.portlet.ActionResponse;
import javax.portlet.GenericPortlet;
import javax.portlet.PortletException;
import javax.portlet.PortletPreferences;
import javax.portlet.PortletSession;
import javax.portlet.PortletURL;
import javax.portlet.RenderRequest;
import javax.portlet.RenderResponse;
import javax.portlet.ValidatorException;
```

```
public class PreferencesValidationPortlet extends GenericPortlet
{
    String VALIDATOR_ERROR = "VALIDATOR_ERROR";
    String FAILED_KEYS = "FAILED_KEYS";

    protected void doView(RenderRequest request, RenderResponse response)
        throws PortletException, IOException
    {
        PortletSession session = request.getPortletSession();

        response.setContentType("text/html");

        Writer writer = response.getWriter();

        writer.write("<H2>Portlet Preferences</H2>");

        //get the user's preferences
        PortletPreferences prefs = request.getPreferences();

        //Write the preferences out
        writer.write("<P>The user's current preferences:");
        Enumeration names = prefs.getNames();

        if (!names.hasMoreElements())
        {
            writer.write("<P>There are no preferences defined for this portlet.");
        }

        while (names.hasMoreElements())
        {
            String name = (String) names.nextElement();
            String value = prefs.getValue(name, "defaultValue");
            writer.write("<P>Name: " + name);
            writer.write("<BR>Value:" + value);
        }

        //check for portlet preferences validation
        String errMsg = (String) session.getAttribute(VALIDATOR_ERROR);
        if (errMsg != null)
        {
            writer.write("<BR>Failed to store any preferences.");
            writer.write("<BR><B>Error: </B>" + errMsg);
            Enumeration failedKeys =
                (Enumeration) session.getAttribute(FAILED_KEYS);
```

```
            while (failedKeys.hasMoreElements())
            {
                String failedKey = (String) failedKeys.nextElement();
                writer.write("<BR>Error with preference: " + failedKey);
            }
        }

        //create a form so preferences can be created
        writer.write("<P><H2>Set Preferences</H2><P>");
        PortletURL url = response.createActionURL();
        writer.write("<FORM METHOD='POST' ACTION='" + url + "'>");
        writer.write(
            "Preference 1: <INPUT NAME='pref1' TYPE='text' SIZE='30'><P>");
        writer.write(
            "Preference 2: <INPUT NAME='pref2' TYPE='text' SIZE='30'><P>");
        writer.write("<INPUT TYPE='submit'>");
        writer.write("</FORM>");

    }

    public void processAction(ActionRequest request, ActionResponse response)
        throws PortletException, IOException
    {
        //get the preference values from the request
        String pref1 = request.getParameter("pref1");
        String pref2 = request.getParameter("pref2");

        PortletPreferences prefs = request.getPreferences();
        PortletSession session = request.getPortletSession();

        //set the preferences
        prefs.setValue("pref1", pref1);
        prefs.setValue("pref2", pref2);

        //store the preferences
        try
        {
            prefs.store();

            //if the store is successful, we can remove any validator
            //error messages in the session

            if (session.getAttribute(VALIDATOR_ERROR) != null)
            {
                session.removeAttribute(VALIDATOR_ERROR);
```

```
                session.removeAttribute(FAILED_KEYS);
            }
        }
        catch (ValidatorException ve)
        {

            session.setAttribute(VALIDATOR_ERROR, ve.getMessage());
            session.setAttribute(FAILED_KEYS, ve.getFailedKeys());
        }
    }
}
```

To use a preferences validator, we had to create a class that implemented the `PreferencesValidator` interface, and then add a reference to the validator to the portlet deployment descriptor.

The `ExamplePreferencesValidator` class simply checks each preference value to see if the length is four or more characters, in which case it passes. If the preference value fails validation, the validator adds the preference name to its collection of failed keys, and then throws a `ValidatorException` when it is done validating all of the preference values. We could have thrown a `ValidatorException` on the first failed preference if we wanted.

```
package com.portalbook.portlets;

import java.util.*;

import javax.portlet.PortletPreferences;
import javax.portlet.PreferencesValidator;
import javax.portlet.ValidatorException;

public class ExamplePreferencesValidator implements PreferencesValidator
{
    public void validate(PortletPreferences prefs) throws ValidatorException
    {
        LinkedList failedKeys = new LinkedList();
        Enumeration names = prefs.getNames();
        while (names.hasMoreElements())
        {
            String name = (String) names.nextElement();
            String value = prefs.getValue(name, "");
            if (value.length() < 4)
            {
                failedKeys.add(name);
            }
        }
```

```
            if (failedKeys.size() > 0)
            {
                String errMsg =
                    "Preference values must be at least 4 characters long";
                throw new ValidatorException(errMsg, failedKeys);
            }

        }
    }
```

Here is the portlet.xml deployment descriptor, with the validator reference:

```
<?xml version="1.0" encoding="UTF-8"?>
<portlet-app xmlns="http://java.sun.com/xml/ns/portlet/portlet-app_1_0.xsd"➥
version="1.0" xmlns:xsi="http://www.w3.org/2001/XMLSchema-instance"➥
xsi:schemaLocation="http://java.sun.com/xml/ns/portlet/portlet-app_1_0.xsd➥
http://java.sun.com/xml/ns/portlet/portlet-app_1_0.xsd">
    <portlet>
        <description>Preferences Validation Portlet</description>

        <portlet-name>PreferencesValidationPortlet</portlet-name>

        <display-name>Preferences Validation Portlet</display-name>

        <portlet-class>com.portalbook.portlets.PreferencesValidationPortlet➥
        </portlet-class>

        <expiration-cache>0</expiration-cache>

        <supports>
            <mime-type>text/html</mime-type>
            <portlet-mode>VIEW</portlet-mode>
        </supports>

        <supported-locale>en</supported-locale>

        <portlet-info>
            <title>Preferences Validation Portlet</title>
            <short-title>Validation</short-title>
            <keywords>Preferences,Validation</keywords>
        </portlet-info>
```

```
        <portlet-preferences>
            <preferences-validator>➥
                com.portalbook.portlets.ExamplePreferencesValidator➥
            </preferences-validator>
        </portlet-preferences>
    </portlet>
</portlet-app>
```

Figure 7-1 shows an example of the validation in action. Figure 7-2 shows our example portlet with some invalid input.

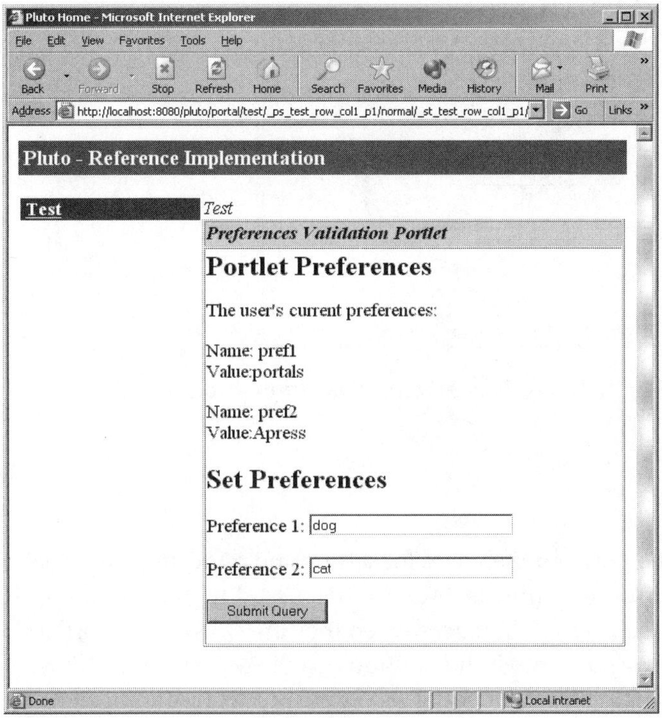

Figure 7-1. Our Preferences Validator Portlet with invalid input and existing values

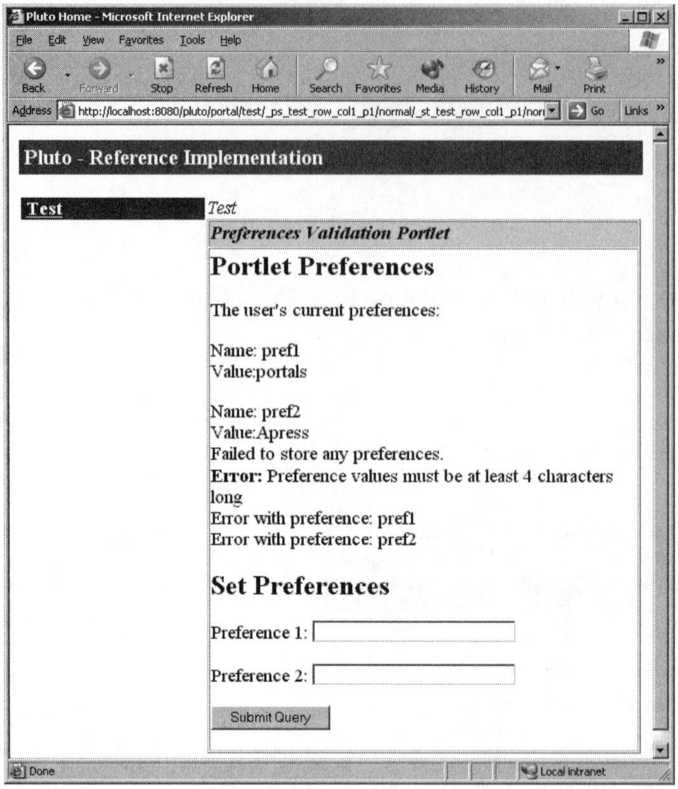

Figure 7-2. Our Preferences Validator Portlet with validation errors

Summary

In this chapter, we covered portlet preferences for setting and retrieving individual user configuration settings for a portlet. We also discussed the preferences validator for verifying each user's preferences when they are stored. The portlet's configuration can be accessed through the methods on the `GenericPortlet` base class if necessary. Information about the portal server the portlet is running in can be retrieved through the `PortalContext` class. This information includes available window states, portlet modes, and portal properties.

CHAPTER 8

Security and Single Sign-On

SECURITY AND SINGLE Sign-On (SSO) are not unique to portlets, but when considering their implementation you must take into account some special advantages, disadvantages, and responsibilities.

A portlet has some security advantages over a conventional application. You do not have to concern yourself with obtaining a login from the user, for example—this is the responsibility of the container.

You do still have some responsibilities; your portlet must manage access to its resources. For example, a corporate address book should probably be accessible only to employees of the company, whereas a private address book should in general be accessible by only one person.

A portlet may obtain information from external resources, so you also need to be aware of the options for passing security information around—possibly over the network.

While the developer's natural inclination is to "Keep It Simple, Stupid" (KISS), it is no longer a safe assumption (if it ever was) that the network is secure by default. Avoiding security vulnerabilities adds a regrettable but necessary level of complexity to the design of any portlet acting as the gateway to sensitive information.

This chapter discusses the standards, protocols, and APIs that are required to implement secure portlets. The security mechanisms specified in the portlet API are the most basic level of portlet security. We discuss SSO strategies for portals, including authentication with Java Authentication and Authorization Services (JAAS). We also demonstrate how to use the Java Generic Security Services Application Program Interface (GSS-API) with Kerberos.

Before we embark on our analysis, let's briefly consider a situation where all of these tools might be required for a truly integrated solution. In the example shown in Figure 8-1, we have users connecting to (and authenticating with) a portal using their normal browser security. This contains a portlet e-mail application, which uses the user's credentials to log into and present a web mail application. This in turn must access a legacy e-mail database, presenting the user's credentials to do so.

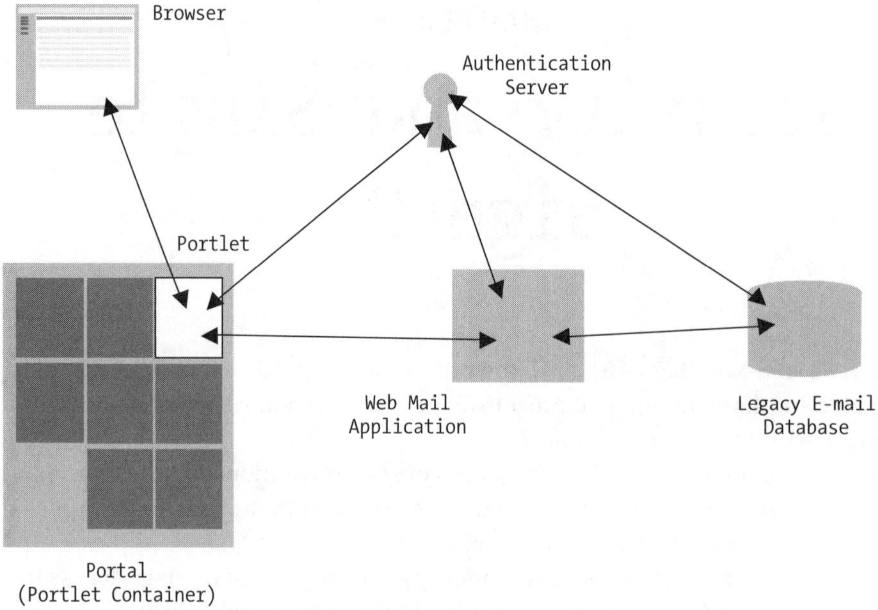

Figure 8-1. Portlet security interactions

E-mail is a very familiar environment for almost all users, and the need for the protection of private messages is obvious. We suggest that you consider this example as you encounter the security technologies available to you when building a portlet.

Portlet Security

Generally, a portlet passively receives user authentication and authorization information from the container. It is often not necessary for your portlet to directly establish the identity of the user. As a result, when designing a simple secured portlet to be entirely portable, you need only concern yourself with the way that your portlet interacts with its security environment.

This holds true only when a portal has its own access control for portlets, either on a per-user or per-group basis. Some portals allow a user to add any installed portlet to the user's portal page. Most portal deployments require some kind of security or access control for administrative portlets. This can be accomplished by allowing only certain users or sets of users to show a portlet on their page, or by having the portlet code check the user's information to determine what they are allowed to view.

Similarities to Servlet Security

Since a portlet is generally contained within a servlet, it should come as no great surprise to discover that a portlet behaves quite like a servlet in its provision of security mechanisms.

The `HttpServletRequest` object provided with requests to a servlet is required to offer the following four methods:

```
public String getAuthType()
public String getRemoteUser()
public boolean isUserInRole(String role)
public Principal getUserPrincipal()
```

The information provided by these four methods is in turn made available directly to a portlet via the `PortletRequest` object. The same four methods are available from the request object during the action handling and during render handling.

Authentication Types

Portlets generally permit four types of authentication. Which of these has been used can be determined by calling `getAuthType()`. This method allows a portlet to determine the quality of the secure relationship and as a result to restrict the set of information that it will permit the user to access.

In Basic authentication, the username and password are obtained from the web client (browser), which manages the mechanism of obtaining them from the user and submitting them to the server. The web browser sends the details as plaintext, so they are vulnerable to "man-in-the-middle" attacks.

> **NOTE** *Man-in-the-middle attacks are a form of security attack where someone sets up a proxy server between an unknowing client and an unknowing server. The proxy server listens to requests from the user and records them. The requests are passed to the server, and the server returns a response to the proxy server. The proxy server also logs the response, and then passes the response back to the client. The "man in the middle" now has all of the user's requests and responses. If the browser has sent any sensitive information as unencrypted text, it is now compromised. The attacker may also alter the user's requests and responses.*

Client Certificate authentication requires the server and, optionally, the client to authenticate each another with public key certificates. The exchange is carried out over Secure Sockets Layer (SSL) to guarantee that it cannot be read if it is intercepted. Client Certificate authentication is managed by the web client.

Digest authentication is about halfway between Basic and Client Certificate authentication. The username and password are not sent in plaintext; instead they are sent as a message digest, which prevents the password from being retrieved. However, as with basic authentication, the identity of the server is not verified and the exchange is carried out over an unsecured connection so there is still some degree of vulnerability.

> **NOTE** *A message digest is an arbitrarily short representation of a message. A "hash function" is applied to the original message to produce this short representation. A trivial example of a hash would be one that counted the number of words in the message.*
>
> *A more typical example is the MD5 algorithm, which will reduce a message of any length to 16 representative bytes. The chances of any two messages producing the same digest are astronomically small, and it is effectively impossible to reverse-engineer the original message from its MD5 hash.*
>
> *This makes the MD5 hash perfect for confirming a password over a network. The remote server will send the client a random "salt" text. This is added by the client to the password, and the digest is computed. The client sends the digest to the server, which will compute the digest independently and compare it with the client's digest. If they match, both machines must know the password, but an eavesdropper cannot reproduce the digest independently (without knowing the password).*
>
> *The use of a salt prevents a third party from simply retransmitting the digest, since it will be different for every salt value.*

Form-based authentication is one of the most commonly used forms of authentication, largely because it can be made secure and offers cosmetic advantages over web client–managed mechanisms. The username and password are submitted as plaintext in a form request. If the POST mechanism is used and the connection is over HTTPS (SSL) rather than HTTP, this cannot easily be intercepted. The `PortletRequest` class provides the constants that are used to identify each authentication type.

It is also possible that no authentication will have been carried out, in which case `getAuthType()` will return null.

Identifying the User

The `getRemoteUser()` method provides the username of the current user of the portal. The username is generally not considered to be a sensitive piece of information; on the contrary, it is normal to use the username extensively as an identifier of objects and in tables. However, you should bear in mind that the username may not be a simple direct representation of the user's name. It may, for example, include the details of the authentication domain that this user is associated with. While you can reasonably expect the username in this form to be unique, confusion can arise. Consider for example:

```
dave@example.com
dave@paperstack.com
```

In these two cases, what one colloquially thinks of as the username is "dave", but in fact two distinct users are identified—one associated with the example.com domain; the other with paperstack.com.

We will not belabor the point, but it is wise to retain the full string returned by `getRemoteUser()` to avoid ambiguities.

Obtaining a Principal

The principal represents a user (or service, or server) whose identity has been confirmed by the portal. It is distinct from a username, because there is no principal for an unauthenticated user. Note that in practice `getRemoteUser()` is likely to return null for unauthenticated users anyway, because the authentication process is often the mechanism by which the user is established.

The `getUserPrincipal()` method therefore returns the `Principal` object associated with the current logged-in user, or null if the user has not been logged in.

You may not immediately see the need for a separate object to represent this—surely one could use a combination of the username and an `isAuthenticated()` method? However, the principal serves an important purpose when you wish to indicate to another service that our service is entitled to act on behalf of the user in question.

> **NOTE** *This sort of situation arises often with portals, because they can aggregate quite distinct systems into a common interface. Take as an example an investment bank's systems. There may be distinct systems for bond and equities trading, and these systems in turn talk to a set of back-end databases. When using a portal to unify the systems, users must first present their credentials to the portal, which in turn establishes a* `Principal`*, which is passed to the bond system and the equities system. These in turn use it to gain access to the back-end databases. By using the end user's credentials all the way through the system, a secure audit trail can be maintained, albeit with a performance penalty.*

The principal is an instance of the `java.security.Principal` interface. You can call the `getName()` method on it, and in general this will return the same string that you would retrieve from a call to `getRemoteUser()`, although it is not required. In the example given in the previous section, the string returned might be "dave@example.com" or just "dave".

Using Roles

Portlet roles work in exactly the same way as servlet roles. Roles are represented by strings, and any given user can be assigned to a specific role, or a group of roles.

The idea is that a role name should represent the rights and duties of a user rather than being the privileges assigned. So for instance, Manager is a good name for a role, whereas ListSalaries is not.

To determine if a user falls within a given role, call the `isUserInRole()` method and pass in the name of the role. The method will return `true` or `false` appropriately. If the current user is null (i.e., not logged in), this method will always return `false`.

Since the mappings of the native security system may not correspond naturally to those of the portlet application (or indeed to those of a servlet application), a facility is provided to allow a security role to be mapped to an additional name, in effect allowing the developer or deployer to assign aliases to roles.

As is normal with servlets, an entry can be placed in the portlet application's web.xml deployment descriptor file to specify a `<security-role-ref>` element for an existing role name. The format is

```
<security-role-ref>
   <role-name>ForumModerator</role-name>
   <role-link>Administrator</role-link>
</security-role-ref>
```

In this example, the native role of Administrator is mapped to the application role of ForumModerator.

Working with portlets you may also specify a mapping in the same form within the `<portlet>` element of the portlet.xml file.

When `isUserInRole()` is called, the system checks each file in turn, so if no suitable role name is listed in the portlet.xml, the system checks the web.xml. If that in turn contains no suitable role name entries, the native security system will be tested for the appropriate principal's role memberships.

Single Sign-On Strategies

SSO is essentially a technical solution to a usability problem. Users are not good at remembering several different passwords, and they dislike being made to enter a password numerous times.

For example, the authors have worked for various companies where this is a problem. Dave used to work for a company where there was a separate login to the workstation, to the e-mail system, to the timekeeping system, to the database, and to each of the six different systems that he was developing interfaces for.

The situation is common on the Internet. Your bank, auction site, web mail account, and so on are likely to have distinct usernames and passwords. Some services have sprung up to try to unify logins between sites. Microsoft Passport and the Liberty Alliance are competing standards in this domain; they are SSO solutions at the interorganizational level.

When building an SSO solution for services accessed via portlets, you have slightly different considerations, and indeed, SSO does not refer to a single technology, or even a single strategy for solving the problem. There are distinct approaches, which we will now discuss in the context of portlets.

Using True SSO

True SSO is the term we will adopt for the "perfect" solution. In this scenario, your user enters a username and password only once—when logging in to the portal.

Problems with this approach arise when legacy systems are involved. Most of our examples will discuss using Kerberos to manage authentication between the portals and external services, but this is a relatively new protocol. Older systems can be difficult or expensive to update to accommodate Kerberos or another standard SSO technology.

> **CAUTION** *Our examples use the Kerberos v5 software from MIT, as this is the reference implementation of the standard. The example code would require changes to work with Microsoft Active Directory.*

Using Proxy SSO

Proxy SSO, as the name suggests, uses a proxy system to carry out sign-ons for us. Users log into the portal with their username and password, and this in turn unlocks a store of usernames and passwords for external systems.

The advantage of this system is that, as presented, it offers the same user experience as True SSO. However, it is something of a compromise and this can cause administrative problems.

The approach necessitates management of the passwords for the systems. Different legacy systems may require password changes at different times. Users will still have to remember (or, dangerously, write down) the individual passwords so that they can change them when they expire, or alternatively the passwords will need to be set not to expire at all, which is in itself a security risk. For seamless integration, the proxy SSO server would need to manage the life cycle for each username and password pair. If the proxy SSO server had rules for each legacy system that dictated the password expiration, the range of valid password values, and the ability to change passwords, this could all be managed for the user. The integration development costs for a project like this would be very high.

Because the passwords must be retrieved in order to present them to the legacy systems, they must be stored by the proxy SSO solution in an encrypted form that decrypts to plaintext. This is generally considered undesirable. More desirable would be a solution that stores a message digest or hash of the password, so the original password cannot be reconstructed.

Using a Common Registry

The common registry approach is something of a compromise between the true and proxy SSO solutions. While it does not require full implementation of a GSS-API–compliant system, it does require some changes to any legacy systems involved.

The idea is that a central system is used to carry out all authentication, but that users are prompted for usernames and passwords each time they access a different system. However, subsequent access to the same systems within the login session does not require reauthentication.

Perhaps the term "Single" Sign-On is a misnomer here, since of course the user is making multiple login efforts, but because a single username and password combination is required, far less is required of the user. In practice this is often a satisfactory solution, and it has the advantage that it is compatible with a migration to the True SSO solution as the legacy systems are retired.

In a portlet environment, the attraction of this approach is less obvious, since it is possible that users would be initially presented with a great number of portlets on their home page, each and every one of which could initially demand a username and password before they can be used!

Authenticating with JAAS

We have encountered a small part of the Java Authentication and Authorization Services (JAAS) in our coverage of the `Principal` object returned by the `getUserPrincipal()` method of the `PortletRequest` object.

The portlet generally obtains a principal in this manner, so you can get by without knowing how to do this manually. However, it is enlightening to see the mechanism used in practice, and in some SSO scenarios—especially the proxy scenario—it can be necessary.

At the point that you conduct a login, some details of the login mechanism must be known. You cannot generally log in to a Unix system using NTLM (Microsoft) authentication, and most authentication systems provide no discovery mechanism to determine the protocol in use.

JAAS is therefore based on an API called Pluggable Authentication Modules (PAM), which allows you to try a login on a system or systems using a variety of different protocols. As a result, you can conduct a JAAS login, at the end of which one or more systems may have vouched for your credentials.

The protocols to be used are generally specified using a configuration file. This can contain individual or multiple entries.

```
// Kerberos.config
ClientAuthentication
{
   com.sun.security.auth.module.Krb5LoginModule required;
};
ServerAuthentication
{
   com.sun.security.auth.module.Krb5LoginModule required storeKey=true;
};
```

Here we have specified two distinct configurations. One is for our client, and the other for a server that we will be demonstrating later in the chapter. For the client authentication, a `LoginModule` has been specified, and we have indicated that a login using this module is required in order to consider the authentication successful. Additional parameters may be provided (as shown in the server example, where the `storeKey` parameter is specified), but are not necessary for our login example.

Login modules are objects that know how to talk the appropriate protocol to establish a login to a particular type of authentication server—in this case a Kerberos v5 server.

> **NOTE** *Kerberos v5 is a well-respected enterprise-grade security system from MIT. Using brief exchanges of information, Kerberos can determine the identity of users without ever needing to see their password. Kerberos can also supply participants with security keys, allowing them to set up a secure channel of communication between participants with a minimal overhead. Kerberos forms the core of the authentication system in Microsoft Active Directory, and implementations exist for most platforms.*

A small set of modules are provided with the Java 2 SDK, and others are available either for free or commercially. For example at `http://free.tagish.net/jaas/index.jsp` a set is available that will permit you to authenticate against Windows NT servers using the NTLM protocol, to authenticate using credentials stored in a text file, or to authenticate against credentials stored in a database table. The login modules in the Java 2 Standard Edition 1.4.2 SDK are contained in the `com.sun.security.auth.module` package. These modules include the Kerberos login module we are using, an NT login module, a Unix login module, and a Java Naming and Directory Interface (JNDI) login module.

The example application to conduct a JAAS login in Kerberos follows:

```
import javax.security.auth.*;
import javax.security.auth.callback.*;
import javax.security.auth.login.*;

public class Authentication {

    public static class KerberosCallbackHandler implements CallbackHandler {
        public KerberosCallbackHandler(String principal, String password) {
            this.principal = principal;
            this.password = password;
        }

        public void handle(Callback[] callbacks) {
            for (int i = 0; i < callbacks.length; i++) {
                Callback callback = callbacks[i];
                if (callback instanceof NameCallback) {
                    ((NameCallback) callback).setName(principal);
                } else if (callback instanceof PasswordCallback) {
                    ((PasswordCallback) callback).setPassword(
                        password.toCharArray());
                }
            }
        }

        private String principal;
        private String password;
    }

    public static void setKerberosSystemProperties() {
        System.setProperty(
            "java.security.auth.login.config",
            "./Kerberos.config");
```

```
        System.setProperty("java.security.krb5.realm", "JETSPEED");
        System.setProperty("java.security.krb5.kdc", "jetspeed");
        System.setProperty("sun.security.krb5.debug", "false");
    }

    public static Subject jaasLogin(
        String context,
        String principalName,
        String password)
        throws LoginException {
        System.out.println("Acquiring context");
        LoginContext lc =
            new LoginContext(
                context,
                new KerberosCallbackHandler(principalName, password));

        System.out.println("Logging in...");
        try {
            lc.login();
            System.out.println("OK, Logged in.");

            System.out.println(
                "Retrieving and returning the Subject from the login context.");
            return lc.getSubject();
        } catch (Exception e) {
            throw new LoginException("Login failed: " + e);
        }
    }

    public static void main(String[] argv) {
        String principalName = "dave";
        String password = "MyPassword";

        setKerberosSystemProperties();

        System.out.println("Attempting jaasLogin");
        try {
            Subject subject =
                jaasLogin("ClientAuthentication", principalName, password);
            System.out.println("Logged in " + subject);
        } catch (Exception e) {
            System.out.println("JaasLogin Failed: " + e);
            e.printStackTrace();
        }
```

```
        System.out.println("OK, Done.");
    }
}
```

In the main method, we provide a principal name (username) and password. We then invoke `setKerberosSystemProperties()` to specify Kerberos configuration values. These could equally well be provided on the command line or extracted from a properties file, but for the sake of clarity we're setting them explicitly in the code. First, we specify the location of the configuration file to use:

```
System.setProperty(
    "java.security.auth.login.config",
    "./Kerberos.config");
```

Then we assign the name of the Kerberos realm that the user should be logged in to:

```
System.setProperty("java.security.krb5.realm", "JETSPEED");
```

This specifies the network name of the Kerberos server that the user should use to log in to (this does not have to have the same name as the realm, but it does need to be a master or slave controller for the realm):

```
System.setProperty("java.security.krb5.kdc", "jetspeed");
```

Kerberos Terminology

Kerberos distinguishes between the realm and the controller that a user logs in to. The controller is a physical machine, identified by a name—for example, the Internet name example.com would be a suitable identifier for a controller. Alternatively an IP address such as 192.168.0.1 could be used. The proper name for such a controller is a Key Distribution Center (KDC). You can have any number of KDCs on a network.

The realm is the logical group that the users log in to. For example, a small company might easily use its domain name, so users would log in to the example.com domain. This name does not have to have a DNS style name, however, so "example" is an equally valid realm name.

In a larger organization, realms are likely to be organized in a way that reflects the company's hierarchy, so one set of users might log in to the ACCOUNTS realm while another logs in to the HUMANRESOURCES realm. A user "bob" who has an account in the HUMANRESOURCES realm is always represented as bob@HUMANRESOURCES even if the physical machine he uses to carry out a login is hr.example.com.

For each realm there will be a master KDC machine (which optionally may be the master for several realms). Principals are managed on this master machine. The master(s) can then distribute key information to any number of slave KDCs to distribute the burden of authentication to a manageable degree.

This specifies that additional debugging information should be switched off (the default). Setting this flag to `true` is a recommended first step when debugging problems:

```
System.setProperty("sun.security.krb5.debug", "false");
```

We then invoke the `jaasLogin()` method to retrieve a subject. The method establishes a `LoginContext` object, which is populated with the name of the entry from our configuration file (`ClientAuthentication`) and a `CallbackHandler`.

When the login method is invoked on the `LoginContext` object, the `LoginModule` specified in the configuration file is instantiated. This then establishes a connection to the appropriate server, and carries out the appropriate login conversation (in our case to a Kerberos 5 server). When additional information is required to complete the login, the `handle(Callback[])` method of our `CallbackHandler`

```
public void handle(Callback[] callbacks)
             throws IOException,
                    UnsupportedCallbackException
```

is invoked with the array populated with suitable `Callback` objects. It is the client's responsibility to populate these `Callback` objects with appropriate data.

In the case of a Kerberos 5 login, we require only a username and password. The following code carries out this task:

```
for (int i = 0; i < callbacks.length; i++) {
    Callback callback = callbacks[i];
    if (callback instanceof NameCallback) {
        ((NameCallback) callback).setName(principal);
    } else if (callback instanceof PasswordCallback) {
        ((PasswordCallback) callback).setPassword(
            password.toCharArray());
    }
}
```

If the login were being carried out on a Swing application (for instance), the handler could block the login process and prompt the user for a password and username at runtime. For a web application, however, the approach of prompting the user for details first and then populating a callback handler prior to login is preferable. Disposing of such a handler as soon as it has served its purpose is advisable, since otherwise the username and password will be retained in clear text in memory indefinitely.

Once the `LoginContext` object had completed its login method successfully (an exception is thrown if the login cannot be completed), a `Subject` object can be obtained from the context and returned.

A subject is used to represent a single entity. In our example, the entity is the user of the system, but it can be a service, or a server on a system. Whereas a principal represents an entity authenticated against a single system, the subject can represent an entity authenticated simultaneously against a variety of different systems.

The subject can therefore contain a number of `Principal` objects, and when the subject is printed via its `toString()` method, you should see something like this:

```
Attempting jaasLogin
Acquiring context
Logging in...
OK, Logged in.
Retrieving and returning the Subject from the login context.
Logged in Subject:
        Principal: dave@JETSPEED
        Private Credential: Ticket (hex) =
0000: 61 81 E5 30 81 E2 A0 03  02 01 05 A1 0A 1B 08 4A  a..0...........J
0010: 45 54 53 50 45 45 44 A2  1D 30 1B A0 03 02 01 00  ETSPEED..0......
0020: A1 14 30 12 1B 06 6B 72  62 74 67 74 1B 08 4A 45  ..0...krbtgt..JE
0030: 54 53 50 45 45 44 A3 81  AF 30 81 AC A0 03 02 01  TSPEED...0......
0040: 10 A1 03 02 01 01 A2 81  9F 04 81 9C C6 44 4B B7  .............DK.
0050: 9B AA 75 AA 9E B8 51 0F  10 95 AA AD 9C 58 3A 6F  ..u...Q......X:o
0060: 42 A7 FF 09 D6 9F 17 81  CF B9 3F 02 84 47 90 B0  B.........?..G..
0070: 92 DD FF F5 9B 29 09 97  F6 90 94 A2 E6 98 3E 0B  .....)........>.
0080: 17 B0 D9 25 FE 08 98 17  6F 9F 36 A1 75 00 18 4B  ...%....o.6.u..K
0090: DA D0 90 E5 29 F3 4A B0  99 95 B8 97 37 E7 30 34  ....).J.....7.04
00A0: 22 16 EC 3E 51 12 F4 59  55 E3 6F 21 31 3B E2 3B  "..>Q..YU.o!1;.;
00B0: 1B 97 2D 79 71 0F 3B 8E  3A AA C7 F2 71 A9 E9 F3  ..-yq.;.:...q...
00C0: F7 05 8D 74 3F 7F BB 63  0D AE 5A 31 6E 35 A5 EE  ...t?..c..Z1n5..
00D0: 81 D0 C2 32 FE EB 93 61  45 6B A4 8F 41 C9 4E 64  ...2...aEk..A.Nd
00E0: 8D 81 61 B7 AD B6 FA F9
Client Principal = dave@JETSPEED
Server Principal = krbtgt/JETSPEED@JETSPEED
Session Key = EncryptionKey: keyType=1 keyBytes (hex dump)=
0000: D0 F1 15 A7 A7 49 52 16

Forwardable Ticket false
Forwarded Ticket false
```

```
Proxiable Ticket false
Proxy Ticket false
Postdated Ticket false
Renewable Ticket false
Initial Ticket false
Auth Time = Sat Apr 17 16:02:17 BST 2004
Start Time = Sat Apr 17 16:02:17 BST 2004
End Time = Sun Apr 18 02:02:17 BST 2004
Renew Till = Null
Client Addresses  Null

   OK, Done.
```

You might be surprised by just how much information the subject contains. There are principals here to represent the user (as expected) dave@JETSPEED, and to represent the client (who happens to be the same person). And there is a principal to represent the server from which we obtained authentication. These in turn contain "ticket" information, which independently allows us to confirm the identity of a principal.

A large part of the complexity in JAAS is due to the need to support otherwise incompatible standards. The protocol for logging into a Windows NT domain differs in almost every respect to those required to log into a Unix system. Even so, the fundamental steps (prepare appropriate module, configure, log in) are simple once you understand the context in which they operate.

Understanding Kerberos

What are the tickets that are contained within the principals? A principal is not obliged to contain any specific item of information, so tickets must be an artifact of the implementation. We are using Kerberos as our authentication system, and indeed, tickets are a fundamental part of the way that Kerberos operates.

The aim of Kerberos is to avoid the need for users ever to send their password in a retrievable form over the network. In order to authenticate, the client follows these steps:

1. The client asks the server for a ticket-granting ticket (TGT). The request is unencrypted, and specifies the username of the client. It does not specify the password.

2. The server issues a TGT to the client. A TGT contains an encrypted "session key." This can be decrypted using the client's password only. Therefore, only our client can obtain the session key even if someone else has been listening to the exchange.

3. Once the client has obtained the session key, it is able to use this to encrypt subsequent communications with the server. The use of the session key demonstrates that the client is who they claim to be (since they could only have acquired this by knowing the user's password, which is assumed to be a secret).

4. Once the client has a session key, they are able to request another type of ticket, the service ticket from the server. This can be used to set up secure lines of communication with other processes, services, and users. Similar exchanges of keys and communication with the server allows third parties to verify the identity of the client as well as communicate securely with it.

Java GSS-API

JAAS is all very well for authenticating a user on our own server, but how does this help when you need to authenticate a user on another system?

One possible answer would be to store the username and password in the client; then make these available to remote systems as and when needed. This is not an especially desirable approach. There are various reasons for avoiding this, but the most compelling is that ultimately if any of the systems involved is compromised in any way (even if the channels of communication between them are otherwise secure), the user's password will become known.

The GSS-API is not a specific mechanism (it does not define a protocol) but rather an API. It dictates how one goes about authenticating your application against a remote system without needing to know how the underlying mechanism is implemented. Once the identity of all parties has been established, the GSS-API also defines a standard for securing (encrypting) communications between them.

The GSS-API itself is dictated in RFC (Request For Comments) document number 1508, and is therefore an open standard. Most of the infrastructure of the Internet is published in these documents and freely available for download from the Internet Engineering Task Force (IETF) web site at `www.faqs.org`.

A series of subsequent RFC documents define the language-specific APIs. We are specifically interested in RFC 2853, which defines the Java bindings. The protocol implementations are then defined in additional documents. For our example we will be using the Kerberos authentication mechanism, which we have already encountered. RFC 1510 defines Kerberos v5, and RFC 1964 defines how GSS should use Kerberos.

It is not necessary to read these in depth, but RFC documents tend to be written in an accessible manner, so it is worth glancing through them for insights into how things work at a level beyond the scope of this book.

The code that follows demonstrates what is required to establish the authenticity of a client with a server using the Java GSS-API. In this example, we want to authenticate the user "dave" with the password "MyPassword" against a service that is authenticated as "login/java" with the password "MyPassword". All authentication is carried out against a Kerberos KDC called "jetspeed" where all users are members of the realm "JETSPEED".

You should run the server before starting the client, and you should place a copy of the configuration file Kerberos.config in the same directory as the applications.

> **TIP** *Running this code with some Kerberos servers, you may encounter the following error message:*
>
> *GSSException: Failure unspecified at GSS-API level (Mechanism level: KDC has no support for encryption type (14))*
>
> *In this case you will need to define the encryption mechanism for your principals (users) as "des-cbc-crc:normal". The error is caused by an incompatibility between the Java GSS implementation and the Kerberos server.*

```
// GSSContextUtil.java
import java.security.PrivilegedExceptionAction;
import javax.security.auth.Subject;
import org.ietf.jgss.*;

public class GSSContextUtil {
    public static GSSContext createIncomingGSSContext(
        Subject subject,
        String credentialPrincipal,
        String contextPrincipal)
        throws Exception {
        GSSContext context =
            (GSSContext) Subject.doAs(
                subject,
                new CreateGSSContextPrivilegedAction(
                    credentialPrincipal,
                    contextPrincipal,
                    GSSCredential.ACCEPT_ONLY));
        return context;
    }

    public static GSSContext createOutgoingGSSContext(
        Subject subject,
        String credentialPrincipal,
        String contextPrincipal)
        throws Exception {
        GSSContext context =
```

```
            (GSSContext) Subject.doAs(
                subject,
                new CreateGSSContextPrivilegedAction(
                    credentialPrincipal,
                    contextPrincipal,
                    GSSCredential.INITIATE_ONLY));
        return context;
    }

    public static class CreateGSSContextPrivilegedAction
        implements PrivilegedExceptionAction {

        public CreateGSSContextPrivilegedAction(
            String clientPrincipal,
            String serverPrincipal,
            int usage) {
            this.credentialPrincipal = clientPrincipal;
            this.contextPrincipal = serverPrincipal;
            this.usage = usage;
        }

        public Object run() throws Exception {
            GSSManager manager = GSSManager.getInstance();

            // Declare OID for Kerberos mechanisms
            Oid krb5Mechanism = new Oid("1.2.840.113554.1.2.2");

            // Identify who the client wishes to be
            GSSName clientName =
                manager.createName(credentialPrincipal, GSSName.NT_USER_NAME);

            // Identify the name of the server.
            GSSName serverName =
                manager.createName(contextPrincipal, GSSName.NT_USER_NAME);

            // Acquire credentials for the user
            GSSCredential userCreds =
                manager.createCredential(
                    clientName,
                    GSSCredential.DEFAULT_LIFETIME,
                    krb5Mechanism,
                    usage);
```

```
            // Instantiate and initialize a security context
            // that will be established with the server
            GSSContext context =
                manager.createContext(
                    serverName,
                    krb5Mechanism,
                    userCreds,
                    GSSContext.DEFAULT_LIFETIME);

            return context;
        }

        private String credentialPrincipal;
        private String contextPrincipal;
        private int usage;
    }

    // This utility class should not be instantiated
    private GSSContextUtil() {
    }
}
```

The `GSSContextUtil` class provides a pair of messages for creating the `GSSContext` objects that we require to carry out the authentication, and a `PrivilegedAction` class that allows us to do the necessary setup while running with the privileges of the `Subject` that we retrieve from JAAS.

To carry out the privileged action for the client, we invoke `createOutgoingGSSContext()`. The meat of this method is the following call:

```
        GSSContext context =
            (GSSContext) Subject.doAs(
                subject,
                new CreateGSSContextPrivilegedAction(
                    credentialPrincipal,
                    contextPrincipal,
                    GSSCredential.INITIATE_ONLY));
```

Here we use the `Subject.doAs()` method

```
public static Object doAs(Subject subject,
                          PrivilegedExceptionAction action)
                   throws PrivilegedActionException
```

to assume the privileges of the logged-in subject. The action that should be carried out is defined by the run() method of an instance of CreateGSSContextPrivilegedAction. We provide this method with the name of the principal associated with the subject, the name of the principal of the context that we would like to establish (effectively the principal that we want to connect to), and the direction in which the operation will take place—in this case, the client is initiating the connection.

The run() method of the privileged action then carries out a number of tasks in its privileged state:

```
public Object run() throws Exception
```

We acquire a GSSManager object, which we will use to obtain other GSS objects to carry out the authentication:

```
GSSManager manager = GSSManager.getInstance();
```

We declare an object identifier (Oid), which represents the GSS mechanism that we want to use to carry out the credential exchange. In our case, we want to use the Kerberos GSS protocol. The "magic number" here is defined in RFC 1964:

```
Oid krb5Mechanism = new Oid("1.2.840.113554.1.2.2");
```

We retrieve an object representing the client principal, and an object representing the server principal, but we do not explicitly use principals here, allowing the underlying mechanism to determine the specifics. We do, however, specify that this is a username, rather than the name of a server or other principal type. The "NT" in NT_USER_NAME stands for "Name Type" rather than having any connection with the Windows NT operating system:

```
GSSName clientName =
   manager.createName(credentialPrincipal, GSSName.NT_USER_NAME);

GSSName serverName =
   manager.createName(contextPrincipal, GSSName.NT_USER_NAME);
```

Now we acquire an object that represents the credentials to initially be associated with the context object that we're creating. This will be the logged-in user associated with the subject:

```
// Acquire credentials for the user
GSSCredential userCreds =
    manager.createCredential(
        clientName,
        GSSCredential.DEFAULT_LIFETIME,
        krb5Mechanism,
        usage);
```

Finally we create a context object to represent the process of establishing the authentication with the server. As yet, this context is unauthenticated, which implies that the user principal is not yet authenticated on both of the machines that will share the context:

```
GSSContext context =
    manager.createContext(
        serverName,
        krb5Mechanism,
        userCreds,
        GSSContext.DEFAULT_LIFETIME);
```

The client and server code invokes the methods of the `GSSContextUtil` class to establish a secure context, and we invoke a method in the `Authentication` class that we've already discussed in order to establish a login prior to this. The code for the client is

```
// AuthClient.java
import java.io.*;
import java.net.Socket;
import javax.security.auth.Subject;
import org.ietf.jgss.GSSContext;

public class AuthClient {
    public AuthClient(String server, int port) throws IOException {
        socket = new Socket(server, port);
        output = socket.getOutputStream();
        input = socket.getInputStream();
    }

    public void close() throws IOException {
        socket.close();
    }

    public void createContext(
        String clientPrincipal,
        String clientPassword,
        String serverPrincipal)
        throws Exception {
        Authentication.setKerberosSystemProperties();

        Subject subject =
            Authentication.jaasLogin(
                "ClientAuthentication",
                clientPrincipal,
```

```
                clientPassword);
        System.out.println("Logged in " + subject);

        serverContext =
            GSSContextUtil.createOutgoingGSSContext(
                subject,
                clientPrincipal,
                serverPrincipal);
        System.out.println(
            "Server context established:" + serverContext.isEstablished());
    }

    public GSSContext handshake() throws Exception {
        System.out.println("Performing handshake");

        serverContext.requestConf(true);
        serverContext.requestMutualAuth(true);
        serverContext.requestReplayDet(true);

        while (!serverContext.isEstablished()) {
            System.out.println("Exchanging tokens");
            serverContext.initSecContext(input, output);
            output.flush();
        }

        System.out.println("Handshake completed");
        return serverContext;
    }

    private Socket socket;
    private GSSContext serverContext;
    private InputStream input;
    private OutputStream output;

    public static void main(String[] argv) throws Exception {

        AuthClient client = new AuthClient("192.168.0.5", 3000);

        System.out.println("Establish server context");
        client.createContext("dave", "MyPassword", "login/java");

        GSSContext ctx = client.handshake();
        System.out.println("Server context established:" + ctx.isEstablished());
```

```
        client.close();
        System.out.println("OK");
    }
}
```

Following through the main method of the client, things progress in a quite straightforward manner.

First we establish a socket connection between the client and server machines. Although we make use of sockets, any medium that is capable of exchanging an array of bytes (bi-directionally) is able to use the GSS-API to establish a secure context, so Remote Method Invocation (RMI) could be used as easily. At a pinch, you could even establish the secure context by e-mail!

```
AuthClient client = new AuthClient("192.168.0.5", 3000);
```

Next we create a context object to represent the authentication that is to be carried out. The username and password of the client principal are required here to obtain a `Principal` object. In your portlets you are able to retrieve a principal by invoking the `getUserPrincipal()` method, so no knowledge of the password is required. For the remote machine, however, we need to specify only the name of the principal. The authenticity of the server will be established with the GSS handshake:

```
client.establishContext("dave", "MyPassword", "login/java");
GSSContext ctx = client.handshake();
```

Finally, we test to confirm that the context was established:

```
System.out.println("Server context established:" + ctx.isEstablished());
```

Assuming that the return from `ctx.isEstablished()` is `true`, we can be confident that the remote server is logged in as "login/java", and that it has authenticated our user as "dave".

We've covered the bulk of the `createContext(String,String,String)` method in our discussion of the `GSSContextUtil` class, so we'll just concentrate on the specifics of the `handshake()` method.

Initially we specify the attributes that we want the secure context to have:

```
serverContext.requestConf(true);
serverContext.requestMutualAuth(true);
serverContext.requestReplayDet(true);
```

We want confidentiality. This allows us to use the credentials of the two parties to encrypt information that is subsequently to be exchanged (requestConf(boolean)).

We want to carry out authentication mutually—that is, we want the server to confirm the client's identity and the client to confirm the server's identity (requestMutualAuth(boolean)).

We also want to be alerted if a third party tries to use previously transmitted tokens to set up the connection (requestReplyDet(boolean)).

Once we know what sort of context we want, we carry out the work to set it up:

```
while (!serverContext.isEstablished()) {
    System.out.println("Exchanging tokens");
    serverContext.initSecContext(input, output);
    output.flush();
}
```

This code could not be simpler—while the context is not established (i.e., not secure), we exchange tokens using our socket's associated streams (and being sure to flush the output stream to compel the server to respond in a timely manner). Once enough tokens have been exchanged to convince both parties of each other's authenticity, the isEstablished() flag returns true, and we return the established context.

If we were dealing with a context exchange over e-mail, or something more exotic (RFC 1149), we could use additional methods in the GSSContext to acquire the bytes representing the appropriate tokens directly. These are comprehensively documented in the JavaDoc for the GSSContext API.

Once run, the output of the client should be something like the following:

```
Config
Acquiring context
Logging in...
OK, Logged in.
Retrieving and returning the Subject from the login context.
Logged in Subject:
        Principal: login/java@JETSPEED
        Private Credential: Ticket (hex) =
0000: 61 81 E5 30 81 E2 A0 03   02 01 05 A1 0A 1B 08 4A  a..0...........J
0010: 45 54 53 50 45 45 44 A2   1D 30 1B A0 03 02 01 00  ETSPEED..0......
0020: A1 14 30 12 1B 06 6B 72   62 74 67 74 1B 08 4A 45  ..0...krbtgt..JE
0030: 54 53 50 45 45 44 A3 81   AF 30 81 AC A0 03 02 01  TSPEED...0......
0040: 10 A1 03 02 01 01 A2 81   9F 04 81 9C 6B AA 82 71  ............k..q
0050: 34 5F D4 7A 96 E4 D1 99   B7 DF D7 3E 6E E3 9F 9A  4_.z.......>n...
0060: 1F 32 74 CE 2F 1B 16 9C   76 21 E6 08 8E 88 CA 78  .2t./...v!.....x
0070: B1 C1 93 D5 9F 80 63 FB   31 4D 2A 96 2D CF F6 1B  ......c.1M*.-...
```

```
0080: 23 8A 16 EC 77 CD 9D 41   8E 7C 39 68 55 6A 1F 05  #...w..A..9hUj..
0090: 76 4D 39 34 88 3A AD 7E   3F 98 A9 B8 D8 8B C0 E8  vM94.:..?.......
00A0: 04 16 BD 1F 56 09 B6 90   A4 2C 66 45 22 F9 17 78  ....V....,fE"..x
00B0: 37 B3 53 BB 57 71 09 FD   64 AD 56 F3 8E F7 8D 01  7.S.Wq..d.V.....
00C0: 69 D5 C2 C3 53 75 40 22   38 20 A2 44 CD 13 66 66  i...Su@"8 .D..ff
00D0: 96 80 B5 2A 44 2D CD CA   71 26 86 E1 0F EB 38 8C  ...*D-..q&....8.
00E0: EF 84 18 1D 6B 63 47 C7
Client Principal = login/java@JETSPEED
Server Principal = krbtgt/JETSPEED@JETSPEED
Session Key = EncryptionKey: keyType=1 keyBytes (hex dump)=
0000: A7 16 D9 98 F4 20 3E DF

Forwardable Ticket false
Forwarded Ticket false
Proxiable Ticket false
Proxy Ticket false
Postdated Ticket false
Renewable Ticket false
Initial Ticket false
Auth Time = Sat Apr 17 15:54:10 BST 2004
Start Time = Sat Apr 17 15:54:10 BST 2004
End Time = Sun Apr 18 01:54:10 BST 2004
Renew Till = Null
Client Addresses  Null
        Private Credential: Kerberos Principal login/java@JETSPEEDKey Version 0key
EncryptionKey: keyType=3 keyBytes (hex dump)=
0000: F2 61 89 1C C4 67 B6 C8


Setting up GSSContexts
Server: sun.security.jgss.GSSContextImpl@14da8f4
Waiting for client connection
Connection established
Establishing client context
Exchanging tokens
Client context established !
Context established by dave@JETSPEED to login/java
OK: Client is authenticated
```

The implementation of our server is similar to that of the client:

```
// AuthServer.java
import java.io.*;
```

```
import java.net.*;
import javax.security.auth.Subject;
import org.ietf.jgss.*;

public class AuthServer {
    public AuthServer(Subject subject, String serverPrincipalName) {
        this.subject = subject;
        this.serverPrincipalName = serverPrincipalName;
    }

    public static void main(String[] argv) throws Exception {
        String serverPrincipalName = "login/java";
        String serverPassword = "MyPassword";

        System.out.println("Config");
        Authentication.setKerberosSystemProperties();

        Subject subject =
            Authentication.jaasLogin(
                "ServerAuthentication",
                serverPrincipalName,
                serverPassword);
        System.out.println("Logged in " + subject);

        System.out.println("Setting up GSSContexts");
        GSSContext serverContext =
            GSSContextUtil.createIncomingGSSContext(
                subject,
                serverPrincipalName,
                serverPrincipalName);

        System.out.println("Server: " + serverContext);

        System.out.println("Waiting for client connection");
        ServerSocket serverSocket = new ServerSocket(3000);
        Socket socket = serverSocket.accept();

        System.out.println("Connection established");
        InputStream input = socket.getInputStream();
        OutputStream output = socket.getOutputStream();

        try {
            System.out.println("Establishing client context");
```

```
            while (!serverContext.isEstablished()) {
                System.out.println("Exchanging tokens");
                serverContext.acceptSecContext(input, output);
                output.flush();
            }
            System.out.println("Client context established !");

            String clientName = serverContext.getTargName().toString();
            String serverName = serverContext.getSrcName().toString();

            System.out.println(
                "Context established by " + serverName + " to " + clientName);

            if (serverContext.isEstablished()) {
                System.out.println("OK: Client is authenticated");
            } else {
                System.out.println("ERROR: Client is NOT authenticated");
            }

        } catch (GSSException e) {
            System.out.println("ERROR: Client is NOT authenticated");

            System.out.println("MajorString:" + e.getMajorString());
            System.out.println("MinorString:" + e.getMinorString());
            e.printStackTrace();
        }

        // Close socket.
        socket.close();
    }
}
```

In our server we have created an incoming rather than an outgoing `GSSContext`, so we don't need to set flags.

Although we have enhanced the error handling slightly, the server introduces no new concepts; despite the naming convention we have used of "client" and "server", the participants are peers, so the operations can be carried out in either direction. It is therefore natural that the configuration of a client and server should be so similar.

When you run the server, you should see something like the following output:

```
Establish server context
Acquiring context
Logging in...
```

```
OK, Logged in.
Retrieving and returning the Subject from the login context.
Logged in Subject:
        Principal: dave@JETSPEED
        Private Credential: Ticket (hex) =
0000: 61 81 E5 30 81 E2 A0 03   02 01 05 A1 0A 1B 08 4A  a..0...........J
0010: 45 54 53 50 45 45 44 A2   1D 30 1B A0 03 02 01 00  ETSPEED..0......
0020: A1 14 30 12 1B 06 6B 72   62 74 67 74 1B 08 4A 45  ..0...krbtgt..JE
0030: 54 53 50 45 45 44 A3 81   AF 30 81 AC A0 03 02 01  TSPEED...0......
0040: 10 A1 03 02 01 01 A2 81   9F 04 81 9C 3B A6 83 82  ............;...
0050: 41 D1 89 BB 13 39 AB AA   F4 79 AE 8A 11 68 1A 91  A....9...y...h..
0060: 0D E2 27 E3 A4 A5 70 8E   80 7F C0 9D 45 8C 13 E2  ..'...p.....E...
0070: 9A 40 16 79 F3 52 DD 41   73 51 C6 8C 9A 5B D4 8C  .@.y.R.AsQ...[..
0080: 1F F5 DB 9B D6 16 BA 34   91 32 37 16 45 BA 67 C4  .......4.27.E.g.
0090: 8C 68 9A 20 72 06 D3 B3   BC 5E D3 15 9E DB B4 BD  .h. r....^......
00A0: D6 A8 A2 E3 21 23 3D 6D   9D 98 1E 71 AD 66 D1 CB  ....!#=m...q.f..
00B0: 36 05 A1 BA 2C 68 8C 80   34 A7 0E 5B E1 B4 7C 8B  6...,h..4..[....
00C0: 3C 1E 00 33 76 71 A0 D9   54 F3 65 43 8B 95 C7 17  <..3vq..T.eC....
00D0: D8 95 77 11 B9 BE BA 1D   61 43 E9 B1 64 0A 10 EC  ..w.....aC..d...
00E0: 49 70 BA 8C 53 D4 98 5A
Client Principal = dave@JETSPEED
Server Principal = krbtgt/JETSPEED@JETSPEED
Session Key = EncryptionKey: keyType=1 keyBytes (hex dump)=
0000: F1 F4 BA 40 A4 45 15 80

Forwardable Ticket false
Forwarded Ticket false
Proxiable Ticket false
Proxy Ticket false
Postdated Ticket false
Renewable Ticket false
Initial Ticket false
Auth Time = Sat Apr 17 15:54:54 BST 2004
Start Time = Sat Apr 17 15:54:54 BST 2004
End Time = Sun Apr 18 01:54:54 BST 2004
Renew Till = Null
Client Addresses  Null

Server context established:false
Performing handshake
Exchanging tokens
Exchanging tokens
Handshake completed
Server context established:true
OK
```

Note that before the handshake is performed and tokens are exchanged, the call to `isEstablished()` for the context returns `false`, and subsequently `true`. Once `isEstablished()` returns `true`, the server can be confident that the client is who they claim to be, and thus the authentication is complete.

Integrated Security

In a real-world situation you are unlikely to be able to dictate the terms of your security environment. While Java security is a major topic in its own right, we will now discuss some of the APIs and protocols that you may encounter in architecting a security solution.

JNDI, LDAP, and Active Directory

Authentication is the process of establishing a user's identity, whereas authorization is the process of granting and denying access to appropriate parts of an application based on that identity.

This chapter has discussed authentication, but only our coverage of roles has touched on authorization. When working with a self-contained portlet, you will be able to work directly with the roles provided by the `isUserInRole()` method, but interfacing with external systems for SSO you may be obliged to acquire role memberships from elsewhere.

Generally speaking, role memberships or security group memberships will be listed in a directory service. A directory is a hierarchical database. Given an appropriate set of keys, you can interrogate it for an associated set of values. The set of keys is usually termed a path. A typical scenario might map the key "/system/security/users/dave" to the values "Manager" and "User".

A directory service that is not directly related to security is the Directory Naming Service (DNS) used to translate names such as example.com to IP addresses like 192.0.34.166 is a directory service. In fact, example.com is a path, but in DNS the keys are separated by dots instead of slashes.

Java provides an API for accessing directory services called Java Native Directory Interface (JNDI). This permits you to access different services using a standardized API, so it is a simple matter to acquire the role memberships from an appropriate directory server.

Probably the most popular directory protocol is Lightweight Directory Access Protocol (LDAP). Among the most common proprietary directory service implementations, Microsoft's Active Directory authentication and authorization servers can be accessed via the LDAP protocol. Free versions are also available, such as the offering from the OpenLDAP Foundation (`www.openldap.com`).

Microsoft's Active Directory can be accessed as a Kerberos server for pure authentication, but its implementation includes a proprietary extension that incorporates role (authorization) information into the security tickets.

The predecessor of Active Directory was Microsoft's NTLM. This was the security system originally built into OS/2. Using third-party tools, it is possible to use JAAS to authenticate against an NTLM domain.

SAML

A technology to augment your authentication systems, Security Assertions Markup Language (SAML) is essentially a standardized XML document for conveying security information.

Because SAML allows standardized transmission of security information, it permits a third-party server to carry out the authentication for a variety of external systems. This allows for the building of interorganizational sign-on systems like that promoted as the Liberty Alliance.

Java ACC

The Java Authorization Contract for Containers (ACC) is a Java Community Process (JCP) set of extensions to the standard methods already discussed in this chapter. It codifies a system that makes more comprehensive use of `Principals` than that currently available with the servlet API.

Although this specification is not yet commonly implemented in servlet containers, you should expect it to become more prevalent. It is likely that portlets will adopt this system of necessity since they rely on the servlet API for most of their services.

The details of the specification can be obtained from the JCP home page at `www.jcp.org`.

Summary

This chapter has discussed the methods that are available to portlets to identify the user. We have described how they relate to the corresponding methods in servlets, and how they can be used to authenticate the user against external services. We have also covered some of the techniques available for assigning and determining the roles of users.

We used the Kerberos v5 protocol to demonstrate SSO authentication using JAAS, and we also used the GSS-API to authenticate a user on another system. The GSS-API is a standard for authenticating users in enterprise applications to a wide range of security mechanisms and protocols.

In the next chapter, we cover syndication of information into and out of your portlets using the RSS protocols.

CHAPTER 9

RSS and Syndication

In this chapter, we describe how portlets can aggregate links to content on external web sites using the group of standards known as RSS. We also discuss how the content of your own portal could be syndicated for convenient inclusion in external sites using the same mechanism.

Overview of RSS

RSS is not a single standard. It is several standards, some closely related, and others more loosely so.

The versions of RSS that are most commonly used are 0.9 and 0.91, both of which were released by Netscape to allow content from external web sites to be aggregated into its My Netscape portal.

Since 0.91, two groups have produced new versions of RSS with varying degrees of backward compatibility. The company UserLand Software carried out early development of RSS for Netscape and has subsequently released versions 0.92, 0.93, 0.94, and 2.0. The RSS-DEV working group (an independent group of developers) released the 1.0 version of RSS stemming from the 0.91 version.

> **NOTE** *Some but not all of these versions are based on the Resource Description Framework (RDF) format. This rather more consistently managed standard from the World Wide Web Consortium (W3C) standards body provided a standard for presenting metadata. A syndication feed is a set of metadata; it does not (generally) provide the articles itself, but will provide their titles, some associated links, and abstracts of the articles.*
>
> *RDF in this respect is ideal—however, it is quite a complex standard; RSS pragmatically provides a reasonable subset of this information oriented specifically toward syndication at the cost of a somewhat fragmented standard.*

Even the naming of the standard reflects the version confusion. Correctly or otherwise, you may see any of these versions referred to as one of "Really Simple Syndication," "Rich Site Summary," or "RDF Site Summary." In practice, it is simplest to refer to RSS by its acronym alone, and use a version number if you feel the need to be specific.

The good news is that amid this riot of colorful standards for RSS, the RSS Portlet that we use to acquire and present syndicated content is quite agnostic. You can import an RSS feed in formats 0.90 through to 2.0. The only thing that you cannot import is invalid XML.

RSS is not the only game in town—there are various other standards for making this type of meta-information available and for syndicating content. Although we won't be covering them any further, you should be familiar with RDF (which we've already mentioned) and the up-and-coming "Atom" standard (in development at `www.atomenabled.org`), which aims to be a more "standard" standard!

Walking Through an Example RSS File

Let's now take a look at some concrete examples of RSS feeds in the most commonly encountered 0.9 and 0.91 formats. Both formats provide a number of optional elements, but for the most part we will ignore these in favor of those most commonly encountered "in the wild."

Version 0.9

The following is a correct RSS 0.9 feed describing the authors' web site, including the compulsory elements and some of the optional ones:

```
<?xml version="1.0"?>

<rdf:RDF
  xmlns:rdf="http://www.w3.org/1999/02/22-rdf-syntax-ns#"
  xmlns="http://my.netscape.com/rdf/simple/0.9/">

   <channel>
      <title>PortalBook Technical Notes</title>
      <link>http://portalbook.com/</link>
      <description>
         Discourse and exposition on Java and
         developing Portlets
      </description>
   </channel>

   <item>
      <title>New version of Jetspeed released</title>
      <link>
         http://portalbook.com/notes/005.html
      </link>
   </item>
```

```
   <item>
      <title>Collections and iterations</title>
      <link>
         http://portalbook.com/notes/004.html
      </link>
   </item>

   <item>
      <title>Deprecated techniques</title>
      <link>
         http://portalbook.com/notes/003.html
      </link>
   </item>

</rdf:RDF>
```

The format is so simple it barely needs explanation, which is indubitably one of the reasons for the enthusiastic early take-up.

The first version of RSS was a valid RDF document. As such it fell within the RDF namespace defined by the W3C. The simple elements required by Netscape's format are specified in the default namespace:

```
<rdf:RDF
  xmlns:rdf="http://www.w3.org/1999/02/22-rdf-syntax-ns#"
  xmlns="http://my.netscape.com/rdf/simple/0.9/">
```

The <channel> element contains the metadata for the feed—its title, the site from which it can be obtained, and a human-readable description of its content. One of the deficiencies of the 0.9 format over later submissions is that it is restricted to a single channel, so a web site proffering diverse subject matter must provide multiple distinct feeds rather than a single RSS feed with multiple channels:

```
<channel>
   <title>PortalBook Technical Notes</title>
   <link>http://portalbook.com/</link>
   <description>
      Discourse and exposition on Java and
      developing Portlets
   </description>
</channel>
```

The <item> element repeats multiple times, once for each article or item of interest that is being publicized in the feed. There is a hard limit of 15 items permissible in the channel. The items includes a title describing the data to be propagated and a link to the data in question. This extremely sparse information is all that is permitted:

```
<item>
   <title>Deprecated techniques</title>
   <link>
      http://portalbook.com/notes/003.html
   </link>
</item>
```

Version 0.91

The following is a correct RSS 0.91 feed describing the authors' web site, including the compulsory elements and some of the optional ones.

```
<?xml version="1.0"?>

<rss version="0.91">
  <channel>

     <title>PortalBook Technical Notes</title>
     <link>http://portalbook.com/</link>
     <description>
        Discourse and exposition on Java
        and developing Portlets
     </description>
     <language>en-us</language>
     <copyright>
        Copyright: (C) 2003 Dave Minter
        and Jeff Linwood
     </copyright>

     <item>
       <title>New version of Jetspeed released</title>
       <link>http://portalbook.com/notes/005.html</link>
       <description>
         We let you know the latest changes
         and improvements to the Jetspeed
         portlet server in the new version.
       </description>
     </item>

     <item>
       <title>Collections and iterations</title>
```

```
      <link>http://portalbook.com/notes/004.html</link>
      <description>
        Misuse of Collections can result in hidden
        nested iterations that rapidly become a
        serious performance drag. We discuss how
        to avoid this and similar pitfalls.
      </description>
    </item>

    <item>
      <title>Deprecated techniques</title>
      <link>http://portalbook.com/notes/003.html</link>
      <description>
        Bad habits die hard. We discuss some of the
        techniques that were legitimate in older
        versions of Jetspeed and the approaches that
        should replace them.
      </description>
    </item>

  </channel>
</rss>
```

This format is not quite as simple as that of version 0.9 but does contain some compensatory features.

The version of RSS is specified in this version, making it a little easier to keep track of what data is incoming:

```
<rss version="0.91">
```

Again only one channel is permitted by the standard. In this version, however, the `<channel>` element encompasses all of the subsequent items along with the channel's metadata:

```
<channel>
```

Rather more information about the channel is available in a 0.91 feed. As well as the title, link, and description, we are provided with an associated language and copyright information:

```
<title>PortalBook Technical Notes</title>
<link>http://portalbook.com/</link>
<description>
   Discourse and exposition on Java
   and developing Portlets
</description>
```

```
<language>en-us</language>
<copyright>
   Copyright: (C) 2003 Dave Minter
   and Jeff Linwood
</copyright>
```

The `<item>` elements are also rather better equipped. In addition to the `<title>` and `<link>` elements, we have a description. This is usually populated with an abstract of the content that is to be covered in the associated link:

```
<item>
   <title>New version of Jetspeed released</title>
   <link>http://portalbook.com/notes/005.html</link>
   <description>
      We let you know the latest changes
      and improvements to the Jetspeed
      portlet server in the new version.
   </description>
</item>
```

This version of the standard is not limited to 15 item elements, but enough software exists that makes this assumption that we figure it is safer to so limit it.

Version 2.0

The following is a correct RSS 2.0 feed describing the authors' web site, including the compulsory elements and some of the optional ones:

```
<?xml version="1.0"?>

<rss version="2.0">
   <channel>

      <title>PortalBook Technical Notes</title>
      <link>http://portalbook.com/</link>
      <description>
         Discourse and exposition on Java and
         developing Portlets
      </description>
      <language>en-us</language>
      <copyright>
       Copyright: (C) 2003 Dave Minter
       and Jeff Linwood
      </copyright>
```

```
      <item>
         <title>New version of Jetspeed released</title>
         <link>
            http://portalbook.com/notes/005.html
         </link>
         <description>
            We let you know the latest changes
            and improvements to the Jetspeed
            portlet server in the new version
         </description>
      </item>

      <item>
         <title>Collections and iterations</title>
         <link>
            http://portalbook.com/notes/004.html
         </link>
         <description>
            Misuse of Collections can result in hidden
            nested iterations that rapidly become a
            serious performance drag. We discuss how
            to avoid this and similar pitfalls.
         </description>
      </item>

      <item>
         <title>Deprecated techniques</title>
         <link>
            http://portalbook.com/notes/003.html
         </link>
         <description>
            Bad habits die hard. We discuss some of the
            techniques that were legitimate in older
            versions of Jetspeed and the approaches that
            should replace them.
         </description>
      </item>

   </channel>
</rss>
```

If you compare this feed with the one demonstrated in the 0.91 version of RSS, you'll see a striking similarity. In fact, they're identical aside from the version number. So what's the point?

RSS 2.0 provides a much larger set of optional elements that can be included in your feed. However, the later the version of RSS that you select for your implementation, the less likely it is that client software will provide compatibility for it. Therefore, you need to weigh this disadvantage against the richer variety of optional metadata (publication dates, unique identifiers, and so forth—for the full list, see the current specification for RSS 2.0 at `http://blogs.law.harvard.edu/tech/rss`) that you can include in a 2.0 feed.

RSS Browsers

As we have discussed, the original purpose of RSS was to allow headlines to be imported into other web pages. However, a number of specialized browsers have appeared that provide a convenient user interface for browsing through these content summaries.

The example shown in Figure 9-1 is for NetNewsWire Lite running on a Macintosh and illustrates the basic functionality you can expect to see in an RSS browser.

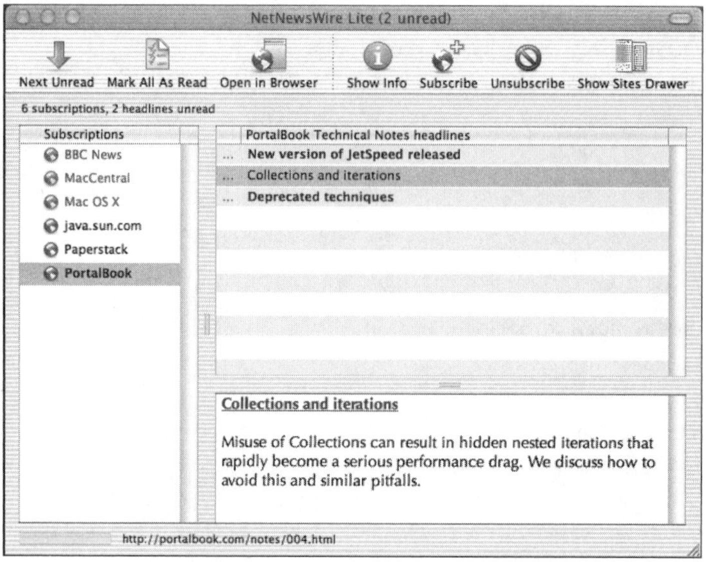

Figure 9-1. NetNewsWire Lite presenting a set of RSS feeds

The browser shown provides a list of sites from which you may choose an RSS feed. Selecting a site lists the article titles available on the site. Selecting a title displays the abstract of the article. A link is provided that will launch a browser with the article in question.

Most of the rest of the example screen shots in this chapter will be taken from a Java Swing-based RSS browser called RSS Viewer, which you can download from `http://sourceforge.net/projects/rssview/`.

RSS Viewer lacks some of the finesse of NetNewsWire Lite, but being Java-based, it will run on any platform. A list of other RSS resources, including RSS browsers for various platforms, is available at `www.lights.com/weblogs/rss.html`.

Displaying Syndicated Information in Portlets

It is possible that your portal will supply a portlet for displaying RSS streams, but failing that, a number of third-party portlets already exist that provide this service. We will discuss a portlet available from the Portlet Open Source Trading (POST) site at `http://portlet-opensrc.sourceforge.net/`.

> **NOTE** *The Portlet Open Source Trading (POST) site provides a set of open source portlets that conform to the Java portlet API or the Web Services for Remote Portlets (WSRP) standard. As of this writing, it has also released a Google portlet, an e-mail portlet, a wizard portlet, and an upload portlet.*

The portlet application we are using is called RSS Portlet and is provided as a WAR file to be deployed in your portal. The open source license for RSS Portlet is a BSD-style license, so you can use it for free as-is, or make any changes you like to it (although under this license if you do so, you're not allowed to call your derivation "RSS Portlet").

The RSS Portlet uses XSL files to translate the incoming RSS feeds into HTML. A style sheet called html.xsl converts 0.9x RSS feeds and a style sheet called Rss20.xsl converts 2.0 RSS feeds. Both of these files are stored in the WEB-INF directory of the portlet.

> **TIP** *At the time of writing, there is a bug in the html.xsl file. If your portlet fails to load and leaves errors like the following:*
>
> ```
> "Can not resolve namespace prefix: im"
> ```
>
> *in your log files, you will need to remove the "im" and "rss-sample" entries from the line beginning "exclude-result-prefixes" so that it now reads:*
>
> ```
> exclude-result-prefixes=
>      "rdf dc dcterms rss content annotate admin image cc reqv"
> ```
>
> *The entries removed from this reference XML namespaces, which have not been included. Earlier versions of the XML parser tolerated this error.*

This portlet makes use of the Xalan XML parser to read and translate the RSS streams. Although the J2SE 1.4 runtime is provided with a version of Xalan, it lacks some of the more up-to-date features required by the RSS Portlet. You may, therefore, need to install the latest Xalan JAR files in your portal.

> **TIP** *If you are using a portlet server based on the Tomcat application server, such as Pluto or Jetspeed, and you are using the 1.4 version of the J2SDK, you will need to take additional measures to have your new Xalan JAR files override the JAR files provided with the SDK. To do this, place the JAR files in the common/endorsed/ directory.*
>
> *An error message like "The output format must have a '{http://xml.apache.org/xslt}content-handler' property!" is indicative of this particular problem.*

The RSS feeds that will appear in the portlet are configured from the "RssXml" preference. The default set of preferences configured in portlet.xml is as follows:

```
<name>RssXml</name>
<value>http://www.theserverside.com/rss/theserverside-0.9.rdf</value>
<value>http://rss.com.com/2547-12-0-20.xml</value>
<value>http://headlines.internet.com/internetnews/top-news/news.rss</value>
<value>http://headlines.internet.com/internetnews/fina-news/news.rss</value>
<value>http://www.sciencedaily.com/newsfeed.xml</value>
```

Naturally you will want to customize the available feeds to suit the audience of your portal.

The default list includes some 0.9-style feeds, as shown in Figure 9-2, along with some 2.0-style feeds, as shown in Figure 9-3.

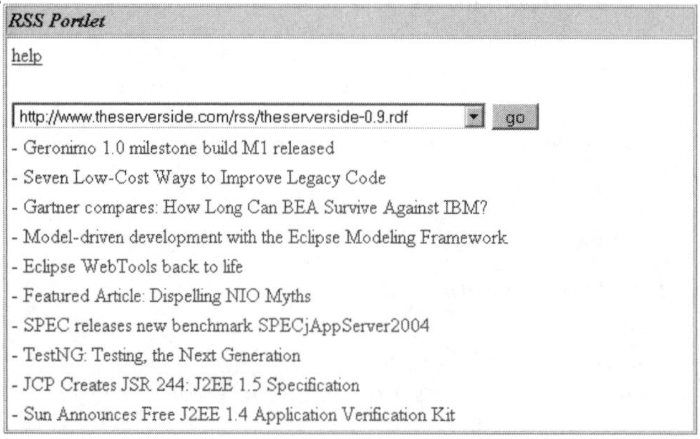

Figure 9-2. Browsing 0.9-style RSS feeds

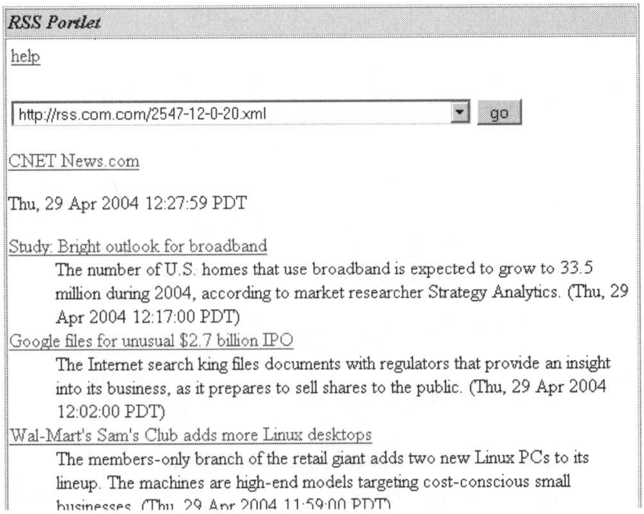

Figure 9-3. Browsing 2.0-style RSS feeds

The RSS Portlet discussed here is not yet a polished piece of work suitable for all situations, but it illustrates the techniques required to display an RSS feed in a portlet. Since it is open source software, it provides an excellent basis for developing a custom RSS portlet for your own purposes.

Syndicating Out

It is possible that you will want to make information from your application available as an RSS stream that third parties may subscribe to. For example, an information portal could represent the names of the available portlets as an RSS feed for interested parties. They would then be aware when new functionality was made available to them.

Probably the simplest way to create a valid RSS stream is to write a JavaServer Pages (JSP) page.

You cannot make an RSS stream available directly from a portlet since a portlet by definition must be displayed as part of a valid HTML page, whereas an RSS stream is an XML document. The RSS stream must be made visible through a servlet (either created directly or as a JSP page).

Although we normally use JSP to generate HTML there is nothing to stop us from using it to generate other document types. A simple example of an RSS 2.0–compliant JSP page follows:

```
<%@
   page contentType="text/xml" session="false"
%><?xml version="1.0" encoding="UTF-8"?>
<%
   java.util.Date today = new java.util.Date();
%>
<rss version="2.0">
   <channel>
      <title>Example Channel</title>
      <link>http://localhost:8080/</link>
      <description>
         The Example Channel discusses exemplary behavior
      </description>
      <copyright>(c) Dave Minter &amp; Jeff Linwood 2004</copyright>
      <lastBuildDate><%= today %></lastBuildDate>
      <generator>Example RSS JSP</generator>
      <managingEditor>tom@example.com</managingEditor>
      <webMaster>dick@example.com</webMaster>

      <% for( int i = 0; i < 10; i++ ) { %>
      <item>
         <title>Example Title Number <%= i %></title>
         <guid isPermaLink="false"><%= i %></guid>
         <link>http://localhost:8080/<%= i %>/</link>
         <pubDate><%= today %></pubDate>
         <description>
            Description for example article number <%= i %>.
         </description>
      </item>
      <% } %>
   </channel>
</rss>
```

While this is not an especially attractive piece of code, it clearly demonstrates the ease of generating an RSS feed. Figure 9-4 shows the generated feed in the RSS Viewer application.

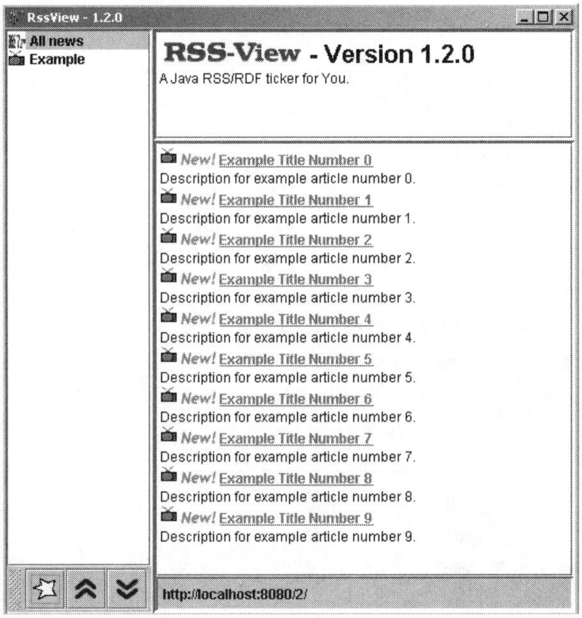

Figure 9-4. Browsing our JSP-generated feed

Alternatively, we can generate our RSS directly from code within a servlet. You could hardcode the XML into your application much as we have done with the JSP page earlier. Alternatively, you could build a Document Object Model (DOM) to represent the XML page directly. Finally, you could use a library specifically oriented to RSS, such as RSS4J, available from `www.churchillobjects.com/c/13005.html`.

RSS4J is yet another open source library, and allows you to model an RSS document rather than the rather more abstract XML document. The library permits you to build a RSS 0.9, 0.91, or 1.0 document, but does not currently allow you to build a 2.0-compliant document.

Here is an example use of the library:

```
import java.io.*;
import javax.servlet.ServletException;
import javax.servlet.http.*;
import churchillobjects.rss4j.*;
import churchillobjects.rss4j.generator.*;

public class RSSExample
   extends HttpServlet
{
    public RSSExample() {
    }
```

```
    public void init() {
        document = new RssDocument();
        document.setVersion(RssDocument.VERSION_91);

        RssChannel channel = new RssChannel();
        channel.setChannelLanguage("en");
        channel.setChannelTitle("The Periodical of the Exemplary Society");
        channel.setChannelLink("http://example.com");
        channel.setChannelDescription(
            "Discourse on the subject, object, and practice of examples");
        channel.setChannelUri("http://example.com/rss/");
        document.addChannel(channel);

        for (int i = 0; i < 10; i++) {
            RssChannelItem item = new RssChannelItem();
            item.setItemTitle("Article number " + i);
            item.setItemLink("http://example.com/" + i);
            item.setItemDescription(
                "Example description of article number " + i);
            channel.addItem(item);
        }
    }

    protected void doGet(
        HttpServletRequest request,
        HttpServletResponse response)
        throws ServletException, IOException {

        try {
            response.setContentType("text/xml");
            OutputStream out = response.getOutputStream();
            RssGenerator.generateRss(document, out);
            out.flush();
        } catch (RssGenerationException e) {
            throw new ServletException("Cannot generate RSS feed", e);
        }
    }

    private RssDocument document;
}
```

In our example, an `RssDocument` is built into the `init()` method (when the servlet is first loaded). This is then rendered every time that the `doGet()` method is invoked. Figure 9-5 shows the generated feed in the RSS Viewer application.

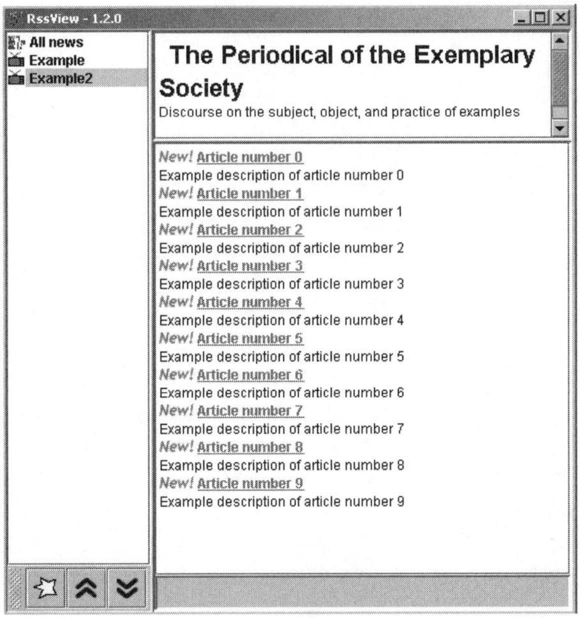

Figure 9-5. Browsing our servlet-generated feed

The major objects used here—`RssDocument`, `RssChannel`, and `RssChannelItem`—correspond exactly with the elements that are required in the RSS feed.

If RSS4J does not meet your needs, it would be fairly easy to extend. Alternatively, the open source Element Construction Set (ECS) from Jakarta at `http://jakarta.apache.org/ecs/` provides a tool for building this sort of document while still avoiding much of the complexity of DOM.

Summary

In this chapter, we discussed the origins of RSS and the various available flavors. We introduced you to an RSS browser application and demonstrated how you can incorporate an RSS feed into your portal. Finally, we showed how you can create an RSS feed from your own applications using the RSS4J library.

In the next chapter, we will show you how to incorporate search tools into your portlets and applications.

CHAPTER 10

Integrating the Lucene Search Engine

Most portal application deployments require a search engine. Portals usually unify content and applications from across an organization, and users may not know where to go to find their information. Deploying a well-thought-out, integrated search engine inside your portal is not just about the search engine technology used—some thought and design has to go into the overall information architecture of the portal and its component portlet applications.

An important consideration is content delivery and display within the portal. How are you going to present the user with HTML content? In our example, we deliver HTML content from the file system through to the portal page when the user clicks on a search result.

Knowledge of information retrieval terms and techniques is extremely useful when designing a search engine implementation, as is an understanding of the user's needs and requirements for search. Launching a limited trial period, a beta, or an initial implementation helps to gather user feedback and real-world results: What terms are users searching for? Do they understand the query language? Are they using the query language or other advanced features? Is the indexed content the set of content they need?

Overview of Lucene

Jakarta Apache Lucene (`http://jakarta.apache.org/lucene`) is an open source search engine written in Java and licensed under the Apache Software License. Lucene is not a full-featured search engine that is ready to plug in to your web application and go, like most commercial search engines. Lucene does not offer a default user interface, and you will need to develop your own integration code to plug it into your portal. Lucene also does not have any web crawlers or spiders, so you will be responsible for providing content to Lucene. Lucene has a well-defined Java API that abstracts most of the underlying information retrieval processing and concepts.

Lucene's advantage is its flexibility. Because it makes no assumptions about what kind of repository your content is in, you can use Lucene in almost any Java application. Another advantage is that Lucene is open source, so if your search results are not what you expect, you can inspect the source code. Lucene also has a thriving community, and several third-party projects and tools are available that could be useful for your application. You'll find a collection of third-party contributions on the Lucene web page (`http://jakarta.apache.org/lucene/docs/contributions.html`).

> **TIP** *If you need a web crawler to spider your web site(s), try the open source project Nutch (`www.nutch.org`). Doug Cutting started the Nutch project and the Lucene project, and Nutch creates Lucene indexes.*

Understanding how Lucene works requires knowledge of the key Lucene concepts, especially creating an index and querying an index. Most of Lucene is straightforward; we've found that Lucene is easy to use once you see how a sample application works.

We use a Lucene tag library in our portlet to speed up the development process—although we used the tag library, you don't have to in your application.

Downloading and Installing Lucene

For this chapter, we use version 1.4 of Lucene. At the time of writing, the current version is 1.4 RC3, but the final release of 1.4 should be available. You can download the latest version of Lucene at the Jakarta Lucene web page (`http://jakarta.apache.org/lucene`) as either a source or binary distribution. Copy the main JAR file (lucene-1.4.jar or similar) to your portlet application's WEB-INF/lib directory. Lucene uses the local file system to store the search engine index, so you will not need to set up a database. Lucene will store its index on the file system or in memory. If you need to use a database, you must create a new subclass of Lucene's `org.apache.lucene.store.Directory` abstract class that stores the index using SQL.

Lucene Concepts

Lucene is a powerful search engine, but developing an application that uses Lucene is simple. There are two key functions that Lucene provides: creating an index and executing a user's query. Your application is responsible for setting up each of these, but they can be treated as two separate parts that share common parts of the Lucene API.

One part of your application should be responsible for creating the index, as shown in Figure 10-1. The index is stored on the file system in its own directory. Lucene will create several files in this directory. While your application is adding or removing documents in the index, other threads or applications will not be able to update the index. Lucene will find documents only in the index; Lucene does not have any kind of live content update facility unless you build it. Your application is responsible for keeping the index up-to-date. If your content is dynamic and changes often, your content update code should probably also update the Lucene index. You can remove an existing document from the Lucene index, and then add a new one—this is called incremental indexing.

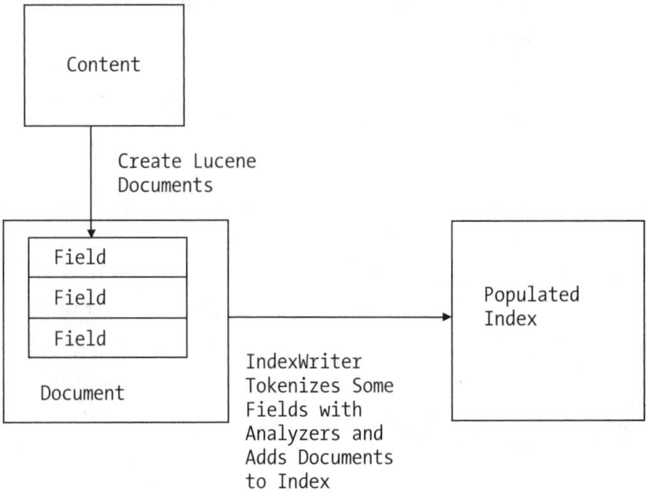

Figure 10-1. Creating the Lucene index

The other half of your application queries the index you created and processes the search results, seen in Figure 10-2. You can pass Lucene a query, and it will determine which pieces of content in the index are relevant. By default, Lucene will order the search results by each result's score (the higher the better) and return an `org.apache.lucene.search.Hits` object. The `Hits` object points to an `org.apache.lucene.document.Document` object for each hit in the search results. Your application can ask for the appropriate document by number, if you want to page your search results.

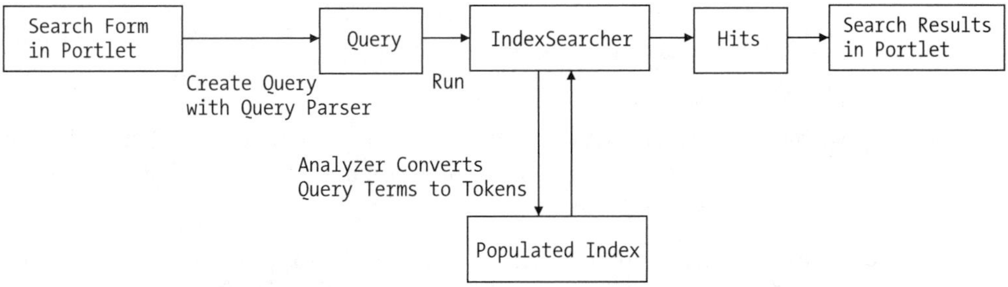

Figure 10-2. Querying the index

Documents

Lucene's index consists of documents. A Lucene document represents one indexed object. This could be a web page, a Microsoft Word document, a row in a database table, or a Java object. Each document consists of a set of fields. Fields are name/value pairs that represent a piece of content, such as the title, the summary, or the primary key. We discuss fields later in this chapter.

The `org.apache.lucene.document.Document` class represents a Lucene document. You can create a new `Document` object directly.

Analyzer

An analyzer uses a set of rules to turn freeform text into tokens for text processing. Lucene comes with several analyzers: `StandardAnalyzer`, `StopAnalyzer`, `GermanAnalyzer`, and `RussianAnalyzer`, among others. The analyzers are in the `org.apache.lucene.analysis` package and its subpackages. Each analyzer will process text differently. Lucene uses these analyzers for two purposes: to create the index and to query the index. When you add a document to Lucene's index, Lucene will use an analyzer to process the text for any fields that are tokenized (unstored and text).

Query

The query comes from a query parser, which is an instance of the `org.apache.lucene.queryParser.QueryParser` class. The portlet creates a query parser for a field in a document, with an analyzer. It is very important to make sure that the analyzer the query parser uses for a field is the same analyzer used for the field when the index was created. If the analyzer is a different class, the results will not be what you expect.

The `parse()` method on the `QueryParser` class returns an `org.apache.lucene.search.Query` object from a search string. Lucene supports many advanced types of querying, including those shown in Table 10-1.

Table 10-1. Different Query Types in Lucene

Search Type	Description
Wildcard searches	Lucene supports the asterisk as a multiple-character wildcard, as in "portal*", or the question mark to replace one character, as in "????let".
Fuzzy searches	You can find terms that are similar to your term's spelling with fuzzy searching. Add a tilde to the end of your search term: "dog~".

Table 10-1. Different Query Types in Lucene (continued)

Search Type	Description
Field searches	If you tell users the names of the fields you used in your index, they can use those fields to narrow down their searches. You can have several terms, all with different fields. For instance, you may want to find documents with the title "Sherlock Holmes", and the word "elementary" in the contents: "title:Sherlock Holmes AND elementary".
Search operators	Lucene supports AND, OR, NOT, and exclude (-). Lucene defaults to OR for any terms, but documents that contain all or most of the terms will generally have higher scores. The exclude (-) operator disallows any hits that contain the term that directly follows the -; for example: "hamlet –shakespeare".

You can pass the `Query` object to an `org.apache.lucene.search.IndexSearcher` object, which is discussed later in this chapter.

Term

The terms of a query are the individual keywords or phrases the user is looking for in the indexed content. In Lucene, the `org.apache.lucene.index.Term` object consists of a `String` that represents the word or phrase, and another `String` that names the document's field. You create a `Term` object with its constructor:

```
public Term(String fld, String txt)
```

The `text()` and `field()` methods return the text and field passed in as arguments to the constructor:

```
public final String text()
public final String field()
```

Many of the `Query` classes take a `Term` argument in their constructor, including `TermQuery`, `MultiTermQuery`, `PrefixQuery`, `RangeQuery`, and `WildcardQuery`. `PhraseQuery` and `PhrasePrefixQuery` have an `add()` method that takes a `Term` object. The query classes reside in the `org.apache.lucene.search` package.

Terms are useful if you are constructing a query programmatically, or if you need to modify or remove content from the index.

Field

A field is a name/value pair that represents one piece of metadata or content for a Lucene document. Each field may be indexed, stored, and/or tokenized, all of which affect the storage of the field in the Lucene index. Indexed fields are searchable in Lucene, and Lucene will process them when the indexer adds the document to the index. A copy of the stored field's content is persisted in the Lucene index, which is useful for content the search results page displays verbatim. Lucene processes the contents of tokenized fields into sets of individual tokens using an analyzer.

The `Field` object is in the `org.apache.lucene.document` package, and there are two ways to create a `Field` object. The first is to use a constructor method:

```
public Field(String name, String string, boolean store, boolean index,
             boolean token, boolean storeTermVector)
```

The other way is to use one of the static methods on the `Field` object. The methods are shown in Table 10-2.

Table 10-2. Static Methods for Creating a Field Object

Method	Description
`Field.Keyword(String name, String value)`	Creates a field that is indexed and stored, but not tokenized. Use the `Keyword()` method if you will need to retrieve metadata such as the last modified date, the URL, or the size of the document. This field is searchable.
`Field.UnIndexed(String name, String value)`	Creates a field that is stored in the index, but not tokenized or indexed. Unindexed fields are useful for primary keys, IDs, and other internal properties of a document. This field is not searchable.
`Field.Text(String name, String value)`	Creates a field that is tokenized, indexed, and stored. Use text fields for content that is searchable text but needs to be displayed in the search results. Examples of text fields would be summaries, titles, short descriptions, or other small amounts of text. Usually, text fields would not be used for large quantities of text because the original is stored in the Lucene index.

Table 10-2. Static Methods for Creating a Field Object (continued)

Method	Description
`Field.UnStored(String name, String value)`	Creates a field that is indexed and tokenized, but not stored. Use unstored fields for large pieces of content that do not need to appear in the search results in their original form. Examples of these would be PDF files, web pages, articles, long descriptions, or other large pieces of text.

Boost

You can improve your search engine's efficiency with the boost factor for a field. If the field is very important in your document, you can set a high boost factor to increase the score of any hits on this field. Examples of important fields include keywords, subject, or summary. The default boost factor is 1.0. The `setBoost(float boost)` method on the `Field` object provides a way to increase or decrease the boost for a given field.

Each Lucene document also has a boost factor, which you can use to selectively increase or decrease the score for some documents. One way to apply this in a portal environment would be to identify a subset of your web pages that are effective landing pages or hub pages for the rest of your content. In your Lucene indexing code, your indexer could set the boost on these pages to a number like 1.5 or 2.0. You can fine-tune your results this way, especially if you would like pages to show up at the top of the results for specific terms.

IndexSearcher

Your application will use the `org.apache.lucene.search.IndexSearcher` class to search the index for a query. After you construct the query, you can create a new `IndexSearcher` class. `IndexSearcher` takes a path to a Lucene index as an argument to the constructor. Two other constructors exist for using an existing `org.apache.lucene.index.IndexReader` object, or an instance of the `org.apache.lucene.store.Directory` object. If you would like to support federated searches, where results are aggregated from more than one index, you can use the `org.apache.lucene.search.MultiSearcher` class. Lucene indexes are stored in `Directory` objects, which could be on the file system or in memory. We use the default file system implementation, but the `org.apache.lucene.store.RAMDirectory` class supports a memory-only index.

To use the `IndexSearcher` object once you create it, call the `search()` method with your query as an argument:

```
public final Hits search(Query query) throws IOException
```

Several other `search()` methods use filters and sorts. Filters restrict the user's query from accessing the entire index, and different sorts return the search results in different orders.

Be sure to call the `close()` method when your application is finished. Because the `search()` methods throw an `IOException`, you should call `close()` from a `finally` block:

```
public void close() throws IOException
```

Hits

The `search()` method on the `IndexSearcher` class returns an `org.apache.lucene.search.Hits` object. The `Hits` object contains the number of search results, a way to access the `Document` object for each result, and the score for each hit.

The `Hits` class is not just a simple collection class. Because a search could potentially return thousands of hits, populating a `Hits` object with all of the `Document` objects would be unwieldy, especially because only a small number of search results are likely to be presented to the user at any one time. The `doc(int n)` method returns a `Document` that contains all of the document's fields that were stored at the time the document was indexed. Any fields that were not marked as stored will not be available.

```
public final Document doc(int n) throws IOException
```

The `length()` method returns the number of search results that matched the query:

```
public final int length()
```

Lucene also calculates a score for each hit in the search results. If you want to show the user of your application the score, you can use the `score(int n)` method:

```
public final float score(int n) throws IOException
```

Stemming

Stemming uses the root of a search keyword to find matches in the indexed content of other words with that stem. The suffix of each word is stripped out, and the results are compared. For instance, a stemming algorithm would consider content with the word "dogs" a valid hit for the search keyword "dog", and vice versa. Other examples of words that would match would be "wandering", "wanderer", and "wanderers". The Porter Stemming Algorithm is one of the most commonly used stemming algorithms for information retrieval. The `org.apache.lucene.analysis.PorterStemFilter` token filter class implements Porter stemming in Lucene.

To use the Porter stem filter, you will need to extend or create your own `Analyzer` class. For more about the Porter Stemming Algorithm, visit Martin Porter's web page (`www.tartarus.org/~martin/PorterStemmer/`).

Building an Index with Lucene

Our Lucene application builds its index from HTML files stored on the local file system. Your application could build an index from products in a database, PDF files in a document management system, web pages on a remote web server, or any other source. Because Lucene does not come with any web crawlers or spiders, you will need to write a Java class that indexes the appropriate content.

The first step is to find all of the content, and the next step is to process the content into Lucene documents. We are going to use the `org.apache.lucene.demo.HTMLDocument` class that comes with the Lucene demo to convert our HTML files into Lucene documents. After we create a document, we will need to add it to our index using the `org.apache.lucene.index.IndexWriter` class. The final steps are to optimize and close the Lucene index.

Creating an IndexWriter

The first thing we need to do is create an `IndexWriter` that will build our index. The `IndexWriter` constructor takes three arguments: the path to the directory that will hold the index, an instance of an `Analyzer` class, and whether or not the index should erase any existing files. Here is the code from our example:

```
writer = new IndexWriter(indexPath, analyzer, true);
```

The `indexPath` variable came from the `main()` method, we created an instance of the `StandardAnalyzer`, and we will erase any existing index.

Finding the Content

Our example indexer reads the list of files in a directory on the file system and indexes all of those files. It takes the path to the directory that contains the content files and a path to the directory that will contain the Lucene index as arguments.

Lucene comes with a demo application that is slightly more advanced than our example; it recursively searches through the directory on the file system to build the list of files. The PDFBox (`www.pdfbox.org`) project has an improved version of the Lucene demo indexer that also uses the PDFBox PDF parser to build Lucene documents.

Building Documents

Because our portlet is going to index HTML content, we need an HTML parser. Indexing the content is more effective if you strip out the HTML tags first. A good HTML parser will also provide access to the HTML tags. In our example, we are going to use the titles of the web pages to display our results.

Rather than write our own class to turn HTML into a Lucene document, we are going to use one of Lucene's bundled classes, `org.apache.lucene.demo.HTMLDocument`. The Lucene demo classes are in the lucene-demos-1.4.jar file, so add this JAR file to your classpath when you run the indexer.

The `HTMLDocument` class uses `HTMLParser`, which is a Java class generated by the Java parser generator JavaCC. The source code and compiled Java class for `HTMLParser` comes with the Lucene distribution; like `HTMLDocument`, it is packaged in the lucene-demos-1.4.jar file.

Inside the `HTMLDocument` class, the static `Document(java.io.File f)` method takes an HTML file and populates a new Lucene document with the appropriate fields. Some of the fields, such as url and modified, come from the `java.io.File` class. The class extracts the title field from the HTML title tag. After stripping the content of its HTML tags, the content is added to the document as the contents field. The `HTMLDocument` class adds the contents field with the `Field.Text()` method, but because it uses a `Reader` object instead of a `String`, the contents are tokenized and indexed but not stored:

```
package org.apache.lucene.demo;

/**
 * Copyright 2004 The Apache Software Foundation
 *
 * Licensed under the Apache License, Version 2.0 (the "License");
 * you may not use this file except in compliance with the License.
 * You may obtain a copy of the License at
 *
```

```
 *      http://www.apache.org/licenses/LICENSE-2.0
 *
 * Unless required by applicable law or agreed to in writing, software
 * distributed under the License is distributed on an "AS IS" BASIS,
 * WITHOUT WARRANTIES OR CONDITIONS OF ANY KIND, either express or implied.
 * See the License for the specific language governing permissions and
 * limitations under the License.
 */

import java.io.*;
import org.apache.lucene.document.*;
import org.apache.lucene.demo.html.HTMLParser;

/** A utility for making Lucene Documents for HTML documents. */

public class HTMLDocument
{
    static char dirSep = System.getProperty("file.separator").charAt(0);

    public static String uid(File f)
    {
        // Append path and date into a string in such a way that lexicographic
        // sorting gives the same results as a walk of the file hierarchy.  Thus
        // null (\u0000) is used both to separate directory components and to
        // separate the path from the date.
        return f.getPath().replace(dirSep, '\u0000')
            + "\u0000"
            + DateField.timeToString(f.lastModified());
    }

    public static String uid2url(String uid)
    {
        String url = uid.replace('\u0000', '/'); // replace nulls with slashes
        return url.substring(0, url.lastIndexOf('/')); // remove date from end
    }

    public static Document Document(File f)
        throws IOException, InterruptedException
    {
        // make a new, empty document
        Document doc = new Document();

        // Add the url as a field named "url".  Use an UnIndexed field, so
        // that the url is just stored with the document, but is not searchable.
        doc.add(Field.UnIndexed("url", f.getPath().replace(dirSep, '/')));
```

```
        // Add the last modified date of the file a field named "modified".  Use a
        // Keyword field, so that it's searchable, but so that no attempt is made
        // to tokenize the field into words.
        doc.add(
            Field.Keyword(
                "modified",
                DateField.timeToString(f.lastModified())));

        // Add the uid as a field, so that the index can be incrementally
        // maintained.
        // This field is not stored with the document; it is indexed, but it is
        // not tokenized prior to indexing.
        doc.add(new Field("uid", uid(f), false, true, false));

        HTMLParser parser = new HTMLParser(f);

        // Add the tag-stripped contents as a Reader-valued Text field so it will
        // get tokenized and indexed.
        doc.add(Field.Text("contents", parser.getReader()));

        // Add the summary as an UnIndexed field, so that it is stored and
        // returned with hit documents for display.
        doc.add(Field.UnIndexed("summary", parser.getSummary()));

        // Add the title as a separate Text field, so that it can be searched
        // separately.
        doc.add(Field.Text("title", parser.getTitle()));

        // return the document
        return doc;
    }

    private HTMLDocument()
    {
    }
}
```

Adding Documents with the IndexWriter

After we create the Lucene document from the file, we need to add the document to the index. We call the `addDocument()` method on the instance of the `IndexWriter` we created:

```
// add the document to the index
try
{
    Document doc = HTMLDocument.Document(file);
    writer.addDocument(doc);
}
catch (IOException e)
{
    System.out.println("Error adding document: " + e.getMessage());
}
catch (InterruptedException e)
{
    System.out.println("Error adding document: " + e.getMessage());
}
```

Lucene makes adding documents to the index easy.

Optimizing and Closing the Index

The last step is to optimize the index, which means that Lucene will merge all of the different segment files it stored in the directory into one file. This improves the performance of queries. We also close the `IndexWriter`, which removes the lock from the index directory. We are using the index directory as the lock directory instead of the default Java temporary directory because our portlet does not share the same Java temporary directory when it runs on Pluto.

```
//optimize the index
writer.optimize();

//close the index
writer.close();
```

If you do not remember to call the `close()` method, your future index updates will fail because of the lock file.

Indexer Java Class

Here is our completed Lucene indexer class:

```
package com.portalbook.search;

import java.io.*;
```

```
import org.apache.lucene.analysis.Analyzer;
import org.apache.lucene.analysis.standard.StandardAnalyzer;
import org.apache.lucene.demo.HTMLDocument;
import org.apache.lucene.document.Document;
import org.apache.lucene.index.IndexWriter;

public class Indexer
{

    protected IndexWriter writer = null;

    protected Analyzer analyzer = new StandardAnalyzer();

    public void init(String indexPath) throws IOException
    {
        //set Lucene lockdir
        System.setProperty("org.apache.lucene.lockdir", indexPath);

        //create a new Lucene index, overwriting the existing one.
        writer = new IndexWriter(indexPath, analyzer, true);
    }

    public void indexFiles(String contentPath) throws IOException
    {
        File contentDir = new File(contentPath);

        if (!contentDir.exists())
        {
            throw new IOException("Content directory does not exist.");
        }

        if (!contentDir.isDirectory())
        {
            System.out.println(contentPath + " is not a directory.");
            return;
        }

        File[] indexableFiles = contentDir.listFiles();
        {
            if (indexableFiles != null)
            {
                for (int ctr = 0; ctr < indexableFiles.length; ctr++)
                {
                    if (indexableFiles[ctr].isFile())
                    {
```

```
                        updateIndex(writer, indexableFiles[ctr]);
                    }
                }
            }
        }

        //optimize the index
        writer.optimize();

        //close the index
        writer.close();

    }

    public void updateIndex(IndexWriter writer, File file)
    {

        // add the document to the index
        try
        {
            Document doc = HTMLDocument.Document(file);

            writer.addDocument(doc);

        }
        catch (IOException e)
        {
            System.out.println("Error adding document: " + e.getMessage());
        }
        catch (InterruptedException e)
        {
            System.out.println("Error adding document: " + e.getMessage());
        }
    }

    public static void main(String args[])
    {

        Indexer indexer = new Indexer();
        try
        {
            String content = "./content";
            String index = "./lucene";
```

```
            if (args.length > 0)
            {
                content = args[0];
                System.out.println(content);
            }

            if (args.length > 1)
            {
                index = args[1];
                System.out.println(index);
            }

            //create the directory for the index if it does not exist
            File indexDir = new File(index);
            indexDir.mkdir();

            indexer.init(index);
            indexer.indexFiles(content);

        }
        catch (Exception e)
        {
            System.out.println(e.getMessage());
        }
    }
}
```

Designing a Portlet to Search the Index

The search portlet will render a small search query content display until the user executes a query. Then the search portlet will render a larger piece of content with the search form and the search results, displaying in the same portlet. Our portlet asks the portal to maximize the search portlet to display the results and the content. If the user selects one of the hits in the search results, it displays in the same portlet.

You can use our search portlet as a starting point to build your own portlet application with Lucene. Because one portlet cannot launch another portlet with the portlet API, we need to build content display technology into the search portlet. To display content, we need to retrieve it, and then render it in the portlet window.

> **TIP** *Future versions of the portlet API will support interportlet communication. It is possible that the ability to create a new portlet from an existing portlet will be added. If we had that capability, we could keep the existing search portlet, and then display a new portlet with the appropriate content.*

Developing a Portlet for Lucene

We start by extending the `GenericPortlet` class, just like we did for our other portlets. This portlet has an `init()` method that we use to configure the location of the Lucene index. When the user first calls the portlet, we display the SearchForm.jsp page in the portlet. After the user sends a search, we process the action and also display SearchResults.jsp. We use a Lucene JSP tag library to execute the query and display the results in the portlet.

Initializing the Portlet

The `init()` method on the `SearchPortlet` class is basic. We check the portlet's `PortletConfig` configuration for an initialization parameter named `indexPath`. If this initialization parameter does not exist, we throw an `UnavailableException` with an informative error.

```
public void init(PortletConfig config) throws PortletException
{
    super.init(config);

    //get the location of the Lucene index from the
    //indexPath initialization parameter
    indexPath = config.getInitParameter("indexPath");

    if (indexPath == null)
    {
        //this portlet requires this parameter
        String errMsg = "The init parameter indexPath must be set.";
        throw new UnavailableException(errMsg);
    }

    //set Lucene lockdir because java.io.tmpdir may not exist in Pluto
    System.setProperty("org.apache.lucene.lockdir", indexPath);
}
```

> **NOTE** *With Pluto, we needed to use a workaround for Lucene 1.4-rc3's lock directory. Lucene uses locks because only one thread can be updating the index at a time. In previous versions of Lucene, the program would check the* `java.io.tmpdir` *Java system property and use the temporary directory for the locks. Lucene 1.4 will use the* `java.io.tmpdir` *as a default, but uses the value of the* `org.apache.lucene.lockdir` *system property if it exists.*
>
> *In our search portlet and our indexer, we use the Lucene index directory for the lock directory. One advantage of this scenario is that portals on different servers can use the same Lucene index on a networked file system, and the servers will respect the Lucene locks. Each server's temporary directory (the* `java.io.tmpdir` *value) would be different, so it is important to map the Lucene lock directory to a shared location. Another possibility would be to create a separate lock directory and use that with all applications that share a Lucene index.*

Here is the relevant section of the portlet.xml deployment descriptor for our portlet's initialization parameter:

```
<portlet-app ...>
    <portlet>
...

        <init-param>
            <description>File system location of the Lucene index</description>
            <name>indexPath</name>
            <value>c:\temp\lucene</value>
        </init-param>
...
    </portlet>
 </portlet-app>
```

You will need to adjust the initialization parameter's value to point to a directory on your file system.

Displaying the Search Form

The `render()` method includes the SearchForm.jsp page in the output. The JSP page is a basic HTML form. The form posts the user's query to the portlet's action URL, so our `processAction()` method can handle the query.

```
<%@ taglib uri='http://java.sun.com/portlet' prefix='portlet'%>

<FORM ACTION="<portlet:actionURL/>">
```

```
Search the Lucene index: <INPUT TYPE="text" SIZE="25" NAME="query">
<BR>
<INPUT TYPE="SUBMIT">
</FORM>
```

Processing the Query

The processAction() method does only two things: increases the portlet's requested size, and sets a render parameter with the query. The portlet requests that the portal maximize the portlet, so it can display the search results, using the setWindowState() method on the ActionResponse. Because the query parameter from the search form's POST request goes to the processAction() method, we need to pass the user's query to the render request. We set a render request parameter named query on the ActionResponse object.

```
public void processAction(ActionRequest request, ActionResponse response)
    throws PortletException, IOException
{

    //increase the portlet's size
    response.setWindowState(WindowState.MAXIMIZED);

    //pass the query to the render method
    response.setRenderParameter("query", request.getParameter("query"));
}
```

Displaying the Results

We used Iskandar Salim's Lucene JSP tag library to display our results. You can download the tag library from its web page, www.javaxp.net/lucene-taglib. The Lucene tag library has an Apache Software Foundation 2.0 open source license.

To use the tag library in this example, add the TLD definition file to the /tld directory under your WEB-INF folder, and add the taglibs-lucene.jar file to your WEB-INF/lib directory.

There are three tags in the JSP tag library: <search>, <index>, and <field>. We are only going to use the <search> tag.

The <search> tag provides us with an easy way to pass a query to an index. We defined the path to the index as a request attribute, so we retrieve it in the scriptlet at the top of the page. The JSP tag takes the name of the field to search as an attribute: field="contents". The <search> tag also takes an attribute for the analyzer, analyzer="standard", for the StandardAnalyzer class. The var attribute names the variable that holds the Hits object. The startRow and maxRow attributes are useful for JSP-based search result paging. The count attribute names the variable used to hold the number of search results.

We use the tag in SearchResults.jsp, which is shown here:

```
<%@ page import="java.util.SortedMap" %>
<%@ page import="javax.portlet.PortletURL" %>

<%@ taglib uri="/WEB-INF/tld/taglibs-lucene.tld" prefix="lucene" %>
<%@ taglib uri='http://java.sun.com/portlet' prefix='portlet'%>
<portlet:defineObjects/>

<%
    String query = request.getParameter("query");
    if (query == null)
    {
        query = "";
    }
    String indexPath = (String) request.getAttribute("indexPath");
%>

<lucene:search var="hits"
    scope="page"
    field="contents"
    analyzer="standard"
    query="<%= query %>"
    startRow="0"
    maxRows="20"
    directory="<%= indexPath %>"
    count="count" />

<p>Total Number of Pages
for <b><%= query %></b> : <%= pageContext.getAttribute("count") %></p>
<% SortedMap[] hits = (SortedMap[]) pageContext.getAttribute("hits"); %>
<% if (hits.length > 0) {   for (int i = 0; i < hits.length; i++) { %>
<p/>
<%
    PortletURL renderUrl = renderResponse.createRenderURL();
    renderUrl.setParameter("contentPath", (String) hits[i].get("url"));
%>
<a href="<%=renderUrl.toString()%>"><%= hits[i].get("title") %></a>
<br/>
<%= hits[i].get("summary") %>
<br/>(Score : <%= hits[i].get("score") %>)
<% } } %>
```

Displaying the Content

Because our content is on the file system, we can open the files with a `FileReader`. We use a `BufferedReader` to write each line of the HTML content to the portlet's writer, which would work well only for HTML.

In a more advanced portlet, we would abstract the content delivery out of the portlet, and return content from a content delivery adapter to the portlet. For instance, HTML pages stored on the file system or in a database could be exposed to the Web with a servlet that also fixes links to work inside the portlet framework. The servlet could also deliver images, PDF files, or Microsoft Office files from the content store. Content that already exists on a web server can be proxied to the portal using a special portlet for web application integration. Jetspeed 1 has a `WebPagePortlet` class that renders applications on other web servers inside a portal, so look for that portlet to be updated for JSR 168 and Jetspeed 2. Other portals use different web clipping portlets to extract content from other web sites for the portal. Check the documentation for your portal, or use an open source web clipping portlet when one is released.

The SearchPortlet Class

Our finished `SearchPortlet` portlet displays a search form so the user can query the index. After the user queries the index, the portlet displays the search form (SearchForm.jsp) again, along with any results (SearchResults.jsp). The `processAction()` method asks the portlet to maximize the portlet by setting a new window state on the action response.

```
package com.portalbook.portlets;

import java.io.*;

import javax.portlet.ActionRequest;
import javax.portlet.ActionResponse;
import javax.portlet.GenericPortlet;
import javax.portlet.PortletConfig;
import javax.portlet.PortletContext;
import javax.portlet.PortletException;
import javax.portlet.PortletRequestDispatcher;
import javax.portlet.PortletSession;
import javax.portlet.RenderRequest;
import javax.portlet.RenderResponse;
import javax.portlet.UnavailableException;
import javax.portlet.WindowState;

public class SearchPortlet extends GenericPortlet
```

```
{
    String indexPath;

    public void init(PortletConfig config) throws PortletException
    {
        super.init(config);

        //get the location of the lucene index from the
        //indexPath initialization parameter
        indexPath = config.getInitParameter("indexPath");

        if (indexPath == null)
        {
            //this portlet requires this parameter
            String errMsg = "The init parameter indexPath must be set.";
            throw new UnavailableException(errMsg);
        }

        //set Lucene lockdir because java.io.tmpdir may not exist in Pluto
        System.setProperty("org.apache.lucene.lockdir", indexPath);
    }

    public void doView(RenderRequest request, RenderResponse response)
        throws PortletException, IOException
    {
        response.setContentType("text/html");

        Writer writer = response.getWriter();

        PortletContext portletContext = getPortletContext();

        PortletSession session = request.getPortletSession();

        PortletRequestDispatcher prd =
            portletContext.getRequestDispatcher("/WEB-INF/jsp/SearchForm.jsp");
        prd.include(request, response);

        String contentPath = request.getParameter("contentPath");

        if (request.getParameter("query") != null)
        {
            request.setAttribute("indexPath", indexPath);
            PortletRequestDispatcher prd2 =
                portletContext.getRequestDispatcher(
```

```
                "/WEB-INF/jsp/SearchResults.jsp");
            prd2.include(request, response);
        }
        else if (contentPath != null)
        {
            File file = new File(contentPath);
            if (!file.exists())
            {
                writer.write("Requested content does not exist.");
                return;
            }

            //write the content of the file out
            FileReader fr = new FileReader(file);
            BufferedReader br = new BufferedReader(fr);
            String line;
            while ((line = br.readLine()) != null)
            {
                writer.write(line);
            }
        }
    }

    public void processAction(ActionRequest request, ActionResponse response)
        throws PortletException, IOException
    {

        //increase the portlet's size
        response.setWindowState(WindowState.MAXIMIZED);

        //pass the query to the render method
        response.setRenderParameter("query", request.getParameter("query"));
    }
}
```

Indexing Other Types of Content

Lucene is capable of indexing any file format for documents, but the application that uses the Lucene search engine is responsible for translating these document types into a format that Lucene can understand. You can use open source or free solutions to index several of these, including HTML, PDF, Word, and Excel. Many Lucene users use more than one of these in their applications. Indexing XML documents usually requires custom development, because XML schemas and

DTDs are different. Table 10-3 shows several open source parsers you can use in conjunction with Lucene to index different file formats.

Table 10-3. Open Source Parsers for Different Types of Documents

Content Type	Name	Description
HTML	JavaCC and IndexHTML	An example that uses JavaCC to parse HTML into Lucene `Document` objects is provided in the Lucene web application demo that comes with the Lucene distribution.
HTML	NekoHTML	The CyberNeko HTML Parser (`www.apache.org/~andyc/neko/doc/html/`) lets you parse HTML documents and remove most of the tags from an HTML document (or all if you want), and then use the ones you left in to help create metadata for your Lucene document. NekoHTML also provides a DOM model for navigating through the HTML.
HTML	JTidy	JTidy (`http://sourceforge.net/projects/jtidy/`) cleans up HTML, and can provide a DOM interface to the HTML files through a Java API.
PDF	PDFBox	PDFBox (`http://pdfbox.org/`) is a Java API from Ben Litchfield that will let you access the contents of a PDF document. It comes with integration classes for Lucene to translate a PDF into a Lucene document.
PDF	XPDF	XPDF (`www.foolabs.com/xpdf/`) is an open source tool that is licensed under the GPL. It is not a Java tool, but there is a utility called pdftotext that can translate PDF files into text files on most platforms from the command line.

Table 10-3. Open Source Parsers for Different Types of Documents (continued)

Content Type	Name	Description
PDF	PDF to HTML	Based on xpdf, there is a utility called pdftohtml that can translate PDF files into HTML files. This is also not a Java application (`http://pdftohtml.sourceforge.net/`).
PDF	JPedal	JPedal (`www.jpedal.org`) is a Java API for extracting text and images from PDF documents.
Word	POI	Jakarta Apache POI has an early development-level Microsoft Word parser for versions of Word from Office 97, 2000, and XP (`http://jakarta.apache.org/poi/`).
Word	TextMining.org	Simple Text Extractor Library (`www.textmining.org`) extracts text from Word 6.0, 97, 2000, XP, and 2003.documents with a Java API.
Excel	POI	Jakarta Apache POI is an excellent Microsoft Excel parser for versions of Excel from Office 97, 2000, and XP (`http://jakarta.apache.org/poi/`).

Lucene and Different Types of Content

Searching every piece of content is useful for general-purpose search engines, but what if you want the user to select groups of content for a personalized search? Or if you have different groups of users, and some can only view certain content? Lucene has no built-in way to restrict content to certain classes of users, so you will have to build a custom solution that maps to your user groups or access control. This is especially important for portals that integrate content management systems. Usually, the content management systems will have their own access control solutions.

There are two key issues here. The first is that users who do not have access to a piece of content should not see that content in their search results, and the second is that users should be able to do a federated search across all content collections that they have access to.

The first step is to sort out which groups of users have access to which collections of content. This is a business-level problem. The next step is to develop Java classes to index each collection of content into a separate Lucene index. Each index should have documents with the same fields, indexed, stored, and tokenized the same way. The indexes should be in separate directories on your file system.

After you've set up your indexes, you will need to create some business logic that determines which indexes a given user has access to. You can then parse the user's query as usual, but instead of using the `IndexSearcher` class to search the index, use the `org.apache.lucene.search.MultiSearcher` class to search over a set of indexes. The hits will be aggregated, so you do not need to do anything special with your search results.

If you just want to create a federated search across multiple indexes, the `MultiSearcher` class will work. You will probably have trouble displaying the results and creating links to content if the documents' fields are different in the indexes—you would just have to write a JSP tag (or another Java class) that displayed the correct search result listing for each different type of document.

Summary

In this chapter, we discussed common Lucene concepts, along with the necessity of building the indexer and the search tools for the Lucene API. We created an indexer class that uses the `HTMLDocument` class from the Lucene demo to parse HTML files into Lucene documents.

The `SearchPortlet` searches the Lucene index our indexer created, and displays the results in a maximized portlet. When the user selects a result, we retrieve the content and display it in the portlet, for a consistent user experience.

This chapter should give you a start on adding search to your portal. Portal search is usually integrated with a content management system. We cover content management integration with the portal in Chapter 15.

CHAPTER 11

Personalization and User Attributes

Because a portlet is generally a minor part of a larger application (the portal), most of the time it will have a strictly limited canvas on which to present its information. So it is vital that the portlet should make the best possible use of this.

A portlet can acquire a considerable body of information with which to tailor its contents to specific users, and in this chapter we discuss how to take advantage of that.

Making a Good Impression

Everybody wants to be remembered. The portlet specification makes allowance for this by suggesting that portals should acquire and then provide to their portlets a set of personal information. This is provided to the portlet in the `PortletRequest` so that it is available to render and action methods.

No mechanism is provided to the portlet to alter this information—it is under the direct control of the portlet container.

The idea is that a portlet will be able to greet users by name and access their personal information silently to avoid the need for tedious form filling. For example, an e-commerce portlet might select the user's home address from the user attributes when dispatching an order. An e-mail portlet would probably make use of the name information.

We Know Who You Are

The portal may know the user because they have just logged in—or it may recall their previous visit to the site by registering a cookie. If the user has never visited the site before and they are not logged in, then no user attribute information is available to the portlet.

The attributes are provided as "key value pairs" so the specification has sensibly selected the standard `Map` interface from the collection classes as the means of accessing them. This map is obtained from the conventional attributes by means of the predefined key `PortletRequest.USER_INFO`.

Quite an array of attributes may be available to you (if you try to get a value from the map using an attribute for which there is no information, null will be returned). These are organized in a hierarchy modeled after the usual Java attribute key convention and grouped into the user's immediate personal information and their (personal and business) contact details. The hierarchy is based on the Platform for Privacy Preferences (P3P) specification from the W3C, which is available in full at `www.w3.org/TR/2004/WD-P3P11-20040427/`.

The attributes available are identical to those offered by the Web Services for Remote Portlets (WSRP) standard (discussed in the next chapter), making it straightforward to make attribute-driven portlets available as services. An exhaustive list of the keys recommended by the standard follows.

The user's immediate personal information:

```
user.bdate
user.gender
user.employer
user.department
user.jobtitle
```

The user's identifying information:

```
user.name.prefix
user.name.given
user.name.family
user.name.middle
user.name.suffix
user.name.nickName
```

The user's personal address information:

```
user.home-info.postal.name
user.home-info.postal.street
user.home-info.postal.city
user.home-info.postal.stateprov
user.home-info.postal.postalcode
user.home-info.postal.country
user.home-info.postal.organization
```

The user's personal telephone details:

```
user.home-info.telecom.telephone.intcode
user.home-info.telecom.telephone.loccode
user.home-info.telecom.telephone.number
user.home-info.telecom.telephone.ext
user.home-info.telecom.telephone.comment
```

The user's personal fax details:

```
user.home-info.telecom.fax.intcode
user.home-info.telecom.fax.loccode
user.home-info.telecom.fax.number
user.home-info.telecom.fax.ext
user.home-info.telecom.fax.comment
```

The user's personal mobile phone details:

```
user.home-info.telecom.mobile.intcode
user.home-info.telecom.mobile.loccode
user.home-info.telecom.mobile.number
user.home-info.telecom.mobile.ext
user.home-info.telecom.mobile.comment
```

The user's personal pager details:

```
user.home-info.telecom.pager.intcode
user.home-info.telecom.pager.loccode
user.home-info.telecom.pager.number
user.home-info.telecom.pager.ext
user.home-info.telecom.pager.comment
```

The user's personal e-mail and web site details:

```
user.home-info.online.email
user.home-info.online.uri
```

The user's business address:

```
user.business-info.postal.name
user.business-info.postal.street
user.business-info.postal.city
user.business-info.postal.stateprov
user.business-info.postal.postalcode
user.business-info.postal.country
user.business-info.postal.organization
```

The user's business telephone details:

```
user.business-info.telecom.telephone.intcode
user.business-info.telecom.telephone.loccode
user.business-info.telecom.telephone.number
user.business-info.telecom.telephone.ext
user.business-info.telecom.telephone.comment
```

The user's business fax details:

```
user.business-info.telecom.fax.intcode
user.business-info.telecom.fax.loccode
user.business-info.telecom.fax.number
user.business-info.telecom.fax.ext
user.business-info.telecom.fax.comment
```

The user's business mobile phone details:

```
user.business-info.telecom.mobile.intcode
user.business-info.telecom.mobile.loccode
user.business-info.telecom.mobile.number
user.business-info.telecom.mobile.ext
user.business-info.telecom.mobile.comment
```

The user's business pager details:

```
user.business-info.telecom.pager.intcode
user.business-info.telecom.pager.loccode
user.business-info.telecom.pager.number
user.business-info.telecom.pager.ext
user.business-info.telecom.pager.comment
```

And finally, the user's professional e-mail address and web site:

```
user.business-info.online.email
user.business-info.online.uri
```

Problems with User Attributes

The main problem with user attributes is that they won't necessarily be available to your portlet. Although support for them is a mandatory part of the JSR 168 specification, all of the individual attributes are optional, so the requirement has very little real force. As a result, your portal may support user attributes in name alone.

> **CAUTION** *At the time of writing, Pluto and most other open source portlet containers do not support user attributes.*

Assuming that user attributes are supported to some extent, you are given only the rather lukewarm assurance that the attributes listed in the previous section are "recommended." If your chosen portal adds other attributes to that list, there is no reason to believe that they will be available in other portals, so you must be careful not to make your portal reliant on them unless you can be certain that it will not be used outside that environment.

Let's suppose for the sake of argument that all of the listed attributes *are* supported by your portal. A user may well balk at entering nearly 70 items of very personal information. This point may be less of an issue in an intranet environment where you will often have all of this information at hand in a directory service of some sort—but if you are operating a portal for external users, you should probably not make the registering of all of this information mandatory for use of the site.

Discounting all the rest of these issues, if the user is not logged in to the portal, there may be no way to associate that user with the appropriate attributes!

The attributes are not very comprehensive—plenty of users will have more than one mobile phone number, and no pager at all. But it may be that you will want to make use of an external directory service such as Lightweight Directory Access Protocol (LDAP) in preference to working within the limitations of the user attributes anyway.

> **CAUTION** *The specification explicitly states that user information is outside its scope and that the user-attributes mechanism will probably be deprecated in favor of a future, more considered mechanism.*

Finally, we note that the specification requires the attribute associated with the user's birth date to be "an integer representing the time in milliseconds since 1970, 00:00:00 GMT." We are concerned that the behavior for dates prior to 1970 has not been defined. Perhaps the obvious solution is to use a negative number, but that which is not defined tends to get interpreted differently by different implementations. 1970 isn't that long ago—while Jeff clears it nicely with eight years to spare, Dave scrapes by with only two—and Dave's brother falls firmly into the problem range.

Note that since the standard requires the value part of each attribute to be a `String` object, the question of rolling over into the next epoch that is an issue with fixed-size time fields does not arise.

Accessing the Attributes

Despite our concerns with the implementation of user attributes, they raise no concerns for the developer from an ease-of-use perspective.

A mapping of the attribute names (as strings) to their assigned values can be retrieved from the portlet requests using the `getAttributes()` method:

```
Map userAttributes = request.getAttribute(PortletRequest.USER_INFO);
```

The retrieved reference may be null if user attributes are unsupported or unavailable; otherwise, a `Map` instance will be provided. The attribute values are then extracted to form the map:

```
String surname = (String) userAttributes.get("user.name.family");
```

The reference returned will be null if the requested attribute is unsupported or unavailable.

To illustrate this process, let's build a simple portlet that looks for and (if found) displays a set of user attributes:

```
package com.portalbook.portlets.custom;

import java.io.IOException;
import java.util.Iterator;
import java.util.Map;
import javax.portlet.GenericPortlet;
import javax.portlet.PortletException;
import javax.portlet.RenderRequest;
import javax.portlet.RenderResponse;

public class UAPortlet extends GenericPortlet
{
   protected void doView(RenderRequest request, RenderResponse response)
         throws PortletException, IOException
   {
      Map ua = (Map) request.getAttribute(RenderRequest.USER_INFO);

      response.setContentType("text/html");
      if ((ua == null) || !ua.keySet().iterator().hasNext())
      {
         response.getWriter().write(
               "<b>No user attributes could be found</b>");
      }
      else
      {
         Iterator i = ua.keySet().iterator();
         response.getWriter().write("<table>");
         while (i.hasNext())
         {
```

```
            String attributeName = (String) i.next();
            String attributeValue = (String) ua.get(attributeName);

            writeAttributeRow(response, attributeName, attributeValue);
         }
         response.getWriter().write("</table>");
      }
   }

   private void writeAttributeRow(RenderResponse response, String name,
         String value) throws IOException
   {
      StringBuffer buffer = new StringBuffer("<tr><td>");
      buffer.append(name);
      buffer.append("</td><td><b>");
      buffer.append(value);
      buffer.append("</b></td></tr>");
      response.getWriter().write(buffer.toString());
   }
}
```

Figure 11-1 shows the output of the portlet when running.

User Attribute Lister
user.name.prefix Mr
user.name.middle Charles
user.name.given David
user.employer Apress
user.name.family Minter
user.department Technical
user.jobtitle Author

Figure 11-1. User attributes revealed

In order to access the user attributes, the portlet has to tell the portal that it's interested in the information. It achieves this by adding <user-attribute> elements at the <portlet-app> level of the portlet.xml file.

Here are the appropriate entries for our example:

```
<portlet-app
   xmlns=http://java.sun.com/xml/ns/portlet/portlet-app_1_0.xsd
   version="1.0"
```

```
    xmlns:xsi=http://www.w3.org/2001/XMLSchema-instance
    xsi:schemaLocation=
     "http://java.sun.com/xml/ns/portlet/portlet-app_1_0.xsd
      http://java.sun.com/xml/ns/portlet/portlet-app_1_0.xsd"
>
    <portlet>
        <description>Portlet Attribute Lister</description>
        <!--The rest of the portlet definition
             has been omitted -->
    </portlet>
    <user-attribute>
        <description>User Given Name</description>
        <name>user.name.given</name>
    </user-attribute>
    <user-attribute>
        <description>User Title</description>
        <name>user.name.prefix</name>
    </user-attribute>
    <user-attribute>
        <description>User Name Suffix</description>
        <name>user.name.suffix</name>
    </user-attribute>
    <user-attribute>
        <description>User Family Name</description>
        <name>user.name.family</name>
    </user-attribute>
    <user-attribute>
        <description>User Middle Name</description>
        <name>user.name.middle</name>
    </user-attribute>
    <user-attribute>
        <description>User Employer Name</description>
        <name>user.employer</name>
    </user-attribute>
    <user-attribute>
        <description>User Department Name</description>
        <name>user.department</name>
    </user-attribute>
    <user-attribute>
        <description>User Job Title</description>
        <name>user.jobtitle</name>
    </user-attribute>

</portlet-app>
```

Making Choices

As we discussed in the introduction to this chapter, your portlet needs to use its screen real estate wisely. Since different users will have different requirements for your portlet, this requires you to adapt the portlet's display dynamically to respond to the current user.

The two main sources of information available to your portlet will be the login information and the user attributes. It is important to remember the distinction between the two, however. The login information is reliable. The portal will have obtained it by secure means, and if a `Principal` is provided, your portlet will be able to verify for itself that this is correct (often this is overkill, since within the portal server the portlet is subject to any of the security flaws in the container).

On the other hand, the user attributes come with no guarantee. The user might be using the same browser (and hence cookies) as some other user, or the user may have lied or misunderstood when filling in the registration form. Do not assume that because the user's name is available from the user attributes that these attributes are correct.

When deciding how to use this information, you will need to consider the business requirements first, and only then encode them in your application. Let's discuss two approaches to this: the traditional "hardcoded" technique and the "softcoded" rules-based approach.

The Traditional Approach

The traditional approach to laying out the display is simply to write code that branches depending on the status of various variables. For example, here is a code fragment that might be used to determine what to render in an online trading portlet:

```
protected void doView(RenderRequest request, RenderResponse response)
      throws PortletException, IOException
{
   Map ua = (Map) request.getAttribute(RenderRequest.USER_INFO);

   response.setContentType("text/html");
   if (ua == null)
   {
      renderDefaultPortlet(request, response);
   }
   else
   {
      if (request.isUserInRole(ADMINISTRATOR_ROLE))
      {
```

```
            renderAdministratorTools(request, response);
        }

        if (request.IsUserInRole(KEY_ACCOUNT_MANAGER_ROLE))
        {
            renderKAMTools();
            renderCustomerTools();
        }
        else if (request.IsUserInRole(SUPPORT_ROLE))
        {
            renderSupportTools();
            renderCustomerTools();
        }
        else if (request.IsUserInRole(HELPDESK_ROLE))
        {
            renderCustomerTools();
            renderHelpdeskTools();
        }

        if (request.IsUserInRole(CUSTOMER_ROLE))
        {
            if (customerNameAvailable(ua))
            {
                renderCustomerName(ua);
            }
            renderCustomerTools();
        }
        else
        {
            renderDefaultPortlet(request, response);
        }
    }
}
```

While this code is sensible, it is not easy to follow. The number of conditions involved makes it difficult to determine whether all of the decisions made are correct. For example, will staff be members of the customer group anyway? If so, then we risk rendering the customer tools twice for some administrative users.

We can hide some of this functionality inside the rendering methods, but this approach won't necessarily shield us from the difficulty of determining whether the application is doing the right thing from a business point of view.

Adding the three standard window states available to a portlet into this already complex situation makes things very much worse. Clearly an alternative approach is required.

Rules-Based Approaches

When the behavior of your application requires a great deal of branching dependent on business requirements, you are essentially coding business "rules" into your system. For example, the very first condition we encounter states in essence is

Unidentified users should see the default portlet.

Taking the remaining rules in our example, we end up with a set of quite simple statements about how the application should behave:

Administrators should see the administrator tools.

Key account managers should see the KAM tools.

Support staff should see the support tools.

Helpdesk staff should see the helpdesk tools.

Customers should see customer tools.

KAM tools include customer tools.

Support tools include customer tools.

Helpdesk tools include customer tools.

This breakdown of the rules is obviously quite programmatic in nature, but it's also close to the way that nontechnical people might think and speak about the business requirements for the portlet—that a key account manager should have access to the customer tools (perhaps to place bids on behalf of a client), but that the administrator who is concerned with determining who is on the helpdesk and who is an account manager and so forth should not.

This technique of rules-based programming is well established, and free tools are available that can help you to accomplish this. The resulting system takes on the form shown in Figure 11-2.

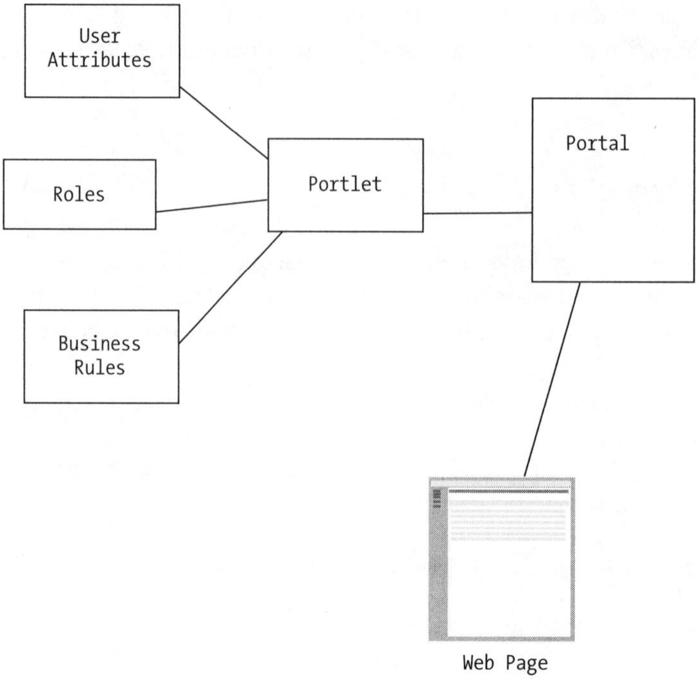

Figure 11-2. Bringing rules into the display logic

The information available to the system, such as the user attributes, the user's role memberships, and other information not shown such as the window state, is combined with the business rules to generate the output.

Most of the solutions available for applying rules-based techniques allow you to create your own business "semantics" for describing business rules. The following XML fragment shows the sort of approach that might be applied to our example problem:

```
<display>
   <tools>
      <role>Administrator</role>
      <output>Administrator</output>
   </tools>
   <tools>
      <role>KeyAccountManager</role>
      <output>KeyAccountManager,Customer</output>
   </tools>
   <tools>
      <role>Support</role>
      <output>Support,Customer</output>
```

```
    </tools>
    <tools>
        <role>Helpdesk</role>
        <output>Helpdesk,Customer</output>
    </tools>
    <tools>
        <role>Customer</role>
        <output>Customer</output>
    </tools>
    <tools>
        <role>user</role>
        <output>general</output>
    </tools>
</display>
```

If a manager decides that the helpdesk should only deal with the simplest queries and have no access to customers' details, it's a simple matter to change the appropriate entry:

```
<tools>
    <role>Helpdesk</role>
    <output>Helpdesk</output>
</tools>
```

We're perhaps not quite at the level where technophobic managers would be willing to create the business rules themselves, but we've certainly arrived at a point where business changes can be accommodated without altering the source code to the original portlet application. This type of XML-oriented presentation adapts itself well to transformation (perhaps via XSL) into formal documentation of the business process.

Although the details of preparing such a business semantics module and integrating it into your code are too extensive to be covered in depth in this chapter, several resources are available to you if you're interested in pursuing this technique.

There is a standard for integrating rules-based systems with Java, JSR 94, which is available from the Java Community Process web site (`www.jcp.org/en/jsr/detail?id=94`), and a reference implementation can be downloaded here. The reference implementation is based on the Jess library from Sandia National Laboratories, which can be downloaded from `http://herzberg.ca.sandia.gov/jess/` (Jess requires a license for commercial uses).

The open source tool DROOLS is available from `http://drools.org/`, and this implements the JSR 94 standard.

Summary

In this chapter we looked at the user attribute information available to an application, and described two techniques for using this information to present a personalized view of your portlet.

In the next chapter, we discuss how you can make your portlet available as a service so that it can be incorporated into other external portals.

CHAPTER 12

Web Services for Remote Portlets (WSRP) and Application Syndication

In this chapter, we discuss the Web Services for Remote Portlets (WSRP) standard. WSRP defines a standard way for portals to handle input and display for a portlet running on a remote portal server. With WSRP, one portal server (or a cluster) is responsible for hosting a portlet, and other portal servers can display the portlet as if it were installed locally. We present an overview of the WSRP standard, along with the steps you need to take as a portlet developer to use WSRP.

We also cover application syndication, just as we covered content syndication in Chapter 9. WSRP is one way to syndicate an application; other ways include integrated frames and proxied web applications. Some of the common problems are branding syndicated applications, Single Sign-On (SSO), and handling personalization for different users.

We are not going to discuss general web services programming for Java in this chapter. If you are interested in developing Java web services with Apache Axis, see *Enterprise Java Development on a Budget* (Apress, 2004).

WSRP Overview

Web Services for Remote Portlets (WSRP) is a standard that defines how one portal will communicate with another to display a remote portlet. The standard is language-independent, but it was codeveloped with the JSR 168 Java portlet API. Other languages and environments can also use WSRP. This standard is useful for interoperability, because portlets written in .NET can appear in a Java-based portal, and vice versa. OASIS (Organization for the Advancement of Structured Information Standards) developed the WSRP specification, and if you are interested in reading the specification, see the WSRP committee home page (`www.oasis-open.org/committees/tc_home.php?wg_abbrev=wsrp`).

Most of the WSRP specification is aimed at software developers who are writing WSRP infrastructure for portal servers. Most portlet developers will not need to know how to call WSRP web services directly—the portlet container will handle all of their portlet application's interaction with WSRP.

WSRP solves an application syndication problem. If one portal serves a portlet application, other portals can display the portlet application as if it were running locally. This puts the burden of hosting the portlet application on one group; others can use the portlet application on their servers without being responsible for ongoing maintenance. This is especially useful if one group has many more technical resources than other groups.

One example of application syndication is if the producer of a product is responsible for creating sales tools for the web sites of partners who sell the product. For instance, an auto manufacturer can create a configuration engine for its product line to enable users to pick valid choices for colors, engines, and other options. The manufacturer may invest a million dollars in this project, so it is not feasible for small auto dealers to replicate the work. Instead, the dealers can license the configuration engine from the manufacturer for use on their web sites. If the configuration engine is installed on several thousand dealer web sites, the auto manufacturer's technical support costs will be huge.

Architecture

WSRP builds on existing standards, such as SOAP (Simple Object Access Protocol) and WSDL (Web Service Definition Language). With WSRP, consumer portals will aggregate portlets from local and remote sources and provide them to the user's web browser as a portal web page. Producer portals publish portlet applications as web services that consumers can access.

We can include any WSRP-compatible portlet in any WSRP-compatible consumer, independent of the content, user information model, or preferences model. WSRP portlets are presentation-oriented, not data-oriented like other web services. We don't have to create a portlet that calls data-oriented web services and assembles the results into content; instead, the WSRP architecture allows the portlet markup to come from a web service directly. No business logic resides on the consumer portal. Figure 12-1 shows a typical application architecture for a WSRP deployment.

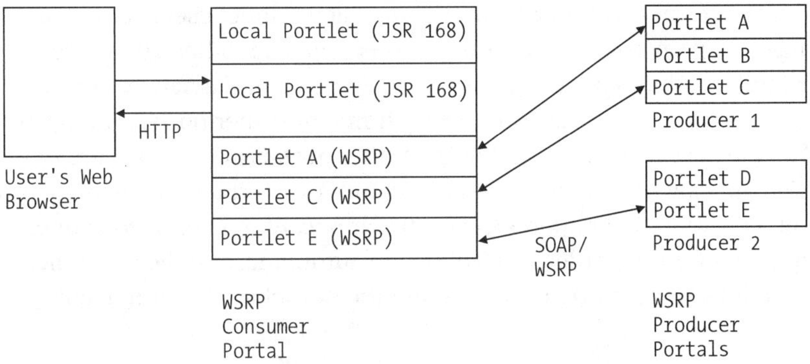

Figure 12-1. Typical WSRP architecture, with two producers and one consumer

The WSRP model should open enterprise architectures to a new range of applications for portals because all portal applications will share a common presentation model. This is important for organizations that have invested in J2EE and .NET environments because portlets running in either display in a consumer portal with WSRP.

Producers

Producers offer portlets to consumers as web services, using SOAP. The WSRP specification defines four web services for producers:

- **Service Description:** Offers information and metadata about the producer to consumers. This service is required.
- **Markup:** Provides content markup fragments for portlets, and processes interaction requests. This service is required.
- **Registration:** Allows consumers to register their information and metadata with the producer, including their capabilities. This service is optional.
- **Portlet Management:** Configures and customizes offered portlets for use by the consumer. This service is optional.

The producer must implement the Service Description and Markup web services, and may optionally implement the Registration and Portlet Management web services.

The producer does not have to be a portal that allows direct user access. For instance, a large company could have a sales portlet application hosted on a server cluster in a central location. The server cluster would be behind a network firewall that allows traffic and access (using WSRP) only from consumer portals run by its customers. The portlet's user accesses the consumer portals and is unaware that the portlet runs on a separate server. This environment has a deployment cost advantage over a solution that requires the portlet application on each consumer portal. Any upgrades for the portlet application are automatic, and the consumer portal administrators do not have to worry about the portlet application details.

Consumers

Consumers call producers to discover portlets, ask for portlet markup, or send portlet events to the producer for processing. They aggregate the portlet markup fragments into a portal page, and return that to the end user's web browser. The portlet markup fragments can come from WSRP portlets or locally running portlets.

In many cases, the consumer will be a proxy portlet that uses the Java portlet API to talk to the local portal and uses WSRP/SOAP to communicate with the producer. Not every consumer will be a portlet or otherwise embedded in a portal. Another scenario is to use the WSRP API to include syndicated applications in a web application. For instance, the navigation for the web page could be generated locally, and the remote portlet can be displayed in the content area. The web application would thus be responsible for much of what a portal does, but would not display any other portlets.

Portlets

WSRP portlets are components running on the producer that process actions and return markup or content. The WSRP portlets can conform to the Java portlet API, or they can be proprietary Java portlets, .NET portlets, or any other language. In addition, software applications that are not portals can be producers of WSRP portlets.

WSRP and the Java Portlet API

The first versions of the Java Portlet API (JSR 168) and WSRP share core portlet concepts, so JSR 168 portlets are compatible with the WSRP standard with no additional code.

WSRP portlets return markup requests, which correspond to the JSR 168 render-handling requests. WSRP portlets also process interactions, which correspond to JSR 168 action-handling requests. WSRP supports JSR 168 portlet preferences. The consumer portal information maps to the Java portlet API `PortalContext` object. This information includes supported portlet modes, supported window states, portal properties, vendor name, and version.

WSRP supports the standard JSR 168 VIEW, EDIT, and HELP portlet modes. The WSRP specification also defines the custom PREVIEW portlet mode for portlets to provide a sample or demo of how they will appear. WSRP supports custom portlet modes.

All of the standard JSR 168 window states are valid WSRP window states (normal, minimized, maximized). In addition, WSRP supports the solo window state for portlets that are the only portlet displaying in a portal page. WSRP also supports custom window states.

WSRP Markup in Content Fragments

The rules for WSRP markup in content fragments are largely the same as markup for Java portlets. One difference is that either the producer or the consumer may do markup encoding and processing for namespaces and portlet URLs.

Namespace Encoding

Namespaces must be encoded in markup for JavaScript and Dynamic HTML (DHTML), so two instances of a portlet running on the same page have unique element names. One difference is that namespaces may be encoded by the producer or by the consumer—Java portlets that use namespace encoding will use producer encoding. If you would like to use consumer encoding, any elements in the markup that need a unique namespace should start with the prefix "wsrp_rewrite_". Then the WSRP consumer is responsible for ensuring that the namespace is unique.

Character Encoding

The consumer and the portlet have to agree on a character encoding for the portlet's content fragment. The consumer tells the portlet which character encoding it would like to use, and the portlet should use that character encoding if possible. If your portlet cannot support the requested character encoding, the portlet may use either UTF-8 or UTF-16 encoding.

Consider your portlet's ability to generate different character sets if your portlet will have an international audience that uses different character encodings.

Portlet URLs

In WSRP, either the consumer or the producer can process portlet URLs for use in the consumer portal page. If a portlet generates a direct link to the producer inside the markup, the link should be intercepted and rewritten, so the user stays inside the portal. Furthermore, a firewall may exist between the user and the producer, so only the consumer can send traffic to the producer. The producer uses SOAP as a protocol, not HTTP, and the producer does not have to be able to handle an HTTP request.

The producer does not have enough information on its own to create the proper links in HTML markup. The producer needs information about the consumer's environment to create links that point to the correct portlet. The producer can get the information from the consumer and create the links itself, or the consumer can process links in the portlet content. If the consumer rewrites the links in the portlet's content markup fragment, the portlet should encode links for rewriting. The WSRP standard supports both of these approaches.

We recommend that your portlets rely on the Java portlet API to create portlet URLs for the portlet content markup fragments. This abstracts the decision on how links look to the portlet container, so your portlets can run unmodified locally or remotely. When servlets or other web applications need to be syndicated out, the application syndication software has to decide how to rewrite the URLs. With the Java portlet API, the portlet container will create the URLs for you at runtime, so the local portal environment is an abstraction.

HTML Tags

The consumer portal aggregates remote portlets' markup fragments into a full web page, just as if the remote portlet was a JSR 168 portlet running on a local portlet server. This means that your portlet cannot display several HTML and XHTML tags in the portlet's content markup. Some portals may strip these tags out of the markup, but for performance reasons, most portals probably will not.

The disallowed tags are:

- `<html>`
- `<head>`
- `<title>`
- `<body>`
- `<frame>`
- `<frameset>`

In addition, some HTML tags should appear only within the `<head>` HTML element. These include `<style>`, `<base>`, `<meta>`, and `<link>`. WSRP does not specifically forbid the portal from aggregating content with these tags into the portal page. Some leading web browsers will use these tags, even if they are not in the head of the HTML page.

Some portlet developers may decide to use these tags inside the portlet markup fragment. We do not recommend this practice, because future revisions of the WSRP standard may not support this.

The HTML tag requirements for the WSRP standard are almost the same as the markup fragment standards for the JSR 168 standard—both of these standards were developed in parallel. The only difference is that the JSR 168 specification does not include the table styles, but most portals will probably have to support the table styles for WSRP anyway. We can hope that portlet standards for other languages and environments (PHP, Python, C#/.NET) will use the same markup rules.

Cascading Style Sheets (CSS)

All of the portlets should use a common set of CSS styles to ensure a unified presentation on the portal page. The consumer portal provides the CSS style sheet that defines the look and feel for each style, so portlets may look different for each consumer portal. The portal administrator can adjust the common CSS style sheet to change the look and feel for all of the portlets.

As shown in Tables 12-1 through 12-6, the WSRP specification defines a set of standard styles that all remote portlets should support. These are the same styles allowed by the Java portlet API. (There are no special CSS styles definitions for links.)

Table 12-1. CSS Font Styles for WSRP Content

Style	Description
portlet-font	The normal font for content without any additional emphasis or markup.
portlet-font-dim	Similar to normal font, but appears lighter. This could be gray instead of black.

Table 12-2. CSS Message Styles for WSRP Content

Style	Description
portlet-msg-status	Current status of the portlet
portlet-msg-info	Useful information or help text
portlet-msg-success	Successful completion of an operation
portlet-msg-alert	Any alert or warning messages
portlet-msg-error	Any error messages

Table 12-3. CSS Section Styles for WSRP Content

Style	Description
portlet-section-body	Normal body text of a section
portlet-section-header	Header for a section
portlet-section-subheader	Subheader text for a section
portlet-section-footer	Text for a section footer
portlet-section-alternate	Used for alternating text (every other row) in a section
portlet-section-selected	Used for the selected text in a section
portlet-section-text	Any text that is not one of the above styles but that is associated with a section

Table 12-4. CSS Table Styles for WSRP Content

Style	Description
portlet-table-body	Normal body text of a table
portlet-table-header	Header for a table
portlet-table-subheader	Subheader text for a table
portlet-table-footer	Text for a table footer
portlet-table-alternate	Used for alternating text (every other row) in a table
portlet-table-selected	Used for the selected text in a table
portlet-table-text	Any text that is not one of the above styles but that is associated with a table

Table 12-5. CSS Form Styles for WSRP Content

Style	Description
portlet-form-label	Text label that describes the form as a whole, such as directions or the form's name
portlet-form-button	Button text
portlet-icon-label	Used for an icon label
portlet-dlg-icon-label	Used for text on a standard dialog button (OK, Retry, Cancel, etc.)
portlet-form-field-label	Used for text on a form input field label
portlet-form-input-field	Style for the text in a text input field
portlet-form-field	Used for text on a form input field, but not a text input field

Table 12-6. CSS Menu Styles for WSRP Content

Style	Description
portlet-menu	Overall style for the menu as a whole
portlet-menu-caption	Caption for the menu
portlet-menu-description	Help or description for the menu
portlet-menu-item	Unselected menu item
portlet-menu-item-selected	Selected menu item
portlet-menu-item-hover	Unselected menu item, with the cursor hovering over the menu item
portlet-menu-item-hover-selected	Selected menu item, with the cursor hovering over the menu item
portlet-menu-cascade-item	Unselected menu item that contains submenus
portlet-menu-cascade-item-selected	Selected menu item that contains submenus

Using WSRP

At the time of this writing, there are two open source projects with WSRP support for Java portlets. WSRP4J (`http://ws.apache.org/wsrp4j`) is an Apache project that was created by IBM. WSRP4J has two components: a producer that runs on Apache Pluto, and a consumer that runs as a Java Swing application. The producer publishes portlets as WSRP web services, and the Swing consumer can display WSRP portlets.

EXO (`http://exoplatform.org/`) has a WSRP producer service to publish portlets. It also comes with a consumer portlet that uses the EXO WSRP consumer service to consume remote portlets.

Other portals, such as Oracle Portal, are going to support WSRP in the future. Because the configuration for each portal will be different, you will need to consult the user documentation for your portal.

Common Problems with Application Syndication

Some of the most common issues with application syndication are applicable to any type of syndication. We discuss several of them, including branding, SSO, flexibility, user attributes, and personalization. WSRP addresses several of these issues at a technical level, but some problems require business solutions.

Branding

One recurring issue with application syndication is branding. Branding is an easy issue for software developers to dismiss as unimportant, but it may be a strong driving force for your portal's business case.

WSRP does not have any built-in support for branding. Your portlet will have to get information about the portlet consumer to determine how to present the portlet to users. One way to customize your application is to store all of the content for each class of portlet consumers in skins, and then send content with the appropriate skin for each user. Another approach is to create all of your content in XML, and then provide an XSLT style sheet for each consumer that customizes their look and feel. If you use the standard portlet CSS styles, each consumer can maintain their own style sheet.

You may have to provide different images for each consumer. We once worked on a project together where each user had to have a completely redone set of images because the colors on the images did not match the user's corporate colors. This was not something we could automate because the images had to be antialiased and we were on a tight budget for software. Try to discourage your business users from changing many images—often just a different logo is good enough.

Single Sign-On and Flexibility

For a coherent user experience, the syndicated application should be so well integrated with other applications and content that the user cannot tell where the application is hosted. This means that if the consumer portal can authenticate the user to the remote application itself, it should do so. We discuss SSO in Chapter 8.

One of the problems with application syndication is flexibility—if developers cannot easily change the remote application, the consumer portal needs to proxy the application. If the login and authentication API is not available, the proxy may need to set HTTP cookies, pass the username and password in a query string or parameters, keep track of session IDs, or strip out unwanted navigation.

User Information and Personalization

Sharing user information from the consumer to the application running on the producer is a common problem with application syndication. The syndication protocol has to allow for sharing of user objects or attributes between the consumer and the producer. This might be for personalization of content or for filling out the syndicated application's user profiles. JSR 168 portlets access user information from the consumer portal through WSRP, so if you use WSRP, user information access will be transparent.

Load Balancing

Many production web-hosting environments use load balancers to distribute incoming client requests to available servers. Load balancers are especially useful to take one server at a time out of the pool for scheduled maintenance or upgrades. The load balancer uses cookies or another tracking method for HTTP requests and responses to ensure that each client's requests go to the same server.

WSRP does not directly address details of load balancing and HTTP cookies for session tracking, but the consumer must return any cookies it receives. The producer may not have actually set the cookie on the HTTP response—it could have been the load balancer. As a portlet developer, you will not have to do anything different for load balancing, but the portal administrator should make sure that the consumer portal is properly handling HTTP cookies on the WSRP SOAP request. This is very important to check when you do system or integration testing because the software vendors may not have tested your combination of consumer portal/load balancer/producer portal.

Future Directions of WSRP

The current version of the WSRP specification is 1.0. The next version of the specification will be 2.0, which will probably be released in the middle of 2005. The WSRP technical committee is working on standards for publishing remote portlet catalogs for a producer, finding a remote portlet on a producer, and binding a consumer to a producer. These technical notes are planned for fall 2004.

Summary

In this chapter, we discussed the overall architecture of WSRP, including producers and consumers. Your Java portlets will be compatible with WSRP, so developers should focus on architectural and design considerations when using WSRP. The portlet container can automatically make these available to WSRP consumers, so application syndication becomes an administrative task, not a development project. We covered some of the markup limitations portlet developers need to take into account. WSRP is not the only kind of application syndication, and we discussed common application syndication issues. These included user information, SSO, and branding.

CHAPTER 13

Exposing an Existing Application As a Portlet

IN THIS CHAPTER WE take an existing web application, the YAZD forum software, and adapt it to provide a portlet front end. Initially, we install the forum software in its unaltered state; then we show the decisions and changes we make in the process of building the portlet.

Overview of the YAZD Forum Software

The YAZD forum software is available from `http://yazd.yasna.com` as an open source product under the Apache License. This means that you are allowed to make any changes you want to the source code as long as you keep all of the original copyright messages and as long as you call your resulting product something different.

This software has quite a few rough edges. Sometimes errors will be displayed to the user instead of being caught and handled nicely. The initial configuration of the application is quite complex. However, the code is readily adaptable and sensibly designed, and the flaws can be fixed in the process of adapting it to a portal environment.

All the code used in this example is available from our web site (`http://portalbook.com/`), and it is the aim of the authors to make a complete package available.

Using YAZD

Before we embark on a conversion of the YAZD application, we need to install and configure it for our purposes. If you want to get a feel for the behavior of the forums before you install them, the YAZD support forums are hosted using YAZD itself.

Installing

To install the YAZD forums, you will need to acquire a database, with a JDBC driver, and an application server such as Tomcat. You will also need a copy of the YAZD application. For our example we've used the MySQL database.

> **CAUTION** *The MySQL database is very popular for small projects—and rightly so, since it is free, easy to configure, and runs on most platforms. However, it has a number of limitations that should make you very cautious about using it for larger projects.*
>
> *If you need a free database for a large project, we recommend the PostgreSQL system (though this is difficult to configure to run on Windows).*

We recommend following the installation instructions available from `http://paperstack.com/yazd` since these are slightly more comprehensive than those available from the `http://yazd.yasna.com` site.

Figure 13-1 shows what you should see once you've got the administration side of things up and running.

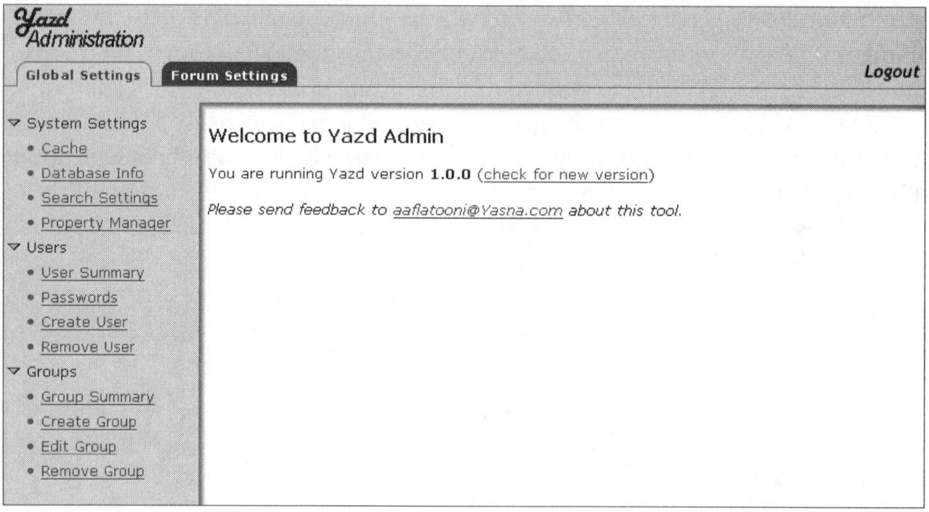

Figure 13-1. The YAZD Administration console

Configuring

Although the "general use" forums are mostly pretty slick, the forum administration page is quite idiosyncratic (probably because it has received less feedback from users). One particularly annoying bug causes a newly created forum to disappear if you haven't assigned it a moderator. To prevent this problem, we recommend that you assign the default Administrator user all privileges immediately after creating a forum.

You should then assign "read messages" and "post messages" privileges to all anonymous users.

Deciding What to Change

If you are building a portlet as a part of a large, well-funded project team—perhaps portletizing a company's premiere project—your aim in the process of portletization will be to keep as much of the existing functionality as possible.

If like most project teams you have limited time and resources, you'll be looking to cut down the scope of the project as much as possible. For our example chapter, we will be drastically trimming functionality from that offered by the complete YAZD forums—we will dispense with the user account management of the system so that only unauthenticated (anonymous) users will have access to the system. We will also omit the search functionality (based on Lucene, which we discussed in Chapter 10).

This leaves our portlet as a tool to allow anonymous users to view and post into the YAZD forums. The basic administration functionality required to create new forums and assign privileges to anonymous users can still be accessed via the original application, since all message and account information is stored in the database.

Giving Up Control

Probably the first thing to remember when you sit down to design the portlet version of an existing application is that your application is not the only game in town. You have given up some control over your environment in return for the additional features offered by that environment.

Your portlet doesn't have the whole browser window to play with when it is in its normal state, so you should endeavor to make it scale as nicely as possible. You should also attempt to limit the amount of information displayed in the portlet so that it will fit into the available space without crowding out other portlets.

Figure 13-2 shows what the application looked like before we started removing functionality.

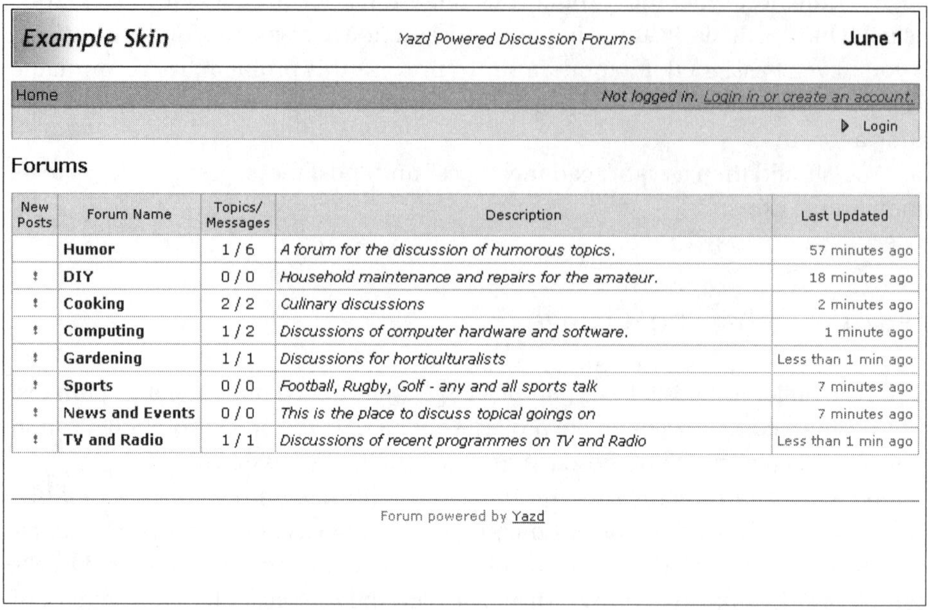

Figure 13-2. The application in its original state

Your portlet has some control over the window state, but you need to make sure that it behaves in a consistent manner when the user clicks a link. Users won't want the application to flicker between normal, maximized, and minimized views unpredictably. Indeed, if your application has a sufficiently adaptable GUI, you might want to relinquish all control over the window state and let the user select this through the portal decorations (maximize, minimize, and normal mode "buttons"), which are usually added to the portlet content.

In our conversion of YAZD, we have decided that it is impractical to carry out most of the functionality of the forums within the limited space likely to be available in the normal window state. We will therefore display a summary of the available forums in this state; then switch users to the maximized state when they follow any of the links in the normal view. To ensure that we don't fill the normal view with dozens of available forums, we will limit the summary to the first five forums available on the system.

Figure 13-3 shows what we end up with in the summary page after we've finished trimming down the application.

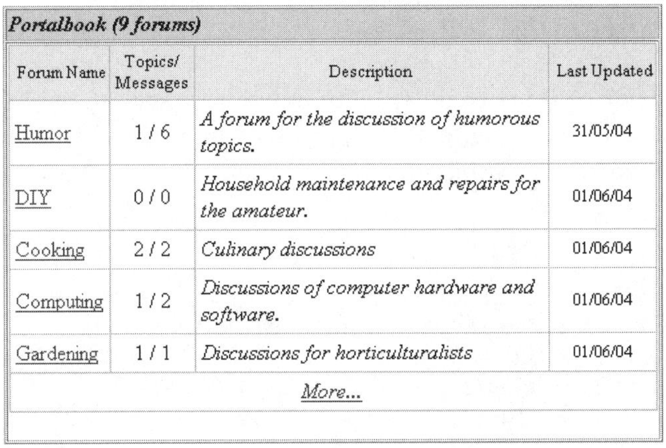

Portalbook (9 forums)

Forum Name	Topics/ Messages	Description	Last Updated
Humor	1 / 6	*A forum for the discussion of humorous topics.*	31/05/04
DIY	0 / 0	*Household maintenance and repairs for the amateur.*	01/06/04
Cooking	2 / 2	*Culinary discussions*	01/06/04
Computing	1 / 2	*Discussions of computer hardware and software.*	01/06/04
Gardening	1 / 1	*Discussions for horticulturalists*	01/06/04
		More...	

Figure 13-3. The application as a portlet

In Figure 13-4, you can see how the portlet presents the expanded list of forums once the More link is selected. Note that this is still not as wordy as the pre-portletization version shown earlier.

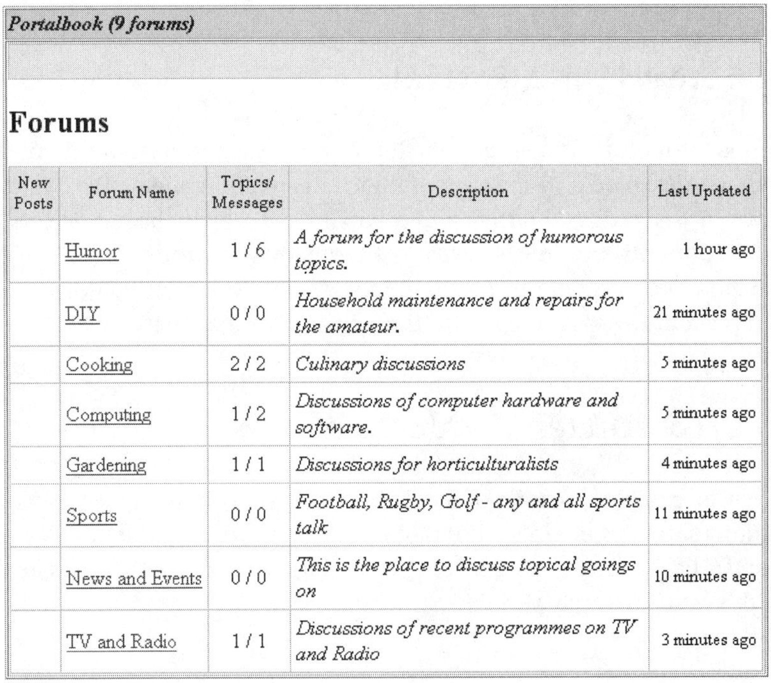

Portalbook (9 forums)

Forums

New Posts	Forum Name	Topics/ Messages	Description	Last Updated
	Humor	1 / 6	*A forum for the discussion of humorous topics.*	1 hour ago
	DIY	0 / 0	*Household maintenance and repairs for the amateur.*	21 minutes ago
	Cooking	2 / 2	*Culinary discussions*	5 minutes ago
	Computing	1 / 2	*Discussions of computer hardware and software.*	5 minutes ago
	Gardening	1 / 1	*Discussions for horticulturalists*	4 minutes ago
	Sports	0 / 0	*Football, Rugby, Golf - any and all sports talk*	11 minutes ago
	News and Events	0 / 0	*This is the place to discuss topical goings on*	10 minutes ago
	TV and Radio	1 / 1	*Discussions of recent programmes on TV and Radio*	3 minutes ago

Figure 13-4. The expanded portlet display

Moving Around the Application

Most of the time, writing a portlet is not so different from writing a servlet, but in one unexpected aspect they really are quite different: you cannot render URLs directly if you want the link to appear within the portlet rather than as a page in its own right.

> **NOTE** *Actually the authors are quite perplexed by just how difficult rendering a portlet URL has been made—sufficiently so that we suspect this is largely an oversight by the developers of the standard.*

The YAZD application has a GUI primarily built from JSP pages, so our solution to this problem has been to create a tag library specifically for rendering links so that the directed page will appear within the portlet.

To recap, one of your tasks when converting an existing application into a portlet will be to determine which links need to leave the user in the portlet rather than directing to an external page, and then rewriting those links appropriately.

Displaying Screens in a Portlet

Our application is to operate as a single portlet, but we want to base it on an application that was designed as a number of JSPs (effectively servlets). We could reconcile the two by discarding the JSPs and rewriting the portlet based on the business logic components, but this is a waste of perfectly good code.

Instead, we build a controller portlet that hides the implementation detail of the JSP files and presents a single portlet for the portal to interact with.

Building Our Controller Portlet

Our controller portlet must be capable of receiving a render request, determining from the parameters passed in which JSP page to dispatch the request to, and responding to any other requests made by the portal during the portlet's life cycle. As it turns out, this is surprisingly simple:

```
package com.portalbook.forums;

import java.io.IOException;

import javax.portlet.GenericPortlet;
```

```
import javax.portlet.PortletConfig;
import javax.portlet.PortletContext;
import javax.portlet.PortletException;
import javax.portlet.RenderRequest;
import javax.portlet.RenderResponse;
import javax.portlet.WindowState;

import com.Yasna.forum.Authorization;
import com.Yasna.forum.AuthorizationFactory;
import com.Yasna.forum.ForumFactory;
import com.portalbook.forums.tags.UrlTag;

public class ForumPortlet extends GenericPortlet
{

   /**
    * Calls the request dispatcher to include a specified JSP path
    * in the portlet output.
    *
    * @param path The path to the JSP to include
    * @param request The request object to pass in
    * @param response The response object to pass in
    * @throws PortletException Thrown if there is a
    *                            problem accessing the context
    * @throws IOException Thrown if there is a
    *                              problem writing the page fragment
    */
   private void include(String path, RenderRequest request,
         RenderResponse response) throws PortletException, IOException
   {
      getPortletContext().getRequestDispatcher(path).include(request,
            response);
   }
```

Here's where most of the work is done—the `doView()` method looks in the parameters supplied with the request for an `HREF` (the JSP page) and the `QUERY` (everything to be appended to the page). These are used to invoke a JSP page stored in the WEB-INF directory, which therefore cannot be loaded directly by the user.

The response from the page is rendered directly into the portlet's response stream.

The result is that we can invoke JSP pages quite simply with a minimal portlet. Most of the additional effort involves adapting the JSP pages to remove unnecessary or harmful tags (such as `<html>`), and rendering links and images. We discuss the latter problems in the next section on building a tag library.

```
/**
 * Invoked by the portal to render our portlet. This should cause
 * the content of an appropriate JSP page to be rendered within
 * the portlet.
 *
 * @param request The request object from the invocation
 * @param response The response object from this portlet
 * @throws PortletException Thrown if there is a
 *                             problem accessing the context
 * @throws IOException Thrown if there is a problem
 *                       writing the page fragment
 */
protected void doView(RenderRequest request, RenderResponse response)
      throws PortletException, IOException
{
   PortletContext context = getPortletContext();
   WindowState state = request.getWindowState();

   // Retrieve the JSP to direct to (if any)
   // (formatted as "path/path/file.jsp")
   String href = request.getParameter(UrlTag.HREF);

   getPortletContext().log("Href retrieved: " + href);

   // Retrieve the query to append (if any) (formatted as "?x=y&z=w")
   String query = request.getParameter(UrlTag.QUERY);
   getPortletContext().log("Query retrieved: " + query);

   if ((href != null) && (query != null))
      href += ("?" + query);
   if (href == null)
      href = VIEW;

   if (state.equals(WindowState.NORMAL))
   {
      include(PORTLET_GUI + NORMAL + href, request, response);
   }
   else if (state.equals(WindowState.MINIMIZED))
   {
      include(PORTLET_GUI + MINIMIZED + href, request, response);
   }
   else if (state.equals(WindowState.MAXIMIZED))
   {
      include(PORTLET_GUI + MAXIMIZED + href, request, response);
   }
```

```
    else
    {
        throw new PortletException(
                "Unrecognized WindowState in View mode: "
                        + state.toString());
    }
}

/**
 * Invoked by the portal to determine the title of
 * the portlet. We return a string identifying the
 * name of the portlet plus the number of forums
 * available to the system.
 *
 * @param request The render request from the portal
 * @return The title String
 */
protected String getTitle(RenderRequest request)
{
    Authorization auth = AuthorizationFactory
            .getAnonymousAuthorization();
    int count = ForumFactory.getInstance(auth).getForumCount();
    return forumName.trim() + " (" + count
            + ((count != 1) ? " forums)" : " forum)");
}

/**
 * Initialize the configuration of the
 * portlet.
 *
 * @param config The configuration object from which
 *               configuration parameters should be
 *               drawn.
 */
public void init(PortletConfig config) throws PortletException
{
    super.init(config);

    // Retrieve the name of the forums for display
    forumName = config.getInitParameter(FORUM_NAME);
    if (forumName == null)
        forumName = "Portalbook";
}
```

```
    // The name of the forums
    private String forumName;

    // The configuration name in the portlet.xml file
    private static final String FORUM_NAME = "title";

    // The location (relative to the portal's webapp) from which to obtain
    // the GUI components which are all written as JSPs
    private static final String PORTLET_GUI = "/WEB-INF/skins/portalized/";

    // The path in the skin directory containing the various
    // window-state versions of the display
    private static final String MINIMIZED = "minimized/";
    private static final String MAXIMIZED = "maximized/";
    private static final String NORMAL = "normal/";

    // The paths in the appropriate skin directories for
    // the mode views of the portlet
    private static final String VIEW = "view.jsp";

    // The identifier for an unknown user
    private static final String UNKNOWN = "anonymous";
}
```

Building a Tag Library

As we've just discussed, our controller portlet looks out for the configuration parameters HREF and QUERY and converts them into a URL, which if followed by the user will render a page within the portlet.

The process of placing these configuration parameters into the JSP pages that build the forum software is rather daunting, however, so we have chosen to simplify the process by means of a custom tag library.

Our tag library will allow us to conveniently provide relative links to resources to be displayed by the portlet. For example, to render the link to the image for the Post New Message button used by the forums, we use the following tag:

```
<img src="<pb:href path="images/postnewmsg.gif"/>" border="0"/>
```

While that looks a little cumbersome, the alternative is the following nugget of JSP:

```
<img src="
   <%=
      ((PortletResponse)response).encodeURL(
```

```
        ((PortletRequest)request).getContextPath() + "images/postnewmsg.gif" )
    %>" border="0"/>
```

We think that does very little to improve the readability of a page. Our custom tag at least has some similarity to the conventional HTML for an image tag.

Because this link-rewriting tag is the simpler of the two in our library, we'll examine its implementation first, and then we'll take a look at the more complex one. We're assuming you're familiar with the basics of tag libraries, so we'll concentrate on the specifics of their interactions with the portlet container and our controller portlet.

The Link-Rewriting Tag (href)

Because a portlet container is permitted to store information about the state of its portlets in the URL used to invoke a page, a simple portlet can have a surprisingly complicated URL—which has no obvious correlation with the URL it occupies on initialization.

Because of this, a relative URL like `images/postnewmsg.gif` cannot be used to reference resources such as images that are not a part of the portlet itself. You might think that you could work out what the "real" URL would be, but since the mechanism used is not mandated by the standard, there's no guarantee that your solution would work on another platform.

To illustrate the mess this can make of your URL, the image mentioned if rendered as a relative URL from the viewForum.jsp page in Pluto could end up as (with line breaks introduced to fit it on the page):

```
http://localhost:8080/pluto/portal/test/_rp_test_row_col1_p3_href/1_post0x2jsp/
_st_test_row_col1_p3/normal/_md_test_row_col1_p3/view/
_pm_test_row_col1_p3/view/_ps_test_row_col1_p3/normal/
_rp_test_row_col1_p3_query/1_forum=2/_pid/
test_row_col1_p3/images/postnewmsg.gif
```

Obviously, there's some method in this madness—we can make out the portlet mode (view) and window state (normal) in there, along with the parts of the URL we tried to add directly, but it's far from obvious that what should have been provided was

```
http://localhost:8080/yazd/images/postnewmsg.gif
```

And even if you knew the rule that Pluto had used to create this, there's no reason to imagine that any other portlet container will use the same mechanism.

We must therefore use the mechanism that we described in the introduction to this section, and we'll build a tag to do this. The following class achieves this:

```
package com.portalbook.forums.tags;

import java.io.IOException;

import javax.portlet.PortletRequest;
import javax.portlet.PortletResponse;
import javax.servlet.jsp.JspException;
import javax.servlet.jsp.tagext.TagSupport;

public class HrefTag extends TagSupport
{

   /**
    * Getter for the attribute used to dictate
    * the path to be rewritten
    *
    * @param path The path to be rewritten as an absolute URL
    */
   public void setPath(String path)
   {
      this.path = path;
   }

   /**
    * Retrieves the attribute used to dictate
    * the path to be rewritten
    *
    * @return The path to be rewritten
    */
   public String getPath()
   {
      return this.path;
   }

   /**
    * Ignores the body of the tag (there shouldn't be one)
    * and generates an absolute URL for the provided path
    * attribute relative to the context in which this
    * portlet is running.
    *
    * @return SKIP_BODY
    * @throws JspException if the output stream cannot be written
    */
   public int doStartTag()
      throws JspException
```

```
    {
        try
        {
            String contextPath = ((PortletRequest) pageContext
                    .getRequest()).getContextPath();
            String absolutePath = ((PortletResponse) pageContext
                    .getResponse()).encodeURL(contextPath + "/" + getPath());
            pageContext.getServletContext().log("Path: " + path);
            pageContext.getServletContext().log(
                    "Context path: " + contextPath);
            pageContext.getServletContext().log(
                    "Absolute path: " + absolutePath);
            pageContext.getOut().print(absolutePath);
            return SKIP_BODY;
        }
        catch (IOException e)
        {
            throw new JspException(
"Could not write to the page buffer while expanding an href custom tag",
                    e);
        }
    }

    // The field to store the path attribute
    private String path;
}
```

The tag's TLD entry follows:

```
<tag>
  <name>href</name>
  <tagclass>com.portalbook.forums.tags.HrefTag</tagclass>
  <bodycontent>NONE</bodycontent>
  <info>
    Rewrite a relative URL so that it refers to the position in the page
    relative to the portlet (this will remove any path information
    donated by the portal to manage the portlet's state).
  </info>

  <attribute>
     <name>path</name>
     <required>true</required>
     <rtexprvalue>true</rtexprvalue>
  </attribute>
</tag>
```

Note that we have flagged that the tag requires the path field (there's no point using the tag without specifying a path to rewrite), that it does not process any body content, and that it should permit the evaluation of runtime expressions for the path attribute, allowing the following sort of invocation:

```
<pb:href path="<%=runtimepath%>"/>
```

This last point is essential, since we are adapting an existing application, which may well generate paths for resources at runtime. By permitting runtime evaluation of the path attribute, we enable the generated path to be used directly.

The Link-Building Tag (url)

The more complex link-building tag is used to allow reasonably efficient generation of links to components of the portlet as JSP pages without substantial rewriting of the JSP page.

For example, the original page might provide a URL linking index.jsp to viewForum.jsp thus:

```
<a href="viewForum.jsp?forum=<%=forumID%>"><%=forumName%></a>
```

where `forumID` and `forumName` are scripting variables.

Because of the relative URL problem described for static resources, we can't use this URL as is, but must instead rewrite it into an absolute URL that describes the portlet view required.

Our tag should look like this:

```
<pb:url mode="VIEW" state="NORMAL" var="link">
  viewForum.jsp?forum=<%=forumID%>
</pb:url>
```

Again, scripting variables must be expanded (although these are now most likely to reside in the body of the tag). The mode attribute defines the `PortletMode` that the portlet will be set to, and the state describes the `WindowState` that the portlet will be set to. We also supply the name of a scripting variable that we would like to contain the generated URL (in fact, a `PortletURL`). This allows us to pre-declare various links using the long syntax and then include them in the output in this way:

```
<a href="<%=link%>">Forum Link</a>
```

Each link must have a distinct scripting variable name.

The code implementing this tag follows:

```
package com.portalbook.forums.tags;

import javax.servlet.jsp.JspException;
import javax.servlet.jsp.tagext.BodyContent;
import javax.servlet.jsp.tagext.BodyTagSupport;
import javax.portlet.PortletMode;
import javax.portlet.PortletModeException;
import javax.portlet.RenderResponse;
import javax.portlet.PortletURL;
import javax.portlet.WindowState;
import javax.portlet.WindowStateException;

public class UrlTag extends BodyTagSupport
{

   /**
    * Getter for the scripting variable attribute
    * @return The name of the scripting variable
    */
   public String getVar()
   {
      return var;
   }

   /**
    * The getter for the mode attribute
    * @return The name of the mode to select
    */
   public String getMode()
   {
      return mode;
   }

   /**
    * The getter for the state attribute
    * @return The name of the window state to select
    */
   public String getState()
   {
      return state;
   }

   /**
    * The setter for the scripting variable attribute
    * @param var The name of the scripting variable
```

```
 */
public void setVar(String var)
{
   this.var = var;
}

/**
 * The setter for the mode attribute
 * @param mode The name of the mode to select
 */
public void setMode(String mode)
{
   this.mode = mode;
}

/**
 * The setter for the state attribute
 * @param state The name of the state to select
 */
public void setState(String state)
{
   this.state = state;
}

/**
 * Determines an initial PortletURL object to refer to
 * the current portlet context. The mode and state
 * attributes are then extracted and applied to the
 * PortletURL.
 *
 * EVAL_BODY_BUFFERED is returned so that the link to
 * rewrite can be determined
 *
 * @return EVAL_BODY_BUFFERED
 * @throws JspException Thrown if the desired mode
   *                        or state cannot be set.
 */
public int doStartTag() throws JspException
{
   // Get the URL representing the portlet
   PortletURL url = ((RenderResponse) pageContext.getResponse())
         .createRenderURL();

   // Get the desired mode and state (if not default) from
   // the attributes
```

```
    PortletMode mode = getModeFromModeName(getMode());
    WindowState state = getStateFromStateName(getState());

    // Set the mode and state
    try
    {
       if (mode != null)
          url.setPortletMode(mode);
       if (state != null)
          url.setWindowState(state);
    }
    catch (PortletModeException e)
    {
       throw new JspException("Could not set portlet mode in url: "
             + mode);
    }
    catch (WindowStateException e)
    {
       throw new JspException("Could not set portlet state in url: "
             + state);
    }

    // Make the URL available as a page variable if
    // the user has requested this.
    if (getVar() != null)
    {
       pageContext.setAttribute(getVar(), url);
    }

    // Evaluate the body (for the link)
    return EVAL_BODY_BUFFERED;
 }

 /**
  * Retrieves the PortletURL created in the start tag
  * and adds to it the HREF and QUERY parts of the
  * desired path. The path is split into two parts because
  * the Pluto portlet container (erroneously?) does not
  * encode the '?' part of the parameter. This must therefore
  * be removed from the parameter data - since otherwise it
  * will be included in the URL when used to invoke the
  * ForumPortlet and the ForumPortlet will only receive
  * those parts of the invoking URL prior to the '?'
  *
  * Returns SKIP_BODY to indicate that the tag has
```

```
     * completed processing of the body.
     *
     * @return SKIP_BODY
     * @throws JspException Thrown if the link cannot be retrieved from the body.
     */
    public int doAfterBody() throws JspException
    {
        PortletURL url = (PortletURL) pageContext.getAttribute(getVar());

        // Retrieve the content of the tag
        BodyContent body = getBodyContent();
        if (body == null)
        {
            throw new JspException("No body (link) provided in tag");
        }

        // Check that we've got a path !
        String path = body.getString();
        if (path == null)
        {
            throw new JspException("No path (link) provided in tag");
        }

        pageContext.getServletContext().log("UrlTag path=" + path);

        // Determine the href part and the query part
        // of the given relative (hopefully) URL.
        int splitAt = path.indexOf('?');

        // The HREF part is from the beginning of the string up to, but
        // not including the '?' (or the whole string if there's no '?').
        String href = (splitAt > 0) ? path.substring(0, splitAt) : path;

        // The QUERY part is from immediately AFTER the '?' to the end
        // of the string (or an empty string if there's no '?')
        String query = (splitAt > 0) ? path.substring(splitAt + 1) : "";

        // Add the parameters to the PortletURL
        // ready for the user to obtain them.
        url.setParameter(HREF, href);
        url.setParameter(QUERY, query);

        // We're done processing the body
        return SKIP_BODY;
    }
```

```
/**
 * Converts the state name as a String into
 * the WindowState object representing it
 *
 * @param name The name of the state
 * @return A WindowState representing the named state
 * @throws JspException Thrown if a non-standard state name is provided
 */
private WindowState getStateFromStateName(String name)
      throws JspException
{
   if (name.equalsIgnoreCase(WindowState.MAXIMIZED.toString()))
   {
      return WindowState.MAXIMIZED;
   }
   else if (name.equalsIgnoreCase(WindowState.MINIMIZED.toString()))
   {
      return WindowState.MINIMIZED;
   }
   else if (name.equalsIgnoreCase(WindowState.NORMAL.toString()))
   {
      return WindowState.NORMAL;
   }
   else
   {
      // Tag can't handle non-standard states
      throw new JspException("Can't handle non-standard state: "
            + name);
   }
}

/**
 * Converts the mode name as a String into
 * the PortletMode object representing it
 *
 * @param name The name of the mode
 * @return A PortletMode representing the named mode
 * @throws JspException Thrown if a non-standard mode name is provided
 */
private PortletMode getModeFromModeName(String name)
      throws JspException
{
   if (name.equalsIgnoreCase(PortletMode.EDIT.toString()))
   {
```

```
            return PortletMode.EDIT;
         }
         else if (name.equalsIgnoreCase(PortletMode.VIEW.toString()))
         {
            return PortletMode.VIEW;
         }
         else if (name.equalsIgnoreCase(PortletMode.HELP.toString()))
         {
            return PortletMode.HELP;
         }
         else
         {
            // Tag can't handle non-standard modes
            throw new JspException("Can't handle non-standard mode: "
                  + name);
         }
      }

      // The field to contain the mode
      // attribute (defaults to VIEW)
      private String mode = "view";

      // The field to contain the state
      // attribute (defaults to NORMAL)
      private String state = "normal";

      // The field to contain the name
      // of the scripting variable - this
      // is a required field.
      private String var = null;

      /**
       * Defines the parameter name for the HREF part
       * of a URL
       */
      public static final String HREF = "href";

      /**
       * Defines the parameter name for the QUERY part
       * of a URL
       */
      public static final String QUERY = "query";
   }
```

Simplifying the Screens

The JSP pages that we have inherited from the YAZD application are part of a full-fledged web application. Our portlet is a small part of the portal. We need to trim anything redundant from our pages.

First, we reduce the number of JSPs required. The original application was formed from the following:

```
breadcrumb.jsp
createAccount.jsp
error.jsp
footer.jsp
header.jsp
index.jsp
login.jsp
post.jsp
search.jsp
toolbar.jsp
userAccount.jsp
userDetail.jsp
viewForum.jsp
viewThread.jsp
```

We can discard any pages that manage account information, such as login.jsp. We have removed the search facility from our design, so search.jsp can go. We also want our page to be an HTML fragment rather than a full page, so the header and footer pages can be deleted. Our remaining set of pages is as follows:

```
error.jsp
index.jsp
post.jsp
toolbar.jsp
view.jsp
viewForum.jsp
viewThread.jsp
```

We'll now discuss the purpose of these remaining pages in turn.

`error.jsp` provides error handling for the user should an unexpected problem arise during processing of the application. We have implemented the bare minimum, and merely report the exception to the user. A professional application should translate this into plain English for the user.

`index.jsp` provides the full listing of forums available to the user and permits them to select a forum for a detailed view of the threads it contains.

`post.jsp` is the page through which messages are added to the forums.

`toolbar.jsp` provides some functionality that is common to all of the major pages.

`view.jsp` offers a summarized view of the forums available to the user. This is the only page that we have added to the design.

`viewForum.jsp` provides a detailed view of the threads contained in a selected forum.

`viewThread.jsp` provides a detailed view of the messages contained in a selected thread.

Once selected, the screens are updated to remove any dependencies on the removed pages, such as variables declared in the removed pages or URLs that link into the removed pages. The implementation of our new view.jsp page follows as an example.

First, we import the libraries that will be needed inline, and declare the page that will handle exceptions thrown while generating the page:

```
<%@   page import="java.util.*,
                    com.Yasna.forum.*,
                    com.Yasna.forum.util.*"


   errorPage="error.jsp"
%>
```

Now we import the tag library to aid in rewriting URLs, and initialize various variables:

```
<%@ taglib uri="portalbook.tld" prefix="pb" %>

<%!  ///////////////////////////////////
   // customize the look of this page

   // Colors of the table that displays a list of forums
   final static String forumTableBgcolor = "#cccccc";
   final static String forumTableFgcolor = "#ffffff";
   final static String forumTableHeaderFgcolor = "#eeeeee";
%>
```

The next item of code obtains a token to identify the user. In our case, this will be the anonymous user, so we have removed any identity checking and replaced it with the following:

```
<%
   Authorization authToken = AuthorizationFactory.getAnonymousAuthorization();
%>
```

Now we obtain an object that we can use to retrieve information from the forum software about the forums and the messages they contain:

```
<%
   ForumFactory forumFactory = ForumFactory.getInstance(authToken);

   User user = forumFactory.getProfileManager().getUser(authToken.getUserID());
   long userLastVisitedTime = SkinUtils.getLastVisited(request,response);
%>
```

Next, we render the list of forums available, starting with the headings for the table:

```
<table bgcolor="<%= forumTableBgcolor %>"
       cellpadding="0"
       cellspacing="0"
       border="0"
       width="100%">
 <td>
  <table bgcolor="<%= forumTableBgcolor %>"
         cellpadding="4"
         cellspacing="1"
         border="0"
         width="100%">
   <tr bgcolor="<%= forumTableHeaderFgcolor %>">
    <td align="center" width="1%" nowrap>
     <small>Forum Name</small>
    </td>
    <td align="center" width="1%">
     <small>Topics/<br>Messages</small>
    </td>
    <td align="center" width="95%">
     <small>Description</small>
    </td>
    <td align="center" width="1%" nowrap>
     <small>Last Updated</small>
    </td>
   </tr>
```

Then we obtain an iterator that will allow us to step through a list of forums obtaining information about each one in turn (and we check to make sure there are some forums to display before proceeding to iterate through them):

```
<%
   Iterator forumIterator = forumFactory.forums();
   if( !forumIterator.hasNext() ) {
%>
      <tr bgcolor="<%= forumTableFgcolor %>">
      <td colspan="6" align="center">
      <br>
      <span class="error">
      Sorry, there are no forums in the YAZD system.
      Please have your forum administrator create some.
      </span>
      <br><br>
      </td>
   </tr>
<%   }

   java.text.DateFormat df =
      java.text.DateFormat.getDateInstance(java.text.DateFormat.SHORT);

   boolean forumLoaded = false;

   int forumCount = 0;
   while( forumIterator.hasNext() ) {
      Forum forum = (Forum)forumIterator.next();
      forumLoaded = true;
      int forumID = forum.getID();
      String forumName = forum.getName();
      String forumDescription = forum.getDescription();
      int threadCount = forum.getThreadCount();
      int messageCount = forum.getMessageCount();
      String creationDate = df.format(forum.getCreationDate());
      String modifiedDate = df.format(forum.getModifiedDate());
%>
```

Since users will be able to select each of our links in turn to drill down into a thread-level view of their chosen forum, we need to use our tag library to generate appropriate URLs to display the next JSP page within the portlet.

Figure 13-5 shows the view of the forum threads.

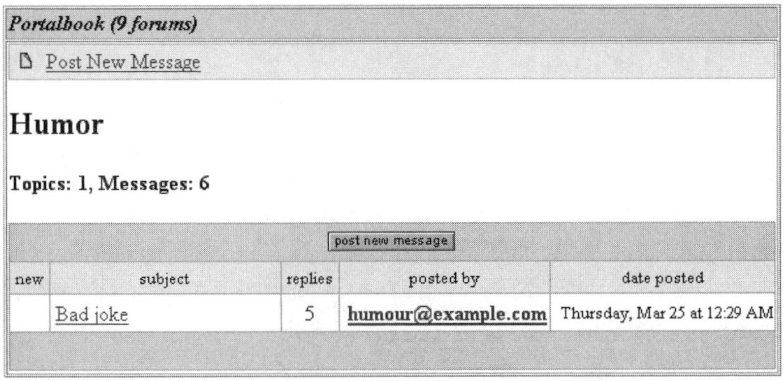

Figure 13-5. Drilling down into a message thread

Note the declaration of the scripting variable in the `var` attribute of the tag, and the subsequent use of it to render a link for the forum name:

```
<pb:url state="NORMAL"
        mode="VIEW"
        var="link">
    viewForum.jsp?forum=<%=forumID%>
</pb:url>
<tr bgcolor="<%= forumTableFgcolor %>">
 <td nowrap><a href="<%=link%>" class="forum"><%= forumName %></a></td>
 <td align="center" nowrap><%= threadCount %> / <%= messageCount %></td>
 <td><i><%= (forumDescription!=null)?forumDescription:" " %></i></td>
 <td nowrap align="center">
  <small class="date"><%= modifiedDate %></small>
 </td>
</tr>
```

If more than five forums are available to users, we will list the first five, then make a link available to users that they can select to view the rest. This restricts the amount of space taken up by our portlet in its "normal" viewing mode.

```
<%
        if( ++forumCount > 4 ) {
%>
   <pb:url state="NORMAL" mode="VIEW" var="more">index.jsp</pb:url>
   <tr bgcolor="<%= forumTableFgcolor %>">
    <td colspan="5" align="center">
     <i><a href="<%=more%>">More...</a></i>
    </td>
   </tr>
<%
```

```
            break;
        }
    }
%>
  </table>
 </td>
</table>
```

Getting Configuration Information

Portlets get the benefit of most of the sources of configuration information that are available to servlets. They also have access to a few more of their own.

Configuration from Portlet.xml

The portlet's XML descriptor is the first place to consider for placing configuration information, which is unlikely to vary between platforms for your portlet.

This allows you to recommend values for the name of the portlet, keywords to associate with it, and user preferences. User preferences are a particularly important resource, as we will discuss in a moment. Here's the portlet.xml file to configure the YAZD portlet application:

```
<?xml version="1.0" encoding="UTF-8"?>
<portlet-app
  xmlns=
   http://java.sun.com/xml/ns/portlet/portlet-app_1_0.xsd
  version="1.0" xmlns:xsi=http://www.w3.org/2001/XMLSchema-instance
  xsi:schemaLocation=
   "http://java.sun.com/xml/ns/portlet/portlet-app_1_0.xsd
    http://java.sun.com/xml/ns/portlet/portlet-app_1_0.xsd">
   <portlet>
      <description>Portalbook Forum Portlet</description>
      <portlet-name>forum</portlet-name>
      <display-name>Portalbook</display-name>
      <portlet-class>
         com.portalbook.forums.ForumPortlet
      </portlet-class>
      <expiration-cache>-1</expiration-cache>
      <supports>
         <mime-type>text/html</mime-type>
         <portlet-mode>VIEW</portlet-mode>
      </supports>
```

```
        <supported-locale>en</supported-locale>
        <portlet-info>
            <title>Portalbook Forums</title>
            <short-title>Forums</short-title>
            <keywords>Forums</keywords>
        </portlet-info>
        <portlet-preferences>
            <preference>
                <name>ForumCount</name>
                <value>5</value>
                <read-only>false</read-only>
            </preference>
        </portlet-preferences>
    </portlet>
</portlet-app>
```

In our example, we configure a portlet preference for the `ForumCount`. We will use this to define the number of forums that can be seen in the normal portlet view of the application.

> **TIP** *Portlet preferences are one of the more impressive ideas to come with the portlet API—so much so that we rather wish they were available from servlets. As well as allowing you to provide a set of basic information with which you can configure your portlet, they also allow you to persist those details once changed by the user in a portal-independent way.*
>
> *This makes it really easy to build lightweight portlets, since persistence tools often take up quite a lot of a small application's logic.*

Here's some JSP logic that uses this to decide when to stop rendering form details in the portlet view:

```
<%
    if( ++forumCount > (c-1) ) {
%>
        <pb:url state="NORMAL" mode="VIEW" var="more">index.jsp</pb:url>
        <tr bgcolor="<%= forumTableFgcolor %>">
            <td colspan="5" align="center">
                <i><a href="<%=more%>">More...</a></i>
            </td>
        </tr>
<%
```

```
        break;
    }
%>
```

In order to allow the user to decide how many forums should be displayed on a page, rather than just sticking with the defaults, we will allow a request parameter to be handled by the `ForumPortlet`. Since this will change the state of the portlet, it needs to be handled as an Action:

```
public void processAction(
    ActionRequest request,
    ActionResponse response)
throws PortletException, IOException
{
    // If the user has requested a different count of
    // forums in the default view, extract and preserve this
    // for subsequent use
    if (request.getParameter("ForumCount") != null)
    {
        String count = request.getParameter("ForumCount");
        getPortletContext().log(
                "Forum Count request retrieved: " + count);
        request.getPreferences().setValue("ForumCount", count);
        getPortletContext().log("Forum Count set as preference");
        request.getPreferences().store();
        getPortletContext().log("Forum Count preference stored");
    }

    super.processAction(request, response);
}
```

Note that as we retrieve the parameter named `ForumCount` we preserve it temporarily by updating the user preferences, and then preserve it permanently by invoking the `store()` method. It is then the responsibility of the portal to ensure that the same value is available for subsequent use of the portlet—and that this survives a restart of the portal!

Our final step is to provide a mechanism by which users can set their preferences, and we do this by rendering a suitable set of `actionURLs`:

```
<b>Forums to view in main page: </b>
<%
    // Determine the number of rows to show
    // the user in small-view mode !
```

```
    for(int i = 1; i <= 10; i++ ) {
        javax.portlet.PortletURL url =
            ((javax.portlet.RenderResponse)
                pageContext.getResponse())
                    .createActionURL();
         url.setParameter(
            "ForumCount",
            Integer.toString(i));

// Render the actual Link:
%>
<a href="<%=url%>"><%=i%></a>
<%
// Place a comma or period after
// each number as appropriate:
        if( i < 10 ) {
%>,<%
        }
        else
        {
%>.<%
        }
    }
%>
```

Configuration from JNDI

The database configuration information for YAZD was originally maintained in a properties file. This is a perfectly workable solution, but it requires the application to provide an administration GUI of its own.

One of the real advantages of the J2EE suite is that by standardizing the behavior of services, it allows for the standardization of the configuration of those services as well. JDBC connection configuration in modern applications is generally a responsibility of the application server, not its client applications.

Tomcat 5 is no exception here—a perfectly serviceable user interface is available to us to configure a JDBC DataSource for the client application. We will therefore strip out the existing YAZD database connection code and replace it with our custom-written alternative.

Figure 13-6 shows the Tomcat 5 administration page for the JNDI setup of a JDBC DataSource.

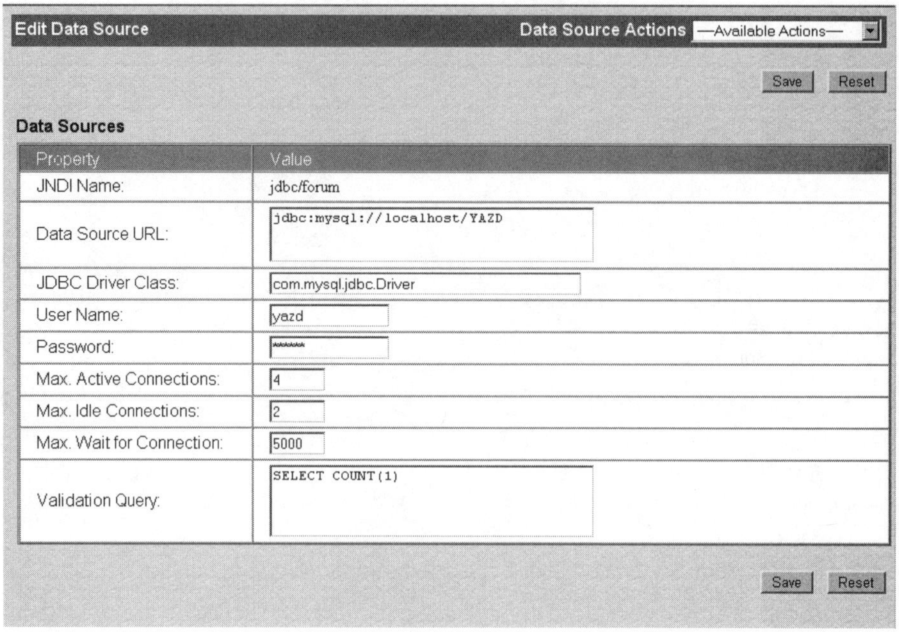

Figure 13-6. Managing JNDI in Tomcat

Note that the JNDI name is given as "jdbc/forum" because the root of the JNDI namespace for Java applications begins at "java:comp/env", giving the full path for our data source (as shown in the application code) as java:comp/env/jdbc/forum.

Fortunately, the database code in YAZD is concentrated in the `DBConnectionManager` class, and a single call to `getConnection()` is used throughout YAZD when a connection is needed.

We remove the body of this method entirely and replace it with a call to the static method `com.portalbook.forums.Environment.getConnection()`:

```
public static Connection getConnection()
   throws ForumException
{
   return Environment.getConnection(Environment.DATABASE_CONTEXT);
}
```

As indicated by the package name, the `Environment` class is our own creation. It implements the `getConnection()` method like this:

```
public static Connection getConnection(String path)
   throws ForumException
{
   // Acquire a connection from the DataSource
```

```
    try
    {
        Context ctx = new InitialContext();
            if (ctx == null)
            throw new ForumException(
                "There was a problem connecting to the database",
            "Null Context retrieved",
                new NullPointerException());

        DataSource ds =
            (DataSource) ctx.lookup(DATABASE_CONTEXT);

        if (ds == null)
            throw new ForumException(
                "There was a problem connecting to the database",
                "Null data source retrieved",
                new NullPointerException());

            return ds.getConnection();
        }
        catch (NamingException e)
        {
                    throw new ForumException(
                "There was a problem connecting to the database",
                "Naming lookup failed", e);
        }
        catch (SQLException e)
        {
            throw new ForumException(
                "There was a problem connecting to the database",
                "SQL failed", e);
        }
}

// This declares the name that will be used to obtain a datasource
// from the Application Server.
public static final String DATABASE_CONTEXT = "java:comp/env/jdbc/forum";
```

With these two quite trivial changes, the application no longer requires an explicit database configuration in the properties file. The context names for DataSources and other resources should be provided with the administrator documentation for your applications so that users deploying an application can configure it appropriately to connect to their database.

Issues Encountered in Our Example

Converting our application was not an entirely straightforward process. We encountered a few problems with some of the technology that we chose to use in our solution.

There is a minor bug in Tomcat 5.0.19 that produces a `NullPointerException` under some circumstances if there is no local session object. Unfortunately, Pluto exercises this particular bug—if you're using this particular combination, you will need to upgrade to version 5.0.25 or higher of Tomcat.

Pluto does not handle parameters quite as expected. Parameters containing a question mark will not be encoded when constructing the URL to invoke the portlet. Since "?" is used in HTTP as the delimiter between the file path part of a URL and the query part, everything subsequent to the question mark is lost from the parameter list of the receiving portlet. The specification does not address the "?" character in URLs explicitly, but would permit encoding of it, so we consider this to be a bug (or at least a quirk) in the current Pluto implementation. We hope that by the time you read this you won't have to jump through quite so many hoops to construct usable URLs.

Summary

In this chapter, we looked at converting an existing application into a portlet. We discussed how to adapt the JSP files to behave as a single portlet, we discussed the configuration of the database connection, and we looked at the creation of tag libraries to interact with the portlet-specific behavior.

In the next chapter, we look at presenting summary information such as charts and reports within a portlet.

CHAPTER 14

Charting with JFreeChart

Many portal applications will have a business requirement to provide charting, reporting, or other analysis tools. These could be part of a sales forecasting system, a financial reporting tool, or a customer service application. In one possible architecture, basic functionality for accessing and modifying charts or reports could belong to a front-end portlet application, with an enterprise information system (EIS) on the back-end.

In many cases, the EIS already exists, either as a custom-built application or as a packaged product. Packaged products may have charting, reporting, or analysis tools, although these may not be completely customizable or deployable in a portlet environment.

If you are developing the EIS at the same time as the portlet application, you can design an API to enable data extraction for charting or reporting. Patching in a data access layer after the EIS is completed will probably be more complicated.

In either case, creating a specification that defines the needed data and goals of the application will help create usable portlets. Sample charts are an easy way to define requirements for the application. By creating examples early in the process, developers and customers can set expectations for the project. Sometimes the charting tools will not be at the level needed for the sample charts. Knowing this ahead of time, developers can factor in additional development time for the project. Choosing a charting component that comes with source code is an efficient way to provide more business value for your customers and speed up your development.

In this chapter, we use an open source product for charting named JFreeChart. Although many other commercial and open source charting products and tools are available, JFreeChart is widely used, has a large selection of charts, and is integrated into several reporting tools, such as Jasper Reports and JFreeReport.

Building Charts and Graphs with JFreeChart

JFreeChart is an open source Java library that you can use to create charts and graphs. The software package can be found at `www.jfree.org/jfreechart/index.html`. The library is licensed under the GNU Lesser Public License. We are using version 0.9.17 for the examples in this chapter. You will need the JFreeChart JAR file (jfreechart-0.9.17.jar). From the JFreeChart distribution's lib directory, we also use the gnujaxp.jar, log4j-1.2.8.jar, and jcommon-0.9.2.jar files.

JFreeChart provides charts for Swing applications, applets, servlets, portlets, or other types of Java applications. The JFreeChart software does not offer any direct support for the portlet API or portal behavior. In this chapter, we focus on understanding how to use the JFreeChart API; then we create a portlet application that displays charts generated with JFreeChart. Our charting portlet creates temporary files for our charts, and a servlet serves the image files to the user.

Chart Types

The common chart types are included with JFreeChart, including bar, pie, area, scatter plots, time series, and area charts. Variations are possible with each chart type, and it is also possible to create 3D pie charts and bar charts. JFreeChart comes with a charting demo application (jfreechart-0.9.17-demo.jar) that has examples of the various charts and styles. You can run the demo application from the root directory of the JFree distribution with this command line (adjust the slashes for your OS if it is not Windows):

```
java -cp lib\gnujaxp.jar;lib\jcommon-0.9.2.jar;lib\log4j-1.2.8.jar➥
;lib\servlet.jar;jfreechart-0.9.17.jar -jar jfreechart-0.9.17-demo.jar
```

> **NOTE** *The previous command should all be one line when you type it, but we had to split it to fit on the printed page.*

From the demo application, Figures 14-1 through 14-6 show examples of charts that JFreeChart can create.

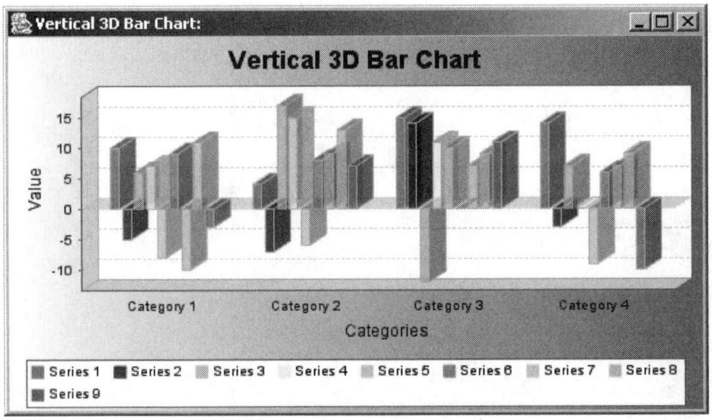

Figure 14-1. A vertical 3D bar chart

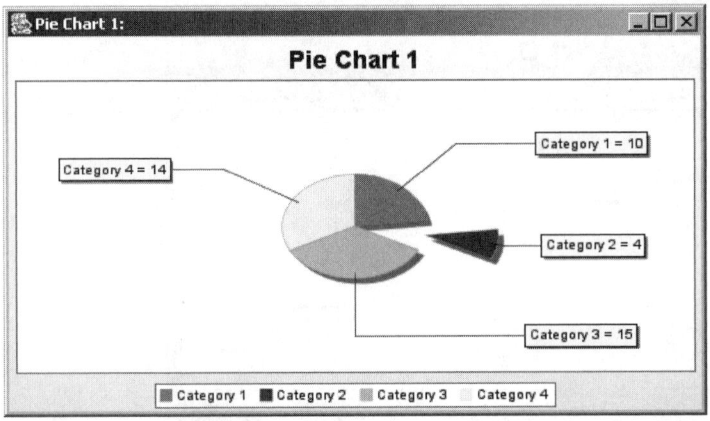

Figure 14-2. A pie chart showing an exploded section

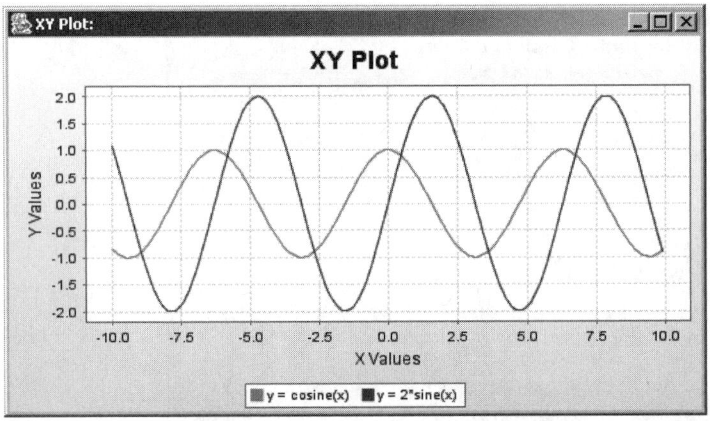

Figure 14-3. An XY chart with a gradient background

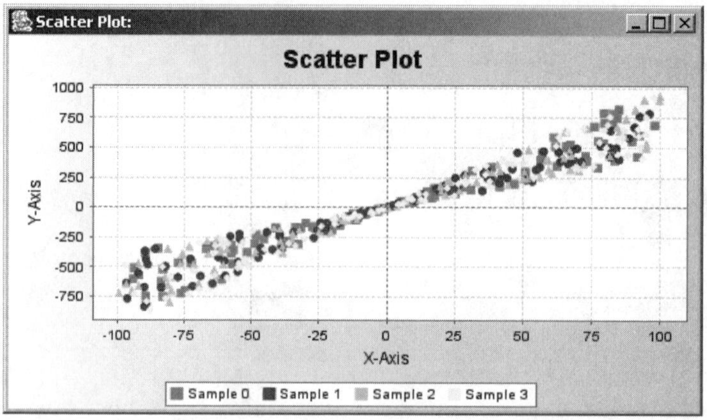

Figure 14-4. An XY scatter plot

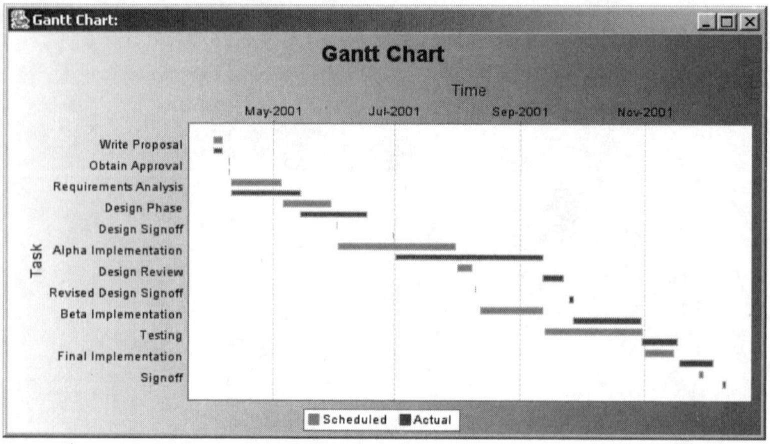

Figure 14-5. A Gantt chart

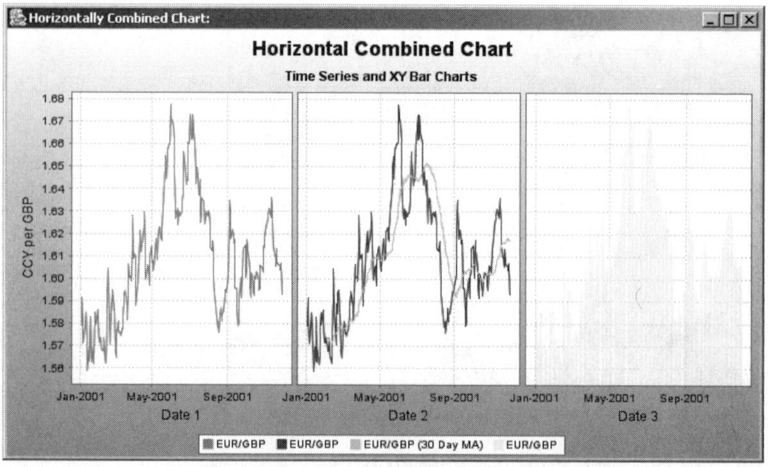

Figure 14-6. A horizontal combined chart, with embedded time series and XY plot charts

If JFreeChart does not have the exact chart type you need, you may be able to customize one of the existing chart types to do what you need. The source code is included with the distribution, so you can look at the existing charts and see how JFreeChart creates its graphs. Additionally, you can customize how JFreeChart draws the chart so that it uses your fonts and colors. It is also possible to set the background image for a chart to anything you like.

Basic JFreeChart Example

Let's now create a 3D bar chart example using JFreeChart. Applications can display the charts in Swing, or export charts to Joint Photographic Experts Group (JPEG) or Portable Network Graphics (PNG) images. Our example will create a PNG file on disk, and you can view the image in your web browser or another application.

The PNG image format looks much better than JPEG-compressed charts, because PNG is lossless compression and JPEG is lossy. JPEG is more suitable for photographic images than for simple charts. Most modern web browsers support PNG images, although it is not as common on web pages as the JPEG and GIF formats.

The `org.jfree.chart.ChartFactory` class provides static methods for creating charts. All of the method signatures are similar, although the inputs needed do vary with the type of chart being created. We use the `createBarChart3D()` method on the `ChartFactory` class for our example:

```
public static JFreeChart createBarChart3D(String title,
                           String categoryAxisLabel,
                           String valueAxisLabel,
                           CategoryDataset dataset,
                           PlotOrientation orientation,
                           boolean legend,
                           boolean tooltips,
                           boolean urls)
```

The first argument, `title`, may be null. The category and value axis labels may also be null. Be sure to keep your category and value axes straight when you create your data set—this is easy to mix up. For a hypothetical bar chart that represents the weather in Austin, Texas, the category axis would be Months in 2004, and the value axis would be Number of Sunny Days.

The 3D bar chart requires a category data set, as an `org.jfree.data.CategoryDataset` object. All of the JFreeChart charts use data sets that inherit from the base `org.jfree.data.Dataset` interface. We discuss data sets in more detail later in this chapter.

The chart can be displayed with a horizontal or a vertical orientation. The createBarChart3D() method takes a PlotOrientation object. The values are available as either the HORIZONTAL or VERTICAL static variable on PlotOrientation. The chart may display a legend if needed. The tooltips on the chart are optional, as is URL generation. Both tooltips and URLs are used for HTML image maps, if the chart is clickable in a web browser. JFreeChart can also use the OverLIB (www.bosrup.com/web/overlib/) JavaScript library to generate tooltips for web images. You will need to include the JavaScript source file overlib.js in your portlet application output.

Data for the 3D Bar Chart

The 3D bar chart requires an org.jfree.data.CategoryDataset object as its data source. The CategoryDataset class is an interface. We use the concrete implementation org.jfree.data.DefaultCategoryDataset class to hold our data. For our purposes, the only method we need to use on the data set class is addValue(double value, Comparable rowKey, comparable columnKey). This method adds our numerical value to the data set, with the row key "2004" and the column key "January", "February", or "March".

The row and column keys refer to the data set's structure, not necessarily the way the chart is rendered. If we use more than one row key in a bar chart data set, we will get multiple bars for each category value. Each bar will have a different color. We could use this for a chart that visualizes monthly rainfall in different years, although other chart types (such as a line chart) would probably be better.

Saving the Chart As a PNG Image File

In our example, we export the chart to a PNG image file on our file system. The chart's filename is barchart3d.png, and will be created in the working directory for this Java application.

The PNG image should load in most modern web browsers and image manipulation tools. The org.jfree.chart.ChartUtilities class provides methods for saving charts as JPEG or PNG images, writing JPEG or PNG to an input stream, and working with image maps:

```
public static void saveChartAsPNG(File file, JFreeChart chart, int width,➥
                                  int height) throws java.io.IOException
```

The saveChartAsPNG() method we use in the SimpleChartDemo example creates a PNG image out of the chart with the width and height in pixels that we specified. The file does not have to exist before this method is called, and any existing files will be overwritten if the file system allows it.

3D Bar Chart Example Source Code

You can execute this charting example from the command line. Your classpath will need to include the libraries distributed with JFreeChart. With JFreeChart 0.9.17, this would be jcommon-0.9.2.jar, jfreechart-0.9.17.jar, log4j-1.2.8.jar, and gnujaxp.jar.

```
package com.portalbook.charting;

import org.jfree.chart.ChartFactory;
import org.jfree.chart.ChartUtilities;
import org.jfree.chart.JFreeChart;

import org.jfree.chart.plot.PlotOrientation;

import org.jfree.data.CategoryDataset;
import org.jfree.data.DefaultCategoryDataset;

import java.io.*;

public class SimpleChartDemo
{

    protected CategoryDataset createChartData()
    {
        DefaultCategoryDataset dataset = new DefaultCategoryDataset();

        dataset.addValue(1.3, "2004", "January");
        dataset.addValue(2.6, "2004", "February");
        dataset.addValue(4.6, "2004", "March");

        return dataset;
    }

    protected JFreeChart createBarChart3D(CategoryDataset dataset)
    {
        String title = "Weather in Austin, Texas";
        JFreeChart chart =
            ChartFactory.createBarChart3D(
                title,
                "Months in 2004",
                "Number of Sunny Days",
                dataset,
```

```
                PlotOrientation.VERTICAL,
                true,
                false,
                false);

        return chart;

    }

    protected void saveChartAsPNG(JFreeChart chart) throws IOException
    {
        File file = new File("barchart3d.png");
        ChartUtilities.saveChartAsPNG(file, chart, 400, 300);
    }

    public static void main(String[] args)
    {
        SimpleChartDemo demo = new SimpleChartDemo();
        CategoryDataset dataset = demo.createChartData();
        JFreeChart chart = demo.createBarChart3D(dataset);

        try
        {
            demo.saveChartAsPNG(chart);
        }
        catch (IOException e)
        {
            System.out.println(e.getMessage());
            e.printStackTrace();
        }
    }
}
```

After this application runs, you should have a file called barchart3d.png in your working directory. Your output should be similar to that shown in Figure 14-7.

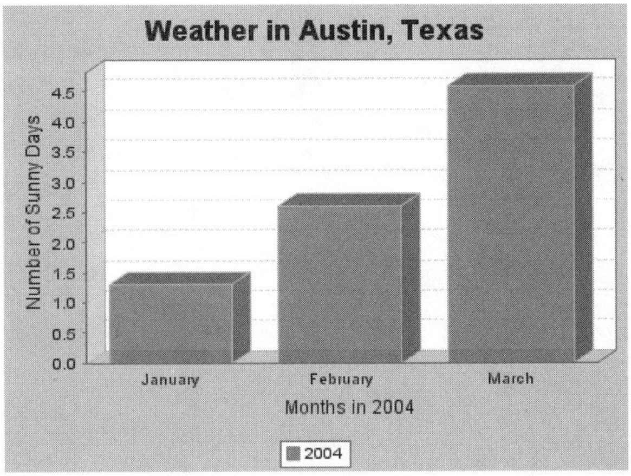

Figure 14-7. 3D bar chart from JFreeChart

Most data sets will not be as simple to integrate as the data we used for our example. Your portlet application is responsible for populating the appropriate data set for your chart.

Providing Data to the Chart

In JFreeChart, the data that a chart uses is contained in an object that implements the `org.jfree.data.Dataset` interface. Each chart type has a corresponding data set interface that extends the `Dataset` interface. You will need to check the JavaDocs for JFreeChart to find the available classes that implement these interfaces. The methods used to add or remove values from the data set differ from class to class, so the JavaDocs are the best place to learn more about a particular data set. Table 14-1 shows the Java interface for each chart's data set.

Table 14-1. Chart Types and Data Set Interfaces

Name of Chart	Corresponding Data Set Interface
Area	`CategoryDataset`
Bar	`CategoryDataset`
Bar 3D	`CategoryDataset`
Box and Whisker	`BoxAndWhiskerXYDataset`
Bubble	`XYZDataset`
Candlestick	`HighLowDataset`
Gantt	`IntervalCategoryDataset`

Table 14-1. Chart Types and Data Set Interfaces (continued)

Name of Chart	Corresponding Data Set Interface
High Low	HighLowDataset
Histogram	IntervalXYDataset
Line	CategoryDataset
Multiple Pie Charts	CategoryDataset
Multiple Pie Charts 3D	CategoryDataset
Pie	PieDataset
Pie 3D	PieDataset
Polar	XYDataset
Scatter	XYDataset
Signal	SignalsDataset
Stacked Area	CategoryDataset
Stacked Bar	CategoryDataset
Stacked Bar 3D	CategoryDataset
Stacked XY Area	TableXYDataset
Time Series	XYDataset
Wafer Map	WaferMapDataset
Waterfall	CategoryDataset
Wind	WindDataset
XY Area	XYDataset
XY Bar	IntervalXYDataset
XY Line	XYDataset
XY Step Area	XYDataset
XY Step	XYDataset

The `org.jfree.data.DatasetUtilities` class contains static methods that simplify working with data sets. There are three methods for creating `CategoryDataset` objects from two-dimensional arrays of numbers. Another set of methods is useful for extracting data for a pie chart from one row or column of a `CategoryDataset`. This might come in handy if you offer drill-down capability for your charts. Several statistical methods are available as well for analyzing the minimum and maximum values in a data set.

Database

Several data set classes use a Java Database Connectivity (JDBC) connection to retrieve data for the chart. The first step is to create a SQL query that will provide the result set you need out of your database. The `JDBCCategoryDataset`, `JDBCPieDataset`, and `JDBCXYDataset` classes in the `org.jfree.data` package all have specific requirements for the JDBC result set. For the JDBC pie data set, the result set should contain two columns. The first column should contain the labels for the pie slices, and the column's data type must be `VARCHAR`. The other column contains the values for the pie chart.

The JDBC data set classes can access the database with a portlet-supplied JDBC `java.sql.Connection` object, or they can create the connection with the JDBC URL, JDBC driver name, and a database user's username and password.

XML

JFreeChart will accept XML in its own format as the data source for the category and pie data sets. The `org.jfree.data.xml.DatasetReader` class provides helper methods for loading data sets from XML files or input streams. The JFreeChart code to parse XML into a data set is not very complicated, so it should be easy to add support for other data set types or XML formats. The XML format used for category data sets and pie data sets mirrors the `CategoryDataset` and `PieDataset` objects.

Here is an XML data source that demonstrates the structure for the `PieDataset`:

```
<?xml version="1.0" encoding="UTF-8"?>
<PieDataset>
  <Item>
    <Key>Winter</Key>
    <Value>110</Value>
  </Item>
  <Item>
    <Key>Spring</Key>
    <Value>180</Value>
  </Item>
  <Item>
    <Key>Summer</Key>
    <Value>220</Value>
  </Item>
  <Item>
    <Key>Fall</Key>
    <Value>175</Value>
  </Item>
</PieDataset>
```

The XML format for the category data set is similar, but the root element is `<CategoryDataset>`, and the children of the root element are `<Series>` XML elements. The `<Series>` elements contain one more `<Item>` element. For an example, see the org/jfree/chart/demo/categorydata.xml file under the src directory in the JFreeChart distribution.

If you already have an XML data format, you have two choices. The first is to develop XML transformation code that will translate your format into the category or pie data set XML format. This is probably more trouble than it is worth, given that JFreeChart supports only two XML markups. The better alternative is to write a Java class that reads your XML and builds up a JFreeChart data set object. Use the `org.jfree.data.xml.PieDatasetHandler` and `org.jfree.data.xml.CategoryDatasetHandler` classes as inspiration, especially if you are using the Simple API for XML (SAX) to parse your XML.

If you are building a business intelligence or digital dashboard portlet application, your portlets will need to integrate with many EISs. One trend in commercial software is that common layers for integrating different systems for analysis are emerging, usually as distinct software products. You could also build this piece yourself, and if most of your back-end systems are proprietary, you might as well. Depending on your needs, you may be able to define a common XML Schema for your charting data. Then you could build an integration adapter for each of your systems that provides real-time data for your charts. These integration adapters could be web services, or they could be as simple as a servlet that builds a web page that consists of XML. Then you could write a custom JFreeChart data set handler (or an existing one) to create your charts. Because your XML is standard across all systems, you are not as locked into one solution. Any deep analysis or business logic should be embedded in a separate layer outside the EISs. This separate layer may reside in the portlet application, but should not use any JFreeChart or portlet classes for portability.

Displaying Charts from a Portlet

JFreeChart can create PNG or JPEG images out of the charts. Web and portal developers have two choices for displaying charts. The first approach is to create an image file on the file system and then serve the file through the web server to the end user. This works well when an image is created on a schedule. An example is a thread that creates a PNG file named last_day_results.PNG on the file system every 24 hours.

> **TIP** *The PNG format is preferable for charts, because it is a lossless format, and the image quality will be much superior to the JPEG file format. Unless you have to support a web browser that does not support PNG images, avoid the JPEG file format for your charts. They will look terrible.*

Usually, developers will choose to use a servlet to create an image dynamically instead. The source of an HTML image tag would be a URL that points to a servlet with several parameters for customization. This approach works in either web applications or portal applications—in both cases, a servlet provides an image. We do not use portlets for this, even though the portlet API supports writing binary output to a render response. Binary output works only for portlets that are contained in an HTML `<IFRAME>` frame within the portal, and this will be a rare deployment scenario. The `<IFRAME>` frame will reset to its starting page whenever the portal page refreshes, which is usually not how the user expects the portal page to behave.

JFreeChart and Servlets

Servlet support comes with JFreeChart. There are three classes in the `org.jfree.chart.servlet` package that servlet or portlet application developers can use. The `ServletUtilities` class provides several utility methods for servlet developers who are serving charts over the Web. The `DisplayChart` servlet reads chart images out of the Java temporary directory and serves them as binary image files. It is ready for inclusion in a portlet or web application. The `ChartDeleter` class is a helper class for the servlet or portlet that is managing the content that includes the charts. When a chart is created in the temporary directory, the servlet or portlet registers the chart's filename with `ChartDeleter` so it is deleted when the user's session expires.

ServletUtilities

The `ServletUtilities` class is useful for developers who need to serve JFreeChart charts from servlets. If the security provided with the `DisplayChart` servlet is not sufficient, you can develop your own image-serving servlet class. `ServletUtilities` also provides methods for portlet or servlet developers to save their charts in the temporary directory.

The `saveChartAsPNG()` and `saveChartAsJPEG()` methods create an image file in the Java temporary directory with the given height and width. They also register the chart for deletion with the user's `ChartDeleter`. The methods retrieve the `ChartDeleter` from the user's session. If the `ChartDeleter` does not exist, it will be created. The `ChartDeleter` is stored in the session with the key "JFreeChart_Deleter".

```
public static String saveChartAsPNG(JFreeChart chart, int width, int height,
                        HttpSession session) throws IOException
public static String saveChartAsJPEG(JFreeChart chart, int width, int height,
                        HttpSession session) throws IOException
```

These methods return the filename on the file system. The `DisplayChart` servlet uses the filename to serve the images out of the temporary directory. When we create the files, the filename will start with the prefix "jfreechart-", followed by a unique number, and then end with the suffix ".png"—for instance, jfreechart-45606.png.

There are also two methods for setting and retrieving the temporary file prefix used by the `saveChartAsPNG()` and `saveChartAsJPEG()` methods. The default prefix is "jfreechart-".

```
public static String getTempFilePrefix()
public static void setTempFilePrefix(String prefix)
```

Three `sendTempFile()` methods stream a file in the temporary directory to a user's web browser. They set the HTTP Content-Length and Last-Modified headers on the HTTP response. If the MIME type of the file is either image/jpeg or image/png, they also set the HTTP Content-Type header.

```
public static void sendTempFile(String filename, HttpServletResponse response)
    throws IOException
public static void sendTempFile(File file, HttpServletResponse response)
    throws IOException
public static void sendTempFile(File file, HttpServletResponse response,
    String mimeType) throws IOException
```

You can use any MIME type passed into the third `sendTempFile()` method listed previously. It is convenient to use the `DisplayChart` servlet class that comes with JFreeChart to serve your images if possible.

DisplayChart

JFreeChart supplies a helper servlet class named `DisplayChart` to serve chart images to the user. The portlet application's web.xml deployment descriptor must contain the `DisplayChart` servlet definition.

```
<servlet>
    <servlet-name>DisplayChart</servlet-name>
    <servlet-class>org.jfree.chart.servlet.DisplayChart</servlet-class>
</servlet>
<servlet-mapping>
    <servlet-name>DisplayChart</servlet-name>
    <url-pattern>/servlet/DisplayChart</url-pattern>
</servlet-mapping>
```

The `DisplayChart` servlet expects to find the filename of the chart image in the filename request parameter. The portlet has to provide this parameter, or the `DisplayChart` servlet will throw an exception. The display servlet looks in the Java temporary directory for an image with that filename. The `java.io.tmpdir` system property defines the temporary directory, which you may need to configure in your portal or application server if you do not want the default. If the user is permitted to view the chart, the `DisplayChart` servlet puts the binary chart data into the servlet response using the `sendTempFile()` method on the `ServletUtilities` class.

> **NOTE** *In the current version of Pluto as of this writing, servlets running outside the portal but inside the same servlet container do not share a session with the portlets in the same portlet application, when we run on Tomcat (5.0.25). The* `DisplayChart` *servlet looks in its* `HttpSession` *for a* `ChartDeleter` *object, so it can determine whether to serve the chart to the user. To use these classes in our portlet application, we had to remove the* `DisplayChart` *servlet's dependency on the* `HttpSession`. *Unfortunately, this means that we also removed the servlet's security features. Other portals or future releases of Pluto may not have the same problem, and you will be able to use the* `DisplayChart` *class as-is. We commented out the security checks in the* `DisplayChart` *class's* `service()` *method. You can find the modified version of* `DisplayChart` *on our web site,* `www.portalbook.com`.

One nice feature of the `DisplayChart` servlet is that it strips any ".." directory references from the filename parameter, so you can prevent unauthorized access to files outside the temporary directory. In addition to this basic security, the display servlet checks the image to see if this user is allowed to access the chart, or if the chart is available to any user. This prevents users from viewing another user's chart by changing the filename parameter on the URL. If you use this servlet to display your charts, you will need to use the `ChartDeleter` class inside your portlet to manage the charts in the temporary directory.

If the `DisplayChart` servlet meets your security needs, you can use it as-is. The source code for the servlet comes with JFreeChart, so it should be easy to make any necessary modifications.

ChartDeleter

The `ChartDeleter` class serves two purposes: disk space management and security for the `DisplayChart` servlet. Your portlet application should clean up the temporary chart image files that it creates. These can easily fill your hard drive, and you will need to come up with a strategy that minimizes disk space demands but that also does not erase an image that might be served to a user right now. One approach is to create a scheduled thread that deletes any chart images in the temporary directory over 24 hours old.

A better approach is to ensure that any charts created for the user be available as long as the user has a valid session. The ChartDeleter class implements the HttpSessionBindingListener interface. Any attributes in the portlet session are also attributes in an HTTP session, so the standard servlet session binding listeners will work. The portlet that is responsible for charting should add an instance of the ChartDeleter object to the user's session if one does not already exist. When the portlet serves a content fragment that includes one or more charts embedded as <IMG> HTML tags, the portlet should register the chart's filename with the user's ChartDeleter using the addChart() method:

```
public void addChart(String filename)
```

The ChartDeleter works only with files in the Java temporary file directory. At any time, the portlet can ask the ChartDeleter if a chart is on the deletion list, using the isChartAvailable() method:

```
public boolean isChartAvailable(String filename)
```

After the user's session has expired, the portlet container will call the valueUnbound() method on the user's ChartDeleter object. This method deletes all of the files registered with the ChartDeleter in the temporary directory.

Portlet Extensions to JFreeChart

The ServletUtilities class relies on the HttpSession class, which is not available from the portlet API. One of the design decisions made for the portlet API was not to have a way to access an underlying HttpSession from a portlet's PortletSession. Servlets and JSPs deployed in the portlet application use an HttpSession that contains the same data as the PortletSession.

We created a PortletUtilities class that is analogous to the ServletUtilities class. The difference is that the saveChartAsPNG() method takes a PortletSession as an argument. The registerChartForDeletion() method also uses a portlet session instead of an HTTP session.

You can download the PortletUtilities class from the book's web site, at www.portalbook.com.

In our next example, we use the PortletUtilities class.

Portlet Example with a 3D Pie Chart

This example displays a 3D pie chart with some expenditures data. The pie chart uses a PieDataset object, which we populated using the setValue() method. Like with the bar chart example earlier, we used the `ChartFactory` class to create our pie chart.

One interesting JFreeChart feature we used was the ability to combine small values in a pie data set into a catch-all category called "Other." The `limitPieDataset()` method on the `org.jfree.data.DatasetUtilities` class takes a pie data set and a cut-off value for small values. In our example, the Recruiting, Turnover, and Corporate Initiatives values were all under 2 percent of the total expenditures. All three were lumped into a slice of the pie called Other:

```
package com.portalbook.portlets;

import java.io.IOException;
import java.io.PrintWriter;

import javax.portlet.GenericPortlet;
import javax.portlet.PortletException;
import javax.portlet.PortletSession;
import javax.portlet.RenderRequest;
import javax.portlet.RenderResponse;

import org.jfree.chart.ChartFactory;
import org.jfree.chart.JFreeChart;
import org.jfree.data.DatasetUtilities;
import org.jfree.data.DefaultPieDataset;
import org.jfree.data.PieDataset;

import com.portalbook.charting.PortletUtilities;

public class ChartingPortlet extends GenericPortlet
{
    public void doView(RenderRequest request, RenderResponse response)
        throws PortletException, IOException
    {

        response.setContentType("text/html");
        PrintWriter writer = response.getWriter();

        PortletSession session = request.getPortletSession();

        PieDataset dataset = createDataset();

        //Lower the number of entries in the pie table by combining
        //the ones that fall under a 2% threshold into "Other"
        dataset = DatasetUtilities.limitPieDataset(dataset, 0.02);
```

```
        JFreeChart chart = createChart(dataset);

        String filename =
            PortletUtilities.saveChartAsPNG(chart, 400, 300, session);

        writer.write("<H1>IT Expenditures Chart</H1>");
        String chartServlet =
            request.getContextPath() + "/servlet/DisplayChart";
        writer.write(
            "<IMG SRC='" + chartServlet + "?filename=" + filename + "'");

    }

    protected PieDataset createDataset()
    {
        DefaultPieDataset dataset = new DefaultPieDataset();
        dataset.setValue("Software", 65.2);
        dataset.setValue("Services", 20.1);
        dataset.setValue("Hardware", 17.3);
        dataset.setValue("Network", 18.9);
        dataset.setValue("Recruiting", 1.3);
        dataset.setValue("Training", 2.8);
        dataset.setValue("Turnover", 1.2);
        dataset.setValue("Corporate Initiatives", 0.5);

        return dataset;
    }

    protected JFreeChart createChart(PieDataset dataset)
    {
        JFreeChart chart = null;
        String title = "IT Expenditures 2003";
        chart =
            ChartFactory.createPieChart3D(title, dataset, true, false, false);
        return chart;
    }
}
```

The portlet uses our `PortletUtilities` class to save the chart to disk as a PNG file. The `DisplayChart` servlet serves the image to the user. The portlet's content fragment contains an `<IMG>` HTML element that references the `DisplayChart` servlet, and passes the servlet a parameter named `filename` that contains the name of the chart in the temporary file directory. Figure 14-8 shows the third pie chart our portlet creates.

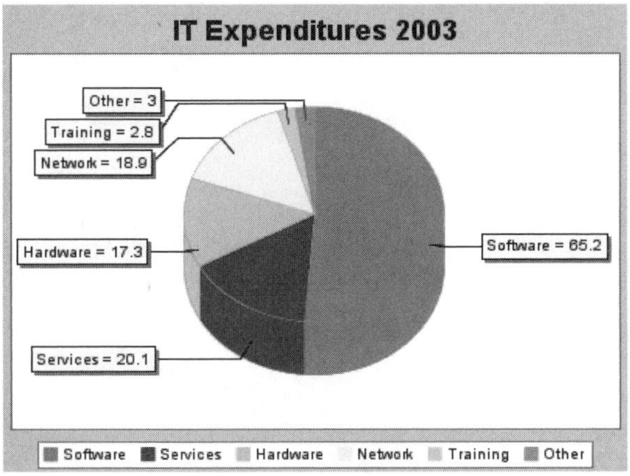

Figure 14-8. 3D pie chart from the example

Summary

JFreeChart is a very useful component for generating graphs and plots. The basic model is to create a data set with the chart's data. Be sure to use the appropriate `Dataset` object for your chart type. Next, you create the chart with the `ChartFactory` class. Finally, you export the chart to the appropriate image format on the hard drive.

You can use the JFreeChart servlet functionality for your projects, or you can write your own servlet to serve image files. We used the `PortletUtilities` class for our example charting portlet. Our portlet created a pie data set, and then consolidated the smaller values in the pie data set into a new data set. The portlet generated the 3D pie chart, and then used the `PortletUtilities` functionality to save the chart image. We added the `DisplayChart` servlet to our web.xml web application deployment descriptor for our charting application. Our portlet placed an image tag that pointed to the `DisplayChart` servlet into its content fragment. We also had to modify the `DisplayChart` servlet to let it run on our version of Pluto and Tomcat 5.0.25.

CHAPTER 15

Content Management Systems

One of the most common uses of a portal is to provide an interface to content management systems (CMSs). Some users may need to get information from the CMS, while others may need to create content. Many portals integrate with a CMS from the same vendor—sometimes the portal ships with the CMS, and in other cases it is a separate product. If you do not have a vendor-supplied integrated solution, you will probably need to develop one using the portlet API and a CMS API.

In this chapter, we discuss the Java Content Repository API (JSR 170), and the WebDAV protocol. We also build a portlet that uses WebDAV to connect to a content store—in this case, the open source CMS Apache Slide (`http://jakarta.apache.org/slide`). Our portlet should work with any WebDAV server, so you can use your own CMS if it supports WebDAV.

Overview of Content Management Systems

Content management is a broad field that encompasses a wide range of software applications. Document management, imaging, product data management, digital media and asset management, knowledge management, and web content management are some of the different types of content management systems. Usually, all of these different systems are grouped together into a field called enterprise content management.

From a technical perspective, many of these systems share a common base of functionality and features. All of them have a content repository, where content is stored on a database or file system. Most systems use some kind of hierarchical organization for the content, although you will certainly find CMS applications where all of the content is at the same level. Most CMS packages with a hierarchical view actually store all of the content in a single database table or directory. The relationships for the hierarchy are stored in the database. This provides advantages for access and retrieval, and allows the same piece of content to appear in two or more different locations.

The next piece of the CMS puzzle is content delivery. Most web content management packages are optimized for content delivery, and can easily be plugged into a web-based application. In some cases, part of the vendor-provided content delivery is a display portlet that can save you a lot of development effort. One disadvantage of CMS tools with content delivery is that they often include page assembly features, for delivering a web page with navigation, headers, and footers. This is not very useful from a portal perspective, where the portal page provides the interface. Usually there is a way to access the raw content directly, without any of the page assembly.

A common use of content management systems is to introduce workflow into the content production process. A classic business use case for a CMS project involves a content producer creating a Microsoft Word file locally and then uploading it into the CMS. His manager gets a review notice through e-mail and logs into the CMS. The manager approves the content inside the CMS, and the content is ready for delivery. Most enterprise CMS applications will have workflow or an approval process for publishing built-in. The level of automation and custom development varies from CMS to CMS. Sometimes it can be very easy to create a complex content review process that turns out to be unwieldy for the end user in practice. Bottlenecks will start to appear, especially with different levels of approval. Creating a "ready for review" portlet for a CMS is usually a straightforward development project involving a proprietary API.

Content production and authoring is a newer technology that has become more popular with the availability of rich text or HTML authoring controls for web pages. These content-creation tools could be Java applets, ActiveX controls, DHTML, Flash, or any other client-side technology. Some CMS applications come with these as part of an authoring workspace. The rapid adoption of WebDAV in desktop applications means that these controls may not be the best solution for your users, especially if they are already familiar with tools like Macromedia Dreamweaver MX. It is easy enough to embed one of the client-side HTML authoring tools into a portlet—saving the HTML onto the server will depend on the CMS.

Personalization is a feature that somewhat overlaps with portals. Your content management system may support varying levels of personalization, some of which may coincide with your portal vendor's personalization product. If you have to choose between the two, the portal's personalization will work for other applications running on the portal, but the CMS personalization will be portable across multiple portals. Ideally, future versions of the portlet API will standardize personalization, so this will become less of a problem.

Almost every CMS includes some level of search support, whether it is a simple SQL query interface or an integrated search engine like Verity or Lucene. The Java Content Repository API defines a standard for queries and query languages that should gain support from Java-based CMS vendors. The trickiest part of external search engine integration with a CMS and a portal will be indexing the CMS properly. If your site includes multiple user groups with different access to content, you should consider a federated search approach, as we described in Chapter 10 for Lucene. Commercial search vendors will have their own recommendations, and will probably offer ready-made JSR 168 portlets either now or in the near future.

Integration with a Content Management System

Most portal deployments require integration with at least one content management system; often, integration with several different vendors' systems is necessary. From a project management perspective, bringing content into a portal requires several steps. The first is to identify which content should be available and where the content is coming from. The next step is to determine which sets of users should see which content. The third step involves identifying which functionality in the content management system belongs in a portlet. After these business process steps are completed, you can start planning the technical architecture of the integration—does the vendor provide a JSR 168 portlet already? Many vendors write portlets for their content management systems, which can make your job much easier. Two commercial vendors with JSR 168 portlets at the time of writing are Stellent and Documentum; other vendors likely have products on the way. If you do not have a ready-made portlet application to roll into your application, you are going to need to look into the integration APIs for the content management system.

There are two major standards for CMS APIs: WebDAV and the new Java Content Repository API (JSR 170). WebDAV is a set of extensions to the HTTP protocol for versioning, accessing metadata, making directories, locking files, and checking files in and out, among other things. WebDAV is not tied to a single platform or architecture, although the CMS must specifically implement a WebDAV layer. The Java Content Repository API (JCR API) is a new standard for Java content management systems. The JCR API defines a standard set of interfaces and classes that CMS clients can use to connect to a CMS and access content and metadata. We discuss both WebDAV and the JCR API in this chapter.

Neither of these APIs covers all of the possible functionality for a CMS. In addition, not every CMS implements one of these APIs—most will have a separate proprietary API, which you will have to implement yourself. If there are any servlet/JSP example applications, they should be easily adapted to a portlet application.

You can pull content out of almost any content management system through its database or file system store, but that should be a last-ditch integration step. Of course, if your CMS is 10 years old, running on a legacy platform, and does not have an open API, this may be your only choice. It is probably better at that point to migrate the legacy CMS to something newer, but for lots of reasons that may not make business sense.

Common Problems with CMS and Portals

Some of the most common technical problems with CMS integration with portals are authentication, access control, link rewriting, and content delivery. We can manage authentication with Single Sign-On (SSO) functionality, which we discussed in Chapter 8. If the application is not suitable for SSO, you can collect the correct CMS credentials from the user once, and then store them in the user's portlet preferences.

Access control partly comes from SSO, especially if you have an enterprise-wide set of permissions for your portal and your CMS. If all of your access control is maintained in one directory, you can cut down on technical support, but your software development costs for integration will be huge. If you do not have an enterprise access control system, most content management systems will only display content that the user has access to. You will have to manage the permissions yourself, either programmatically or through an administrative GUI.

Link rewriting is another common problem. The links in your CMS content will not stay in the portal. You could write a set of content display adapters that rewrites your HTML content with the appropriate portlet URLs for links. Another approach would be to standardize on an enterprise-wide XML format for content. Each content delivery or content authoring system would be responsible for rendering the XML correctly for display in that system, but creating the correct links would be easy.

Any content that relies on JavaScript will probably not work, unless the JavaScript is completely contained in the piece of content. Because you may want to use the content in more than one location, you probably do not want JavaScript embedded in your content. Convince your content producers that they do not need to use scripts—one way to encourage this is to provide support for custom HTML or XML tags, such as `<PrinterFriendly>`, `<PopupWindow>`, `<DynamicMenu>`, or similar tags. Your content delivery applications would render these tags in the appropriate manner for display, or ignore them altogether. This puts more control on the systems side, and takes control away from the content creators. Portals especially need this type of control over content because the content needs to appear in a portlet.

You will have to determine how content delivery through a portal will work. You could display all of your content in new browser windows that open up outside of the portlet window. If you take this path, your CMS portlets would open links to web applications that display the content correctly, with working links, styles, and images. Another approach is to display HTML or XML content inside the portlet, and rewrite the links to any binary data such as PDF files or images to use a servlet for access. Your portlet cannot stream binary data to the user's web browser directly, so an approach like this is necessary. You could also look into ActiveX controls for PDF files, Microsoft Office files, and the like.

Java Content Repository API (JSR 170)

The Java Content Repository API (JCR API, `www.jcp.org/en/jsr/detail?id=170`) is a common interface to content management systems, just like the portlet API is a common interface for portals. The JCR API is Java Specification Request 170

(JSR 170), and at the time of this writing, it was in public review. Similar to the portlet API, the motivation for the JSR 170 standard was that each CMS vendor used a different API. Writing applications on top of these proprietary APIs was difficult because the application ran only on one CMS or because porting and maintaining compatibility required lots of development resources. Imagine trying to build an application (for instance, a search engine) that ran on a number of portals and used several different content management systems. Then imagine supporting that application for all the combinations of systems your customers might have.

The advantage of the JCR API is that more applications can take advantage of content management systems—the barrier to entry is lower, and there is less worry about proprietary lock-in. A client application does not have to know the details of how the JSR 170 implementation works on the content management system. The JCR API does not specify a client/server protocol. Because some CMSs organize content in a hierarchy of folders and content items, and others organize content in a flat set, the JCR API can use either type of structure.

The JCR API does not cover all of the possible functions of a content management system. The standard covers the most common functionality for a content repository, but does not include such areas as personalization, publishing, workflow, or taxonomies. There are two levels of the JCR API. The first level is Level 1, and it includes basic content repository functionality. The main features it includes are

- Retrieving content
- Writing content
- Removing content
- Serializing content
- Searching content
- Changing and retrieving different content types

The more advanced functionality is grouped into Level 2. Level 2 is not required because not every CMS needs that level of complexity. The advanced features in Level 2 are

- Transactions
- Versions
- Observation

- Access control
- Locks

JCR API Concepts

The JCR API uses several key classes for access to most of the content repository functionality. These classes model the content management system's internal structure, but building this API on top of a legacy CMS may be difficult. Some of the JCR API classes may not be a one-to-one match for existing classes, and some of the APIs and key concepts might be implemented differently in the CMS.

You should understand how the concepts described next map onto your CMS, especially noting which functionality is unavailable through the JCR API.

Repository

The `javax.jcr.Repository` interface models a Java content repository. The repository represents all of the content, relationships, and metadata in the content management system. The content repository contains content workspaces. Your portlets will ask this class for a ticket that represents access to a workspace for an authenticated user. The repository will need a valid set of credentials for the user.

Ticket

Tickets map authenticated users to workspaces. Ticket objects implement the `javax.jcr.Ticket` interface. A ticket maps to a single workspace. Each ticket provides access to the repository for the user, but the ticket will keep any changes queued until the portlet either reverts or saves the changes.

Credentials

The `javax.jcr.Credentials` interface represents the user authentication information for the user. If the credentials are valid, the repository will return a valid ticket that grants access to a workspace. Your CMS will implement the interface with whatever information it needs to grant access—this will usually include a username and password, and could include a group or a domain, or other custom authentication attributes.

Workspace

Use the `javax.jcr.Workspace` interface to get access to a content workspace. The repository holds one or more workspaces. Each workspace has a tree of items, which are organized under a root node.

Each `Workspace` object for an authenticated user maps to a `Ticket` object.

Item

The `javax.jcr.Item` interface is the base class for nodes and properties. The workspace consists of a tree of items.

Node

Nodes represent individual entities in the content management system, and are implementations of the `javax.jcr.Node` interface. They could be pieces of content, folders, documents, products, or anything else. Each node can have zero or more child nodes. With CMS support, nodes may also have more than one parent node. Nodes can have zero or more properties.

Each node has one primary node type, but can also have multiple *mixin* node types. Mixin types describe additional information about a node, beyond its primary node type. Each primary node type inherits from the `nt:base` node type, which must be supported. The CMS may define its own node types below the hierarchy. Some predefined (but optional) node types are `nt:file`, `nt:folder`, `nt:version`, and `nt:query`. Certain primary node types require mixin types, and others allow only certain mixin types. Nodes can have versions, although the node must have the mixin node type `mix:versionable`.

Property

Properties are children of nodes, and have only one parent node. The property interface is `javax.jcr.Property`. Properties represent pieces of metadata about nodes. The values of properties must conform to allowed property types, which include strings, binary data, dates, longs, doubles, and booleans. Properties may also be soft links or references. Soft links are links to paths in the content repository. These are soft references; the linked content may be moved, deleted, or may not even exist. The soft link's path can be absolute or relative. References are hard links to nodes. They link by the node ID (UUID), and they must exist. If a reference exists to a node, that reference must be deleted before the node may be moved or deleted. Some properties may have multiple values.

Path

A path points to an item in the repository. Paths may be either relative or absolute. /Engineering/Reports/11222.doc is an example of an absolute path in the repository. ../Reports/11222.doc is a relative path, just like a file system. Your portlet may get a node through the ticket by its absolute path. If two or more nodes under the same parent node have the same name, the path can be tricky. You will have to use array-based notation (starting at 1, not 0) to reference the node you want.

Search

One of the most interesting features of the JCR API is its search support. Because JCR defines a standard set of query interfaces, it should be possible to create a search portlet that can execute a search and display search results for any content management system. Compare that with the Lucene portlet we built in Chapter 10. The Lucene portlet's basics are the same for every CMS, especially if you use a standard set of fields. The difficulty with Lucene is writing classes that synchronize the contents of the CMS with the Lucene index, especially if you are integrating multiple systems. We expect that many JCR API implementations will use Lucene to provide search capabilities.

The JCR API defines two query languages for the search function:

- **JCRQL (with SSES):** Java Content Repository Query Language (with Simple Search Engine Syntax) is similar to SQL, but has extensions for the hierarchical content model and also supports standard search query terms.

- **XPath:** XPath 2.0 is an XML technology for searching through a hierarchical XML document and extracting elements that match an XPath expression. The JCR API XPath query language supports a subset of the XPath 2.0 functionality plus some extensions needed for the JCR API.

Each content repository has to support at least one of these query languages. Each CMS can also support additional languages—for instance, a Google-style query language, or a Lucene query language with named fields. This means your application will need to know which query language the CMS supports. The `javax.jcr.query.QueryManager` class has a `getSupportedQueryLanguages()` method that will return the supported languages. If you are building a general-purpose application, you will probably need to support both of the standard query languages. This way, your application will run on any JCR API–compliant CMS. Your support may just be limited to different help files for the search engine because the `QueryManager` class also parses the query from the user's statement.

Development with the JCR API

The JCR API classes belong to the `javax.jcr` package and its subpackages. To start developing with the JCR API, you will need to select and install a server that implements the standard. The standard is still quite new, so we expect that a reference implementation of the JCR API will be released around the time that this book is published. Some of the details of the API may have changed since the public review, but all of the major concepts should be the same.

The first step with the JCR API is to obtain a `javax.jcr.Repository` object. Your content management system should include directions for getting an instance of `Repository`, because this is one area of the API that is not standardized. The authors of the specification expect that a JNDI lookup will be a common approach. `Repository` is an interface with one method, `login()`:

```
public Ticket login(Credentials credentials, String workspaceName)
        throws LoginException, NoSuchWorkspaceException
```

The `login()` method takes a set of credentials and a workspace name. The `javax.jcr.Credentials` interface consists of a `getUserId()` method; a `getPassword()` method; and several methods for storing, setting, and removing attributes on the credentials. The JCR API provides a basic implementation of the `Credentials` interface with the `javax.jcr.SimpleCredentials` class. You can create a new instance of `SimpleCredentials` by calling its constructor and passing a user ID and password as arguments. Upon successful authentication, the `login()` method returns a `Ticket` object.

The `javax.jcr.Ticket` class is the main gateway for your client to access the content repository. From the ticket, you can get the root node of the workspace, or you can get a node by its absolute path. You can also import an XML document that represents new items.

Once you have a node, you can continue traversing the tree by relative paths. The `Node` class has methods for retrieving and setting the node's properties. You can also create new nodes or add existing nodes as children. After you make any changes, you will have commit your changes by saving the node. You can also save all of your changes for the workspace by calling the `save()` method on the ticket.

Retrieving a document out of a content repository with the JCR API is simple. When you have a node with the primary type `nt:file`, that node will have a child node called `jcr:content`. The `jcr:content` node holds the content in one of its properties, which could be called `data`. You could get the value of the `data` property, and then pass it back through to the portlet.

WebDAV

WebDAV (`www.webdav.org`) is a commonly implemented protocol for connecting to content management systems and other content stores. The WebDAV specification (RFC 2518) can be found at `www.webdav.org/specs/rfc2518.htm`. Many applications and operating systems are WebDAV compatible. A non-exhaustive list of compatible client applications follows:

- Microsoft Word
- Microsoft Excel
- Adobe Photoshop
- Macromedia Dreamweaver
- Apple Mac OS X
- Microsoft Windows XP
- Altova XML Spy 2004

All of these applications are able to connect to a WebDAV-compatible server. Apache Tomcat comes with a WebDAV servlet that provides WebDAV access to files on the file system. Apache Slide (`http://jakarta.apache.org/slide`) is an open source content management system that has a WebDAV server and a command-line WebDAV client. Slide also has a WebDAV client library for Java, which we will use to build a WebDAV client portlet.

WebDAV is an extension of the HTTP 1.1 protocol, so it is relatively easy to implement.

WebDAV Methods

If you are already familiar with the GET and POST HTTP methods, the WebDAV methods will look very similar. WebDAV adds many new methods beyond GET,

POST, HEAD, and the other standard HTTP methods. The biggest difference is that WebDAV supports, and for some methods, requires, an XML message body for the WebDAV methods.

We explain some of the most commonly used WEBDAV methods in this section. Other methods in the WebDAV specification are MOVE, COPY, LOCK, and UNLOCK. The versioning extensions to WebDAV (RFC 3253) also define the VERSION-CONTROL, REPORT, CHECKOUT, CHECKIN, and UNCHECKOUT methods. Other related specifications are WebDAV Ordered Collections (RFC 3648) and WebDAV Access Control (RFC 3744).

PROPFIND

Use the PROPFIND method to access the properties of a resource. The client will ask for a set of properties by name for a given WebDAV resource. The server can also return all of the properties for the resource.

The client may also ask for all of the resource's properties along with all of its children's properties up to a given depth. The depth may be 0, 1, or infinity. An infinity depth returns the properties of all resources under the named resource.

If your WebDAV client needs to browse through content in the server's repository, the PROPFIND method is useful for determining what the current resource's properties are and the names and types of resources under the current resource. You can easily create a directory listing style interface. If you use a depth of 1 or infinity, your application could cache the properties to improve performance.

PROPPATCH

Client applications use the PROPPATCH method to create, modify, or remove properties on a resource. You can both set and remove one or more properties in a single request. The PROPPATCH method is an all or nothing proposition—if any of the requests to set or modify a property fail, none of the requests will be permanent. Any changes before the failed request will be set back to the way they were. If a PROPPATCH call fails, you will get an error message back explaining what the problem was.

MKCOL

The MKCOL method creates a new collection resource. The request's path should not already exist. If the path does exist, the MKCOL method will not work. Another condition to consider is that the specified path's parent collections must already exist—only one collection will be created.

DELETE

The DELETE method removes the non-collection resource at the specified path. If the resource is a collection, the DELETE method will remove the collection and all resources under the collection. This is a very powerful method.

PUT

The PUT method creates a new resource at the given path, or it replaces the contents of the existing resource. The PUT method works only for non-collections. If you need to create a new collection, use the MKCOL method.

Slide WebDAV Client Library

The client distribution for Apache Slide includes a command-line client and a WebDAV client library. We will use both to build a portlet that communicates with a WebDAV server. Both the WebDAV client library and the command-line client are open source projects licensed with the Apache Software License. The Java WebDAV client API is straightforward, once you understand the basics of the WebDAV protocol.

The WebDAV client library is in the jakarta-slide-webdavlib-2.0.jar file. You need to copy that file into your WEB-INF/lib folder. The source distribution of the Slide client includes the source code of the command-line client. The command-line client is the best source for information on how to use the WebDAV client library, so we used its source code as a model for our portlet.

The WebDAV client library classes are in the `org.apache.webdav.lib`, `org.apache.webdav.lib.methods`, and `org.apache.webdav.lib.properties` packages. Your application will create an `org.apache.webdav.lib.WebdavResource` object that represents a resource on the remote server. You will need the URL of the remote resource, along with the username and password (if necessary). If the resource does not exist, you can create it once you have the object.

Once you have an object that represents a resource, you can execute the WebDAV methods we discussed in the previous section. The WebDAV methods are available directly on the `WebdavResource` object (`mkcolMethod()`, `moveMethod()`, `deleteMethod()`, etc.). Other methods on the WebdavResource object use WebDAV indirectly, or return information that already exists on the object. These include `list()`, `listBasic()`, and `listWebdavResources()`. Each of these methods returns information about the child resources of the current resource if the current resource is a collection. The `list()` method returns a `String` array of pathnames to the children. The `listBasic()` method returns the child resources' path names, content length, either collection or a content type, and the last modified date. This information is stored in an array for each resource, and then each array is stored in a `Vector`. If you would like to get an array of `WebdavResource` objects that represents each of the child resources in the collection, use the `listWebdavResources()` method.

WebDAV Portlet

We are going to build a portlet that connects to a WebDAV server. You will need to install a CMS that supports WebDAV. We used the open source Apache Slide server. The easiest way to get started is to download the Slide binary distribution that bundles the compiled version of Slide with an installation of Apache Tomcat. You will need to edit the port numbers for Slide's Tomcat if you run Slide side by side with Pluto on the same computer, so they do not conflict. Another option is to install the Slide web application on an external installation of Tomcat. We used Slide 2.0, running on port 9080.

Use your operating system's built-in WebDAV support to add some files and folders to the Slide content repository. Documentation for both Windows and Mac OS X is available on the Slide web site. You can also use the command-line Slide WebDAV client. Our portlet only allows content browsing and viewing, although we could certainly add more file management support.

We are using several open source libraries for our WebDAV portlet. The first is the WebDAV client library we discussed previously. That library is packaged in the jakarta-slide-webdavlib-2.0.jar file. It also requires the Jakarta Commons HTTP client library and the Jakarta Commons logging libraries. The correct versions are in the Slide client binary distribution. The other libraries we will use are the JSP Standard Tag libraries, for our JSP files. We use the Jakarta Commons Standard Tag Library, version 1.0.4 (the same as Chapter 5). We will need the jstl.jar and the standard.jar files. All of these libraries should go in your WEB-INF/lib directory.

Our portlet will display the available resources for a collection, or it will display the contents of a noncollection resource. If you select a collection, the portlet will update its internal pointer to a WebDAV resource, and then display the resources in the collection. If you select a file, the portlet will retrieve its contents as a string, and then display them in the portlet window. You may also navigate back up the hierarchy with the parent folder link at the bottom of the page.

We created one portlet class, `CMSPortlet.java`. It responds to action requests and render requests. The `WebDAVHelper` class encapsulates the WebDAV functionality. `WebDAVHelper` is a bridge between the portlet and the client library, and it includes some utility methods. Our JSP file, ListFiles.jsp, uses the portlet and standard JSP tag libraries to display the resources for a collection.

CMSPortlet.java

The CMSPortlet class initializes itself from the initialization parameters on the portlet deployment descriptor. Three parameters, URL, username, and password, contain the connection information for the WebDAV server.

The doView() method looks at the current WebDAV resource to determine if it is a collection. If it is a collection, it dispatches the request to the ListFiles.jsp page. If it is not a collection, it asks for the contents of the resources as a String, and displays them in the portlet output. We could also have created links in the JSP file that would show the contents of the resources in a new window if the resource was an image, PDF file, or another binary file.

The processAction() method looks at the COMMAND parameter and then performs an action based on the command. All of our commands change the current WebDAV resource.

```
package com.portalbook.portlets;

import java.io.*;

import javax.portlet.ActionRequest;
import javax.portlet.ActionResponse;
import javax.portlet.GenericPortlet;
import javax.portlet.PortletConfig;
import javax.portlet.PortletContext;
import javax.portlet.PortletException;
import javax.portlet.PortletRequestDispatcher;
import javax.portlet.RenderRequest;
import javax.portlet.RenderResponse;
import javax.portlet.UnavailableException;

import org.apache.webdav.lib.WebdavException;
import org.apache.webdav.lib.WebdavResource;

public class CMSPortlet extends GenericPortlet
{
    public static final String COMMAND = "COMMAND";

    public static final String CHANGE_COLL = "CHANGE_COLLECTION";
    public static final String DISPLAY_CONTENT = "DISPLAY_CONTENT";
    public static final String DISPLAY_PARENT = "DISPLAY_PARENT";
    public static final String PATH = "PATH";

    WebDAVHelper helper;
```

```
public void init(PortletConfig config) throws PortletException
{
    super.init(config);

    helper = new WebDAVHelper();

    try
    {
        String url = config.getInitParameter("URL");
        String username = config.getInitParameter("username");
        String password = config.getInitParameter("password");
        helper.openURL(url, username, password);
    }
    catch (IOException e)
    {
        System.out.println(e.getMessage());
        e.printStackTrace();
        throw new UnavailableException(e.getMessage());
    }

}

protected void doView(RenderRequest request, RenderResponse response)
    throws PortletException, IOException
{
    response.setContentType("text/html");

    Writer writer = response.getWriter();

    PortletContext portletContext = getPortletContext();

    WebdavResource resource = helper.getResource();

    request.setAttribute("resource", resource);
    System.out.println("name: " + resource.getName());

    if (resource.isCollection())
    {
        PortletRequestDispatcher prd =
            portletContext.getRequestDispatcher(
                "/WEB-INF/jsp/ListFiles.jsp");

        prd.include(request, response);
```

```
        }
        else
        {
            writer.write(resource.getMethodDataAsString());
        }

    }

    public void processAction(ActionRequest request, ActionResponse response)
        throws PortletException, IOException
    {
        String cmd = request.getParameter(COMMAND);
        System.out.println("Command: " + cmd);

        if (CHANGE_COLL.equals(cmd))
        {
            String path = request.getParameter(PATH);
            if (path != null)
            {
                System.out.println("path: " + path);
                try
                {
                    helper.setPath(path);
                }
                catch (WebdavException e)
                {
                    System.out.println(e.getMessage());
                    e.printStackTrace();
                }
            }
        }
        else if (DISPLAY_CONTENT.equals(cmd))
        {
            String path = request.getParameter(PATH);
            if (path != null)
            {
                System.out.println("path: " + path);
                try
                {
                    helper.setPath(path);
                }
                catch (WebdavException e)
                {
```

```
                    System.out.println(e.getMessage());
                    e.printStackTrace();
                }
            }
        }
        else if (DISPLAY_PARENT.equals(cmd))
        {
            String path = request.getParameter(PATH);
            if (path != null)
            {
                System.out.println("path: " + path);
                try
                {
                    helper.setPath(helper.getParentPath(path));
                }
                catch (WebdavException e)
                {
                    System.out.println(e.getMessage());
                    e.printStackTrace();
                }
            }
        }
    }
}
```

WebDAVHelper.java

The `WebDAVHelper` class is a utility class we created to simplify our interactions with the WebDAV client library. We have several methods to make working with paths easier because the slashes can become tricky.

The `openURL()` method creates a new `HttpURL` object that represents the URL to the WebDAV server. Because our WebDAV server is protected with HTTP authentication, we set the user info on the `HttpURL` object with the user's username and password.

```
package com.portalbook.portlets;

import java.io.*;

import org.apache.commons.httpclient.HttpException;
import org.apache.commons.httpclient.HttpURL;
```

```
import org.apache.webdav.lib.WebdavException;
import org.apache.webdav.lib.WebdavResource;

public class WebDAVHelper
{
    private WebdavResource resource = null;

    protected void openURL(String uri, String username, String password)
        throws HttpException, IOException
    {
        HttpURL url = new HttpURL(uri);

        if (resource == null)
        {
            url.setUserinfo(username, password);
            resource = new WebdavResource(url);
        }
        else
        {
            resource.close();
            resource.setHttpURL(url);
        }
    }

    protected void setPath(String path) throws WebdavException
    {
        try
        {
            String collPath = fixPath(path);
            resource.setPath(collPath);
            if (!resource.exists())
            {
                throw new WebdavException("Path does not exist.");
            }
        }
        catch (Exception e)
        {
            throw new WebdavException(e.getMessage());
        }
    }

    protected String getParentPath(String path)
    {
        path = fixPath(path);
```

```
        //for the root and any paths right beneath it.
        if (path.lastIndexOf('/') == path.indexOf('/', 1))
        {
            return path;
        }

        //our paths have a trailing slash
        int trailingSlashIndex = path.lastIndexOf('/');
        String cleanedPath = path.substring(0, trailingSlashIndex);

        int lastSlashIndex = cleanedPath.lastIndexOf('/');
        String parentPath = cleanedPath.substring(0, lastSlashIndex + 1);

        System.out.println("parent path: " + parentPath);
        return parentPath;

    }

    protected String fixPath(String path)
    {
        if (!path.startsWith("/"))
        {
            path = resource.getPath() + "/" + path;
        }

        //clean up any double slashes
        path = path.replaceAll("//", "/");

        return path;
    }

    public WebdavResource getResource()
    {
        return resource;
    }
}
```

ListFiles.jsp

This JSP page displays the contents of the WebDAV collection. The hardest part of writing this page was creating the working links and mixing the JSP expression language with the regular JSP. We used the portlet tag library to create portlet action tags. We also used the JSP standard tag library to iterate through the items in the WebDAV resource collection and determine whether they are collections.

```
<%@ taglib uri="/WEB-INF/tld/c.tld" prefix="c" %>
<%@ taglib uri='/WEB-INF/tld/portlet.tld' prefix='portlet'%>

<%@ page import="org.apache.webdav.lib.WebdavResource" %>
<%@ page import="java.util.Vector" %>
<%@ page import="javax.portlet.PortletURL" %>

<%
    WebdavResource resource = (WebdavResource) request.getAttribute("resource");
    Vector children = resource.listBasic();
    pageContext.setAttribute("resource", resource);
    pageContext.setAttribute("children", children);

%>

<c:forEach var="child" items="${children}" varStatus="status">
  <c:set var="path" value="${resource.path}/${child[0]}"/>
  <c:choose>
    <c:when test="${child[2] == 'COLLECTION'}">
      <a href="<portlet:actionURL>
                  <portlet:param name="COMMAND" value="CHANGE_COLLECTION"/>
                  <portlet:param name="PATH"
                    value="<%=(String)pageContext.getAttribute("path")%>"/>
              </portlet:actionURL>">
              <c:out value="${child[0]}"/>
      </a>
    </c:when>
    <c:otherwise>
      <a href="<portlet:actionURL>
                  <portlet:param name="COMMAND" value="DISPLAY_CONTENT"/>
                  <portlet:param name="PATH"
                    value="<%=(String)pageContext.getAttribute("path")%>"/>
              </portlet:actionURL>">
              <c:out value="${child[0]}"/>
      </a>
      <c:out value="${child[1]}"/>
    </c:otherwise>
  </c:choose>
  <c:out value="${child[3]}"/>
  <br>
</c:forEach>
<p/>
```

```
<a href="<portlet:actionURL>
            <portlet:param name="COMMAND" value="DISPLAY_PARENT"/>
            <portlet:param name="PATH" value="<%=resource.getPath() + "/"%>"/>
        </portlet:actionURL>">
        Back to parent collection
</a>
```

Finally, here is our portlet.xml portlet deployment descriptor, showing the three initialization parameters. You will need to change the URL initialization parameter to point to your installation of Slide or another WebDAV server. If you are using Slide 2.0, the root/root username and password combination will work fine.

```
<?xml version="1.0" encoding="UTF-8"?>
<portlet-app xmlns="http://java.sun.com/xml/ns/portlet/portlet-app_1_0.xsd" ➥
version="1.0" xmlns:xsi="http://www.w3.org/2001/XMLSchema-instance" ➥
xsi:schemaLocation="http://java.sun.com/xml/ns/portlet/portlet-app_1_0.xsd ➥
http://java.sun.com/xml/ns/portlet/portlet-app_1_0.xsd">

    <portlet>
        <description>CMS WebDAV Portlet</description>

        <portlet-name>CMSPortlet</portlet-name>

        <display-name>CMS WebDAV Portlet</display-name>

        <portlet-class>com.portalbook.portlets.CMSPortlet</portlet-class>

        <init-param>
            <description>URL to the WebDAV server</description>
            <name>URL</name>
            <value>http://localhost:9080/slide/</value>
        </init-param>

        <init-param>
            <description>User name for the WebDAV server</description>
            <name>username</name>
            <value>root</value>
        </init-param>

        <init-param>
            <description>Password for the WebDAV server</description>
            <name>password</name>
            <value>root</value>
        </init-param>
```

```
        <expiration-cache>0</expiration-cache>

        <supports>
            <mime-type>text/html</mime-type>
            <portlet-mode>VIEW</portlet-mode>
            <portlet-mode>EDIT</portlet-mode>
        </supports>

        <supported-locale>en</supported-locale>

            <portlet-info>
                <title>CMS Portlet</title>
                <short-title>CMS</short-title>
                <keywords>CMS,WebDAV,Slide</keywords>
            </portlet-info>

    </portlet>

</portlet-app>
```

Summary

In this chapter, we examined the two major standards for integrating content management systems into portlets: Java Content Repository API and WebDAV. Although the JCR API is a new standard, we expect that CMS vendors will adopt the standard quickly. Many client and server applications already use WebDAV. We discussed the Apache Slide WebDAV client library, and then used the library in a CMS portlet. Our portlet displays the content available through WebDAV, along with its size and last modification date. We can browse through the folders to find a piece of content we like, and then view it inside the portlet.

Index

Symbols and Numbers

A

B

C

D

E

F

N

O

P

T

U

V

W

X

Y